Allan Kardec (1804-1869)

L'ÉVANGILE

SELON

LE SPIRITISME

CONTENANT

L'EXPLICATION DES MAXIMES MORALES DU CHRIST

LEUR CONCORDANCE AVEC LE SPIRITISME

ET LEUR APPLICATION AUX DIVERSES POSITIONS DE LA VIE

PAR ALLAN KARDEC

Auteur du *Livre des Esprits.*

Il n'y a de foi inébranlable que celle
qui peut regarder la raison face à face,
à tous les âges de l'humanité.

QUATRIÈME ÉDITION

PARIS

LES ÉDITEURS DU *LIVRE DES ESPRITS*

35, QUAI DES AUGUSTINS

DENTU, FRÉD. HENRI, libraires, au Palais-Royal

Et au Bureau de la REVUE SPIRITE, 59, rue et passage Sainte-Anne

1868

THE GOSPEL

ACCORDING TO SPIRITISM

Contains explanations of the moral maxims of Christ, accordance with Spiritism and their application in various circumstances of life.

By

ALLAN KARDEC

(Author of THE SPIRITS' BOOK)

Unshakeable faith is only that which can meet reason face to face in every Human epoch.

This English translation was taken from the 3rd edition of the original French, as being the one containing all of Allan Kardec's final revisions, published in 1866.

Original title: *L'Évangile selon le Spiritisme*
First published in France, 1864. Definitive French edition: 1866.

1st Edition in English 1987 - published by the HEADQUARTERS PUBLISHING CO LTD, London, UK.

2nd Edition 1993 - published by the ALLAN KARDEC Publishing Ltd., London, UK

3rd Revised Edition 2003 published by the International Spiritist Council, Brazil.

4th Final Revision 2019 published by British Union of Spiritist Societies, www.buss.org.uk

Translated by Janet Duncan
2019 - COPYRIGHT donated to the Allan Kardec Study Group-UK Centre for Spiritist Teachings, International Spiritist Council, British Union of Spiritist Societies, Irish Spiritist Federation, Le Mouvement Spirite Francophone.

ISBN 978-1-9999043-3-3

Cover design by: Konrad Jerzak vel Dobosz.

Printed by:
OFICYNA WYDAWNICZA RIVAIL Konrad Jerzak vel Dobosz
Ul. Walbrzyska 11/85
02-739 Warszawa - Poland
www.rivail.pl
Tel: +48 502651666

INDEX

TRANSLATOR'S PREFACE

This is no ordinary book. This is not a book that is usually read from cover to cover, afterwards to be placed on a bookshelf and forgotten. This is a book for daily use, for moments of trouble, when we feel in need of orientation and guidance, a bedside book, a book to be constantly on hand, to take with us in our hand luggage when we travel. In other words, this is a book offering something very special to each person who may read and study it. This book brings peace of mind and comfort in times of bereavement. It is even a book for those who have only a faint knowledge or belief in God and Jesus. It can change lives by bringing tranquillity out of chaos, certainty out of disbelief, as well as compensation for both material and spiritual losses. However, most importantly, it brings us the answers to many questions that we may have been asking, famous questions such as 'Who and what am I?' 'Where did I come from?' 'What am I doing here?' 'Where am I going?' It brings us rational and logical explanations of such matters as reincarnation, inequality of wealth in the world, the reasons why we sometimes hate certain people on sight, and the many disharmonies that exist between husband and wife, brother and sister, parents and children, and much more.

Probably this book will play its greatest part in helping humanity towards a better understanding of LIFE and lead towards spiritual enlightenment when used as readings in Churches and Study Groups. It can also be of great help in times of personal stress, grief or when we are at a loss to know what to do next. If we just lift up our thoughts towards the Heavens - holding the book in our hands - and after a moment of thought open it casually; then read wherever our eyes fall upon the page. Surprisingly we will find it is giving us answers or guidance very applicable to the moment in question. Finally, but certainly not the least of its uses is that it brings us the 'key' to Bible parables we could never fully understand, in everyday language, together with the deep meanings behind the teachings of Jesus.

This is the third book of the Spiritist Doctrine as codified by ALLAN KARDEC whose real name was HYPOLITE LÉON DENIZARD RIVAIL and we offer here a brief biography of this remarkable and dedicated man.

He was born in Lyon, France on 3rd October 1804 into a family who for many generations had been either lawyers or magistrates. He was an intelligent child and was taught high principles of honour and moral by his parents. At an early age, he showed strong inclinations towards the sciences and philosophy. When he was ten years of age, he was sent to the Institute of Pestalozzi at Yverdon in Switzerland, where he soon acquired the habit of investigation and learnt the art of freethinking. At the age of fourteen, he began to give free lessons to schoolmates who were less advanced. On occasion, Rivail was asked by Pestalozzi to teach officially in his absence, due to his natural ability in this field. He became a fervent disciple of Pestalozzi and was much loved by the great man.

In 1822 at the age of eighteen, Hypolite returned to France. A year later, he took up residence in Paris and in 1824, he published his first book entitled: 'A Theoretical & Practical Arithmetic Course.' This was so successful that it continued to be reprinted till as late as 1876. He had an instinct for methodology and this was only the beginning, for he was to publish many other books on varying subjects including 'A classical Grammar of the French Language' (1829). The French University adopted some of these books and their sale rendered him a sufficient income to live on, while he continued to give free lessons to school-children. He taught Chemistry, Mathematics, Astronomy, Physics, Rhetoric, Comparative Anatomy and Physiology. He spoke fluent Italian and Spanish, had a profound knowledge of German, English and Dutch, with some knowledge of Latin, Greek and Gaelic. He also translated a number of books, choosing those that he liked best, including several by Fénelon, which he translated into German.

He married Amélie Gabrielle Boudet on 6th February 1832. She was nine years his senior, a writer, teacher of fine arts, a poet and artist. She was the perfect companion and helper, being dedicated and uncomplaining. She played an important part in all of her husband's activities and sustained him through many financial difficulties encountered during his life, and greatly assisted him in his teaching.

This extraordinary man could have become renowned and wealthy through his various talents, but this was not to be. He was a man with a mission! Between 1848 and 1850, an explosion of spirit phenomena occurred in America and even more strongly in Europe. In the last book of the codification 'Posthumous Works' published by Amélie after his death, Kardec (As he had become known) had written, "It was in 1854 that I first heard about Table turning." When his good friend Mr Fortier brought him the initial news of these extraordinary happenings telling him "The tables also talk!" Kardec's reply to this was, "I will only believe when I see it and when it can be proved to me that a table has a brain that can think, plus nerves to feel with and can also become somnambulic. Until then, allow me to see nothing more than fantasy in these stories!" He had always been a disbeliever of such things as ghosts.

After various encounters with his good friend Mr Fortier in 1855, he was finally persuaded to attend a séance and his curiosity was immediately aroused. He then became a frequent visitor at the séances held in the house of a certain Mr Baudin. It was in fact here that he began his studies and research. He was never to become a medium, but little by little became quite intuitive. On 30th April 1856, a medium in his group received the first indications of his mission from Spirit. His wife always accompanied him to all the meetings and eventually became his secretary, upholding him in every aspect of his work. He adopted the '*nom de plume*' of <u>Allan Kardec</u> at the suggestion of Spirit, so that the works of the codification should not be confused with his own works. The first book of the codification (*The Spirits' Book*) was first published in 1857. That same year he also began meetings in his own home. A year later, he founded '**The Parisian Society for Spiritist Studies**'.

The remaining years of his life were dedicated to his spiritual work, being the completion of the five main books of the Codification, and to lecturing on Spiritism and its philosophy. He also made exhaustive journeys across Europe in order to take the word to as many places as possible, all of which he completed at his own expense. In 1867, he briefly met Léon Denis, who after his death became his disciple, and later published a series of classic works on Spiritism.

On March 31st, 1869, having just finished drawing up the Constitution and rules for a new society that he planned to form, while seated in his usual chair at his study-table in the Rue Sainte Anne, in the act of tying up a bundle of papers, his busy life was suddenly brought to an end. The passing from Earth into the Spiritual World was instantaneous, a peaceful falling asleep - a fitting end to a life well lived. Although the physical man is no longer with us, he lives on in Spirit, continuing his work by inspiring, stimulating and encouraging us to continue our search for knowledge.

In his Introduction to THE SPIRITS' BOOK, Allan Kardec expresses his opinion that new ideas need new terms and so he formulated the words **SPIRITIST** and **SPIRITISM** to give a clear and precise meaning to these Teachings. In his day, the word Spiritualist, meant the opposite to Materialist, but it did not follow that a Spiritualist believed in the existence of spirits or the possibility of communication with the invisible world. He employed the word Spiritism to stipulate the fundamental principle of the Spiritist theory, which is the interaction of the material world with Spirits or the beings of the invisible world. A Spiritist is one who adheres to these teachings. We continue to use these terms today, as the ideas they represent become better understood. Amongst those ideas is the study of the scientific, philosophical and religious aspects of existence; the ever pressing need for Humanity to instruct itself, to cast aside all mystery and superstition and accept responsibility for how we treat our planet and all the life upon it. Eventually recognising we will be required to answer for our actions in all aspects.

As life gathers momentum, as the world goes from crisis to crisis at this time, we are more and more conscious of the reality of the truths contained in Kardec's books.

As a New Epoch dawns, we are beginning to realise the need for all humanity to grow towards this knowledge and seek enlightenment to be prepared. When this time will finally be upon the world then people will be able to appreciate the greatness of this man's vision into the future.

However, we must not forget the important fact that in order to meet the future with confidence we must make adequate preparations today! Each moment that passes cannot be recovered, therefore we must make use of every instant to grow spiritually! To open up our horizons, to broaden our minds, to seek and cultivate our spirituality! We are Spiritual Beings, we are all immortal creatures! If we are to one-day find peace and happiness then we must consider our whole being! While we go on thinking of ourselves as material people, we are only looking at half of ourselves and here lies the secret of so many mistakes, so much unhappiness and so many failures.

For every person this wider and deeper knowledge of LIFE carries with it the need for self-analysis, self-correction and self-improvement. Without these aspects, we are all standing still, marking time, and going nowhere! If this book helps but one person to take just a small step forward, then it will have done its work. God never demands the impossible of any of us. Nor does He give us burdens for which we have no strength. Therefore, if we try to make a conscious effort to better ourselves and cultivate more faith, then we have begun our journey into the future towards the LIGHT, where one-day victory, peace and joy will be ours.

London, 2019

** ** ** ** **

Translator's Acknowledgements

Over the many years and various editions of this special book, the list of helping hands has been extensive and I never cease to be thankful and pray for each one. However, for this final edition I wish to thank Charles Kempf, who has been my right hand helper for all the many hours of tireless work for pagination and corrections in order that the book should continue to offer a clear and inviting design for the reader. In addition, I wish to thank Konrad Jerzak vel Dobosz for his special inspiration for the cover. Without the willing and happy collaboration of these two people, I would not have been able to complete my final task. May God and Jesus bless them now and always.

Also, I wish to say how much joy this work has brought me over the years and I can only hope that all who come to read it may receive comfort and enlightenment, that they be strengthened and upheld along life's troubled pathways, just as I have been.

Finally, may all who read, study and try to put these Teachings into daily practice receive constant blessings and bring them much spiritual progress.

PREFACE

The Spirits of the Lord, who are the Virtues of Heaven, move as does an immense army upon receiving orders from their commander. They spread out over the face of the Earth and similar to the stars, which fall one after another from the skies, are come to illumine pathways and open the eyes of those who cannot see.

In truth I say unto you the times are come when all things will be established in their true light, when the darkness shall be dissipated, the prideful confounded and the just glorified.

The great voices of Heaven reverberate like the sound of trumpets, and the choirs of Angels assemble. Human beings, we are inviting you to this divine concert. Take up the harp and lift up your voices in unison so that, in a sacred chorus, the sound may extend and re-echo from one extreme of the universe to the other.

Fellow beings, beloved brothers and sisters, we are here beside you. Love one another and say sincerely from the bottom of your hearts "Lord! Lord!" In so doing you fulfil the wishes of the Father who is in Heaven; then you too may enter into the kingdom of heaven.

THE SPIRIT OF TRUTH

NOTE: The above instructions, which were received by means of mediumship, are a precise summary of the true character of Spiritism and the finality of this work. They have been placed as the Preface for this reason. A. K.

INTRODUCTION

1. The objective of this work. - 2. The authority of the Spiritist teachings. The Universal control of the Teachings given by the Spirits. - 3. Historic facts. - 4. Socrates and Plato, the forerunners of the Christian idea and Spiritism.

1. THE OBJECTIVE OF THIS WORK

The Gospel can be divided into five parts: *The events in the life of Christ; the miracles; the prophecies; the words taken by the Church on which they base their dogmas; and the moral teachings*. The first four have been the object of controversies. However, the last has remained constantly inviolate. Before this divine code, even incredulity bows down. This is the common ground where all cults may be united; this is the flag under which all may gather whatever their creeds. For it has never been a matter of religious dispute, which has always and in all places originated from dogmatism. Moreover, if it had been discussed, then all cults would have found their own condemnation within it, seeing that, in the majority, they have held on to the more mystical rather than the moral part that demands an intimate reform from each one. Specially prepared for humankind, it constitutes a code of rules on how to behave in every circumstance of both private and public life. It offers the basic principles for all social relations founded on rigid justice. Finally and above all, it is the infallible route to lasting happiness and the uplifting of a corner of the veil that hides the future life. This is what forms the exclusive objective of this work.

Everyone admires the morality of the Gospel; everyone proclaims its sublimity and the need we have of it. However, of the many who proclaim their faith, believing what others have said or relying on maxims that have become proverbs, few know the basis and even fewer understand it or are able to deduce the consequences of it. In many cases, the reason for this is in the difficulty in understanding the Gospel, which for many is quite unintelligible. The allegorical form used and the intentional mysticism of the language make it something we read because we feel we ought to, because our conscience tells us to or because we are obliged to. However, we often do so as one would read prayers, without understanding them and consequently without taking any benefit from them. In this way, the moral precepts go unnoticed, scattered here and there between a mass of narrative. This makes it impossible to get the general idea of the whole or to take these ideas as specific subjects for reading and meditation.

It is true that various works have already been written concerning the Gospel morality. Nevertheless, after being put into modern prose they have lost their primitive simplicity, which at the same time constituted both their charm and their authenticity. Many others also deal with the best-known maxims reduced to the simplest form of a proverb. These then are no more than aphorisms, deprived of part of their value and interest due to the lack of accompanying accessories and the circumstances of the enunciation.

In order to avoid these undesirabilities, we have collected together in this work all the subjects that go to form a universal moral code, without distinction as to creed. In these citations, we have kept all that is useful to the development of these ideas, putting aside only that which does not pertain directly to the matter. Apart from this, we have kept scrupulously to the translations by Sacy[1] and to the division of the verses. But instead of following a chronological order, which would have been impossible and have made no sense, we have methodically grouped and classified the various maxims according to their respective natures so that they follow on, one from the other, as much as possible. An indication of chapters and verses permit reference to the original texts whenever desired.

These details refer only to the material side of the work, which on its own would be of secondary importance. The main objective was to put these Teachings within easy reach of everyone by means of clear explanations, especially those passages that until now have remained obscure. Thus revealing the full consequence of these Teachings and the manner in which they may be applied to all lifestyles. This is what we have attempted to do, together with the help of the Good Spirits who assisted us.

Many points in the Gospel, *the Bible*[1] and the writings of the sacred authors are in general unintelligible, some even appearing nonsensical for lack of a key that would help in understanding their true meaning. This key is to be found in its most complete form within Spiritism, as those who have already made a serious study of it can verify, and as many more in the future will come to recognise. Spiritism can be found throughout ancient times and repeatedly during the different epochs of humanity. We find vestiges in many places in the form of writings, in beliefs and in monuments. This is the reason why at the same time it is opening new horizons for the future, it is also projecting a no less brilliant light upon the mysteries of the past.

---

[1] Kardec used *Le Maistre de Sacy's* version of the Bible. For this Edition of the English translation, the traditional King James Version is quoted. Moreover, under guidance from Spirit some small changes have been made to replace archaic words with modern language, as being more readily understandable. (Tr.)

As a compliment to each precept, we have added some well-chosen instructions from amongst those dictated by Spirits[2] in various countries, through different mediums. If they had been taken from only one origin they would probably have suffered the influence either of the person or the ambient, whereas the diversification of origins proves that the Spirits give teachings without distinctions and that no one person is specially privileged.[3]

This work is for the use of everyone. From it we may all discover the means by which we may apply Christ's moral teachings to our daily lives and how best to go about it. This applies very specially to Spiritists. The relationship between humans and the invisible world has therefore been established on a permanent basis. Thus the Law of the Gospel, which the Spirits have taught to all nations, will no longer be a matter of dead words because each person will be able to understand them. They will see themselves incessantly compelled to put them into practice according to counselling from the spiritual guides. These instructions, coming from the Spirits, are really *the voices from*

---

[2] In using the word 'Spirits' with a capital letter indicates the group of more advanced Spirits that assisted Kardec throughout the process of revealing the Spiritist Teachings. (Tr.)

[3] It would have been possible, without doubt, to have presented many more communications from Spirits on each subject, all of which were received in cities and centres other than those cited. We wished, however, to avoid monotony and useless repetition so have limited our choice to those that, from their base and form, apply more adequately within the plan of this work, reserving for future publication those we have not been able to use here.

With respect to the mediums, we have refrained from naming them. In most cases, they themselves asked not to be mentioned, so we have made no exceptions. It is also a fact that the names of these mediums would not add more value to the work of the Spirits. The mentioning of them by name would only be an incentive to personal pride, to which serious mediums give no importance. They understand fully that their part in the work, being merely passive, in no way exalts their personal merit. It would be foolish to allow oneself to become vain about an intelligent work to which one had only lent mechanical assistance.

Heaven that have come to enlighten humankind and invite them to *put the Gospel into practice.*

2. THE AUTHORITY OF THE SPIRITIST TEACHINGS

The universal control of the teachings as given by the spirits

If the Spiritist Teachings was of a purely human conception it would offer no more guarantee than the enlightenment of those who actually conceived it; but no one on Earth could seriously contemplate the pretension of possessing exclusive and absolute truth. If the Spirits who made these revelations had manifested to only one person there would be no guarantee of their origin, since we would need to believe one person's word alone. Even if we accepted perfect sincerity on their part, the most they could do would be to convince their circle of acquaintances. This person would be able to form a sect, but never be able to form a world congregation.

God wished the *New Revelation* to reach humanity by the quickest and most authentic path, so He entrusted the Spirits to deliver them from pole to pole, manifesting everywhere without conferring the exclusive privilege of entrusting these words to only one individual. A single person might be deceived or could even deceive him or herself, but this could not happen when hundreds of people see and hear the same thing. This constitutes a guarantee for each one and for all. For the rest, it is possible to make one person disappear, but it is not possible to make everyone disappear. It is possible to burn books, but you cannot burn Spirits. Even if all the books were burnt, the base of the Teachings would still be inexhaustible because it is not to be found on Earth, and it would reappear in every place so that all might partake of it. If there is a shortage of people to diffuse it, there will always be

Spirits whose action reaches everyone, even those whom no person can reach.

In reality then, the Spirits themselves do the propagating, with the help of innumerable mediums, disseminating all over the world. If there had been but one interpreter, however favoured they might have been, Spiritism would barely be known. To whatever class the person belonged, that interpreter would have been the object of caution for many people and not every nation would have accepted them, whereas Spirits communicate to the four corners of the Earth, to all peoples, to all sects, to all parties and everyone accepts them. Spiritism has no nationality and does not stem from any known cult that might exist; nor is it imposed by any social class, seeing that any person may receive instructions from parents, relatives and friends from the beyond. This is how it had to be accomplished if it was to lead all humanity towards unity. If it did not maintain itself in neutral territory, it would nurture dissensions instead of pacifying them.

The force of Spiritism, as well as the cause of its rapid spread, resides in these universal Teaching. Where the word of one solitary person, even with the help of the press, would take centuries to become known, millions of voices are making themselves heard simultaneously in every corner of the planet. All are proclaiming the same principles and transmitting them on all levels, from the scholarly down to the most ignorant, so that no one is disinherited. This is an advantage that no other teaching has to offer. Therefore, if Spiritism is the truth, it will not fear the ill will of humanity, modern revolutions or the physical subversions of this globe, because nothing can touch the Spirits.

However, this is not the only advantage that comes from this exceptional situation. It also offers an unattackable guarantee against all misgivings that might arise from someone's ambition or through the contradictions of some Spirits. We cannot deny that these contradictions are obstacles, but they bring their own remedy with them alongside the malady.

We know that Spirits, due to differences in their various individual capacities, do not possess all the truth and do not claim to. It is not given to all to be able to penetrate certain mysteries. The knowledge of each one is proportional to their purification. Ordinary spirits know nothing more than humans do, but amongst them, as amongst men and women, there are those who are presumptuous and falsely wise, who think they know everything, but who in fact are ignorant. These are the systematic ones who take their own ideas to be the truth. In short, it is only highly evolved Spirits, who are almost completely dematerialised, who find themselves free from earthly ideas and prejudices. It is also known that less scrupulous spirits do not hesitate to deceive, by taking names that do not belong to them, in order to impose their utopian ideas. Because of all this, and in relation to all that is outside the exclusive field of moral education, the revelations that any one medium may receive will have an individual character. They will be without any stamp of authenticity and should be considered merely as personal opinions from this or that spirit. It would be imprudent to accept them or thoughtlessly propagate them as absolute truths.

The first corroborative test to be undertaken is without doubt that of reason, to which it is wise to submit, without exception, all that comes from the spirits. Any theory in evident contradiction to good sense, rigorous logic or positive facts that have been previously accepted should be rejected, however apparently respectable is the name by which it is signed. This test will no doubt be left incomplete due to the lack of illumination of some people and the tendency of many to take their own opinions as judgements of truth. That being the case, what of those who deposit absolutely no faith in themselves to do? They should seek what seems to be the majority and take this as a guide. This is the way you should proceed when judging what is said by Spirits, who are the first to offer the means of so doing.

Concordance amongst spiritual Teachings is the best proof of authenticity. However, it is important that this should happen only under determined conditions. The least secure method of concordance is when the actual medium, of his/her own accord, interrogates many different Spirits about a doubtful point. It is evident that, if the medium is under an obsessing influence or dealing with a mystifying Spirit, then that Spirit may say the same thing under different names. Neither is it an adequate guarantee of conformity when different mediums at the same centre receive similar communications, because they may be under the same influences.

The only sure guarantee for Spirit Teachings is the concordance that exists between revelations that have been received spontaneously by large numbers of medium, not known to each other and located in different places.

It should be understood that we are not referring to those communications that deal with secondary interests, but those referring to the basic principles of the Teachings. Experience has taught us that when a new principle is to be presented, it always happens *spontaneously* in different places at the same time in an identical manner, if not in actual form at least in general content. On the other hand, if by chance a Spirit formulates an eccentric doctrine based exclusively on its own ideas and excluding the truth, you may be sure that this idea will remain confined. Undoubtedly, it will collapse when confronted with instructions received from many other places, similar to many examples already known. This exclusiveness destroyed all the biased doctrine that sprang up at the time of the initiation of Spiritism, when each one explained the phenomena according to their own beliefs, before the Laws that govern the relationship between the visible and invisible worlds became known.

This is what we have based ourselves upon when formulating a principle for the Spiritist Teachings. We do not insist on it being true just because it might be in accordance with our own ideas. Neither do we have the least desire to uphold ourselves as being the sole possessor of the whole truth nor have we ever said to anyone, "Believe in this because it is I who tell you." We consider that our own opinion is nothing more than personal, which might be true or false, as we are no more infallible than anyone else is. Nor because we were taught a principle that we believe to be true; it is because it has received the sanction of concordance.

The position in which we find our self in, is that of receiving communications from almost a thousand serious Spiritual Centres, scattered over highly diversified areas of this planet. This gives us the possibility of observing on which principles concordance is established. Concordance has guided us until today and will go on guiding us in new fields still to be explored. We have noticed while studying these communications, coming from France and outside, that due to the very special nature of the information a new path is being sought and that the moment has arrived to take a step forward. These revelations, many times given through veiled words, have frequently passed unperceived by many who have received them. Others have thought themselves to be the sole receivers. Taken in isolation, we would have given them no importance and it is only coincidence that proves their seriousness. Later, when these new teachings reach the general public many will remember having received the same information. The general movement that we are studying and observing, together with the assistance of our spiritual Guides, is what helps us to judge whether it is the correct moment to do something or not.

This universal verification is the guarantee of the future unity of Spiritism and will annul all contradictory theories. It is here that in the future we shall find our criteria for the truth. The cause of the success of these Teachings as put forth in *THE SPIRITS' BOOK* and *THE MEDIUMS' BOOK* was because everyone had received confirmation directly from Spirit, of what these books contain. Whereas if all the Spirits had come to contradict them they would have received the same fate suffered by others who expounded imaginary concepts. Not even the support of the press would have saved them from a shipwreck. On the contrary, deprived as they were of this support, they nevertheless opened new paths and made rapid advancement. This is because the Spirits offered their support and goodwill, which not only compensated but also surpassed the lack of goodwill on the part of humans. This is what will happen to all ideas, whether emanating from either humans or Spirits that cannot withstand this confrontation. This is the final test whose strength no one can deny.

Suppose it pleased some spirits to dictate a book, under whatever title, offering contrary information; let us suppose their intention was hostile, with the object of discrediting the Teachings and maliciously provoking apocryphal communications. What influence could these writings exercise if all other Spirits refuted them? Anyone wishing to launch a doctrine in their own name should first seek assurance in combined concordance from the Spirits. There is no comparison between systems devised by only one person to that of another devised by everyone. What can the arguments of slanderers, wishing only to belittle, achieve against the opinion of the masses, if millions of friendly voices from space make themselves heard in opposition in every corner of the Universe, as well as in family homes? What happens to the innumerable publications that have the pretension of destroying Spiritism? Which of them has as much as caused a hesitation in its march? Until now, no one has considered the matter from this point of view without forgetting the most important fact - each one has been depending on themselves alone, without counting on the Spirits.

The principle of concordance is also a guarantee against any alterations to which Spiritism might be subjected by other sects wishing to take possession of it for their own ends, and so change it to suit their own ideas. Whosoever tries to divert Spiritism from its providential objective will never succeed, for the simple reason that the Spirits, as a universal body, will cause any ideas contrary to the truth to fall.

From all this stands out the main truth; that is, a person who wishes to oppose the established and sanctioned ideas could cause a localised perturbation lasting but a short while, but could never dominate the whole, not even for a moment and even less into the future.

We should also like to point out that instructions given by Spirits on points not yet elucidated by the Spiritist Teachings should not be considered as law until these instructions have been duly isolated and proven. Neither should they be accepted except with all due reserve and under the heading of 'awaiting confirmation.'

From this, we understand the need for greater prudence before making any such communications public. If they are deemed fit to be publicised they should be presented as mere individual opinions, possibly true, but awaiting confirmation. It will be necessary to wait for this confirmation before proclaiming it as a complete truth, unless you wish to be accused of levity or of thoughtless credulity.

Superior Spirits proceed with extreme wisdom in their revelations. They never touch on the most important questions, except gradually, until our intelligence shows itself ready to accept a more advanced truth and when circumstances show themselves to be favourable to a new idea. This is why they did not reveal everything from the outset and still have not told everything. They never give themselves to impatience, like some who want to eat the fruit before it is ripe. It is useless to try to hurry things forward beyond the time designated by Providence for its revelation. If you do, serious Spirits will always deny their assistance. Frivolous spirits however are not in the least preoccupied with the truth and consequently will give answers to anything and everything. Therefore, it is in this manner that whenever a question is premature, contradictory answers will always be found.

The principles mentioned above have not been formed as the result of a personal theory; they are consequences that have been forced upon us from the varying conditions within which Spirit communication is manifest. It is quite evident that if one spirit says one thing and thousands of other spirits say something different, we presume the truth does not lie with the solitary communicant. For someone to imagine they possess the truth against all the rest would be quite illogical, be it a person or a Spirit. Ponderous Spirits, if they do not feel completely or sufficiently clarified about any subject, never give a definite answer, but declare they are merely giving their own point of view and suggest awaiting the necessary confirmation.

However large, beautiful or just an idea may appear, it is impossible to unite opinions right from the first moment. The conflicts that arise in this case are the inevitable consequences that such a movement would cause. They are necessary so that the truth may be emphasised and the sooner this happens the better, so that any false ideas may be discarded. Any Spiritist who feels worried by this situation may be tranquil, as all those isolated claims will fall before the enormous and discerning force of universal concordance.

It is not the opinion of any one person that will produce unity, but the unanimous voices of the Spirits. It will not be any one person, *least of all I,* who will destroy the Spiritist orthodoxy, neither a spirit wishing to impose in any way. This unity will be accomplished by the universal gathering of Spirits who communicate throughout the world, by order of God. This is the essential character of the Spiritist Teachings; this is its force and its authority. God desired that His Law be set upon an immovable base and so did not trust these fundamentals to only one fragile being.

Before such a powerful tribunal, where conspiracy, rivalries, sects or nations are unknown, all opposition, ambition and those who seek individual supremacy will fail. *We ourselves will fall if we try to substitute our own ideas for those of God.* He alone will decide all lawful questions, impose silence on disagreement and give reason to those who have it. Before this imposing accord from the voices of Heaven, what value has an opinion of a mere man or woman or that of one Spirit? It makes no more impression than a drop of water in the ocean and even less than a child's voice in a tempest.

Universal opinion, like that of a supreme judge, is one that is pronounced last, being formed from all the individual opinions. If one of these contains the truth, it merely shows its own relative weight in the balance. If it is false, it cannot prevail against the rest. In this immense concourse, all individuality disappears and this constitutes yet another disappointment for humanity's pride.

This harmonious assemblage is already being formed and before the turn of this century, we shall see its full brightness shining forth in such a manner as to dissipate all doubt. The field is prepared and from now on potent voices will receive the mission of making them heard in order to congregate humanity under one banner. However, until this actually happens, all those who fluctuate between two opposing points of view can observe in which way general opinion forms. This will be the correct indication as to the declaration of the majority of Spirits on the varying subjects, upon which they communicate, and an even more accurate sign as to which of the two systems will prevail.

3. HISTORIC FACTS

In order to understand the Gospel better, it is necessary to know the true meaning of many of the words frequently used, which bear relation to the customs and the Jewish society of the time. Some of these words no longer have the same meaning and have frequently been misinterpreted, which in turn has led to uncertainty. When the full meanings are explained, it shows the real sense behind certain maxims that at first sight appear rather strange.

SAMARITANS - After the division of the ten tribes, Samaria became the capital of the dissident kingdom of Israel. Destroyed and rebuilt at various times, under Roman rule it became the administrative head of Samaria, one of the four divisions of Palestine. Herod the Great beautified Samaria with sumptuous monuments, and to gratify Augusto gave it the name of Augusta, in Greek 'Sebaste'.

The Samaritans were almost constantly at war with the kings of Judah. Profound aversion dating from the time of the separation perpetuated between the two tribes, causing them to avoid any kind of reciprocal relations. In order to widen the schism, and to avoid going to Jerusalem for religious festivities, they built themselves a private temple and adopted some reforms. They only admitted the Pentateuch, that contained the laws of Moses, rejecting all other books to which these had been annexed, and their sacred books were all written in ancient Hebrew characters. According to Orthodox Jews, they were heretics and consequently despised, excommunicated and persecuted. The antagonism between the two nations was founded exclusively upon their religious divergences, despite the fact that the origin of their belief was the same. They were the *Protestants* of their time.

Some Samaritans are still to be found in certain regions of the Levant, especially near Nablus and in Jaffa. They observe the laws of Moses more strictly than other Jews and only marry amongst themselves.

NAZARITES - The name given in olden times to Jews who took the vow, either temporary or perpetual, to remain in perfect purity. They promised to observe chastity, abstain from alcoholic drinks and not to cut their hair. Samson, Samuel and John the Baptist were Nazarites.

Later on, the Jews gave this name to the first Christians, alluding to Jesus from Nazareth. This was also the name given to a heretical sect from the first phase of the Christian epoch and who, like the Ebonites, from whom they adopted certain principles and mixed the practice of the Mosaic Law with those of Christian dogmas. This sect disappeared during the fourth century.

PUBLICANS - In ancient Rome, this was the name given to those who rented out the collection of public taxes and all kinds of incomes, either in Rome itself or in other parts of the Empire. They were like the general collectors and auctioneers of taxes in the ancient system in France, which still exists in some regions (1865). The risks they ran made most people close their eyes when it came to their frequently amounted riches that for some were the fruits of levies and scandalous gains. Later on the name *'publican'* was extended to all those who superintended public monies and their underling agents. Today, this term is employed in a disparaging way, to denote financiers and agents with very few scruples. It is said "Greedy as a publican" or "Rich as a publican" referring to their ill-gotten gains.

During Roman rule, the question of taxes was what the Jews found most difficult to accept, causing great irritation amongst them. Many revolts resulted from this problem, so turning it into a religious question, as it was considered to be against the Law. Indeed, a powerful party was formed headed by a certain citizen named Judah the Guiltier, whose objective was to abolish all taxes.

The Jews despised the taxes and all those entrusted with collecting them. Thence sprang up the aversion shown to publicans of all categories, amongst whom could be found many people of esteem, but who due to their functions, were despised together with whoever kept company with them. Prominent Jews considered it a compromise to have any personal relationship with these people.

TAX COLLECTORS - These were the lower-class collectors, entrusted principally with the collection of tolls on entering cities. Their function was more or less similar to those of customs officials and the granting of passes. They shared the rejection suffered by publicans in general. This is the reason why, in the Bible, we frequently meet the word *publican* alongside the expression - sinful people. This did not imply debauchery or vagrancy but was a term of scorn, a synonym for *people who kept bad company,* people unworthy to mix with decent people.

PHARISEES (From the Hebrew *Parasch*, meaning division or separation.) Tradition is an important part of Jewish theology. It consists of a compilation of the successive interpretations given to the Scriptures that became articles for dogmas. Amongst scholars, this was the subject for interminable discussions, most of which were over simple questions as to the meaning of words and their form, just like theological disputes and subtleties of scholastics in the Middle Ages. From all this resulted different sects, each one wishing to have the monopoly of the Truth and consequently detesting one another, as so often happens.

Among these sects, the most influential were the *Pharisees*, whose chief, *Hillel*, a Jewish doctor born in Babylonia some 180 or 200 years before Jesus Christ. He was the founder of a famous school where it was taught that faith should be put only in the Scriptures. The Pharisees were persecuted in various epochs, especially under Hyrcania[4] – who was sovereign pontiff and king of the Jews – Aristobulus[5] and Alexander, who was a king of Syria. However, Alexander granted them honours and restored their properties, making it possible for them to reacquire their old powerful status. This continued until the *ruin of Jerusalem* in the year 70 AD., at which time the name disappeared because of the scattering of the Jews.

The Pharisees took an active part in the religious controversy. They were faithful practitioners of exterior cults and ceremonies, full of ardent zeal and proselytism, enemies of innovations, maintaining great severity of principles. Nevertheless, behind the cover of punctilious devotion lay dissolute habits, a great deal of pride and above all an excessive desire to dominate. Religion was actually a means to an end, rather than an object of sincere faith. It possessed nothing of virtue beyond outward appearances and ostentation. Nevertheless, they exercised a great influence over the people, in whose eyes they were sacred. This is the reason they were very powerful in Jerusalem.

They believed, or at least made out they believed, in Divine Providence, the immortality of the soul, eternal punishment and the resurrection of the dead. (See chap. IV, item 4) Jesus, who esteemed above all simplicity and the qualities of the heart,

---

[4] Hyrcania I or John Hyrcania was a Sovereign Priest and King of the Jews (134-104 BC), expanded Judea and took it to independence. (Tr.)

[5] King of Judea (67 – 63 BC). He was poisoned by the Pompeian's. (Tr.)

showed preference within the Law for *the spirit that vitalises*, to the word that kills. Therefore, He applied Himself throughout His mission to the unmasking of their hypocrisy and because of this he was considered by them to be their enemy. This is the reason why the Pharisees, together with the High Priests, incited the people to eliminate Him.

THE SCRIBES - This name was given in the main, to the secretaries of the kings in Judea and to scholars certain people who understood matters relating to the Jewish army. Later it was applied to those who taught the Law of Moses and interpreted it to the People. They joined in common cause with the Pharisees, sharing their principles as well as their aversion to all innovations. This is why Jesus included them when He launched criticism against the Pharisees.

SYNAGOGUE (From the Greek *Sunagoguê* meaning assembly, congregation.) There was only one temple in Judea, that of Solomon in Jerusalem, where all the great ceremonies of worship were held. Every year all the Jews would go there on pilgrimage for the principal festivals, such as Passover, the Dedication and the Feast of the Tabernacle. It was on these occasions that Jesus would also be present. The other cities did not have temples, only synagogues, buildings where the Jewish people would collect for their Saturday meetings and public prayers, under the leadership of their Elders, the scribes, or scholars versed in the Law. It was due to this fact that Jesus, although He was not a priest, was able to teach in the synagogues on Saturdays.

Ever since the ruin of Jerusalem and the dispersal of the Jews, the synagogues in the cities where they went to live became temples for the celebration of their cults.

SADDUCEES - Another Jewish sect founded about 24 BC whose name came from *Sadoc,* its founder. They believed in neither immortality nor resurrection, nor in good and bad angels.

However, they did believe in God, but they expected nothing after death, they served Him having in mind only temporary recompenses that according to them were limited by Divine Providence. With these thoughts in mind, their main objective in life was the satisfaction of all physical senses. As to the scriptures, they followed the texts of the old laws. They would not accept traditions or any form of interpretation. They put good works and the pure and simple observance of this law before all outward practices of worship. They were, as you see, the materialists, deists and sensualists of their time. This sect had few followers, but amongst them were some important personages and it became a political party constantly in opposition to the Pharisees.

ESSENES - They were a Jewish sect founded about the year 150 BC during the time of the Maccabees. Their members lived in types of monasteries, forming amongst themselves a kind of moral and religious association. They distinguished themselves by their pacific ways and austere virtues. They taught the love of God and of one's neighbour, the immortality of the soul and believed in the resurrection. They were celibate, condemned war and slavery, held all their possessions in common and devoted themselves to agriculture. Contrary to the Sadducees, who were very sensual and denied immortality and the Pharisees of rigid external practices and only apparent virtues, the Essenes never took part in the disputes that caused antagonism between the other two sects. In their way of life, they were similar to the first Christians. The moral principles they professed caused many people to suppose that Jesus had belonged to their community before He began His mission. It is certain that He knew them, but there is nothing to prove that He was related to them, so all that has been written to this effect is simply hypothetical.[6]

THERAPEUTICS (From the Greek *thérapeutaï*, formed from *thérapeueïn* to serve, meaning: servants of God or Healers.) These were Jewish sectarians and contemporaries of Christ, being mostly established in Alexandria, in Egypt. Like the Essenes, whose principles they adopted, they also practised all the virtues. They were extremely frugal in their eating habits, were celibate, dedicated to meditation, lived solitary lives and constituted a truly religious order. Philo, a platonic Jewish philosopher from Alexandria, was the first to speak of the Therapeutics, whom he considered as a Jewish sect. Eusebius, Saint Jerome and other originators of the Church believed them to be Christians. Whether they were, or whether they were Jewish, the fact remains that, like the Essenes, they represent a link in the union between the Jewish and Christian faiths.

4. SOCRATES AND PLATO, THE FORERUNNERS OF THE CHRISTIAN IDEA AND SPIRITISM

From the mere fact that Jesus knew the Essenes, it is erroneous to conclude that His teachings were derived from this sect and that if He had lived in another environment He would have professed other principles. Great ideas have never appeared suddenly. Those founded on truth have always had their predecessors, who partially prepared the path. Later, at the appointed time, God sends someone who has the mission of resuming, coordinating and completing those scattered elements and uniting them into a teaching. In this way, when the idea arrives it finds Spirits

---

[6] 'THE DEATH OF JESUS', supposedly written by an Essene, is an entirely apocryphal work whose only objective was to serve one opinion. It carries with it the proof of its modern origin.

disposed to accept it. This also happened with the Christian idea, which had been foreseen many centuries previously, before either Christ or the Essenes, having had Socrates and Plato as its principle predecessors.

Socrates, like Christ, wrote nothing himself or at least left nothing written. Just as Christ, he also suffered the death of a criminal, a victim of fanaticism, because he had dared to attack existing beliefs and for having put virtue above hypocrisy and the image of the form, in other words for having combated religious prejudice. Also in the same manner as Jesus, Whom the Pharisees accused of corrupting the people by His Teaching, Socrates was accused by the Pharisees of his time, seeing that they have always existed in all epochs. They accused him of proclaiming the dogma of the unity of God, the immortality of the soul and the future life. Just as the Teachings of Jesus became known only through the writings of His disciples, so the Teachings of Socrates became known through his disciple Plato.

For these reasons, we judge it appropriate to offer a brief summary of the most prominent points of Socrates' teachings in order to show the concordance with the Christian principles. To those who consider this parallel a profanity, claiming there can be no similarity between a pagan doctrine and that of Christ, we would say that the teachings of Socrates were not pagan because he objectively combated paganism. As to the teachings of Jesus, which are complete and pure, they have nothing to lose by this comparison, as it is impossible to diminish the greatness of Christ's Divine mission. For the rest we are dealing with a historical fact that no one can obliterate. Humanity emerges from 'beneath the bushel' of its own accord, because it has reached sufficient maturity to be able to meet truth face to face, and it will be worse for those who do not wish to see this. The time has arrived to consider matters in a more ample and evolved manner, not from the point of view of narrow and diffident interests of sects and castes. Moreover, these citations will prove that if Socrates and Plato presented Christian ideas, they also gave us the fundamental principles of Spiritism in their writings.

A SUMMARY OF THE TEACHINGS OF SOCRATES AND PLATO

1. *A living being is an incarnate soul. Before its incarnation, it existed in union with primordial types, to ideas of truth, goodness and beauty. Then separating from them, it incarnates and on remembering its past, it becomes more or less tormented by the desire to return to it.*

The independence and distinction between the basic principle of intelligence and those of matter could not be more clearly expressed. Apart from this, it is also the teachings of pre-existence, of humanity's vague intuition of another world to which it aspires, and of leaving the spirit world in order to incarnate, including its return to the spirit world after death. Finally, it also expressed the doctrine of the fallen angels.

2. *The soul becomes perturbed and confused when it uses the body in order to consider an object. It becomes dizzy as if intoxicated because it holds on to things that, by their very nature, are subject to change. Whereas, when humanity contemplates its very essence, it directs itself to that which is pure, eternal and immortal and seeing that its soul is of this nature, it remains joined to this state as long as it can. The perturbations then cease because it is joined to that which is immutable and this is the state of the soul called wisdom.*

Thus, people who consider things in a down-to-earth fashion are only deceiving themselves. To see things in their true perspective they must look upon them from high up, that is to say from the spiritual point of view. Those who are in possession of true wisdom must then isolate the soul from the body in order to be able to see with the eyes of the Spirit. This is what Spiritism also teaches. (See Chap. 2, item 5.)

3. *While we have our physical body and our soul is immersed in this corruption, we can never possess the object of our desire, which is Truth. In fact, the body stirs up thousands of obstacles due to the necessity we have of caring for it. Moreover, it fills us with desires, appetites, and doubts, a thousand fancies and foolish things, in such a way that we find it impossible to be wise, even for an instant. Nevertheless, if it is not possible to know anything in its entirety while the soul remains joined to the body, either we shall never know the truth, or we shall only know it after death. Freed from the misleading ideas of the body, we hope it will be permissible to talk with men and women who have been liberated. So understanding for ourselves the essence of things. This is the reason why true philosophers prepare themselves for death, as dying represents nothing to them, and in no way is it to be feared.*

Here we have the principles of the faculties of the souls being obscured by the corporeal organs and the expansion of purified souls. This does not happen to impure souls. (See HEAVEN & HELL by ALLAN KARDEC-1st part, Chap. 2; & 2nd part, Chap. 1.)

4. *The soul in its impure state finds itself oppressed and is once again attracted to the visible world by the fear of that which is invisible and immaterial. It is a mistake then, to say that the gloomy ghosts sometimes seen around tombs and monuments must be the souls of those who have left their bodies without being absolutely pure, and so still conserve part of their material form, which makes them visible to the human eye. In fact, they are not good but evil souls, dragging with them the penalties of their first life, who find themselves forced to wander in such places. They will continue to wander until their appetites, inherent to the material form with which they are clad, recalls them to another* *body. Then, beyond doubt, they will return to the same habits that were the object of their preferences during their first life.*

Not only is the principle of reincarnation clearly shown here, but also the state of those souls who maintain themselves under the restrictions of matter, as described to us in spiritual communications. Furthermore, it says that reincarnation in a material body is the consequence of the impureness of the soul, whereas the purified soul finds itself exempt from further reincarnations. This is exactly what Spiritism teaches, only adding that the soul, having made good resolutions while in the spiritual world and possessing some acquired knowledge, brings fewer defects, more virtues and intuitive ideas on being reborn than it had in the preceding incarnation. In this way, each existence shows both intellectual and moral progress. (See HEAVEN & HELL, 2nd part, Examples.)

5. *After our death, the genie (*daimon, devil*), that had been assigned to us during our life, will take us to a place where all, who must go to Hades in order to be judged, are gathered. The souls, after having been in Hades the necessary length of time, are then returned to this life for* long periods and multiple times.

This is the teaching of the Guardian Angels or Protecting Spirits and of successive reincarnations after intervals of varying lengths in the spirit world.

6. *Devils occupy the space that separates Heaven from Earth; this constitutes the link that unites the Universe with itself. The Divinity never enters into direct contact with human beings, which is done through the mediation of the devils with whom the gods have dealings, and who occupy themselves with him during both waking and sleeping.*

In ancient times the word '*daimon*', from which the term *evil* was derived, was not used in the bad sense as it is today. Nor was it used exclusively for evil beings, but for spirits in general. Within which were included Superior Beings called *gods,* as well as the less elevated, the actual devils, who communicated directly with humans. Spiritism also says that spirits populate space and that God only communicates with human beings through the intermediary of pure Spirits, who are entrusted to transmit His wishes. Spirits can also communicate with human beings during the sleep state, as well as while awake. If we put the word *Spirit* in place of the word *devil* we have the Spiritist Teachings and by putting the word *Angel,* we have the Teachings of Christ.

7. *The constant preoccupation of the philosophers (as understood by Socrates and Plato) is to take great care of the soul, less with respect to the present life, which lasts but an instant, but more with respect to eternity. As the soul is immortal, would it not be more prudent to live our lives bearing this fact in mind?*

Both Spiritism and the Christian faith teach the same thing.

8. *If the soul is immaterial, then after this life it will have to go to a world that is equally invisible and immaterial, the same way as the body decomposes and returns to matter. However, it is very important to clearly distinguish the pure soul that is truly immaterial and nourishes itself, as God does, from thoughts and the sciences; from that of the soul that is more or less stained by impurities of a material nature. This impedes elevation to all that is divine and in fact causes it to be retained in its earthly surroundings.*

As we can see, both Socrates and Plato understood perfectly the different levels of the dematerialised soul. They insisted on the varieties of situations resulting from its *more* or *less* purified states. What they said though intuition, Spiritism proves by the numerous examples that it places before us. (See HEAVEN & HELL, 2nd part.)

9. *If death meant the complete dissolution of the person, then the evil spirits would have much to gain from death, as they would find themselves at the same time free from body, soul and vices. Only those who adorn their soul, not with strange ornaments, but with those that are appropriate, may wait the hour of their return to the other world with tranquillity.*

This is equal to saying that materialism, that proclaims there is nothing after death, annuls all previous moral responsibility. This would consequently be inductive to evilness and that evil has everything to gain from nothingness. Only the person who has divested themselves of all vice and become enriched with virtues can await the awakening in the other life with tranquillity. By means of examples, which are offered to us daily, Spiritism shows how painful it is for those who are evil to pass over into this other life. (See HEAVEN & HELL, 2nd part, Chap. 1.)

10. *The body retains the well-impressed vestiges of the care it received, as well as the marks of all accidents suffered. The same applies to the soul. When it disposes of the body it maintains in evidence the features of its character, its affections, as well as the marks that have been left on it by all the various occurrences during its lifetime. Thus, the worst thing that can happen to a man or woman is to return to the other world with his or her soul laden with crimes. You see, Calicles, which neither you nor Pollex, nor Gorgias, can prove that we should lead a different life that can be useful when we find ourselves on the other side. From so many different opinions, the only one that is unshakeable is* that it is better to receive than to commit an injustice. *That, above all else, we must be careful not just to seem like, but also to actually be men and women of goodness.* (Taken from a dialogue between Socrates and his followers when he was in prison.)

Here we are faced with yet another point of capital importance which experience has proved to us: that the soul which is not yet purified retains the ideas, tendencies, character and passions that it had while on Earth. Is not the maxim - *It is better to receive than to commit an injustice* - entirely Christian? Jesus expressed the same thought when He said, "If someone strikes you on the right cheek, then offer him the other one as well." (See Chap. 12, items 7 & 8).

11. *One of two things - either death is the absolute destruction or it is the passing of the soul into another place. If everything is extinguished, then death would be like one of those infrequent nights when we do not dream nor have any consciousness of ourselves. However, if death is but a change of habitation, the passageway to the place where the dead must meet, what happiness to find there all those we have known! My greatest pleasure would be to closely examine the inhabitants of this other home and to distinguish there, as we do here, which of those who deem themselves worthy are actually so considered. But it is time to part, me to my death and you to live.* (Socrates to his judges.)

According to Socrates, those who live upon the Earth meet again after death and recognize each other. Spiritism shows that relationships continue to the extent that death is not an interruption nor the cessation of life, but rather an inevitable transformation without any discontinuity.

If Socrates and Plato had known what Christ was to teach five hundred years later, and which Spiritism now spreads, they would have said exactly the same things. However, there is nothing surprising in this fact, if we consider that all great truths are eternal and all advanced Spirits had to know them before they came to Earth in order to be able to deliver them. We may consider even further that Socrates and Plato, together with all the other great philosophers of those great times, could have later been among those chosen to uphold Christ in His Divine Mission, being chosen precisely because they were more apt to understand His sublime teachings. It also appears highly probable that today they participate in the Host of Spirits charged with teaching humanity these same truths.

12. *Never return one injustice with another, nor harm anyone, no matter what harm they may have done to us.* Few, however, will admit this principle and those who disagree will, beyond doubt, do nothing but despise one another.

Is this not the principle of charity, which prescribes that we do not return evil for evil and that we forgive our enemies?

13. *We recognise the tree according to its fruit. Every action should be qualified by what it produces: to qualify as evil when it causes evil and as goodness when it produces something that is good.*

The maxim, "It is by the fruits that we know the tree," is repeated many times throughout The Gospel.

14. *Riches are a great danger. People who love riches do not love themselves nor what they possess; they love something that is even more strange than that which they possess.* (See Chap. 16.)

15. *The most beautiful prayers and the most beautiful sacrifices mean less to God than a virtuous soul who has struggled to be like Him. It has been a grave error to think that the gods dispense more attention to their offerings than to our souls. If that were the case then the greatest culprits would become favoured. But no, it is the truly just and upright who, by their words and deeds, fulfil their duties to the gods and humanity.* (See Chap. 10, items 7 & 8.)

16. *We call the person who loves their body more than their soul, depraved. Love is everywhere in Nature and it calls us to use our intelligence; we even find it in the movements of the planets. It is love that covers Nature with its richest carpet; it is a decoration and makes its home where there are flowers and perfumes. It is* *also love that gives peace to humanity, calms the seas, silences the storm and gives sleep to pain.*

It is Love that will unite humanity through a fraternal link that is the consequence of Plato's theory on universal love, as a Law of Nature. Socrates said, "Love is neither a god nor a mortal, but a great devil," that is to say a Great Spirit that presides over universal love. This proposition was held against him like a crime.

17. *Virtue cannot be taught, but comes as a gift from God to those who possess it.*

This is almost the Christian doctrine of grace; but if virtue is a gift from God, then it is a favour and we may ask why it is not conceded to all. On the other hand, if it is a gift then there is no merit on the part of those who possess it. Spiritism is more explicit in saying that those who possess a virtue have acquired it through their own efforts during successive lives, by ridding themselves, little by little, of their imperfections. Grace is a force that God gives to a well-meaning man or woman so that he or she may expunge their evilness and so be able to practice Goodness.

18. *The natural disposition shown by all is to perceive our defects far less than we see those of others.*

The Gospel says, "You see the speck of sawdust that is in the eye of your neighbour, but you do not see the plank that is in your own eye." (See Chap. 10, items 9 & 10.)

19. *If doctors are unsuccessful in treating the majority of ailments it is because they treat the body without treating the soul. If the whole is not in good condition, then it is impossible that part of it should be well.*

Spiritism offers the key to the relationship that exists between the soul and the body, so proving that one of them is constantly reacting over the other. This idea opens up a new field of Science. With the possibility of showing the real cause of certain ailments, the way of curing them becomes easier. When Science takes into account the spiritual element in the organism, then failures will be much less frequent.

20. *Right from infancy, humans commit far more evil than good.*

In this sentence, Socrates touches on the grave question of the predominance of evil on Earth. This question is insoluble without knowledge of the plurality of worlds and the destiny of our planet Earth, inhabited as it is by only a fraction of Humanity. Only Spiritism gives us a solution that is more fully explained in Chaps. 3, 4 & 5.

21. *There is wisdom in not believing in that what you know not.*

This is directed at those who offer criticism about matters that are unknown to them, even in basic terms. Plato completes this thought of Socrates by saying, "In first place, if it is possible, we must make them more honest in their words; if they are not, *we shall not bother with them*, and we shall seek nothing but the truth. We shall do our best to instruct them, *but shall not insult them.*" This is how Spiritism should proceed in relation to those who contradict, whether in good or bad faith. If Plato were to reappear today, he would find things almost as they were in his time and he would be able to use the same words. Socrates would also meet creatures that would jeer at his belief in spirits and would believe him to be mad, together with his disciple Plato.

It was for having professed these principles that Socrates saw himself ridiculed, accused of impiety and condemned to drink hemlock. So assuredly, these great new truths, by calling up against themselves interests and preconceptions that hurt, will not be accepted without a fight or without making martyrs.

THE GOSPEL
ACCORDING TO SPIRITISM

CHAPTER 1

I HAVE NOT COME TO DESTROY THE LAW

The three revelations: Moses, Christ and Spiritism. - The Alliance of science and religion. - INSTRUCTIONS FROM THE SPIRITS: The New Era.

1. Think not that I am come to destroy the law, or the prophets, I am not come to destroy but to fulfil. For verily I say unto you, Till heaven and earth pass, not one jot or one tittle, shall in no wise pass from the law, till all be fulfilled. (MATTHEW 5:17 & 18.)

MOSES

2. There are two distinct parts to the Mosaic Law: the Law of God as promulgated on Mount Sinai and the civil or disciplinary law decreed by Moses. The first is invariable; the other, being appropriate to the customs and character of the people, modifies itself with time.

The Law of God is formulated on the following Ten Commandments:[7]

I. -   *I am the Lord your God, which have brought you out of the land of Egypt, out of the house of bondage. You shall have no other gods before me. You shall not make for yourself any graven image, or any likeness of any thing that is in heaven above or that is in the earth beneath, nor that is in the waters under the earth. You shall not bow down yourself to them, nor serve them.[8]*

II. -   *You shall not take the name of the Lord your God in vain.*

III. -   *Remember the Sabbath Day, to keep it Holy.*

IV. -   *Honour your father and your mother, so that you may live long in the land the Lord your God will give you.*

V. -   *You shall not kill.*

VI. -   *You shall not commit adultery.*

VII. -   *You shall not steal.*

VIII. - *You shall not bear false witness against your neighbour.*

IX. -   *You shall not covet your neighbour's wife.*

X. -   *You shall not covet your neighbour's house, or his manservant or maidservant, his ox, nor his donkey, or anything that belongs to your neighbour.*

---

[7] All Bible extracts are taken from THE HOLY BIBLE as Authorised by King James, published 2003, by Thomas Nelson, US. (Translator's comment.)

[8] Allan Kardec thought fit to quote only the first part of this verse (five). We would therefore call attention to the great significance of this unquoted section that states that the sins of the fathers will be visited upon the third and fourth generations according to the original translations, and not the first and second generations as is stated in some of the recent translations.

In fact, this was a veiled teaching of reincarnation. By the third or fourth generation the sinner has had time to reincarnate yet again, which logically means that the one who originally sinned will pay his or her own debts. This is far more in keeping with God, Who is all loving and merciful, than the suggestion that He would vent the sins of the fathers on the children who had nothing to do with the matter. (Translator's comment.)

This Law is for all times and all countries and because of this it has a divine character. All other laws were decreed by Moses, who found it necessary to restrain his people through fear due to their turbulent and undisciplined nature, and to combat the abuses and prejudices acquired by them during the period of slavery in Egypt. To give authority to his laws, he had to give them a divine origin, as did other legislators of primitive peoples. The authority for Humankind needed to base itself on the authority of God. Only the idea of a terrible God could impress ignorant peoples in whom the sentiments of true justice and morality were very little developed. It is evident that He, Who included amongst His commandments *'You shall not commit murder or cause damage to your neighbour'* could not then contradict Himself by making extermination a duty. The Mosaic Laws themselves thus had an essentially transitory character.

CHRIST

3. Jesus did not come to destroy the Law, that is to say God's Law. He came to fulfil and develop it, to show its real meaning and to adapt it to the degree of advancement of human beings at that time. That is why we find within the Law the principle of our duty to God and our fellow beings to be the base of His Teachings. Regarding the laws devised by Moses, we find that he, on the contrary, modified them profoundly, both in form and in substance. While constantly combating the abuses of exterior practices and false interpretations, he was unable to make the people go through a more radical reform than that of reducing the Law to the order: *'Love God above all things and your neighbour as yourself,'* adding *'this is all the law and the prophets'*.

By the words, 'Heaven and Earth will not pass till everything is fulfilled, even to the last jot,' Jesus wished to say it was necessary for God's Law to be completely implemented and practised over all the Earth in all its pureness, with all its amplifications and consequences. In effect, what use would it have been to promulgate the Law if it were only to benefit one nation or only a few people? Humankind, being sons and daughters of God, is without distinction and so subject to the same solicitude.

4. But the role of Jesus was not simply that of a moralist legislator, merely offering His word as exclusive authority. It fell to Him to complete the prophecies, which had announced His advent, by means of the exceptional nature of His Spirit and His divine mission. Jesus came to teach human beings that true life is not the one lived here on Earth, but rather the life lived in Heaven. He came to show the pathway to this Kingdom, how to be reconciled with God and to present these facts as part of things to come which would enable people to fulfil their destiny. However, He did not explain everything, but limited Himself to offering only the initial part of the truth on many subjects, saying that people as yet could not understand the whole truth. Nevertheless, He talked about all things in implied terms. In order for people to be able to understand the hidden meaning of His words, it was necessary for new ideas and knowledge to mature. Thus bringing the indispensable key, as these things could not appear before the human spirit had achieved a certain degree of maturity. Science still had to play an important part in the emergence and development of these ideas; therefore, it was necessary to give time for Science to progress.

SPIRITISM

5. Spiritism is the new Science that has come to reveal to humanity, by means of irrefutable proofs, the existence and nature of the spiritual world and its relationship with the physical world. It appears not as something supernatural, but on the contrary, as one of the living and incessantly active forces of Nature. As the

source of an immense number of phenomena, which still today are not fully understood, and because of this they are relegated to the world of fantasy and miracles. Christ alluded to this situation on several occasions and it is the reason why much of what He said remained unintelligible or has been wrongly interpreted. Spiritism offers the key by which all can easily be explained.

6. The law of the *Old Testament* was personified in Moses and that of the *New Testament* in Christ. Spiritism is then the third revelation of God's Law. However, no one personifies it because it represents teaching given not by Humans, but by the spirits who are the *voices of Heaven,* to all parts of the world through the co-operation of innumerable intermediaries. In a manner of speaking, it is a collective work formed by all the Spirits who bring enlightenment to humanity by offering the means of understanding their world and the destiny that awaits each individual on their return to the spiritual world.

7. Just as Christ said, "I am not come to destroy the Law but to fulfil it," so Spiritism says, "We have not come to destroy the Christian Law but to carry it out." It teaches nothing contrary to what Christ taught. Rather it develops it and explains it in a manner that can be understood by everyone. It completes what had previously been known only in its allegoric form. Spiritism has come at the predicted time to fulfil what Christ announced and to prepare for the achievement of future things. It is then, the work of Christ Who, as He also announced, presides over the regeneration that is now taking place that will prepare for the reign of the Kingdom of God here on Earth.

THE ALLIANCE OF SCIENCE AND RELIGION

8. Science and religion are the two levers of human intelligence; one revealing the laws of the material world, the other revealing those of the moral world. *Nevertheless, seeing that*

these laws have the same principle, which is God, they cannot contradict themselves. If they contradict one another, it would stand to reason that one was right and the other wrong. However, God could not have intended the destruction of His own work. Therefore, the incompatibility that apparently exists between these two ideas proves that they have been incorrectly interpreted, due to excessive exclusiveness on both sides. For this reason, we have a conflict that has given rise to incredulity and intolerance.

We have now reached a phase upon this planet when the teachings of Christ must be completed and the intentional veil cast over some parts of these teachings lifted. A time when Science must desist in its exclusive materialism, so taking into consideration the spiritual element; when Religion must cease to ignore the organic and immutable law of matter, so that both may become two forces, each leaning on the other and advancing together in mutual concourse. Then religion, no longer being able to oppose the overwhelming logic of the facts and no longer discredited by science, will acquire an unshakeable power because it will be in agreement with reason.

Science and religion could not come together until this time as they could only see matters according to their own exclusive points of view, which in turn caused them to be reciprocally repelled. Something more was needed to enable them to close the gap that separated them, something which could unite them. This missing link is contained in the knowledge of the laws that govern the spiritual universe and its relationship with the world of matter. These laws are as immutable as those that govern the movement of the planets and the existence of all beings. Once this relationship had been proven by experiments, a new light began to shine and faith was directed towards reason. On encountering nothing illogical in faith, then finally reasoning was able to defeat materialism. However, as in many other matters, there are always those who remain behind until the general wave of movement towards progress drags them along. If they choose to resist instead of accompanying this movement they will eventually be crushed. So, after an elaboration that has lasted for more than eighteen centuries, a moral revolution is now in progress, operated and directed by Spirit, as Humanity reaches the climax of its present potentialities and marches towards a New Era. It is easy to forecast the consequences, which will cause inevitable changes in social relations and be impossible to withstand, because they are determined by God and derived from the Law of Progress that is one of God's Laws.

INSTRUCTIONS FROM THE SPIRITS

THE NEW ERA

9. God is unique, and Moses was a Spirit whom He sent on a mission to make known His presence, not only to the Hebrews but also to the entire pagan world. The Hebrew peoples were God's instrument to enable Him to manifest through Moses and the prophets. The vicissitudes suffered by these peoples were meant to attract their attention and so help disclose the existence of the Divinity.

God's commandments, as revealed through Moses, contain the essence of the most comprehensive Christian morality. However, the biblical commentaries and annotations restrict their meaning, because if they had been put into action in all their pureness they would not have been understood. Nevertheless, these Ten Commandments have become a brilliant frontispiece and a beacon destined to light up the pathway which humanity must follow.

The morality taught by Moses was appropriate to the state of advancement of the people he proposed to regenerate. These people were semi-barbaric with respect to the perfecting of the soul and would not have understood that God could be worshipped by other means than a holocaust, or that it is necessary to forgive one's enemies. From the materialistic, scientific and artistic points of view, their intelligence was remarkable, but they were morally backward and would never have been converted by a wholly spiritual religion. Therefore, it was necessary that they were offered a semi-materialistic form of religion, as is presented in the Hebrew faith. The holocausts spoke to their senses at the same time that the idea of God touched their spirits.

Christ was the initiator of the most pure and sublime morality. That is to say, the morality of the evangelical Christian will renew the entire world by bringing together all human beings and turn them into brothers and sisters. It will cause charity to blossom forth in all hearts as well as love for one's neighbour, so establishing a common solidarity between all peoples. Finally, from this morality, which will transform the whole Earth, the planet will become the home of Spirits far superior than those that have inhabit it until now. This is the law of progress, that will be accomplished and to which nature is submitted. *Spiritism* is the lever that God is using to enable humanity to advance.

The time has come in which moral ideas must be developed to bring about the progress determined by God. These ideas will follow the same route as that taken by the ideas of liberty, its predecessor. Do not think however, that these developments will be effected without a fight. No, in order to reach maturity these ideas will need discussion and conflicts so they may attract the attention of the masses. Once achieved, the beauty and sanctity of this morality will touch all spirits, who will in turn embrace a science that will give them the key to a future life and open the doors to eternal happiness. Moses showed humanity the way; Jesus continued this work; Spiritism will finish it. - AN ISRAELITE SPIRIT (Mulhouse, 1861).

10. Once, in His undying charity, God permitted humankind to see the truth pierce the darkness. That day was the advent of Christ. After the living Light had gone, the darkness returned; having been given the alternatives of truth or obscurity the world once again lost itself. Then, similar to the prophets of the Old Testament, the Spirits began speaking and finally gave warning that the world is trembling on its very foundations and thunder will resound. Remain steady!

Spiritism is of a divine order as it is based upon the actual Laws of Nature, and you may be certain that everything of a divine nature has a great and useful objective. Your world was losing itself yet again because science, developed at the cost of all that is moral, was only inducing you to material well being, resulting in benefit for the Spirits of darkness. Ah, eighteen centuries of blood and martyrs, and still Christ's reign has not yet come! Christians, return to the Teacher who wishes to save you! It is easy for those who believe and who love. Love fills us with indescribable happiness. Yes, my children, the world is shaking as the Good Spirits have repeatedly warned. Bend with the wind that announces the storm, so that you will not be thrown down. That is to say, prepare yourselves so as not to be like the foolish virgins who were taken by surprise at the arrival of their husbands!

The revolution that prepares itself is more moral than material. The Great Spirits, who are divine messengers, instil faith amongst you so that all who are enlightened and zealous workers may make their humble voices heard, seeing that all humanity are like grains of sand, without which there would be no mountains. Thus the words 'we are so small' lack significance. To each one their mission, to each their work. Does not the ant build its republic, and other imperceptible animals raise continents? The new crusade has begun! Apostles, not of war, but of universal peace, modern Saint Bernards, look ahead and march forward! The law of the worlds is a law of progress. - FÉNELON (Poitiers, 1861).

11. Saint Augustine is one of the greatest propagators of Spiritism. He has manifested himself in almost every part. The reason for this is found in the life story of this great Christian philosopher. He belongs to a vigorous phalanx known as Fathers of the Church, to whom Christianity owes its most solid bases. Like many others, he was uprooted from Paganism, or rather from the most profound godlessness, by the splendour of truth. When suddenly, in the midst of dissipations, he felt a strange vibration in his soul that called him to himself; and made him understand that happiness was not to be found in debilitating and escapist pleasures. Finally, he too had a similar experience to Paul, who heard saintly voices calling to him on the road to Damascus saying "Saul, Saul, why do you persecute me?" When Saint Augustine heard his voices, he exclaimed "Dear God! Dear God! Forgive me! I believe; I am a Christian!" From this moment on, he became one of the greatest supporters of the Gospel. You may read the notable confessions left by this eminent Spirit, the characteristic and prophetic words he uttered after the death of Saint Monica, *"I am convinced that my mother will visit me and give me advice, revealing to me what awaits us in the future life."* What great teaching in these words! What resounding foresight of the teachings that was to come! This is the reason why today, seeing that the time has come to spread the truth as he predicted, he has become its ardent disseminator and as it were, multiplied himself in order to be able to reply to all who call him. - ERASTUS, disciple of Saint Paul (Paris 1863).

NOTE: Would it be possible for Saint Augustine to demolish what he himself had built? Surely not, but, just as many others before him, he now sees with the eyes of spirit what he could not see while he was a man. In freedom, his soul sees new brightness and understands what previously had been impossible to understand. New ideas have revealed to him the true meaning of certain words. On Earth, he judged things according to the knowledge he possessed at that time. However, ever since he saw the new light he could appreciate those words more judiciously. Thus, he had to revise his beliefs regarding incubus and succubus spirits, as well as the condemnation that he had launched against the theory of the antipodes. Now that he can see Christianity in its true light and in all its pureness, it is acceptable that on some points he thinks differently from when he was alive, which in no way prohibits him from continuing to be a Christian apostle. He may even establish himself as a disseminator of Spiritism without renouncing his faith, because he has seen that which had been forecast come to pass. Therefore, by proclaiming these Teachings today, he only leads us towards a more correct and logical interpretation of the texts. The same also occurs with other Spirits who find themselves in a similar position.

CHAPTER 2

MY KINGDOM IS NOT OF THIS WORLD

The future life. - The kingship of Jesus. - A point of view. -
INSTRUCTIONS FROM THE SPIRITS: An earthy kingship.

1. Then Pilate entered into the judgement hall again, and called Jesus, and said to him, Are you the king of the Jews? Jesus answered, My Kingdom is not of this world. *If my kingdom were of this world, then would my servant's fight, that I should not be delivered to the Jews: but now my kingdom is not here."*

Then Pilate said, "So you are king!" Jesus answered, "You say that I am king. For this reason I was born, and for this reason I came into the world, to testify to the truth. Everyone on the side of truth listens to me. (JOHN, 18:33, 36 & 37.)

THE FUTURE LIFE

2. With these words, Jesus clearly refers to *a future life,* which He presents in all circumstances as the goal to be reached by Humanity and which should be our greatest preoccupation here on Earth. All of his maxims refer to this great principle. Indeed, without a future life, there would be no reason to have the majority of these moral precepts. This is why those who do not believe in a future life cannot understand, or think the matter foolish because they imagine that Jesus was only speaking of the present life.

This dogma can be considered as the basis of Christ's teaching, the central pivot. Therefore, it has been placed as the first item in this work. It must be the point to be most closely looked at, as it is the only one that justifies the anomalies and irregularities of earthly life and shows itself to be in accordance with the justice of God.

3. The Jews had only very vague ideas regarding a future life. They believed in angels, whom they considered privileged beings of the creation; they did not know, however, that men and women could one day become angels and so participate in the same happiness. According to them, the observance of God's Law would bring worldly recompense, the supremacy of their nation, and victory over their enemies. The public calamities and downfalls were a punishment for disobedience to these laws. Moses could say no more than this to those who were mostly shepherds or ignorant people who needed to be touched, before anything else, by worldly things. Later, Jesus revealed that there exists another world where God's justice follows its course. He promises this world to all those who obey the commandments of God and where those who are Good find recompense. This is His kingdom, where He will be found in all His glory and to which He returned when He left Earth.

However, when adapting His teachings to the conditions of humanity at that time, Jesus did not consider it convenient to give them all the truth. For He saw they would only be dazzled by it and unable to understand, so He limited Himself, in a manner of speaking, to the presentation of a future life as a principle, as a Natural Law whose action no one could escape. Therefore, every Christian firmly believes in a future life. However, the idea that many people hold is still vague, incomplete, and because of this, quite false on various points. For the majority of people, it is nothing more than a belief, void of absolute certainty, so this is why there are doubts and even incredulity.

Spiritism has come to complete this point, as well as many others touched on by the teachings of Christ, now that human beings are sufficiently mature as to be able to learn the truth. With Spiritism, a future life is no longer an article of faith, a mere hypothesis. It becomes a material reality, as facts demonstrate, because those who have described it to us have all been eyewitnesses. So not only is doubt no longer possible but also anyone of whatever intelligence is able to get an idea of its many varied aspects; in the same way that we can imagine what a country we have never visited is like by reading a detailed description of it. This description of the future life is circumstantiated to such an extent and the conditions of existence for those who reside there, be they happy or unhappy, are so rational that we are bound to agree that it could not be otherwise. It patently represents the true justice of God.

THE KINGSHIP OF JESUS

4. We can all recognize that the Kingdom of Jesus is not of this world, but could He not also have a kingdom on Earth? The title of 'King' does not always imply temporary authority. We give this title by unanimous consent to anyone who rises to the highest level of whatever idea dominates the times and influences human progress. In this way, we frequently use the expression of 'king' or 'prince' for philosophers, artists, poets, writers, etc. In many cases, this kind of royalty, coming from personal merit or having been consecrated by posterity, reveals supremacy far greater than that circling a royal crown. The first is but a toy of the vicissitudes, whereas the second is imperishable. The generations that follow the first sometimes have cause to curse, whereas those who follow the second always bless themselves. The earthly one extinguishes with life; but the sovereignty of morality continues and maintains its reign, ruling above all after death. From this aspect then, is not Jesus a mightier and more powerful King than all the sovereigns of the Earth? It was with good reason that He said to Pilate: "I am a King, but my Kingdom is not of this world".

A POINT OF VIEW

5. The clear and precise idea that can be formed of a future life provides an unshakable faith in what is to come. This faith places enormous consequences upon the moralization of humans because it completely changes *the point of view as to how life on Earth is regarded.* For those who place themselves by means of thought in the spiritual life, which is undefined, bodily life becomes a mere temporary stay in an ungrateful country. The vicissitudes and tribulations of this life become nothing more than incidents, which can be supported with patience, as they are known to be of short duration and will be followed by a more amenable state. Death no longer has terror attached to it; it ceases to be a door opening on to nothingness and becomes a door that opens to liberation, through which the exile enters into a well-blessed mansion, and there finds peace. Knowing that the place where we find ourselves now is only temporary, and not definite, makes us pay less attention to the preoccupations of life, resulting in less bitterness and a more peaceful state of mind.

Simply by doubting the existence of a future life, people direct all their thoughts to earthly existence. Without any certainty of what is to come, they give everything to the present. With the mistaken idea that there is nothing more precious than earthly things, they behave as a child who can see only its toys and is prepared to go to any length to obtain the only possessions they judge to be solid. The loss of even the least of these causes pungent hurt, be it a mistake, a deception, an unsatisfied ambition, an injustice to which the person has fallen victim, hurt pride or vanity just to name a few. These are some of the torments that turn existence into an eternal agony. So in this manner causing *self-inflicted torture at every step.* From the point of view of earthly life, in whose centre we place ourselves, everything around us begins to assume vast proportions. The harm that reaches us, as well as the good that touches others, takes on a great importance in our eyes. It is like the person who, when in the middle of a great city sees everything on a large scale, but who, when looking down from a mountain top sees things in only minute form.

This is what happens when we look at life from the point of view of a future existence. Humanity, just as the stars in space, loses itself in the great immensity. We begin to see that great and small things are confounded, like ants on top of an anthill; that proletarians and potentates are of the same stature. We lament that so many short-lived creatures give themselves over to so much labour in order to conquer a place that will do so little to elevate them, and which they will occupy for so short a space of time. From this, it follows that the value given to earthly things is completely in reverse to that which comes from a firm belief in a future life.

6. If everybody thought in that manner, it could be argued that everything on Earth would be endangered, because no one would bother about anything. However, each person instinctively looks after their own well-being; even if it were known it was only for a short time people would still do their best. There is no one who, when finding a thorn in their hand, will not take it out so as not to suffer. Well then, the desire for comfort forces people to improve all things, seeing that we are impelled by the instinct of progress and conservation that are elements of the Laws of Nature. Therefore, humanity labours not only through necessity, but also from enjoyment and a sense of duty, so obeying the designs of Providence that has placed humans on Earth for that purpose. Only those who occupy themselves with the future can give relative importance to the present. These people are easily consoled in all of their failings and misfortunes by thinking of the destiny that waits.

Accordingly, God does not condemn all earthly pleasures and possessions, but only condemns the abuse of these things in detriment to the soul. All those who take these words of Jesus for themselves *"My Kingdom is not of this world"* are guarding against these abuses.

Those who identify themselves with a future life are as a rich person who loses a small sum without emotion. Those whose thoughts are concentrated on earthly things are as the poor man who loses all he has and so becomes desperate.

7. Spiritism opens up and broadens out the thought process, offering new horizons. In place of a short-sighted vision concentrated only on the present, it makes this fleeting moment passed on Earth the unique and fragile axis of our eternal future. Spiritism shows us that this life is nothing more than a link in the magnificently harmonious assembly that is God's work. It also shows us the solidarity that joins together all the different existences of one being, of all beings of the same world and all the beings of all the worlds. It offers the base and the reason for universal fraternity, whereas the teaching of the creation of the soul at the birth of the body makes each creature a stranger one to the other. This solidarity between parts of a whole explains what is inexplicable when only one of these parts is considered. This entirety would not have been possible to understand at the time of Christ, and for this reason, He waited until later to make this knowledge known.

INSTRUCTIONS FROM THE SPIRITS

AN EARTHLY KINGSHIP

8. Who better than I to understand the truth of these words of Our Lord, *"My Kingdom is not of this world"*? When on Earth, I

lost myself through pride. Who then can understand the total lack of value of an earthly kingdom better than I? What was I able to bring with me of my earthly regality? Nothing! Absolutely nothing! Moreover, as if to make my lesson more terrible, it did not even accompany me to my tomb! A queen amongst men, I thought to enter Heaven as a queen. What a disillusion! What a humiliation when, instead of being received as a sovereign, I saw above me, a long way above me, those whom I had judged insignificant and had despised because they were not of noble blood. Oh! How I understand now the barrenness of honours and splendour so eagerly courted on Earth!

In order to win a place in this kingdom, it is necessary to show abnegation, humility, benevolence and charity in all its most celestial forms. They do not ask who you are, or what position you occupied. Instead, they ask what good you have done, how many tears you dried.

Oh Jesus! You said that Your Kingdom was not of this world because it is necessary to suffer in order to reach Heaven, and one cannot reach there by means of the steps to a throne. Only the most painful paths lead to it. Seek your path then, through briars and thorns and not amongst the flowers.

Men and women hurry back and forth with the hope of acquiring earthly possessions as if they would be able to keep them forever. Here, however, illusions disappear and it is soon perceived that they had only been chasing shadows. Then it becomes apparent that the only truly golden possessions, the only ones that can be made use of in their heavenly home, the only ones that can offer the possibility of entry, have been despised.

Have pity on those who have not entered into Heaven. Help them with your prayers, because prayer helps to bring all souls closer to the Most High; it is what links Heaven and Earth. Do not forget! - A QUEEN OF FRANCE (Havre, 1863).

CHAPTER 3

IN MY FATHER'S HOUSE
ARE MANY MANSIONS

The different states of the soul in its spiritual wanderings. - The different categories of inhabited worlds. - Earth's destiny. - The cause of human miseries. - INSTRUCTIONS FROM THE SPIRITS: Superior and inferior worlds. - Worlds of tests and atonement. - Regenerating worlds. - The progression of the worlds.

1. *"Let not your hearts be troubled. You believe in God, believe also in me. In my Father's house are many mansions: If it were not so, I would have told you. I am going to prepare a place for you. And if I go and prepare a place for you, I will come again, and receive you unto myself: that where I am, you may be also."* (JOHN, 14:1 - 3).

THE DIFFERENT STATES OF THE SOUL IN ITS SPIRITUAL WANDERINGS

2. The house of the Father is the Universe. The 'different mansions' are the worlds that circulate in infinite space and offer the spirits who incarnate on them dwelling places corresponding to their progress.

Apart from the diversity of the different worlds, the words of Jesus also refer to the fortunate or wretched states of the soul in the spiritual world. Conforming to whether the soul is more or less purified and detached from material ties, the ambient in which it finds itself will vary infinitely in the aspects of things, in the sensations it feels and in the perceptions it has. While some cannot leave the ambient where they live, others raise themselves and travel to other worlds and all over space. While some guilty spirits wander in darkness, there are others who have earned happiness, and these rejoice in a state of shining brightness, while they contemplate the sublime spectacle of the great infinity. Finally, while inferior spirits are tormented by remorse and grief, frequently isolated without consolation, separated from those who were the object of their affections and punished by the iron gauntlet of moral suffering, the just Spirits, together with their loved ones, enjoy the delights of an indescribable happiness. Also in that sense, there are many mansions, although they are not circumscribed or localized.

THE DIFFERENT CATEGORIES OF INHABITED WORLDS

3. As a result of teachings from the Spirits, we know that the conditions of the various worlds differ one from the other with respect to the degree of elevation or inferiority of their inhabitants. Amongst these are those inferior to the inhabitants of Earth, both physically and morally. Then there are some in the same category and yet others which are more or less superior in every aspect. In the inferior worlds, existence is all material, passions are sovereign and morality is almost nil. As souls progress, material influences diminish to such an extent that in the elevated worlds, life is by way of saying, all spiritual.

4. On intermediate worlds, good is mixed with evil, one or the other predominating, according to the degree of advancement of the majority of the inhabitants in any one locality. Although it is not possible to make an absolute classification of all the different worlds, we can at least divide them in general terms by virtue of the state in which they are in and the destiny they bring with them. Based on the most predominant features upon each planet, we may surmise them in a general manner: primitive worlds, destined to receive the initial incarnations of human souls; worlds of tests and

atonements, where evil predominates; regenerating worlds, where souls who still have to atone may absorb new strength by resting from the fatigue of fighting; happy worlds, where goodness outweighs evil; celestial or divine worlds the home of purified spirits, where goodness reigns exclusively. The Earth belongs to the category of worlds of tests and atonements, being the reason why humanity lives exposed to so many miseries.

5. Spirits who find themselves incarnated in any world are not bound to that same world indefinitely, nor do they go through all the phases of progress needed to achieve perfection in that one world. When, in one world, they reach the maximum degree of advancement that world has to offer, they then pass on to a more elevated one, and so on successively until they reach the state of purified Spirits. These different worlds are stations where in each one they find elements for progress they need, in accordance with their degree of perfection. For the spirits it is a recompense to ascend to a world of higher elevation, just as it is a punishment to prolong their stay in a miserable world or to be relegated to another even unhappier than the one they were forced to leave, due to persisting in evil.

EARTH'S DESTINY.
THE CAUSE OF HUMAN MISERIES

6. Many are surprised that on Earth there is so much evil, so many crude passions, so many miseries and every kind of sickness. From this, they conclude, the human species is a very miserable one. This judgment comes from the very narrow point of view of those who emit it, which gives a false idea of the whole. We must consider, however, that in fact the entirety of Humanity is not all on Earth, but only a small fraction of the total. In effect, the human species covers all endowed with a capacity for reasoning that inhabit the innumerable orbs of the Universe.

What then is the mere population of the Earth when compared with the total population of all the worlds? Much less than that of a very small village compared to a great empire. The material and moral situations of terrestrial Humanity are not surprising when we take into consideration the destiny of the Earth and the nature of its inhabitants.

7. It would be a great mistake to judge all the inhabitants of a city by those who inhabit the lowest and most sordid places. In a hospital we see none but the sick and mutilated; in a prison, we find gathered together all kinds of vileness, baseness and many vices; in unhealthy regions, the inhabitants are, for the most part, pale, puny and sickly. Well then, picture the Earth as a combination of a suburb, a hospital and an unhealthy place, because it is all of these put together. Then it can be understood why afflictions outweigh pleasures, for we do not send those who are healthy to a hospital, nor do we throw those who have practised no wrong into houses of correction.

Neither can hospitals and houses of correction be places of delight. Therefore, in the same way that the total population of a city is not found in its hospitals and prisons, neither do we find the entirety of population here on Earth. Just as the sick leave hospital when they are cured and those who have served their term leave prison, when a person is cured of all their moral infirmities they will also leave the Earth environment to go to happier worlds.

INSTRUCTIONS FROM THE SPIRITS

SUPERIOR AND INFERIOR WORLDS

8. In qualifying inferior and superior worlds, there is nothing absolute. A world is relatively inferior or superior only in relation

to those other worlds, which may be above or below it on the scale of progression.

In taking the Earth as a comparison, we may get an idea of what an inferior world is like by supposing its inhabitants to be similar to the primitive races or members of the barbaric nations. Examples are still found amongst us today, these being the remnants of the primitive state of this planet. In the most backward worlds, the inhabitants are, to a certain extent, rudimentary creatures, having human form but devoid of all beauty. Their instincts have not yet softened to any sentiment of delicacy or benevolence, nor have they acquired any notions of justice or injustice. Brute force is the only known law. Without either industry or inventions, they pass their time in the conquest of food. However, God does not abandon even one of His creatures; at the bottom of the darkest intelligence lurks a seed, sometimes more, sometimes less developed, of a vague intuition of a Supreme Being. This instinct is enough to make them superior one from another and to prepare their ascension to a more complete life. They are not degraded beings, but children who are growing. Between inferior and elevated levels are innumerable others. From the pure Spirits, dematerialized and brilliant with glory, it is impossible to recognize the primitive beings they once were; just as from the adult, it is difficult to recognize the embryo.

9. In worlds that have reached a superior level, the moral and material state is very different from that existing on Earth. As everywhere, the form is always human, but it is more beautiful, more perfected and above all else, purified. The body possesses nothing of earthly materiality and consequently is not subject to the same necessities, sicknesses or deteriorations, which the predominance of matter provokes. Due to the higher refinements, the senses are able to capture perceptions that the gross matter of this world obstructs. The specific lightness of body permits rapid and easy locomotion. Instead of dragging painfully over the

ground the body floats, as it were, above the surface or glides through the air with no effort apart from that of desire; just as the angels are depicted as doing, or as the manes on the Elysian fields. According to their wishes, humans keep the features of their past migrations and show themselves to their friends as they had known them, but illuminated by a divine light, transfigured by interior impressions that are always of an elevated nature. In place of countenances discoloured and dejected by suffering and passions, life and intelligence now sparkle with a splendour that painters have shown through the halo or aureole of the Saints.

Very advanced Spirits suffer only slight resistance to matter, thus allowing body development to be extremely rapid, making infancy short and almost non-existent. With the absence of worry and anguish, life is proportionally longer than on Earth. In principle, longevity is in proportion to the degree of advancement of each world. Death in no way conveys any horror of decomposition. Far from causing terror, it is considered a happy transformation because there is no doubt as to the future. During life, the soul, being no longer constricted by compact matter, expands itself and delights in a lucidity that places it in an almost constant state of emancipation, allowing completely free transmission of thought.

10. In blissful worlds relationships between peoples and individuals are always friendly, never perturbed by ambition to enslave their neighbour or make war. There are neither masters nor slaves and none privileged by birth, only moral and intellectual superiority, establishing all conditions and ultimately giving supremacy. Authority receives and deserves the respect of everyone, being given only to those who merit it and thus always exercised with justice. *People do not try to elevate themselves above one another, but only above themselves by striving for perfection.* Their objective is to ascend to the category of Pure Spirits. This desire is never a torment but rather a noble ambition

that induces the person to study ardently in order to become an equal. In these worlds, all the delicate and elevated sentiments of human nature find themselves exalted and purified. Hate is unknown, as are petty jealousies and the covetousness of envy. The ties of love and unity bind all humanity together so that the strong help the weak. Through a greater or lesser degree of intelligence, humanity acquires possessions of a smaller or larger quantity. However, nobody suffers from want, as no one needs to make atonement. In short, evil does not exist in these worlds.

11. Evil is still needed on your world in order to make goodness felt; night in order to be able to admire light; sickness to be able to appreciate health. In those other worlds, there is no need for these contrasts. Eternal light, eternal beauty and eternal serenity of the soul offer proportional eternal happiness, free from the perturbations caused by the anguish of material life and the contact with evil, which finds no access into these realms. These are the things that human spirits find most difficulty in understanding. Humanity has been sufficiently ingenious as to paint the torments of hell, but could never imagine the glories of Heaven. Why not? Because, being inferior, only pain and misery have been known and the celestial brightness has never been seen, so one cannot speak of that which is unknown. However, according as to humanity is raising itself up and cleansing its soul, horizons are expanding and people begin to compare the goodness that is in front of them, as well as the evil that lies behind them.

12. Meanwhile, the happy worlds are not privileged orbs, as God is not partial to any one of His children. To each one He gives the same rights and the same opportunities wherein to reach these worlds. He makes each one start at the same point and gives no one more than another. Even the highest categories are accessible to all. It only depends on the individual to conquer their place in them by means of work, so reaching it more quickly or remaining

inactive for centuries and centuries in the quagmire of humanity. *(This is a summary of the teachings of all the Superior Spirits.)*

WORLDS OF TESTS AND ATONEMENT

13. What more is there to say about worlds of atonement that you do not already know, since you have only to look at the one in which you live? The great number of superior intelligences amongst your inhabitants indicates that the Earth is not a primitive world, destined to receive beings that have recently left the hand of the Creator. The innate qualities that they bring with them constitute proof of their having already lived and achieved a certain degree of progress. However, the number of vices to which they are subject also shows their great moral imperfections. This is why God has placed them in an ungrateful world, in which they can make atonement through hard work and suffer the miseries of life until they deserve to ascend to happier planets.

14. Nevertheless, not all the spirits that have incarnated on Earth came to atone. The races that are called savage were formed from spirits who had only just left their infancy, and who found themselves, as it were, on an educational course for development through contact with more advanced Spirits. Later came the semi-civilized races, made up of the same spirits as they travelled along their paths to progress. In general, these are the indigenous races on Earth, who will raise themselves little by little through the centuries, some of whom have already managed to reach an intelligent state equal to those who are more enlightened.

The Spirits who are in atonement are, if we may use the term, the exotic ones of the Earth. They have already lived in other worlds where they were excluded for persisting in wickedness, or for having been the cause of perturbation to the good people in those worlds. Therefore, they had to be exiled for a time to an ambient of spirits that are more backward. Thus receiving the mission of helping them to advance as they bring with them a more developed intelligence and the germs of the knowledge they have acquired. This then is how spirits under punishment are found amongst the most intelligent races, and why the misfortunes of life seem so very bitter to them. This is because they have a greater degree of sensitivity and so are more highly tested by contrarieties and sorrows than the primitive races, whose moral sense is still obtuse.

15. Consequently, the Earth offers an example of a world of atonement and although the variety is infinite, they all have one thing in common: they all serve as places of exile for those spirits who rebel against the Law of God. This means that these spirits have at the same time to fight against the perversity of humankind and the inclemency of nature that is doubly arduous, but which will develop the qualities of heart and intelligence simultaneously. God then, in all His goodness, allows punishment to become something that will benefit the spirit's progress. - SAINT AUGUSTINE (Paris, 1862.)

REGENERATING WORLDS

16. Among the many scintillating stars in the blue canopy of the sky, there are many worlds like yours, destined by God to serve as atonement and probation! Nevertheless, although there are some that are more miserable, there are also others that are happier, like those of transition, which can be called worlds of regeneration. Each planetary vortex, moving in space around a common centre, drags with it its own primitive worlds of exile, probation, regeneration and happiness. We have spoken to you of worlds where newly born spirits are placed when they are still ignorant of both good and evil, but where they have the possibility of travelling towards God, being in possession of themselves through free will. We have also revealed to you the fact that ample

faculties are given to each soul to enable it to practice the Good. But alas, there are those who succumb! So then God, Who does not desire their annihilation, permits that they go to these worlds where from one incarnation to another they are purified and regenerated, returning worthy of the glory for which they were destined.

17. Regenerating worlds serve as transition phases between those of probation and happiness. The penitent soul rests on them, finds calm and continues the purifying process. Beyond doubt, human beings still find themselves subject to the laws that rule matter; Humanity still experiences sensations and desires, but is liberated from the ungoverned passions to which you have become enslaved. They no longer have the pride that silences the heart, the envy that tortures or the hate that suffocates. The word 'love' is written on every brow. Perfect equity governs all social relationships; everyone recognizes God and tries to travel towards Him, by fulfilling His laws.

However, perfect happiness still does not exist in these worlds, only the dawning of happiness. Human beings are still made of flesh and blood and because of this, are subject to vicissitudes from which only the completely dematerialized beings are liberated. There are still tests to suffer, although without the pungent anguish of atonement. Compared to the Earth, these worlds are very pleasant and many of you would be happy to inhabit them, because they represent the calm after the storm, convalescence after cruel sickness. Therefore, being less absorbed by material things, humans there perceive the future better. They comprehend the existence of other pleasures, promised by God to those who show themselves worthy when death has once again released them from their bodies, in order to bestow upon them the true life. It is then that, being free, the soul hovers above all the horizons; no longer the feelings of gross matter, only the sensation of a pure and celestial perispirit absorbing emanations direct from

God, in the fragrance of love and charity coming straight from His breast.

18. But alas! Humanity is still fallible even in these worlds; the spirit of evil has not completely lost its empire. Not to advance is to fall back, so if humanity is not firmly placed along the pathway to righteousness they may return yet again to a world of atonement, where new and more terrible tests await. So at night, at the time of prayer and repose, contemplate the full canopy of the sky and the innumerable spheres that shine over your head. Ask yourself which ones lead to God and ask Him for one of these regenerating worlds to open to receive you after your atonement here on Earth. - SAINT AUGUSTINE (Paris, 1862.)

THE PROGRESSION OF THE WORLDS

19. Progress is a law of nature. All beings of creation animated or not, have been submitted to this Law through the bounty of God, Who wishes everything to be exalted and to prosper. Even actual destruction that appears to be the end of everything, is only a means of reaching a more perfected state through transformation, seeing that everything dies only to be reborn again, suffering no consequence from the annihilation.

At the same time as living beings progress morally, so the worlds in which they live progress materially. If we were to accompany a world during its different phases, from the first instant the atoms destined to its construction began to agglomerate, we would see it travelling along on a constantly progressive scale. Although these steps would be imperceptible to each generation, it would offer its inhabitants a more agreeable home as the generations pass, according to the manner by which they themselves advance along their pathway to progress. Therefore, we find that together with humans, the animals that are their helpers, the vegetables and the habitations, are all constantly marching along because nothing in Nature remains stationary. How glorious this idea is and so worthy of the grandeur of the Creator! It would be paltry and unworthy of His power if, on the contrary, He concentrated His solicitude and Providence on an insignificant grain of sand, which is this planet, so restricting humankind to the few people who inhabit it!

According to this Law, Earth has been in a materially and morally inferior position to that which it finds itself in today and it will lift itself up in both these aspects in order to reach a more elevated degree in the future. The time has now been reached for one of these periodic transformations, which will move the Earth upward from a world of atonement to that of a regenerating planet where humanity will be happy because God's laws will reign. - SAINT AUGUSTINE (Paris, 1862.)

CHAPTER 4

NO ONE CAN REACH GOD'S KINGDOM IF THEY ARE NOT BORN AGAIN

Resurrection and reincarnation. - Reincarnation strengthens family ties,
whereas a single life would destroy them. - INSTRUCTIONS FROM THE SPIRITS:
Limits of incarnations. - The need for incarnation.

1. When Jesus came into the coasts of Caesarea Philippi, He asked His disciples saying, whom do men say that I the Son of Man am? And they said, some say that you are John the Baptist; some, Elijah; and others Jeremiah, or one of the prophets. He said to them, but whom do you say I am? And Simon Peter answered and said, you are the Christ, the Son of the living God. And Jesus answered and said to him blessed are you, Simon Barjona: for the flesh and blood did not reveal it to you, but my Father which is in Heaven! (MATTHEW, 16:13-17; MARK, 8:27-30)

2. And king Herod heard of him, (for his name was spread abroad) and he said, That John the Baptist was risen from the dead, and therefore mighty works do show forth themselves in him. Others said, That it is Elias. And others said, That it is a prophet, or as one of the prophets. And Herod said, John have I beheaded; but who is this, of whom I hear such things? And he desired to see Him. (MARK, 6:14-15; LUKE, 9:7-9)

3. (After the transfiguration) And His disciples asked Him, saying, why then say the scribes that Elijah must first come? And Jesus answered and said to them, Elijah truly shall first come, and restore all things. But I say to you, that Elijah is come already, and they knew him not, but have done to him whatsoever they wished. Likewise shall also the Son of Man suffer of them. Then the disciples understood that he spoke to them of John the Baptist. (MATTHEW, 17:10-13; MARK, 9:11-13.)

CHAPTER 4

RESURRECTION AND REINCARNATION

4. Reincarnation was part of the Jewish dogmas that were taught under the name of *resurrection*. Only the Sadducees, who believed that everything ended with death, did not accept this idea. Jewish ideas on this point, as on many others, were not clearly defined because they had only vague and incomplete notions with regard to the soul and its connection with the body. They believed that people could live again without knowing exactly the manner by which this could happen. They used the name *resurrection* for what Spiritism more correctly calls *reincarnation*. Effectively *resurrection* presupposes a return to the same physical body, whereas science demonstrates that this is materially impossible; especially when that same body has decomposed and long since been dispersed and reabsorbed. *Reincarnation* is the return of a soul, or spirit, to physical life in another body which has been newly formed for it, and which has nothing to do with the previous one. The word 'resurrection' can be applied to Lazarus but not to Elias, or to the other prophets. If, according to their belief, John the Baptist was Elias, then the body of John could not have been the body of Elias because John was seen as a child and his parents were known. John then could be Elias *reincarnated* but not *resurrected*.

> 5. *There was a man of the Pharisees named Nicodemus, a ruler of the Jews; The same came to Jesus at night, and said to him, "Rabbi, we know you are a teacher come from God: for no-one can do these miracles you are doing except God be with him."*
>
> *Jesus answered and said to him, "Verily, verily, I say to you* except a person be born again, they cannot see the Kingdom of God."
>
> *Nicodemus said to him, "How can a person be born when they are old? Can they enter a second time into their mother's womb and be born?"*

Jesus answered, "Verily, verily, I say to you, Except a person be born of water and of the Spirit, he cannot enter into the Kingdom of God. That which is born of the flesh is flesh; and that which is born of the Spirit is spirit. Marvel not that I said to you that you must be born again. The wind blows wherever it pleases and you hear the sound of it, but you cannot tell where it comes from or where it is going. So it is with everyone born of the Spirit."

Nicodemos answered and said to him, "How can these things be?" - Jesus answered and said to him, "Are you a master of Israel and do not know these things? Verily, verily, I say to you, We speak that we do know, and testify that we have seen; and you receive not our witness. I have told you earthly things, and you believe not; how shall you believe if I tell you of heavenly things?" (JOHN, 3:1-12).

6. The idea that John had been Elias and that the prophets could relive again on Earth is found in many passages of the New Testament, but is most notably quoted in the above extract. (See verses 1, 2, & 3.) If this were an erroneous belief, Jesus would have combated it as He did many others. But according to this, He gave it complete sanction and authority by making it a basic principle and a necessary condition when He said *"No one may reach the Kingdom of God if he is not born again."* Further insisting when He added *"Do not be surprised when I say it is necessary to be reborn."*

7. The words, *"If a person is not born again of water and of Spirit,"* have been interpreted in the sense of regeneration by means of the water of Baptism. However, in the original text it was said simply: *"not born of water and of spirit,"* whereas in some translations the words *"of spirit"* have been substituted by *"Holy Spirit,"*[9] which does not correspond to the original meaning.

---

[9] The translation by Osterwald is according to the original text. It says: NOT BORN OF THE WATER AND OF THE SPIRIT. That of Sacy says: OF THE HOLY SPIRIT, and that of Lamennais: OF THE HOLY SPIRIT.

This capital point stands out from the first comments that the Gospels raised and will one day be confirmed beyond all possible doubt.

8. To enable the real meaning of these words to be reached it is also necessary to pay attention to the significance of the word *water*, which is not used here in its usual sense.

The knowledge of physics was imperfect in ancient times when it was believed that the Earth had risen out of the water. Therefore, water was considered to be the exclusive primitive generating substance. This is why we read in the book of Genesis, "The Spirit of God moved upon the face of the waters; it floated above the waters; - Let there be firmament in the midst of the waters; - Let the waters under the heaven be gathered together into one place, and let the dry land appear; - Let the waters *bring forth* abundantly the moving creatures that have life, and fowl that may fly over the Earth and under the firmament."

According then to this belief, water represented the nature of matter, just as the spirit represented the nature of intelligence. The words: "If a person is not reborn of the waters and of the Spirit, or in water and in Spirit," thus signify, "if a person is not born with their body and their soul." These words were originally understood in this manner.

This interpretation is wholly justified by these other words, "*What is born of the flesh is flesh and what is born of spirit is spirit.*" Here Jesus established a clear distinction between body and spirit. "*What is born of the flesh*" clearly indicates that only the body generates from the body and that the spirit is independent.

9. The words, "The wind blows wherever it pleases and you hear the sound it makes, but you cannot tell where it comes from or where it is going." are referring to the Spirit of God, who gives

life to whom He wishes, or rather to the soul of a person. The words "you know not where it comes from or where it goes," signifies that we do not know who the spirit had been previously or who it will be in the future. If the spirit or soul were created at the same time as the body, we would know where it came from, because we would know its beginning. Whichever way you look at this passage, it confirms the principle of the pre-existence of the soul and subsequently the plurality of existences.

> 10. And from the days of John the Baptist, until now, the kingdom of heaven has suffered violence and the violent take it by force. For all the prophets and the law prophesied until John. And if you will receive it, this is Elias who was to come. He who has ears, let him hear. (MATTHEW, 11:12-15.)

11. Even if the teaching of reincarnation as expressed in John might be interpreted in principle in a purely mystical sense, the same could not happen with this passage from Matthew, which does not permit any ambiguity 'HE is Elias, who was to come'. Here there is nothing figurative, nothing allegorical, only a complete affirmation. "Since the time of John the Baptist until today the kingdom of heaven is seized by violence." What do these words mean when John the Baptist was still alive at that moment? Jesus explains them to us when He says "if you wish to understand what I am saying, this is Elias who was to come." Therefore, if John was Elias, Jesus alluded to the time when John was living under the name of Elias. "Till the present time the kingdom is seized by violence," is another allusion to the violence of the Mosaic laws, which ordered the extermination of infidels so that the rest might attain the Promised Land, the Paradise of the Hebrews. Whereas according to the new law Heaven was to be won by charity and mildness.

Jesus then added, "He who has ears, let him hear." These words are frequently used by Him and tell us that not everyone was in a condition to understand certain truths.

12. Those of your people who were killed will live again. Those who have been killed around me will be resuscitated. Awaken and sing praises to God all you who are living in the dust. For the dew that falls upon you is a dew of light, which will destroy the earth and the kingdom of the giants. " (ISAIAH, 26:19.)

13. This passage from Isaiah is also explicit, "Your dead *will live again.*" If the prophet had wished to speak of a spiritual life, if he had intended to say that those who had been executed were not dead spiritually speaking, he would have said 'They are still alive,' and not *'They will live again.'* In the spiritual sense, these words would be a contradiction, because they imply an interruption in the life of the soul. In the sense of *moral regeneration* they would be a denial of eternal suffering because they establish in principle that *all those who are dead will one day come back to life.*

14. "But when a man has died once, *when his body, separated from his spirit, has been consumed, what happens to him? Having died* once, *can a man* live again? *In the war in which I find myself each day of my life, I await my mutation".* (JOB, 14:10 & 14. Translation taken from Le Maistre de Sacy)

When a man dies, he loses all his strength, expires, afterwards, where is he? If a man dies, will he live again? *Will I wait all the days of my combat, until there comes some mutation?* (Id. Taken from the Protestant translation of Osterwald.)

When a man is dead, he lives forever: when my days of existence on Earth *have finished, I will wait, seeing that* I shall return again. (Id. Taken from the Greek translation.)[10]

---

[10] The King James translation (traditional) says: BUT MAN DIETH AND WASTETH AWAY: YEA, MAN GIVETH UP THE GHOST. AND WHERE IS HE? IF A MAN DIES, SHALL HE LIVE AGAIN? ALL THE DAYS OF MY APPOINTED TIME WILL I WAIT, TILL MY CHANGE COME. (Translator's addition for comparison – 1987.)

15. In these three translations, the principle of the plurality of existences is clearly expressed. Nobody can imagine that Job was referring to regeneration from baptismal water, which certainly he had never heard of. 'Man having *died once*, can he *live again*?' The idea of dying once and reliving implies dying and living many times. The Greek version is even more explicit, if that is possible. "When my days of *existence on Earth* are finished, I will wait, for I will *return again*" or return again to Earth. This is so clear, as if someone were saying: I leave my house, but I will return.

"In the war in which I find myself each day of my life, *I await my mutation*." Here Job evidently was referring to his struggles against the miseries of life, "I await my mutation" meaning he was resigned. In the Greek version, *I will wait*, seems to apply more preferably to a new existence: "When my existence has ended, *I will wait*, seeing that I shall return again." It is as if after death Job places himself in the interval that separates one life from another and says that it is there he will wait until the moment of return.

16. So there is no doubt that under the name of resurrection, the principle of reincarnation was a fundamental belief of the Jews. A point which Jesus and the prophets in general confirm. From which it follows that to deny reincarnation is also to deny the words of Christ. One day, however, when they have been well meditated upon, without preconceived ideas, His words will be recognised as an authority on this point, as well as on many others.

17. From the religious point of view, we add to this authority the philosophical viewpoint of the proofs resulting from the observance of the facts. When we try to discover from the effects what the causes might be, reincarnation becomes an absolute necessity, an inherent part of humanity, in a word: a Law of Nature. By its very results, it becomes evident in a material manner, so to speak, in the same way that a hidden motor reveals itself by its movement. It is only through reincarnation that human

beings can find out where they came from, where they are going and why they are here on Earth and still be able to justify the many abnormalities and all the apparent injustices that present themselves during life.[11]

Without the principle of the pre-existence of the soul and the plurality of existences, the maxims of the Gospel in the most part become unintelligible, which is the reason why they have given rise to so many contradictory interpretations. This is the only principle that will restore them to their true and original meaning.

REINCARNATION STRENGTHENS FAMILY TIES, WHEREAS A SINGLE LIFE WOULD DESTROY THEM

18. Family ties are not destroyed through reincarnation, as some would believe. On the contrary, they become stronger and closer. Where as the opposite principal would certainly destroy them.

In space, spirit entities form groups or families bound together by affection, sympathy towards each other and by similar inclinations. Happy at being together, these spirits seek each other out. Incarnate life separates them only for a while, so on returning to the spiritual world they again reunite as friends who have just returned from a journey. Frequently they will even follow each other into the incarnate form, coming here to be united in the same family or the same circle of friends and acquaintances, in order to work together for their mutual progress. When some members of the same spiritual family become incarnate and others not, they then continue their contact by means of thought. Those who are free watch over those who are captive. Those who are more advanced do everything they can for the less advanced, so helping

---

[11] See THE SPIRITS' BOOK, chapters 4 & 5; WHAT IS SPIRITISM, chap. 2, by Allan Kardec and also LA PLURALITÉ DES EXISTENCES by Pezzani, for further information on reincarnation.

them to progress. After each physical existence, all have made some advancement, even if it is only a step along the path to progress. As they become less bound by matter, their affections become more real and more spiritually refined, because they are not perturbed by selfish or violent passions. This then allows them to live many lives in the flesh without suffering any loss of mutual esteem.

It is understood of course that we refer to real affection, soul to soul, being the only love that survives after the destruction of the body. Therefore, it follows that those of this world, who join because of physical attraction, will have no motive to look for each other in the spirit world. The only lasting relationships are those linked by spiritual affection, all carnal affections being extinguished together with the cause that brought them about, in other words, the physical body. Understand by this that the physical cause no longer exists in the world of spirits, while the soul exists eternally. With regard to those who join exclusively out of interest, they clearly mean nothing to each other. Death separates them both on Earth and in Heaven.

19. The union and affection, which can exist between relatives, is an indication of former sympathies that have brought them together. This is why, when referring to someone whose character, tastes and inclinations hold no similarity to other members of the same family, it is customary to say that they do not belong to that family. When saying this, the truth is being expressed far more profoundly than suspected. God permits that in certain families these spirits, who are uncongenial or strangers to each other, reincarnate with the dual purpose of serving as a test for some members of that family and as a means of progress for others. In this manner, due to contact with Good Spirits and the general care dispensed to them, little by little the evil or wicked spirits get to be better. Their characters grow milder, their habits become more refined and aversions are dissipated. This is how the various

fusions of different categories of spirits are accomplished, as is done with different races and peoples on the planet.

20. The fear that some people may have with regard to the indefinite increase in relationships due to reincarnation is selfish, proving a lack of love sufficiently ample as to be able to embrace a large number of people. Does a father who has many children love them any less than he would if there was only one? Selfish people may be tranquil because there is no reason for such a fear. The fact that a person may have had ten incarnations does not mean that in the spirit world they will find ten fathers, ten mothers, ten wives and a prodigious number of children and relatives. There they will encounter only those who had been the object of their affections, some of whom they would have been linked to here on Earth in various relationships, or perhaps even the same ones.

21. Let us now look at the consequences of an anti-reincarnationist doctrine. By necessity, it annuls all previous existences of the soul, seeing that under these ideas the soul would be created together with the body. No previous links would exist and all would be complete strangers one to another. The father or mother would be strangers to their children. The relationships between families would be reduced to mere physical relationships without any spiritual links whatsoever. Therefore, there would be no motive at all for anyone to claim the honour of having had such-and-such a person for his or her ancestor. Whereas with reincarnation, ancestors and descendants may have known each other, lived together, loved one another and will reunite later on in order to increase the links of sympathy even more.

22. All that refers to the past. So now, let us look at the future. According to one of the fundamental dogmas that come from the idea of non-reincarnation, the destiny of all souls is irrevocably determined after only one existence. This fixed and definite idea

of fate implies the ending of all progress, because when there is still some form of progress, then there is no definite fate. Depending on whether we have lived a good or bad life, either we should go immediately to the home of the blessed or to eternal hell, *we should then be immediately and forever separated, without hope of ever being united again.* In this way fathers, mothers and children, husbands and wives, brothers and sisters, and even friends, would never be sure of seeing each other again; this then means the absolute rupture of all family ties.

However, with the acceptance of reincarnation and consequential progress, all those who love one another will meet again on Earth and in space, gravitating together in the direction of God. If some weaken along the path they will delay their progress and their happiness, but there will never be a total loss of hope. Helped, encouraged and sustained by those who love them, they will one day be able to extricate themselves from the quagmire into which they have allowed themselves to fall. With reincarnation there is perpetual solidarity between incarnates and discarnates constantly consolidating the links of affection.

23. In conclusion, four alternatives present themselves to humans for their future beyond the tomb: Firstly - nothingness, according to the materialist doctrine; Secondly - absorption into the universe, according to the pantheistic idea; Thirdly - individuality with a fixed and definite destiny, according to the Church; fourthly - individuality with constant progress according to the Spiritist Teachings. In the first two alternatives, family ties are interrupted at the time of death, and no hope exists for these souls of ever meeting again in the future. With the third alternative, there is a possibility of meeting again, if each has gone to the same region, which might be either Heaven or Hell. With the plurality of existences, which is inseparable from gradual progression, there is certainty of the continuity of relationships

between those who love, and this is what constitutes the true family.

INSTRUCTIONS FROM THE SPIRITS

LIMITS OF INCARNATIONS

24. What are the limits of incarnation?

In fact, incarnation does not have clearly defined limits, if we are thinking only of the envelope that constitutes the physical covering of the spirit, since the materiality of this covering diminishes in proportion as the spirit purifies itself. In certain worlds more advanced than Earth, this covering is already less compact, less heavy, more refined and consequently less subject to vicissitudes. In worlds of still higher elevation, it is translucent and almost fluidic. It dematerialises by degrees and finally becomes absorbed by the perispirit. According to the kind of world it is taken to live in, the spirit takes on a covering appropriate to that world.

The perispirit itself also undergoes successive transformations. It becomes more and more etherealised, until it reaches complete purification, which is the state of all immaculate Spirits. If special worlds are destined for more highly advanced Spirits, they do not remain prisoners there as in the inferior worlds. The special state of detachment in which they find themselves, allows travel to any part of the Universe to which they may be called on mission.

If we consider incarnation from the material viewpoint, such as can be verified here on Earth, we can say that it is limited to inferior worlds. However, it depends on each spirit to liberate itself more or less quickly, by working towards purification. We should also consider that in the discarnate state, that is to say in the intervals between bodily existences, the situation of each spirit depends on the nature of the world to which it is linked by the degree of advancement it has acquired. Thus, in the spiritual world we are more or less happy, free or enlightened, according to the degree of dematerialization achieved. - SAINT LOUIS (Paris, 1859.)

THE NEED FOR INCARNATION

25. *Is incarnation a punishment and are guilty spirits bound to suffer them?*

The passing of spirits through corporeal life is necessary in order that they may fulfil, by means of a material action, the purpose to which God assigned them. This is necessary for their own good, as the activity they are obliged to perform will help the development of their intelligence. Being just, God must distribute everything in equal parts to all His children. Therefore, it is established that everyone starts from the same point, with the same aptitudes, the same obligations to fulfil and having the same liberty to proceed. Any type of privilege would be an injustice. Nevertheless, for all spirits incarnation is a transitory state. It is a task imposed by God at the beginning of life, as a primary experiment in the use of free will. Those who discharge this task with zeal pass over the first steps of their initiation quickly, less painfully, and so are able to reap the fruits of their labour at an earlier date. Those who, on the contrary, make bad use of the liberty that God has granted them, delay their progress and according to the degree of obstinacy demonstrated, may prolong the need for reincarnating indefinitely, in which case it becomes a punishment. - SAINT LOUIS (Paris, 1859.)

26. NOTE - A common comparison would make this difference more easily understandable. The scholar cannot reach superior studies in science if he has not passed through the series of classes that lead to that level. These classes, whatever may be the work demanded, are the means by which the student will reach their

objective and are not a punishment that is inflicted. If they are diligent, they can shorten the path and consequently encounter fewer thorns. However, this does not happen to the one who is negligent and lazy, which will oblige them to repeat certain lessons. It is not the class work that is the punishment, but the necessity to recommence the same work over again.

This is what happens to humanity on Earth. For the primitive spirit, who is only at the beginning of their spiritual life, incarnation is the means by which they can develop their intelligence. Nevertheless, it is a punishment for an enlightened person, in whom a moral sense has been broadly developed, to be obliged to live over again the various phases of a corporeal life full of anguishes, when they could have arrived at the end of a need to stay in inferior and unhappy worlds. On the other hand, if they work actively towards moral progress, they not only shorten the period of material incarnations, but also they may jump over the intermediate steps that separate them from the superior worlds.

Is it possible for Spirits to incarnate only once in any one world and then fulfil their other existences in different worlds? This would only be possible if every person were at exactly the same point in both intellectual and moral development. The differences between them, from the savage to civilised person, show the many degrees that must be ascended. Besides, an incarnation must have a useful purpose. However, what of short-lived incarnations of children who die at a tender age? Have they suffered to no purpose, for themselves or for others? God, Whose laws are wise, does nothing that is useless. Through reincarnating on the same globe, and by being once again in contact with each other, He wishes these same spirits to have the desire to repair reciprocated offences. With the help of past relationships, He wishes to establish family ties on a spiritual basis, founded on the principles of the natural laws of solidarity, fraternity and equality.

CHAPTER 5

BLESSED ARE THE AFFLICTED

The justice of afflictions. - Causes of present-day afflictions. - Past causes of afflictions. - Forgetfulness of the past. - Motive for resignation. - Suicide and madness. – INSTRUCTIONS FROM THE SPIRITS: To suffer well or badly. - Evil and its remedy. - Happiness is not of this world. - Losing loved ones. Premature deaths. - If they had been a good person, they would have died. - Voluntary torments. True misfortunes - Melancholy. - Voluntary trials. The true hair shirt. - Should we end our neighbour's probation? - Would it be licit to hasten the death of someone incurably sick who is suffering? – Sacrificing one's own life. - Making one's own suffering useful to others.

1. Blessed are they that mourn: for they shall be comforted. Blessed are those, which do hunger, and thirst after righteousness: for they shall be filled. Blessed are they, which are persecuted for righteousness sake: for theirs is the Kingdom of Heaven. (MATTHEW 5:4, 6 & 10.)

2. And he lifted up his eyes on his disciples and said, 'Blessed be the poor; for yours is the Kingdom of God. Blessed are you who hunger now: for you shall be filled. Blessed are you that weep now: for you shall laugh. (LUKE, 6:20 & 21.)

But woe unto you that are rich! For you have received your consolation. Woe unto you that are full! For you shall hunger. Woe unto you that laugh now! For you shall mourn and weep." (LUKE, 6:24 & 25.)

THE JUSTICE OF AFFLICTIONS

3. The compensation promised by Jesus to the afflicted of this Earth can only be effected in a future life. Without the certainty of this future these maxims would be a contradiction; still more, they would be a decoy. Even with this certainty, it is difficult to

understand the convenience of suffering in order to be happy. It is said that it is to acquire greater merit. Then we ask why do some suffer more than others do? Why are some born in misery and others in opulence without having done anything to justify this situation? Why is it that some never manage to achieve anything, while for others everything seems to smile? Yet what is even less understandable is why benefits and misfortunes are divided so unequally between vice and virtue. Why do we find virtuous people suffering side by side with the wicked who prosper? Faith in the future can console and instil patience, but it does not explain these irregularities, which appear to contradict God's justice.

However, once God's existence has been admitted one cannot conceive Him as being less than infinitely perfect. He is naturally all-powerful, all just and all goodness, without which He would not be God. If He is supremely good and just, then He cannot act capriciously, nor yet with partiality. *The vicissitudes of life derive from a cause, and as God is just* so *then that cause must also be just.* We must convince ourselves of this fact. Through the Teachings of Jesus, God started humanity on the path to find that cause, and now that people are sufficiently mature as to be able to understand, He has revealed the cause by means of *Spiritism.* That is to say, through the voice of the *Spirits.*

CAUSES OF PRESENT-DAY AFFLICTIONS

4. The vicissitudes of life are of two kinds, or if you prefer, stem from two different sources that are important to distinguish. Some have their cause in present-day life, while others arise outside this present life.

On going back to the origins of earthly misfortunes, it must be recognised that many are natural consequences of character and the behaviour of those who suffer them.

How many fail through their own fault? How many are the victims of their own thoughtlessness, of their pride and ambition?

How many destroy themselves through lack of discipline, misconduct or from not knowing how to limit their desires?

How many disastrous marriages are due to the fact that they were built on calculated interest or vanity, in which the heart took no part?

How many disagreements and fatal disputes could have been avoided with the aid of a little moderation and less susceptibility?

How many illnesses and diseases stem from intemperance and excesses of all kinds?

How many parents are unhappy with their children because they did not combat their bad instincts from an early age? From either weakness or indifference, they allowed the germs of pride, selfishness and stupid vanity to grow in them, so causing their hearts to dry and shrivel. Later on, when reaping what they have sown, they are surprised and afflicted by the lack of gratitude and the indifference with which they are treated.

We ask each one whose heart has been hurt by vicissitudes or deceptions, to study their own conscience closely; to go back, step by step, to the origins of each misfortune which is torturing them. Like as not they will be able to say '*if I had done or not done such and such a thing, I would not be where I am now.*'

Who then is responsible for humanities afflictions if not humanity itself? So then, in a great number of cases we are the cause of our own misfortunes. Instead of recognising this fact, we find it easier and less humiliating to our vanity to accuse our bad luck, providence or even our unlucky star, when in fact our unlucky star is our own carelessness.

When reckoning with the misfortunes of life, suffering of this nature undoubtedly forms the greatest part of all vicissitudes. Only when humankind works at bettering itself, both morally and intellectually, will it be able to avoid this category of suffering.

5. Human law covers various faults and prescribes punishment. In these cases it is possible for the condemned person to recognise that they are suffering the consequences of the wrong committed. However, the law does not or cannot, reach every wrong; it falls principally upon those who cause damage to society and not upon those who only cause damage to themselves. God, however, does not allow any detour from the straight and narrow path to go unpunished. There is no wrong or infraction of His Law, however small, that does not carry with it the inevitable consequence that may be more or less deplorable. From this, it follows that in small things, as in great matters, humanity is always punished according to the manner in which it has sinned. The suffering that follows is always a warning that wrong has been done. This offers experience and makes people feel the difference between right and wrong, good and bad, so that in the future these sources of bitterness may be avoided; but without which there would be no motive for betterment. If humanity were to be confident of immunity, it would only delay its own progress and therefore its future happiness.

Nevertheless, sometimes experience arrives rather late, when life has already been wasted and become disordered, when strength is already spent and the person is no longer able to remedy the wrongdoing. Then the person will frequently say 'If I had known then what I know now how many false steps would have been avoided! *If I had to begin again* I would act differently, but now there is no more time!' Like the lazy worker who says 'I have wasted my day', the person also says, 'I have wasted my life!' Just as the sun rising on a new day allows the worker the possibility of repaying any lost time, so it is with humanity.

Because after a period of time in the tomb a new life shines forth that will enable advantage to be taken from past experience and good resolutions for the future to be put into practice.

PAST CAUSES OF AFFLICTIONS

6. Although there are misfortunes in life caused principally by human beings, there are also others that, at least according to appearance, seem to be completely strange that strike like fate. For example, the loss of a loved one or the breadwinner of a family. Still others, like accidents that no amount of foresight could have prevented. In addition, reverses in fortune that precautions and judicial counselling could not avoid, natural disasters, infirmities from birth, especially those that make work or the earning of a livelihood impossible, like deformities, insanity, idiocy, etc.

Those who are born with restricting conditions like those mentioned, have done nothing in their present life to deserve such a sad fate that they could not avoid and are very impotent to change, leaving them at the mercy of public commiseration. Why then are there these unhappy beings, when beside them, under the same roof, in the same family, are others who have been blessed in every way?

In short, what can be said of children who die at a tender age and who, during their short life, knew only suffering? These are problems that as yet no philosophy has been able to find a solution for, anomalies that no religion has been able to justify and which appear to be a contradiction of God's goodness, justice and Divine Providence. If the hypothesis of the soul being created at the same time as the body and that of destiny being irrevocably determined after but a few instants upon Earth were to be verified, this would indeed be the case. If these creatures had just left the hands of the Creator, what had caused them to come into the world to face such misery? How could they have received any recompense or punishment seeing that they had been unable to practice either good or evil?

Nevertheless, by virtue of the axiom according to which *every effect has a cause,* these miseries are effects that have to have a cause, and if we admit that God is just, then that cause must also be just. Therefore, as an effect is always preceded by a cause and if that cause is not to be found in the present life, then it follows it must come from before this life, that is to say from a preceding life. On the other hand, God, being unable to punish goodness that has been done or badness that has not been done, it follows that if we are being punished then wrong must have been committed. If that wrong is not of the present life then it must come from a past existence. This is an alternative that no one can avoid and where logic determines on which side God's justice lies.

We are not always punished or completely punished in the present life, but we cannot escape the consequences of our faults indefinitely. The prospering of evil is only momentary; for if the person does not atone today then they will atone tomorrow. Misfortunes, which at first sight appear to be undeserved have their reason to be. Therefore, those who find themselves in a state of suffering may always say, "Lord forgive me, for I have sinned."

7. Sufferings due to causes prior to the present existence, as well as those originating from present causes, are frequently the consequences of errors that have been committed. This is to say that through the action of a rigorously distributive justice, we come to suffer what we have made others suffer. If we have been hard and inhumane, we may be treated with harshness and inhumanity. If we were too full of pride, we may be born in humble circumstances. If we have been miserly, selfish or made bad use of our riches, we may find ourselves deprived of the necessary means of survival. If we have been a bad son or a bad daughter, we may suffer from the behaviour of our children.

It is only through the plurality of existences and the destiny of the planet, as a world of atonement that it now is that we can explain the abnormalities in the distribution of happiness or unhappiness amongst good and evil people alike. Nevertheless, these abnormalities exist only in appearance, due to the fact that they are considered solely from the point of view of the present. If we elevate ourselves, by means of thought, in such a way as to see a succession of existences, we will perceive that to each one is given what is deserved, after taking into consideration that which was gained in the spiritual world. Only then does it become apparent that God's justice is uninterrupted.

Human beings must never forget that they find themselves on an inferior world to which they are confined due exclusively to their imperfections. Each time a vicissitude is suffered, they must remember that if they belonged to a more advanced world these things would not be happening; that it depends completely on themselves to see that they never return to this world by working harder to improve themselves.

8. Tribulations may be imposed on spirits who are ignorant or who have become hardened, in order to induce them to make a choice with knowledge of what they are doing. Spirits who are *repentant*, wishing to repay the evil they have committed, who desire to behave better, are free to make their own choices. Such was the understanding of one spirit who, after having failed to complete a task, asked to be allowed to repeat it so as not to lose the benefit of its work. Therefore, tribulations are at the same time atonements for the past, for which we receive the deserved retribution, and tests relating to the future we are preparing. We offer thanks to God Who, in His goodness, helps humans to repay their debts and does not irrevocably condemn the first fault.

9. However, it is not to be thought that all suffering in this world denotes the existence of a determined shortcoming. Many

times, it is simply an ordeal requested by the spirit that will help it towards purification and active progress. Therefore, atonement is always a test, but a test is not always an atonement. Although tests and atonements are always signs of a relative inferiority, as that which is perfect needs no testing. Nevertheless, it is possible that a spirit having reached a certain degree of elevation, and being desirous of further progress, may request a mission or task to perform. Depending on whether or not they are victorious, and according to the difficulty of the requested test, they will be more or less compensated. These then, are those people who have naturally good instincts, whose souls are elevated and who possess inborn sentiments. They apparently bring nothing from their past existences and who, despite great torments, suffer with true Christian resignation, asking only that God help them to support their trials without complaining. On the other hand, we may consider as atonements those afflictions that provoke complaint and cause a revolt against God.

Beyond doubt, the suffering that does not provoke complaints can also be considered as atonement. However, this indicates it was voluntarily sought rather than imposed. This constitutes a test of our strength of resolution and a sign of progress.

10. Spirits cannot aspire to complete happiness until they become pure. Any kind of stain prohibits entrance into the blissful worlds. It is like passengers on a plagued ship who find themselves prohibited from entering port until they have undergone a cleansing. These imperfections are slowly overcome by means of various corporeal lives. When well supported, the tribulations help them towards progress. They erase faults and find purification by means of atonement, which is the remedy that cleanses the sores and heals the sick person. The more grave the illness, the more energetic the remedy needs to be. Therefore, those who suffer greatly must realise that they have much to atone for and should rejoice in the proximity of the cure. It will depend

on each one to take every advantage from the suffering by being resigned and not spoiling things with impatience, seeing that to the contrary they will have to begin all over again.

FORGETFULNESS OF THE PAST

11. It is useless to object that forgetfulness constitutes a barrier to the utilisation of experience acquired in past lives. If God considers it convenient for a veil to be cast over the past, it is because this will be to our advantage. In fact, remembrance would be a very great inconvenience. It could, in certain cases, cause a person great humility or perhaps make them prideful, which would interfere with their free will. In any case, it would certainly cause inevitable perturbation in social relationships.

A spirit is frequently reborn in the same ambient where it had previously lived, establishing once again the same relationships in order to repay any evil that might have been done. If there was any recognition of these same people, who perhaps had previously been hated, it would only serve to rekindle that emotion. In any case, humiliation would be felt on confronting those who had been offended.

Therefore, in order that we can improve ourselves, God has bestowed upon us precisely what we need being that which is sufficient and nothing more. This being none other than the voice of conscience and our instinctive tendencies. We are only deprived us of what would be prejudicial.

On being reborn, a person brings with them what they have already acquired. They are born exactly the way they have made themselves. Each life is begun from a new starting point. It matters little to know what they had been before. If they are being punished it is because they did something wrong. Actual evil tendencies indicate what is still to be corrected and it is upon this they should concentrate all their attention; because no trace is left of what has already been rectified. The good resolutions the person feels bound to make are the voices of conscience, calling attention to what is right and what is wrong, so giving strength to resist temptation.

Moreover, this forgetfulness only occurs during bodily existence. On returning to the spiritual life, the remembrance of the past is regained. So it is only temporary, a slight interruption similar to that which occurs during sleep, but which does not prevent the remembrance on the subsequent day of what was done on the previous one.

However, it is not only after death that the spirit may recover remembrance of their past. It can be said that it is never lost, even whilst incarnate, as experience demonstrates that during the sleep state, being a period when the spirit enjoys a certain amount of liberty, it is conscious of its past acts. It knows why it is suffering and that it suffers justly. Memory is only extinguished during the course of exterior existence, in the life of relationships. Nevertheless, during these partial remembrances, which, if it were otherwise might cause added suffering and harm social relationships, the spirit absorbs new strength in these moments of emancipation, if it knows how to take advantage of them.

MOTIVES FOR RESIGNATION

12. With the words: *Blessed are the afflicted for they will be consoled,* Jesus indicates the compensation that awaits those who suffer and the resignation that leads us to bless suffering as a prelude to the cure.

These words can also be understood in this manner: that one should be content to suffer, seeing that the pain of this world is the payment for past debts that were incurred. Patiently supported here on Earth, these pains will save centuries of future suffering. One should be happy that God is reducing the debt by permitting payment now, thereby guaranteeing a tranquil future.

The sufferer is like a debtor who owes a large sum and to whom the creditor says, "If you pay me even a hundredth part of your debt today, I will exonerate you and you will be free. But if you do not, then I shall torment you till you pay every last penny." Would not the debtor feel happy in supporting all kinds of hardships in order to be liberated, so paying only a hundredth part of what they owed? Instead of complaining to the creditor, would they not be grateful?

This is the meaning of the words, 'Blessed are the afflicted for they shall be consoled'. They are happy because they are paying their debts and because after payment they will be free. However, if on acquitting themselves on the one side, a person becomes indebted on the other, they will never find liberation. Therefore, each new fault only increases the debt, there being not even one that does not entail a compelling and inevitable punishment. If not today, then tomorrow; if not in this life, then in another. Amongst the list of failings, it behoves a person to put the lack of submission to God's Will in first place. Therefore, if we complain about our afflictions, if we do not accept them with resignation, or if we accuse God of being unjust, we contract new debts, which in turn make us lose the fruits that should have been gathered from these sufferings. This is why we must begin again from the beginning, exactly as if after paying part of a debt to a creditor who has been tormenting us, we then took out another loan.

On entering into the spiritual world, we are like the labourer who arrives on the day of payment. To some God will say, "Here is your recompense for the days you have worked." While to others, the so-called lucky ones on Earth who have lived in idleness, or those who have built their happiness on the satisfaction of their own self-esteem and on worldly pleasures, He will say, "There is nothing more to come: you have already received your salary on Earth. Go and begin your task again."

13. We can soften or increase the bitterness of our trials according to the manner in which we regard earthly life. Our suffering will be even more depending on how long we imagine it to be. But those who can see life through a spiritual prism understand bodily existence at a glance. They see that life is but a point in eternity; they comprehend the shortness of its duration and recognise that this painful moment will soon pass. The certainty of a happier future sustains and animates them and far from complaining, they offer thanks to God for the pain, which will permit them to advance. On the other hand, for all those who see only bodily life before them, the duration seems interminable and the pain oppresses with all its weight. The result of looking at life from a spiritual way is a diminishing in importance of all worldly things. Thus, we feel ourselves compelled to moderate our desires and to be content with our position without envying others. This, in turn, enables us to receive weakened impressions of reverses and deceptions that may be experienced. From these attitudes comes calmness and resignation, so useful to bodily health, as well as to the soul; whereas from jealousy, envy and ambition we voluntarily condemn ourselves to tortures, increased miseries and anguish during our short existence.

SUICIDE AND MADNESS

14. The calm and resignation that can be acquired regarding the way terrestrial life is viewed, together with confidence in the future, give the spirit a serenity that is the best preventive measure against *madness and suicide*. To be sure, it is certain that the vast majority of cases of madness are due to the commotion produced by vicissitudes that people have not had the strength to support.

However, if the things of this world were regarded from the point of view with which the Spiritist Teachings regard them, then all the reverses and deceptions that in other circumstances would cause people to become desperate can be received with indifference, even with happiness. It is evident then that this inner strength puts us above these happenings, so protecting us from shocks to the mind, which if it were not for this, would cause serious disturbance.

15. The same applies to suicide. Leaving aside those that occur due to drunkenness or madness that can be classified as unconscious it is certain that in every case the cause is discontentment, whatever the private motives may be. However, for those who are sure they will only be unhappy for a day, and that the days to come will be much better, it is easy to be patient. People only become desperate when they can see no end to their suffering. What is a lifetime compared to eternity? Is it not less than a day? Nevertheless, for those who do not believe in eternity and judge that everything ends with life, who become dejected, grief-stricken or heartbroken, death appears to be the only solution for so much sorrow. Expecting to receive nothing, it seems natural and even logical to them to shorten their miseries by means of suicide.

16. Lack of belief, simply doubting as to the future or having materialistic ideas, are in fact the greatest of all incitements towards suicide because they cause *moral cowardice*. Upheld by the authority of their knowledge, Scientists do their best to prove to those that will listen or read what they write, that we have nothing to expect after death. Are they not in fact leading us to deduce that if we are wretched then the best thing to do is to kill ourselves? What can they offer as a reason to turn away from this conclusion? What compensation do they have to offer? What hope can they give? None at all, except nothingness! From this, we should conclude that if nothingness were the only heroic remedy,

the only prospective, then it would be better to seek it immediately and not later on, so as to suffer less.

So then, the dissemination of such materialistic doctrines is the poison that inoculates the idea of suicide into the majority of those who actually come to commit this act. Therefore, those who become disciples of such doctrines assume tremendous responsibilities. With Spiritism, however, this doubt is impossible and the aspect of life changes completely. For the believer, existence prolongs itself after the so-called death, although in many varied conditions. From this belief stems patience and resignation that naturally leads all thought away from the idea of suicide. This then is the process that enables us to acquire *moral courage.*

17. In the same aspect, Spiritism produces yet another equally positive result, one that is perhaps even more decisive. It presents these actual suicides, who inform us of the unhappy situations in which they find themselves, so proving that no one violates God's laws with impunity. God prohibits human beings to cut short their own life. Among suicides, there are those whose suffering, even when only tempory, are none the less terrible and of such a nature as to make those who might be considering this act, stop and reflect before leaving this world sooner than God ordained. The Spiritist moreover, has various reasons against the idea of suicide. First, the *certainty* of a future life in which it is *known* that happiness will be in proportion to the misfortunes and the degree of resignation shown while on Earth. Combined with a *certainty* that if they abbreviate their life they will reap the exact opposite to that desired. By liberating themselves from a trial in this manner, they will consequently encounter another one far worse in its place, longer and more terrible, causing them to reflect that it is not worthwhile to leave this world before the appointed time set by God. The Spiritist then has various reasons against the idea of committing suicide; such as the *certainty* of a future life, during

which they *know* they will be that much happier according to how unhappy, but resigned, they had been while on Earth. They understand that it is a mistake to imagine that by killing themselves they will reach heaven more quickly, because suicide is an obstacle that will prevent them from joining those they love and hope to meet on the other side. The consequences of all this will only bring deceptions, and therefore are against their best interests. From these reasons, the number of people already saved from suicide is quite considerable. Thus, we may conclude that when all men and women are Spiritists, conscious suicide will cease to exist. When comparing the results of materialist doctrines with those of the Spiritist Teachings, on this one point alone we are forced to recognise that whereas the logic of the first leads towards suicide, the logic of the second prevents suicide, which is a proven fact confirmed by experience.

INSTRUCTIONS FROM THE SPIRITS

TO SUFFER WELL OR BADLY

18. When Christ said, "Blessed are the afflicted, for the kingdom of heaven belongs to them", He did not refer to all those who suffer, seeing that everyone on Earth suffers, whether they are seated upon thrones or lie upon straw. But alas! So few suffer well! A mere handful understands that only trials that have been well supported can lead to the Kingdom of God. Despondency is a fault, and God will refuse consolation to those who lack courage. Prayer supports the soul; however, alone it is not enough. It is also necessary to have a firm belief in the kindness of God as the basis for deep faith. You have heard it said many times that He does not put a heavy burden on weak shoulders. The burden is always in proportion to the strength, just as the recompense depends on the degree of resignation and courage. The more painful the affliction

the greater the recompense. It behoves us then to make ourselves worthy, and it is for this purpose that life presents itself so full of tribulations.

The soldier who was not sent to the front is discontent, because by resting in camp he will never receive promotion. So then, be like soldiers and do not desire repose, which will only allow the body to become debilitated and the soul become numbed! Be content when God sends you into battle because this is not a battle of the firing line, but the bitterness of life, during which sometimes there is need for even greater courage than in a bloody battle. A person who can stand firm before an enemy often weakens when confronted with the tenacity of moral suffering. Although there is no reward for this kind of courage on Earth, God will reserve the laurels of victory and a place of glory for those who withstand. When facing sufferings or obstacles, if you are able to place yourself above the situation, by managing to dominate the impulses of impatience, anger and despair, then you may say to yourself with just satisfaction, 'I was the stronger.'

So then, the words *blessed are the afflicted* should be understood in the following manner: blessed are those who have occasion to prove their faith, firmness, perseverance and submission to the Will of God. Because they will have multiplied a hundred times the happiness they lacked on Earth, for after labour comes repose. - LACORDAIRE (Havre, 1863.)

EVIL AND ITS REMEDY

19. Is the Earth a place of enjoyment and a paradise of delights? Does the voice of the prophet no longer re-echo in your ears? Did He not proclaim there would be weeping and gnashing of teeth for those who were born into this valley of pain? So then, all who live here must expect bitter tears and suffering. Nevertheless, no matter how acute or how deep the pain, lift up your eyes to the heavens

and offer thanks to the Lord for wishing to test you! ... Oh humanity! Can you not recognise the power of our Lord except when He cures the sores of your bodies and crowns your days with beauty and fortune? Can you not recognise His love except He adorns you with all the glories, and restores the brilliance and whiteness? You should imitate the one who was given as an example. Having reached the final degree of abjection and misery, while laying upon a dung heap, he said to God, "Lord, I have known all the delights of opulence and You have reduced me to the most absolute misery; thank you, thank you, my Lord, for wishing to test your servant!" How long will your eyes remain fixed upon the horizon limited by death? When will your soul finally decide to launch itself beyond the limits of the tomb? Nevertheless, even if you suffer and cry the whole of this life, what is that compared to the eternal glory reserved for those who suffer their trials with faith, love, and resignation? Seek consolation for your ills in the future, which God will prepare for you and search for the causes in the past. Moreover, you who have suffered the most, consider yourselves the blessed of this Earth.

As discarnates, when floating in space, you chose your own trials, judging yourselves sufficiently strong to support them. Why then do you complain now? You asked for riches and glory because you wished to hold fight with temptation and overcome it. You asked to fight with body and soul against both moral and physical evil, knowing that the harder the trial the greater and more glorious the victory. Despite the fact of your body ending up on a dung heap at death, as long as you have triumphed, it will release a soul of radiant whiteness purified by the baptism of atonement and suffering.

What remedy can be prescribed for those attacked by cruel obsessions and mortifying evils? There is but one infallible way, through faith that is the appeal to Heaven. If at that moment of highest poignancy in your suffering you intone hymns to the Lord, then the angel at your bedside will show you the sign of salvation and the place that you will one day occupy... Faith is the only sure remedy for suffering. It will always show the infinite horizon before which the few cloudy days of the present will vanish. Therefore, do not ask what the remedy is for an ulcer or a sore, for temptations or trials, but remind yourselves that those who believe are strengthened through the remedy of faith. Those who doubt its efficiency, even for an instant, will be punished immediately because they will quickly feel the pungent anguishes of affliction.

The Lord has put His seal upon all those who believe in Him. Christ told you that it was possible to move mountains by faith alone, and I tell you that those who suffer yet have faith to uphold them, will remain under the protection of the Lord and will suffer no more. The moments of greatest pain will become the first happy notes of eternity. The soul will detach itself from the body in such a manner that, while the latter is still writhing in convulsions, it will be gliding into the celestial regions, singing hymns of gratitude and glory to the Lord, together with the angels. Fortunate are those who suffer and weep! Happy are these souls because God will heap blessings upon them. - SAINT AUGUSTINE (Paris, 1863.)

HAPPINESS IS NOT OF THIS WORLD

20. "I am not happy! Happiness was not made for me!" people from all lifestyles frequently proclaim this fact. This, dear children proves, better than any possible form of reasoning the truth of the maxim from the book of *Ecclesiastics*: "Happiness is not of this world." Indeed, not riches, power or even the blossom of youth, are essential conditions for happiness. Furthermore, not even by uniting these three elements, so desired by many, can happiness be assured because we are constantly hearing people of all ages, even

those from the most privileged classes, bitterly complaining about the situation in which they find themselves.

Before this fact, it is inconceivable that the militant and working classes envy, with a great desire, the positions of those who are apparently favoured by fortune. In this world, despite what anyone can do, each must face their own part of work and misery, their quota of suffering and deceptions. From which it is easy to reach the conclusion that the Earth is a planet of trials and atonement.

So then, those who preach that the Earth is Humanity's only home and that it is here during only one existence that people can reach the highest level of happiness possible to their nature, are merely deluding themselves and those who listen to them. It has been demonstrated through multi-secular experiences that only in exceptional cases can this globe offer the necessary conditions for complete happiness for any one individual.

In general, it is possible to affirm that happiness is a Utopia, whose conquest has been striven after by successive generations without ever having been able to reach their objective. If a sensible man or woman is a rarity in this world, then the completely happy person has never been found.

Happiness on Earth consists of something so fleeting for those who are not guided by ponderation, that but for a year, a month or a week of complete satisfaction the rest of their existence is a series of bitter deceptions. In addition, note dear children, that I refer to those who are considered the lucky ones of the Earth, those who are the envy of the masses.

Consequently, if the earthly dwelling-place is specifically for trials and atonement, then we must admit that somewhere there are more favourable dwelling places; where the human spirit, although still a prisoner in a material body, may possess the delights of human life in all its fullness. This is the reason why God has planted those beautiful superior planets in your vortex, towards which your efforts and tendencies will one day cause you to gravitate, when you have become sufficiently purified and perfected.

However, do not deduce from my words that the Earth is perpetually destined to remain a penitentiary. No, certainly not! From the progress that has already been achieved, we may readily infer further progress in the future; from the various social betterments already obtained new and more fertile improvements. This is the immense task to be realised by these new Teachings that the Spirits have revealed to you.

So then, my dear children, may a saintly emulation animate you and that each one of you may energetically change your ways. Everyone should dedicate himself or herself to the propagation of Spiritism that has already begun your own regeneration. It is your duty to help your brothers and sisters to participate in the rays of this sacred light. Accordingly set to work, dear children! Let us hope that within this solemn reunion all hearts may aspire to this great objective of preparing a world for future generations where the word happiness is no longer meaningless. - *François-Nicolas-Madeleine*, Cardinal MORLOT (Paris, 1863.)

LOSING LOVED ONES - PREMATURE DEATHS

21. When death cuts down a member of your family, carrying off the youngest before the oldest without discrimination, you are accustomed to say that God is not just, because He sacrifices one who is strong and has all their future before them. Thus, leaving those who have lived many years and are full of deceptions. Also, because He takes those who are useful and leaves behind those who are no longer able to work and breaks the heart of a mother by depriving her of the innocent creature who was her only joy.

Humans, it is on this point that you must lift yourselves above commonplace thoughts about life, in order to be able to understand that goodness is frequently where you judge there to be evil, and the wisdom of Providence where you think you perceive the blind fatality of destiny. Why do you evaluate divine justice by your own ideas? Do you suppose that the Lord of the Worlds applies justice through mere caprice, in order to inflict cruel punishment? Nothing happens that has not an intelligent meaning and no matter what happens there is always a reason for it. If you scrutinise better all the pain that redounds to you then you would surely find Divine reason, regenerating reason, wherein you would see the worthlessness of your interests that consequently, would become so secondary as to be cast into the last place.

Believe me, in the case of an incarnation of twenty years, death is preferable to any of the shameful dissipations that bring untold distress to respectable families, break the hearts of mothers and cause parents' hair to whiten before their time. Premature death is frequently a great blessing that God concedes to those who depart, so preserving them from the miseries of life or the seductions that possibly occasioned the loss of life. The person who dies in the flower of youth is not a victim of fate. God judges that it is not suitable for that person to remain longer on Earth.

What a terrible tragedy, you say, to see cut the thread of life that was so full of hope! To what hope are you referring? That of the Earth? Where the one who departed could perhaps have shone or made their way and become rich? Always there is this restricted vision that prevents a person from rising above that which is material. Who can tell what might have been the actual fate of that life you thought so full of hope? How do you know that it would not have become saturated with bitterness? Do you then disdain the hopes offered by the future life, to the point of preferring this fleeting existence here on Earth? Do you suppose that a high position amongst humans is worth more than an elevated place amongst the blessed Spirits?

Instead of complaining, rejoice when it pleases God to withdraw one of His children from this vale of miseries. Would it not be selfish to wish they continued suffering at your side? Ah! This is the pain conceived by those lacking in faith, who see death as an eternal separation! However, those of you who are Spiritists know that the soul lives better when it is separated from its material form. Mothers, know that your beloved children are near you, yes, very near. Their fluidic bodies embrace you, their thoughts protect you and the remembrances that you keep delight them with happiness; but your unreasonable pain afflicts them, because it reveals a lack of faith, so constituting a revolt against the Will of God.

Those who understand the meaning of spiritual life, listen to the beatings of your heart calling to these loved ones. If you ask God to bless them, you will feel great consolation, the kind that will dry your tears; you will feel magnificent aspirations that will show you the future that our Supreme Lord has promised. - SAMSON, ex-member of the Spiritist Society of Paris, (1863.)

IF THEY HAD BEEN A GOOD PERSON THEY WOULD HAVE DIED

22. When speaking of an evil person who has escaped some danger, it is customary to say that *if they had been a good person they would have died*. Well then, in saying this you are speaking the truth, because it frequently happens that God bestows a longer trial on a spirit who is only commencing their path to progress than He would give a Good Spirit who, by merit of their worthiness, receives the blessing of the shortest possible period of atonement. Consequently, whenever you use that aphorism you unsuspectingly commit a blasphemy.

If a good person dies, having as neighbour someone who is considered as evil, it is soon remarked that it would have been better *if the neighbour had died.* By saying this, you are committing a very big mistake, because the one who has departed had completed his or her tasks and the other, who is left, has perhaps not even begun. Why should you wish the bad person to be denied the necessary time to complete their tasks, while condemning the good person to remain an unnecessary prisoner on Earth? What would you say about a prisoner that continued to be held in prison after having served their sentence when another person, who had no right, was set at liberty? It must be understood that true liberty for a spirit is the breaking of the ties that keep it captive within a physical body and that while upon Earth, it is really a prisoner.

Accustom yourselves then not to censure the things you do not understand. More especially to believe that God is just in all things and that on many occasions what appears to be an evil is really a blessing. Because your faculties are so limited, it is not possible for you to have a clear vision of the whole, nor can it be felt by your obtuse senses. However, if you strive to reach beyond your limited sphere, by means of thought, you will find that the importance of all material things diminishes according to the manner in which you are able to lift up your thoughts. In this way, life presents itself as a mere incident in the infinite course of spiritual existence, which is the only true life. - FÉNELON (Sens, 1861.)

VOLUNTARY TORMENTS

23. Human beings are incessantly searching for happiness that always escapes them, because pure happiness does not exist here on Earth. However, despite the vicissitudes that form an inevitable procession throughout earthly life, they may at least enjoy relative

happiness, if they do not search for it within perishable things that are subject to the same vicissitudes; that is to say within material enjoyments, instead of seeking it within the delights of the soul. The only real happiness in this world comes from having *peace of mind*. Instead of which people are constantly seeking all things that agitate and perturb and, strangely enough, it seems as if they create many of the problems and torments themselves, on purpose, when it is up to each one to avoid them.

Are there any worse torments than those created by envy and jealousy? For those who are envious or jealous, there is no rest; they suffer a state of perpetual fever. The possessions of others cause sleepless nights; the success of rivals provokes giddiness; in their eyes emulation is epitomised in eclipsing those around them; all their happiness consists in provoking a rage of jealousy in those as imprudent as themselves. They are indeed poor foolish beings! Never imagining that perhaps tomorrow they will have to leave behind all these trifles, being the covetousness that has poisoned their lives. The words: 'Blessed are the afflicted for they shall be consoled' certainly do not apply to these people, seeing that their preoccupations are not those that receive recompense in Heaven.

On the other hand, many torments will be avoided by those who are content with what they have, who can see things they do not possess without envy and who do not try to appear better than they are. These will be constantly rich, since by looking below oneself, it is always possible to see others with less than we have. These kinds of people are calm, because they do not create imaginary necessities for themselves. Is calmness then not happiness in the midst of life's turmoil? - FÉNELON (Lyon, 1860.)

TRUE MISFORTUNES

24. Everyone talks about misfortune, everyone has experienced it and judges they understand its multiple characteristics. I have

come to tell you that almost everyone is deluded, as real misfortune is not what the world, that is to say those people who are unfortunate, believes it to be. They see as misfortune the unheated stove, the threatening creditor, the empty cradle, tears, the funeral procession and those following with broken hearts, the anguish of betrayal, the stripping of pride from those who would wish to be dressed in the purple, but who can barely hide their nudity beneath the ragged tatters of their vanity. To all this and much more, humanity gives the name of misfortune. Yes, it is misfortune for those who only see the present. However, real misfortune is in the consequences of these facts, rather than in the facts themselves. Tell me then, if a happening that at the time was considered a happy event, but which later caused disastrous consequences, is not more calamitous than another that initially caused contrariety, but finally produced benefits? Tell me also, is a storm that uproots trees but purifies the air and dissipates unhealthy miasmas that can cause death, not more of a blessing than unhappiness?

In order to be able to judge, one must first consider the consequences. Thus in order to more fully appreciate what is really fortunate or unfortunate for humanity, we must transport ourselves beyond the vision of this life, for it is only there that the consequences can begin to be felt. Therefore, everything called unhappiness according to the short sightedness of human beings ends with the body, and receives its compensation in the future life.

I will reveal misfortune to you in yet another light, in the form of beauty and colour, that is accepted and even earnestly desired by your poor deluded souls. Pleasure, commotion, unnecessary agitation and the satisfaction of stupid vanities are the true misfortunes; causing human beings to ignore their conscience, prevents the process of thought and leaves them in a dazed state with regard to their future. These unhappinesses, so ardently sought after, are nothing more than the opium of forgetfulness.

Have hope all you who cry! Tremble all who laugh because their body is satiated! It is not possible to deceive God or to escape one's destiny. Afflictions, those creditors more pitiless than the wolf pack, unloosed by your miseries, are constantly lurking behind the illusion of repose only to suddenly emerge in the form of agony and real unhappiness, for all who have allowed their souls to become flabby through indifference and selfishness.

Therefore, let Spiritism offer enlightenment and establish truth and error in their real formats that until now have been so singularly deformed by your blindness! Act like brave soldiers who, far from running away from peril, prefer the dangerous fight rather than peace, which will bring them neither glory nor promotion! What does it matter to the soldier if he loses weapons, baggage and uniform if he comes out of battle the winner, covered with glory? What does it matter to those who have faith in the future, if they leave riches and their physical bodies on the battlefield of life, provided their soul enters radiantly into the Celestial Kingdom? - DELPHINE DE GIRARDIN (Paris, 1861.)

MELANCHOLY

25. Do you know why sometimes a vague sadness fills your heart, leading you to consider that life is bitter? This is because your spirit, aspiring to happiness and liberty, on finding itself tied to the physical body that acts like a prison, becomes exhausted through vain efforts to seek release. On recognising that these attempts are useless the soul becomes discouraged and as the body suffers the influence of the spirit, it feels weary, apathetic, full of despondency and it is then that you judge yourself unhappy.

Believe me when I tell you to resist these tendencies with all your strength, as they only weaken your willpower. Aspirations for a better life are inborn in all humanity, but do not seek them in this world. Now that God is sending His Spirits to instruct you about the happiness He has reserved for you, wait with patience for the time when the liberating angel will come to help you break away from the ties that hold your spirit captive. Remember, during your exile here on Earth, you have a mission to fulfil that you do not even suspect; be it dedicating yourself to your family or fulfilling the various obligations bestowed upon you by God. If within the course of this exiled probation, while seeking exoneration, you feel about to collapse through anxiety, uneasiness or tribulations, be strong and courageous enough to support these pressures. Stand up to them with resolution for they will soon pass. These are the only means by which you can reach those for whom you pine and who, jubilant at seeing you once again, will hold out their hands towards you to guide you to regions inaccessible to earthly afflictions. - FRANÇOIS DE GENÈVE (Bordeaux.)

VOLUNTARY TRIALS - THE TRUE HAIR SHIRT

26. You ask if it is licit for a person to lessen his or her own probation. This is equal to another question such as is it licit for drowning people to save themselves? Should we take a thorn from our hand? Should we call a doctor when we are ill? The reason behind our trials is to help us to use our intelligence, patience and resignation. It may happen that someone is born into a difficult and painful situation precisely to make them look for the means of alleviating these problems. The merit is in suffering the consequences that cannot be avoided *without complaining*, in persevering with the fight and in not allowing oneself to become desperate when one is not successful. It is never to be found in negligence, which is more laziness than virtue.

This quite naturally leads to another question: if Jesus said 'Blessed are the afflicted,' can merit be gained by seeking afflictions that could aggravate our trials by means of voluntary suffering? To this, we can reply very decidedly yes, there is great merit provided the suffering and privations are of benefit to others; this is charity through suffering. However, not when the suffering and privations are of benefit to the inflictor; this would only be fanatical selfishness.

It is necessary to make a clear distinction in this matter. Regarding yourself personally, be content with the trials and problems that God sends. Do not seek to increase this volume, as it alone may at times be extremely heavy to bear. Accept it without murmuring but with faith; that is all that God asks. Do not weaken your body with useless privations and mortifications that have no objective, because you will need all your strength if you are to fulfil your work here on Earth. To torture and martyr the body voluntarily is to go against God's Law. He has given humanity the means to sustain life, so to weaken the body needlessly is true suicide. Use it, but do not abuse it, that is the Law. The abuse of the best thing God has given you will bring inevitable consequences as a punishment.

Nevertheless, quite the contrary occurs when people impose suffering upon themselves in order to alleviate that of others. If you support cold and hunger in order to offer heat and sustenance to another, thereby causing your body to be affected, you are making a sacrifice that God will bless. When you leave your perfumed homes to go to an infected hovel so as to console; dirty your hands to treat wounds; lose sleep so as to hold vigil at the bedside of the sick; who after all are your brothers and sisters in God; put your health in jeopardy for the purpose of practising the Good, then it is here that you find your hair shirt, the true and blessed hair shirt. You have not allowed the delights of this world to shrivel your heart, nor have you slept upon the voluptuous breast of riches. Rather you have become a consoling angel to the sadly deserted.

However, you who retire from the world to live in isolation in order to avoid its seductions, what utility do you serve here on Earth? Where is the courage to face your problems? You have merely run away from the fight and deserted the combat. If you wish to make a sacrifice, then apply it to your soul and not to your body. Mortify your spirit, but not your flesh; whip your pride, receive humiliations without murmur, scourge yourself of self-love, harden yourself against the pain of insult and slander, which is more pungent than physical pain. It is in these things that you find your true hair shirt, whose wounds will be taken into account because they will testify to your courage and submission to God's Will. - *A Guardian Angel* (Paris, 1863.)

SHOULD WE END OUR NEIGHBOUR'S PROBATION?

27. *Should anyone put an end to another's probation when they can, or should God's purpose be respected, so leaving things to take their own course?*

We have already said repeatedly that you are upon this planet of atonement to conclude your trials, and everything that happens is a consequence of past lives. This is the interest on the debt you must pay. However, in some people this fact provokes reflections that should be combated, due to the disastrous effects that might be caused.

Some people think that by being on Earth for the purpose of atonement all probation must follow its course. Then there are others who believe that not only should nothing be done, but also they should help others to benefit by making these sufferings more active, more intense. This is a very big mistake. It is quite true that trials must take their course as marked by God, but how do we know what God has designed? Do we know to what extent they must reach? What if our merciful Father designated that this or another suffering should only reach a certain point? How do you know whether Divine Providence has placed you, not as an instrument of torture to aggravate the suffering of the culprit, but as the soothing balm of consolation to help heal the wounds? So therefore, never say "It is God's justice and must follow its course." On the contrary, rather say, "Let me see what means our merciful Father has put within my reach so I may lessen the suffering of my brother or sister." Let me see if my moral consolations, my material help or my counselling can help them overcome this test with more energy, patience and resignation. Perhaps God has put in my hands a way to stop suffering; perhaps even He has given me this possibility as a test, or perhaps an atonement, to deter evil and substitute it with peace.

Therefore, always help each other mutually in your tests and never consider yourself an instrument of torture. Every person who has a heart should revolt against such an idea. Especially Spiritists because they, more than anyone else, understand the infinite extension of God's Goodness. Every Spiritist should be convinced that their whole life must be an act of love and devotion; that whatever they might do to oppose God's wishes, these wishes will always be fulfilled. Therefore, they should apply maximum strength to attenuate the bitterness of atonement without fear, because only God has the right to shorten or prolong a trial, as He sees fit.

Would it not be immense pride on the part of human beings to consider that it is right, in a manner of speaking, to turn the knife in the wound? To increase the dose of poison in the viscera of the one who is suffering, under the pretext that it is part of their expiation? Oh! Always consider yourselves as instruments for the alleviation of pain! To summarise: all are on Earth for atonement and all, without exception, must strive to lessen the atonement of one's fellow beings, which is in accordance with the law of love and charity. - BERNARDIN, a Protecting Spirit (Bordeaux, 1863.)

WOULD IT BE LICIT TO HASTEN THE DEATH OF SOMEONE INCURABLY SICK WHO IS SUFFERING?

28. *A person is agonising under cruel suffering. Their state is known to be desperate. Would it be licit to save them a few instants of anguish by hastening their end?*

Who has given you the right to prejudge God's purpose? Can He not conduct a person to the very brink of the grave and then withdraw them, in order that they may awaken and recognise the need to change their ideas? Even when a dying person has reached the last extremes, no one can be sure the final hour has arrived. Has science never been wrong in its predictions?

Of course, there are cases that with good reason, can be considered desperate. Even if there is no hope of a definite return to life and health, there always exists the possibility, testified on many occasions, of a sick person recovering their faculties at the last instant. Well then, this is the hour of grace conceded by God that may be of extreme importance. You do not understand the reflections that the spirit may have during those last agonising convulsions, nor how a lightning repentance may save them from many torments.

The materialist, who only sees the body and does not take into consideration the spirit, is not apt to understand these things. However, the Spiritist, who knows what happens in the afterlife, comprehends the value of these last thoughts. Therefore, mitigate the last sufferings as much as you can, but guard yourself against abbreviating life, be it even for a minute, as this minute can be the means of avoiding many tears in the future. - SAINT LOUIS (Paris, 1860.)

SACRIFICING ONE'S OWN LIFE

29. *Are those who are tired of life, but who do not wish to extinguish it by their own hands, guilty if they seek death on a battlefield with the intention of making their death useful?*

Whether people kill themselves, or cause others to kill them, the intention is always to abbreviate life. Therefore, there is intentional suicide even if there is no actual fact. The idea that this death would serve some purpose is mere illusion, just a pretext to cover up the act and for the person to excuse themselves in their own eyes. If they seriously wished to serve their country, they would do their best to stay alive so they might be able to defend it, rather than seek death, because if they are dead they can no longer be of help. Real devotion consists in not being afraid of death when it is a matter of utility, of facing danger and, when necessary, in sacrificing one's life without thinking about it. However, in seeking death with a *premeditated intent* by exposing oneself to risk, even if it were in service, annuls all merit for the action. - SAINT LOUIS (Paris, 1860.)

30. *If someone exposes them self to imminent danger in order to save the life of a fellow being, knowing that they will succumb, will this act be considered as suicide?*

If there is no intention to seek death in this act, then there is no suicide, only devotion and abnegation, even though there is a certainty of death. But who can be sure? Who can say that Providence has not reserved an unexpected means of salvation at the last moment? Is it not possible even to save one who is before the cannon's mouth? On many occasions, it happens that Providence wishes to take a trial of resignation to the extreme limits, in which case an unexpected circumstance will ward off the fatal blow. - SAINT LOUIS (Paris, 1860.)

MAKING ONE'S OWN SUFFERING USEFUL TO OTHERS

31. Do not those who accept their suffering with resignation, because they are submissive to God's wishes and are mindful of their future happiness, work only for their own benefit? Is it not possible for them to make their suffering useful to others?

These sufferings may be useful to others both materially and morally. In a material sense, by the work, privations and sacrifices they impose upon themselves that can contribute to the material well being of their fellow companions. In the moral sense, by the example they offer of their submission to God's Will. By showing the strength of the Spiritist faith, many unfortunate and wretched people can be induced to resign themselves, so being saved from despair and its disastrous consequences. - SAINT LOUIS (Paris, 1860.)

CHAPTER 6

CHRIST THE CONSOLER

The gentle yoke. - The promised Consoler. – INSTRUCTIONS FROM THE SPIRITS: The advent of the Spirit of Truth.

THE GENTLE YOKE

1. Come unto me, all you that labour and are heavy laden and I will give you rest. Take my yoke upon you and learn from me, for I am meek and lowly in heart: and you will find rest for your souls. For my yoke is easy, and my burden is light. (MATTHEW, 11:28 - 30)

2. All sufferings such as miseries, deceptions, physical pain and loss of loved ones will find consolation from faith in the future and from confidence in God's justice, all of which Christ came to teach humanity. On the other hand, for those who expect nothing after this life or who simply doubt, afflictions will seem heavier to them, as they do not have any hope of mitigating their bitterness. This is what prompted Jesus to say, "Come to me all who are weary and I will give you rest."

Meanwhile, the assistance and happiness promised to the afflicted depends on one condition that is found in the law He taught. His yoke is the observance of this law, but the yoke is light and the law gentle because it only imposes love and charity as its obligations.

THE PROMISED CONSOLER

3. "If you love me keep my commandments. And I will pray to the Father, and He shall give you another Comforter that he may abide with you forever; Even the Spirit of Truth, whom the world cannot receive, because it sees him not, neither knows him: but you know him: for he dwells with you, and shall be in you. But the Comforter, which is the Holy Ghost, whom the Father will send in my name, he shall teach you all things, and bring all things to your remembrance, whatsoever I have said to you. (JOHN, 14:15-17 & 26.)

4. Jesus promises another Consoler the *Spirit of Truth,* which the world did not yet know because it was not sufficiently mature to be able to understand. This is the Consoler, sent by the Father to teach humanity all things and to call to mind all that Christ had said. Therefore, if the Spirit of Truth was to come at a later date to teach these additional matters, then it was because Christ had not told everything. But if the Spirit of Truth was to come to remind us of what Christ had said, that is because it had been forgotten or not properly understood.

Spiritism has come at the predicted time to fulfil Christ's promise. Presided over by the Spirit of Truth, it calls humanity to observe the Law and reveals all manner of things so making understandable what Jesus had said only in the form of parables. Christ Himself had given the warning, "Listen, all those who have ears to hear." Spiritism has come to open the eyes and ears of earthly humanity because it speaks without figuration or allegory, so lifting up the veil that had been intentionally cast upon certain mysteries. Finally, it has come to bring supreme consolation to the disinherited of this Earth and to all who suffer, by showing them the just causes of their suffering and the useful purpose of all pain.

Christ said, "Blessed are the afflicted for they will be comforted." But how can anyone feel happy if they do not know why they suffer? Spiritism shows the cause of suffering to be in past existences and the destiny of this planet, upon which human beings make atonement for their past. It explains the object of suffering by showing it as a salutary process that produces a cure and as a means of purification, both of which guarantee future happiness. From this, it becomes possible for human beings to understand that they deserve the suffering and that this is just. Humans also learn that suffering and pain will help towards progress and so are able to accept it without complaining, just as a worker accepts the work that will guarantee their salary. Spiritism gives an unshakable faith in the future so that they are no longer troubled by a consuming doubt within their souls. Thus, on being enabled to see things from a higher level makes the importance of earthly vicissitudes disappear on the vast and splendid horizon that Spiritism sets before us. The prospect of the happiness that awaits gives humans patience, resignation and courage to continue to the end of their pathway.

In this manner, Spiritism realizes what Jesus said of the promised consoler, by bringing knowledge of those things that allow human beings to know where they have come from, where they are going and why they are on Earth. Thus calling attention to the true principals of God's Laws and offering consolation through faith and hope.

INSTRUCTIONS FROM THE SPIRITS

THE ADVENT OF THE SPIRIT OF TRUTH

5. I have come, as I came on another occasion, to those misguided sons and daughters of Israel, to bring the truth and to dissipate the darkness. Listen to me! Just as my words in the past did, so today Spiritism must remind the incredulous that above them reigns the immutable truth that is the existence of the Good God, the great God, who causes the plants to germinate and the waves to rise up. I revealed the Divine Teachings. As a reaper, I have gathered into sheaves the scattered goodness in the breasts of human beings and said, "Come unto me, all who are suffering!"

However, ungrateful humanity has moved away from the straight and wide path that leads to the Kingdom of my Father, becoming lost along the rough and narrow pathways of impiety. My Father does not wish to annihilate the human race. He wants the living and the dead, that is to say, those who are dead according to the flesh because death does not exist, to assist each other mutually. Listen no more to the voices of the prophets and apostles, but listen instead to those who no longer live upon the Earth who proclaim, "Pray and believe! Death is the resurrection and life is an ordeal you seek, during which the virtues you have cultivated will grow and develop, even as the cedar tree."

Those of you, who are weak and know the obscurity of your own minds, do not deviate from the beacon that divine clemency has put into your hands to enlighten your pathway and reconduct you, who are lost children, once again to the bosom of the Father.

I am too much overcome with compassion for your miseries and by your immense weakness, not to extend a helping hand to all those who have unhappily been misguided who, while looking up to Heaven, have fallen into the pit of error. Believe, love, and meditate on these things that are revealed to you. Do not mix the chaff with the good seed or the Utopias with the truth.

Spiritists! Love one another, that is the first precept; educate yourselves is the second. Within Christianity, you will find all the truths. The errors in which people have become enrooted are all of human origin. Here from beyond the grave, where you thought there was nothing, voices call out to you, "Brothers and sisters! Nothing perishes! Jesus Christ is the victor over all evil; you can be the victors over impiety." - THE SPIRIT OF TRUTH (Paris, 1860.)

6. I have come to instruct and console the poor and humble people who are the disinherited. I have come to tell them to raise up their resignation to the level of their trials; to weep, for pain

was consecrated in the Garden of Olives; but also to have hope, for the consoling angels will come to them and dry their tears.

Workers, plan your pathway! Recommence the following day the wearisome labour of the previous one. The work done by your hands furnishes the body with earthly bread; however, your souls have not been forgotten. I, the Divine Gardener, cultivate them in the silence of your thoughts. When the time comes for repose, the thread of life slips through your fingers and your eyes are closed to the light, you will feel the surging within and the germination of My precious seed. Nothing is lost in the Kingdom of our Father. Your sweat and miseries form the treasure that will make you rich in the superior spheres, where light substitutes the darkness and where the most naked of you will perhaps become the most resplendent.

In truth, I say to you that those who bear their burdens and help their brothers and sisters are beloved by Me. Instruct yourselves in the precious Teachings that dissipate the errors of revolt and show the sublime objectives of human trials. As the wind sweeps the dust, so the breeze of the spirits dissipates your resentment against the riches of the world, that is frequently very pitiable, since they are subject to more dangerous trials than yours. I am with you and my apostle will instruct you. Therefore, you who are kept captive by life, drink from the living spring of love and be prepared to one-day launch yourselves, free and happy, upon the bosom of He Who created you weak so that you might become perfect. Who desires that you model your own pliable clay in order to be the author of your own immortality. - THE SPIRIT OF TRUTH (Paris, 1861.)

7. I am the great doctor of souls and I have come to bring you the remedy that will cure. The weak, the suffering and the sick are My favourite children and I am come to save them. Come then to Me all who suffer or find yourselves oppressed and you will be

alleviated and consoled. Do not search for strength and consolation elsewhere, as the world is impotent to offer them. God directs a supreme appeal to your hearts by means of Spiritism. Listen to Him! Eradicate impiety, lies, error and incredulity from your aching souls. These are like monsters that suck the purest of your blood and open wounds that are usually mortal. Thus, in the future, when you have become humble and submissive to the Creator, you will keep His Divine Laws. Love, pray and be gentle with the Spirits of the Lord and call unto them sincerely from the bottom of your hearts. Then He will send His beloved Son to instruct you and to say these goodly words, "I am come because you called Me." - THE SPIRIT OF TRUTH (Bordeaux, 1861.)

8. God consoles the humble and gives strength to the afflicted when they ask. His power covers the Earth and in every place with each tear shed, He places a consoling remedy. Abnegation and resignation are a continuous prayer and contain profound teaching. Human wisdom resides in these two words. Would that all suffering spirits could understand this truth, instead of clamouring against their pain and the moral sufferings that it behoves them to partake. So, take these words for your motto: *devotion and abnegation.* Then you will be strong, as they resume all the obligations that charity and humility impose. The sentiment of fulfilled duty will give repose and resignation to your spirit. Then your heart will beat more steadily, your soul will become more tranquil and your body will be protected against despondency; because the body suffers more when the spirit is profoundly stricken. - THE SPIRIT OF TRUTH (Havre, 1863.)

CHAPTER 7

BLESSED ARE THE POOR IN SPIRIT

How to understand the words 'poor in spirit.' - He who exalts himself shall be debased. - Mysteries that are hidden from the learned and prudent. - INSTRUCTIONS FROM THE SPIRITS: Pride and humility. - The mission of the intelligent person on Earth.

HOW TO UNDERSTAND THE WORDS 'POOR IN SPIRIT'

1. Blessed are the poor in spirit: for theirs is the kingdom of heaven. (MATTHEW, 5:3)

2. Incredulity has mocked this maxim: *Blessed are the poor in spirit* as it has mocked many other things it does not understand. By the words '*poor in spirit*', Jesus did not mean those devoid of intelligence, but those who are humble; in as much as He said that the kingdom of heaven would be for them and not for the prideful.

People of knowledge and imagination, so called by public conviction; generally hold such high opinions of themselves and their superiority that they consider everything divine as being undeserving of their consideration. By concentrating all their attention upon themselves, they are then unable to lift up their eyes to God. This tendency to believe they are superior to everything and everyone, very frequently leads them to deny anything that might be above them, even Divinity itself, for fear it might belittle them. If they condescend to admit its existence, they then contest one of its most beautiful attributes that is providential action over things of this world, because they think they alone are sufficient to govern. Taking the intelligence they possess as a measure of universal intelligence and judging themselves able to understand everything, they are unable to believe in the viability of that which they do not understand. They consider their judgement to be the law.

If they refuse to admit the existence of the invisible world and an extra-human power, it is not because it is beyond their capability, but because their pride makes them revolt against the idea of something above which they are unable to place themselves, that would bring them down from the pedestal upon which they like to contemplate. Hence, they only have scorn for everything that does not belong to the visible and tangible world. They attribute to themselves such imagination and learning that they cannot believe in things that, according to their way of thinking, are only good for simple people, taking for poor in spirit all who take such matters seriously.

However, say what they like, they will inevitably be drawn into this invisible world they scoff at, together with everyone else. It is there that their eyes will be opened, so making them realise their errors. Nevertheless, God being just, He cannot receive those who have denied His majesty in the same manner as those who submit to His laws with humility, nor can He give them equal share.

By saying that the kingdom of heaven belongs to those who are simple, Jesus shows us that no one will be admitted to this kingdom without simplicity of heart and humility of spirit. That the ignorant person who possesses these qualities will be preferred to a wise person who believes more in themselves than in God. In all circumstances, Jesus puts humility into the category of virtues that brings us near to God and pride into the category of vices that keep us away from God. The reason for this is clear, for to be humble is an act of submission to God, whereas pride is a revolt against Him. Therefore, there is far greater value for our future happiness when people are poor in spirit - in a worldly sense - and rich in moral qualities.

HE WHO EXALTS HIMSELF SHALL BE DEBASED

3. At the same time came the disciples to Jesus, saying, who is the greatest in the kingdom of heaven?' And Jesus called a little child to him, and set him in the midst of them, And said, Verily I say to you, except you are converted, and become as little children, you shall not enter into the kingdom of heaven. Whosoever, therefore, shall humble himself as this little child, the same is greatest in the kingdom of heaven. And whoso shall receive one such little child in my name receives me. (MATTHEW, 18:1-5.)

4. Then came to him the mother of Zebede's children with her sons, worshipping him. And he said to her, What do you want? She said to him, Grant that these my two sons may sit, the one on your right hand, and the other on the left, in your kingdom. But Jesus answered and said, You know not what you are asking. Are you able to drink from the cup that I shall drink from, and be baptised with the baptism that I am baptised with? They said to him, We are able. And he said to them, you shall drink indeed from my cup, and be baptised with the baptism that I am baptised with: but to sit at my right hand, and on my left hand is not mine to give, but it shall be given to them for whom it is prepared by my Father. And when the ten heard it, they were moved with indignation against the two brothers. Nevertheless, Jesus called them to him and said, You know that the Princes of the Gentiles exercise dominion over them, and they that are great exercise authority over them. But it shall not be so among you: but whosoever will be great among you, let him be your minister; And whoever will be chief among you, let him be your servant: Even as the Son of man came not to be ministered to, but to minister, and to give his life a ransom for many. (MATTHEW, 20:20-28)

5. And it came to pass, as he went into the house of the chief Pharisee to eat bread on the Sabbath day, that they watched him. And he put forth a parable to those which were bidden, when he marked how they chose out the chief rooms; saying to them, When you are invited of any man to a wedding, sit not down in the highest room; lest a more honourable man than you be invited by him; and he that invited you and him come and say to you, Give this man place; and you begin with shame to take the lowest room. But when you are invited, go and sit down in the lowest room; that when he that invited you cometh, he may say to you, Friend, go up higher; then you will have worship in the presence of them that sit at meat with you. For whosoever exalted himself shall be abased; and he that humbles himself shall be exalted. (LUKE, 14:1 & 7-11.)

6. These maxims stem from the principle of humility that Jesus was constantly presenting as an essential condition for the happiness promised to the chosen of the Lord, which He presented in this manner, "Blessed are the poor in spirit, for theirs is the kingdom of heaven." He took a child as a symbol of simplicity of heart when He said, "The greatest in the kingdom of heaven will be those who are humble and *small as a little child.*" That is to say, those who hold no pretension to superiority or infallibility.

We find the same fundamental idea in the following maxim: Whoever wants to be first must be your slave and also in this: He who humbles himself will be exalted and he who exalts himself will be humbled.

Spiritism confirms this theory through examples when it shows that those who are great in the spiritual world are those who were small on Earth. That frequently those who were great and powerful on Earth find themselves extremely small in the spiritual world. This is because on dying, people take with them only that which makes for greatness in Heaven, that which is never lost being their virtues. All earthly greatness, such as riches, titles, glory, nobleness of birth, etc., is impossible to take with them. On reaching the other side, if humans have nothing apart from these qualities, they find themselves destitute of everything, like shipwrecked people who loses everything, even to their clothes. The only item still retained is pride that makes the position even worse, more humiliating, when it is found that those they trod underfoot on Earth have been raised to places of glory far above.

Spiritism also shows another side of this principle within the process of successive reincarnations. When those who had raised themselves to high positions in one life, then find that in a succeeding existence they are born into lowly conditions, if they had allowed themselves to be dominated by pride and ambition. Therefore, do not seek the highest positions on Earth, nor place yourself above others if you do not wish to be obliged to descend. On the contrary, seek the most humble and modest positions, seeing that God will then give you a more elevated place in heaven if you deserve it.

MYSTERIES ARE HIDDEN FROM THE LEARNED AND PRUDENT

7. At that time Jesus answered and said: thank thee, O Father, Lord of Heaven and Earth, because you have hidden these things from the wise and prudent, and have revealed them to little children. (MATTHEW, 11:25.)

8. It may appear quite singular that Jesus gives thanks to God for having revealed these things to the *meek* and *humble*, who are the poor in spirit, and for having hidden them from *the learned* and *prudent*, who apparently are more able to understand. Nevertheless, we must recognise that the former are those who are submissive, who *humble themselves* before God and do not consider themselves superior. The latter are those who *are arrogant and full of pride* for their worldly knowledge, judging themselves prudent because they deny God or who, when they are not refusing to accept Him, treat Him as an equal despite the fact that in ancient times '*learned*' was a synonym for '*wise*'. This is why God has left them to discover the secrets of the Earth and

revealed the secrets of Heaven only to the humble, who bow down before Him.

9. The same thing has happened today with the great truths revealed by Spiritism. Many of those who are incredulous are surprised by the fact that the Spirits take so little trouble to convince them. The reason for this being that it is preferable to look after those who seek with good faith and humility, rather than offer enlightenment to those who suppose they already possess it; who perhaps imagine that God should be very thankful for having managed to attract their attention by proving His existence to them.

The power of God manifests itself in all things, from the smallest to the greatest. He does not hide His light, but rather disperses it in constant waves to every corner of the Universe; to such an extent that only those who are blind do not see. *God does not wish their eyes to be opened by force, seeing that they desire to keep them shut.* Their time will come. First, it is necessary that they feel the anguish of darkness and so *recognise it is God and not mere chance that hurts their pride.* In order to overcome this incredulity, God uses the most convenient means according to each individual. It is not their incredulity that prescribes what is to be done, nor is it up to them to say, "If you want to convince me, then you must do this or that on a certain occasion because this is what could persuade me."

Therefore, those who are unbelievers should not be surprised if neither God nor the Spirits, who execute His wishes, do not submit to these demands. Instead, they should ask themselves what they would say if the lowest of their servants tried to impose upon them in whatever form. God imposes the conditions and does not accept those who wish to impose conditions on Him. He listens kindly to those who direct themselves to Him with humility and not to those who judge themselves greater than He.

10. It is often asked if God could not touch these people personally by means of clearly evident manifestations, before which even the most obstinate unbeliever would be convinced. Beyond all doubt He could. In this case, what merit would be gained and more importantly, what use would it be. Do we not see people every day who do not bow down even before such evidence and who say, "Even if I saw I would not believe because I know it is impossible?" If they deny the truth in such a manner, it is because their spirits have not yet reached sufficient maturity to enable them to understand or their hearts able to feel. *Pride is the cataract that covers their vision.* What good does it do to show a light to one who is blind? Rather it is first necessary to cure the cause of the ill. This is why, just as a skilful doctor, He first punishes their pride. He will never abandon any of His children since eventually, their eyes will be opened, but He wishes this to happen of their own free will. Then defeated by the torments of incredulity, they will throw themselves into His arms of their own accord, begging to be forgiven just as did the prodigal son.

INSTRUCTIONS FROM THE SPIRITS

PRIDE AND HUMILITY

11. My dear friends, may the peace of the Lord be with you! I have come in order to encourage you to follow the good pathway.

Humble Spirits, who in other times inhabited the Earth, have been commissioned by God to enlighten you. Blessed be the Lord for the grace that He has granted us of being able to help you improve. May the Holy Spirit illuminate me, so helping to make my words understandable and grant me the favour of being able to put them within reach of all! To you who are incarnate, who are undergoing trials and searching for the light, I pray that the will of

God comes to my aid so that I may make His Teachings shine before your eyes!

Humility is a virtue much forgotten amongst you. Of the many examples given very few have been followed. However, is it possible to be charitable to your neighbour without being humble? Of course not, because this sentiment reduces humankind to the same level by telling them they are brothers and sisters who should help one another mutually, which leads them to a state of Goodness. Without humility, you are merely adorning yourself with virtues you do not possess, as you use clothes especially to hide some physical deformity. Remember He who saved us; remember His humility, which was so great as to put Him above all the prophets!

Pride is the terrible adversary of humility. If Christ promised the kingdom of heaven to the very poor, it was because the great ones on this Earth imagine their titles and riches are recompenses, conferred upon them due to merit. Therefore, they consider themselves to be of an essence much purer than that of the poor. They judge that the titles and riches are due to them, in view of which, when God takes them away, they accuse Him of injustice. Oh! What a mockery of God's justice, what blindness! Does God then distinguish by means of the body? Is not the physical covering of the poor person just the same as that of the rich person? Has the Creator made two kinds of humanity? Everything made by God is wise and great. Therefore, never attribute to Him those ideas created by your own prideful minds.

Oh! You who are rich! While sleeping beneath your golden roofs, safe from the cold, are you aware that thousands of your brothers and sisters, who in God's eyes are worth just as much as you sleep upon beds of straw? Are not those who go hungry your equals? I know that your pride revolts at my words. You agree to give alms, but you will never shake their hands! "Why me!" you will say "I, who am of the noblest blood, one of the great of this Earth, equal to those miserable wretches covered in rags! This is a vain Utopia of pseudo-philosophers! If we are equal, why would God have placed them so low and me so high?" It is true that your clothes are not alike, but if you undressed what difference would there be between you and them? Nevertheless, those of noble blood would say there is a chemical difference. However, until today no such difference has even been discovered between the blood of a lord and that of a common person, or that of a master and that of a slave. Who can guarantee that in the past you too were not as wretched and unfortunate as he was? That you too did not beg for alms. Who can say that one-day in the future you will not beg alms of the one you despise today? Are riches eternal? When the body extinguishes itself, do they not disappear? After all, the body is nothing more than the perishable covering of the spirit! Ah! Cover yourselves with a little humility! Cast your eyes finally on the reality of the things of this world; on what leads to greatness on the one hand and humility on the other. Remember you will not be spared from death, for no one is; nor can your titles be preserved from its blow that might strike today, tomorrow or at any hour. If you bury yourself in your pride, then I feel sorry for you because you will be deserving of pity!

You who are so full of pride! What were you before you became noble and powerful? Probably you were beneath the lowest of your servants. Therefore, bow down your haughty brows, for God can cause you to fall at the exact moment when you most exalt yourselves. All human beings are equal on the divine scale of justice; only virtue marks the distinction in the eyes of God. All spirits come from the same essence and all bodies are formed from the same matter. Your titles and names modify nothing. They remain in the tomb and in no way contribute to the possibility of enjoying the happiness promised to the chosen.

Their titles of nobleness are based solely upon their humility and acts of charity.

Poor creature! You are a mother! Your children suffer! They are cold and hungry while you, bent under the burden of your cross, go out to humiliate yourself in order to bring them bread! Oh! I bow down before you! How saintly and noble you are, how great in my eyes! Pray and wait; happiness still is not of this world. But God will grant the Kingdom of Heaven to the poor and oppressed who have confidence in Him.

And you, a young maiden, poor child, thrust into work and privations. Why do you have such sad thoughts? Why do you cry? May your eyes be lifted up with serenity and pity to God. He feeds the small birds. Believe in Him; He will not abandon you. The sound of parties and the joys of this world make your heart beat faster. You wish to adorn your hair with flowers and join together with the fortunate of this world. You say to yourself that, like the women you see passing by, free of cares and full of laughter, you too could be rich. Oh! Dear child, do not say such things! If you only knew how many tears and what unspeakable pain are hidden beneath those embroidered dresses, and how many sobs are muffled by the sound of that noisy orchestra, you would prefer your humble position and pauperism. Maintain yourself pure in the eyes of God, if you do not want your Guardian Angel to return to Him, covering its face with its white wings, leaving you to your remorse on this planet, without a guide, without support, where you will be lost and where you will be forced to await punishment in the next world.

All you who suffer injustice from your fellow creatures be indulgent with the faults of your brothers and sisters, pondering that you are not exempt from guilt. This is charity and humility. If you suffer from slander, bow down your head before this trial. What importance does the slander of this world have for you? If your conduct is pure, cannot God recompense you? Support courageously the humiliations put upon you by humanity; be humble and recognise that only God is great and powerful.

Oh dear God! Will it be necessary for Christ to return to Earth a second time in order to teach His Laws because humanity has forgotten them? Will He once again have to expel the merchants from the temple for defiling His house that should have been kept exclusively for prayer? Ah, who knows? Oh Humanity! If God granted this grace once more would you not reject Him yet again! Would you not accuse Him of blasphemy because He would humble the pride of modern Pharisees! Perhaps it is even possible that you would make Him follow the road to Golgotha again.

When Moses climbed Mount Sinai to receive God's commandments, the people of Israel being left to themselves abandoned the true God. Men and women gave whatever gold they possessed in order that an idol could be made for them to worship. Today civilised humanity still behaves in the same way. Christ bequeathed His Teachings to you, giving examples of all the virtues, but you have abandoned these examples and precepts. Each one of you, charged with passions, has made a god in accordance with your desires; for some, bloody and terrible; for others, indifferent to the interests of the world. Nevertheless, the god you have fabricated is still the golden calf which each adapts to his or her own tastes and ideas.

My friends, my brothers and sisters, awaken! Let the voices of the Spirits echo in your hearts. Be generous and charitable without ostentation, that is to say, do Good with humility. Let each one, little by little, begin to demolish the altars erected to their pride. In a word, if you are a true Christian you will possess the kingdom of truth. Do not continue to doubt the goodness of God, when He is giving so many proofs of this fact. We have come to prepare the way so that the prophecies may be fulfilled. When the Lord gives you a more resounding demonstration of His clemency, may His celestial messenger find you all gathered together in a great family. It is hoped that by then, your hearts being gentle and mild, you will be worthy to hear the divine words He will offer. May the Chosen One encounter only laurels in His path that have been laid there by your having returned to goodness, charity and fraternity amongst all humans. Then will your world become an earthly Paradise. However, if you remain insensitive to the voices of the Spirits who have been sent to purify and renew your civilised society, which although rich in science, is so poor in noble sentiments, then sadly there will be nothing left for you but tears and groans of unhappiness. However, that will not happen! You will return to God the Father, and all of us who have contributed to the fulfilling of His wishes will join together in singing a hymn of thanksgiving for His unbounded goodness, to glorify Him throughout all the coming ages. So be it. - LACORDAIRE (Constantine, 1863.)

12. Humans, why do you complain about the calamities that you yourselves have heaped upon your heads? You despise the saintly and divine morality of Christ; so do not be surprised that the cup of iniquity should overflow on all sides.

Trouble has become generalised. Who is to blame if not you, who have unceasingly tried to crush each other? It is impossible to be happy without mutual benevolence; but how can benevolence coexist alongside pride? Pride! This is the root of all your troubles. Apply yourselves therefore to destroying it, if you do not wish continually to perpetuate these fatal consequences. There is only one way that offers itself for this purpose, but it is infallible: take Christ's Law as your invariable rule of conduct, that very same Law that you have spurned or falsified in its interpretation.

Why do you hold that which shines and enchants the eyes in higher esteem than that which touches the heart? Why do you make the vice of opulence the object of your adulations, whereas you are disdainful of true merit when it is obscure? Whenever a rich debauchee appears, even though they be lost in body and soul, all doors open, all rush to give them attention; whereas a godly person who lives by their work is hardly given a greeting! When the consideration dispensed to others is measured by the gold they possess or the name they use, what interest can they have in correcting their defects?

This situation would be very different if the many degrading and immoral practices that are gilded over were censured by public opinion, as much as is the failing of poverty. However, pride shows itself ever indulgent to all who flatter it. You say that this is the century of cupidity and money. Beyond doubt; but why allow material necessity to overshadow your good sense and reason? Why must each one wish to place themselves above their brother or sister? Society today is suffering the consequences of this fact.

Never forget that this state of affairs is always a sign of moral decay and decline. When pride reaches extremes it is an indication of an imminent fall, for God never fails to punish the arrogant. If He sometimes allows them to rise, it is only in order to give time for meditation, and to mend their ways under the blows that come to strike their pride from time to time, to serve as warnings. Instead of becoming humble, they rebel. Thus, when the cup is full God will cause them to descend and according to how high they have risen, the more terrible will be their fall.

Poor suffering humanity, whose selfishness has corrupted all pathways, we beg you to renew your courage despite everything. In His infinite mercy, God has sent you a powerful remedy for all your ills, an unexpected help for all your miseries. Open your eyes to the light! Here are the souls of those who no longer live upon the Earth, who have come to call you to the fulfilment of your duties. They will tell you, with the authority of experience, how the vanities and grandeur of this passing existence become mere trifles when faced with eternity. There, in the beyond, the greatest is the one who has been the humblest amongst the most humble in your world. They will tell you that the ones who have most loved their fellow beings will be the best loved in Heaven. That the most powerful on Earth, if they abuse their authority, will be obliged to obey their own servants. Lastly, humility and charity, who are as two brothers or sisters, going hand in hand, are the most effective titles in obtaining grace before He who is Eternal. - ADOLF, Bishop of Algiers. (Marmande, 1862.)

THE MISSION OF THE INTELLIGENT PERSON ON EARTH

13. Never be prideful of what you know, because that knowledge has very restricted limits in the world in which you live. Even supposing you were a prominent intellectual celebrity on this planet, still, you would have no right to be proud. If God, within His designs, causes you to be born in an ambient where you could develop this intelligence, then it was because He wished you to use it for the benefit of everyone. You have been given a mission by the fact of God having placed an instrument in your hands that can be used to develop the retarded intelligences around you, and so conduct them to God. Is not the nature of the instrument an indication as to the purpose for which it should be used? Does not the hoe, which the gardener gives to his assistant, show to what use it should be put? What would you say if instead of working with the hoe, he raised it against his master with a desire to injure him? You would say it was monstrous, that the person should be expelled. Well then, is it not the same for the person who uses their intelligence to destroy the idea of God and Providence amongst their fellow beings? Does not the person who

had been given a hoe to till the soil then raise it against their master? Have they then the right to receive the promised salary? On the contrary, do they not deserve to be expelled from the garden? Do not doubt that they will be! Then they will pass through many miserable existences full of humiliations until they finally bow down before Him to whom they owe everything.

Intelligence is rich in future merits, provided it is well employed. If all men and women who possessed it used it in conformity with God's wishes, then it would be easy for the Spirits to perform their task of helping humanity advance. Unhappily, many have become instruments of pride and perdition against themselves. Humanity abuses intelligence as it does all the other faculties. Nevertheless, there is no lack of Teachings to warn of a powerful Hand that may withdraw what has been granted. FERDINAND, a Protecting Spirit. (Bordeaux, 1862.)

CHAPTER 8

BLESSED ARE THE PURE IN HEART

Simplicity and pureness of heart. - Sinning by means of thought. Adultery. -
True pureness. Unwashed hands. - Offences. If your hand is the cause of an
offence, cut it off. - INSTRUCTIONS FROM THE SPIRITS: Let little children come
to me. - Blessed are those whose eyes are closed.

SIMPLICITY AND PURENESS OF HEART

1. Blessed are the pure in heart: for they will see God.
(MATTHEW, 5:8.)

*2. And they brought young children to Him, that He should touch
them; and His disciples rebuked those that brought them. But
when Jesus saw it, He was much displeased, and said to them,
Suffer the little children to come to me, and forbid them not: for
such is the Kingdom of God. Verily I say to you, Whosoever shall
not receive the Kingdom of God as a little child, he shall not enter
therein. And He took them up in his arms, put His hands upon
them, and blessed them.* (MARK, 10:13-16).

3. Pureness of heart is inseparable from simplicity and
humbleness. It excludes all ideas of selfishness and pride. This
was why Jesus took infancy as the symbol of purity and
humbleness.

It might appear unjust to make this comparison seeing that the
spirit of a child could be very old, and on being reborn to
corporeal life might bring with it the imperfections that it had not
been able to cast off during previous incarnations. Only a spirit
who has reached perfection can offer an example of true purity.
However, from the point of view of our present life, it offers an
exact comparison because a child, having had no opportunity yet

to manifest any perverse tendencies, presents us with an image of innocence and purity. So it becomes clear that Jesus did not say *the kingdom of heaven was meant for children, but for those who resemble them.*

4. Since the spirit of a child has lived before, why does it not show itself as it really is right from birth? Everything in God's work is full of wisdom. A child needs special care, which only a mother's tenderness can bestow; tenderness that stems from the frailty and ingenuousness of the child. For a mother, her child is always an angel and this is the way it must be in order to captivate concern. She would not be able to offer the same solicitude if, in place of ingenuousness, she saw virility and adult ideas in the infantile features, nor if she came to know the past of that incarnated spirit.

From the moment of birth, ideas gradually take on shape and impulse according to the development of the organs, from which it is possible to say that during the first years the spirit is truly a child because all ideas that form the true character remain dormant. During this period of dormancy, in which the instincts are also latent, the spirit is more malleable, more accessible to impressions that can modify the character and help the spirit to progress. All of which makes it easier for the parents to educate the child at this stage.

The spirit then wears a temporary tunic of innocence; so Jesus was right when, not withstanding the anteriority of the soul, He takes a child as the symbol of purity and simplicity.

SINNING BY MEANS OF THOUGHT. - ADULTERY

5. You have heard it was said by them of old time, You shall not commit adultery: but I say to you, That whosoever looks on a woman to lust after her has committed adultery with her already in his heart. (MATTHEW, 5:27 & 28).

6. Under no circumstance should the word *adultery* be accepted in the exclusive sense to which it is commonly applied, but rather it should be understood in terms that are more general. Jesus used it many times in an extensive sense to designate evil, sin and every type of bad thought. As for example in this passage: "Whosoever therefore, shall be ashamed of Me and My words in this adulterous and sinful generation, of him shall the Son of Man be ashamed, when He comes in the glory of His Father with the holy angels." (MARK, 8:38.)

True pureness is not only in behaviour but also in thought, since the person who has a pure heart does not even think evil. Jesus wished to say that He condemned sin even in thought because it is a sign of impurity.

7. This principle naturally leads to the following question: *Do we suffer any consequence for a bad thought, even if it is not followed by the actual action?*

At this point, it is necessary to make an important distinction. As the soul advances along its path to evolution and spiritualisation, it will slowly become enlightened and so little by little divest itself of its imperfections according to the greater or lesser goodwill it demonstrates within its freewill. Therefore all evil thoughts result from the imperfections of the soul. However, according to the strength of the desire to purify itself, the evil thought becomes a means of advancement when it is energetically repelled. This is an indication of a positive action by the soul in order to extinguish a blemish. In this way, it will not give in to the temptation to satisfy an evil desire, and having resisted, the soul feels itself to be stronger and content with the victory.

On the contrary, the person who has made no resolutions will look for every opportunity to practice evil, and if this is not achieved it will not be for the wanting, but for the lack of opportunity. This person then will be just as guilty as if he or she had actually committed evil.

To summarise, the person who does not conceive the idea of committing evil has already achieved a certain degree of progress. For the person who feels the urge but constantly repels it, progress is in the process of realisation. However, for the person who thinks in terms of evil, taking pleasure in these thoughts, then the evil still exists in all its strength. In the one, the work has been done, whereas in the other it is still to be started. But being just, God takes into account all these gradations when it comes to individual responsibilities for acts and thoughts.

TRUE PURENESS. UNWASHED HANDS

8. Then came to Jesus scribes and Pharisees, which were in Jerusalem, saying, Why do your disciples transgress the tradition of the elders? For they wash not their hands when they eat bread.

But He answered and said to them, Why do you also transgress the commandments of God by your tradition? For God commanded, saying, honour your father and mother; and, he that curses father and mother, let him die the death. But you say, Whosoever shall say to his father or his mother, it is a gift, by whatsoever you may be profited by me; and honour not his father or his mother shall be free. Thus, you have made the commandment of God of no effect by your tradition.

You hypocrites, well did Esaias prophesy of you saying, These people draw near to me with their mouth and honour me with their lips; but their heart is far from me. But in vain do they worship me, teaching for doctrine the commandments of men.

And He called the multitude, and said to them, Hear, and understand: Not that which goes into the mouth defiles a man; but that which comes out of the mouth, this defiles a man. Then came his disciples, and said to Him, knowest you that the Pharisees were offended, after they heard this saying? But He answered and said, every plant, which my heavenly Father did not plant, shall be rooted up. Leave them alone: they are blind leaders of the blind. And if the blind lead the blind, both shall fall into the ditch (MATTHEW, 15:1-20).

9. And as He spoke, a certain Pharisee invited Him to dine with him: and he went in and sat down to meat. And when the Pharisee saw it, he marvelled that He had not first washed before dinner. And the Lord said to him, Now do you Pharisees make clean the outside of the cup and the plate; but your inward part is full of ravening and wickedness. You fools, did not He that made that which is without make that which is within also? (LUKE 11:37-40).

10. The Jews had scorned God's true commandments in order to cling to the practice of regulations established by human beings and had made the rigid observance of these regulations a matter of conscience. The original simple substance became lost beneath complicated forms of ritual, as it was much easier to practice exterior cult than to effect moral reform, *to wash hands instead of cleansing the heart*, thus humanity became deluded, believing they were exonerated before God by conforming to these practices. Seeing that the people were taught that God demanded nothing more of them, they remained the same as they had always been. Hence the prophet said, *"But in vain do they worship me, teaching for doctrine the commandments of men."*

The verification of this can also be found in the moral Teachings of Christ, which has ended up in second place and as a result, many Christians, just like the ancient Jews, consider that salvation is better guaranteed by means of external practice rather than by moral practice. It is to these fabricated additions to God's law that Jesus referred to when He said, *"Every tree that my heavenly Father has not planted will be rooted up."*

The objective of religion is to conduct humanity towards God. Well, God can only be reached through perfection. Therefore, any religion that does not make people better than they are now, will never reach this objective. Everything that a person judges will support them in committing evil is either false or has had its principles falsified. Such is the result for all religions where the form surmounts the base. Belief in the efficiency of exterior manifestation is invalid if it does not oppose the acts of murder, adultery, robbery and the causing of slander or damage in whatever form to whomsoever it may be. These kinds of religions never create godly men and women, only people who are superstitious, hypocrites and fanatics.

The mere appearance of pureness is not enough, because above all else it is necessary to have a pure heart.

OFFENCES. - IF YOUR HAND IS THE CAUSE OF AN OFFENCE, CUT IT OFF

11. But whoso shall offend one of these little ones which believe in me, it were better for them that a millstone was hanged about their neck, and that they were drowned in the depth of the sea.

Woe to the world because of offences! For it must needs be that offences come; but woe to the person by whom the offences come!

Take heed that you despise not one of these little ones; for I say to you, That in heaven their angels do always behold the face of my Father that is in heaven. For the Son of man is come to save that which was lost.

And if your right hand offends you, cut it off, and cast it from you: for it is profitable for you that one of your members shall perish, and not that your whole body should be cast into hell. And if your right eye offends you, pluck it out and cast it from you: for it is profitable for you that one of your members should perish and not that your whole body should be cast into hell. (MATTHEW, 18:6-9; 5:29 &30).

12. In its most usual meaning, the word *scandal* is any action that goes extensively against morality or decorum. The offence is not in the action itself so much as in the repercussion it may cause. The word always implies a certain amount of commotion and dispute. Many people are content if they avoid causing a *scandal* in public, because this would cause them to suffer a loss of prestige, so hurting their pride. They do their best to hide their mistakes, as this is sufficient to quieten their consciences. They are, as Jesus said: "As white sepulchres which are full of rottenness, like vessels which are clean without, but dirty within."

However, in the evangelic sense, the accepted meaning of the word scandal, used so repeatedly, is very much more generalised and this is why in certain cases its meaning is not understood. It becomes not only that which affects the conscience of another person but also everything that is the result of vice and human imperfections, as well as every bad reaction from one individual to another, with or without repercussion. *In this case, the scandal is the effective result of bad morality.*

13. Jesus said: *It is necessary that offences exist in the world* because, due to the many imperfections of those on Earth, humanity shows itself inclined to practice evil and because bad trees only bring forth bad fruits. From these words then, we must understand that evil is the consequence of humanity's imperfections and not that there exists an obligation to practice evil.

14. *It is necessary for scandals to come* seeing that here on Earth humanity is making atonement. Human beings are being punished through contact with their own vices, thus becoming their own victims, from where they will finally come to understand the inconvenience of this way of life. When people are

tired of suffering due to evil, they will seek a remedy in Goodness. Therefore, the reactions caused by these failings serve for some as a punishment and for others as a test. This is how God gets good out of evil and how humanity itself profits from utilising both bad and useless things.

15. It could be said then that evil is necessary and that it will last forever, seeing that if it disappears God would be deprived of a powerful means of being able to correct the guilty. It could also be said that it is useless to try to make Humanity better. However, if we ceased to have culprits then it would be unnecessary to have any kind of punishment. Let us suppose that Humanity becomes transformed, so becoming composed only of good men and women, where no one would think of doing evil to their neighbour and all would be happy to be Good. This is the condition found on advanced worlds, where evil has been excluded. This is what will happen here on Earth, when humanity has made sufficient progress. However, while some worlds are advancing, others are forming, populated by primitive spirits which also serve as places of exile and as places of atonement for those spirits who are imperfect, rebellious and persistent in evil, who have been expelled from worlds that have become places of happiness.

16. *But woe to that person by whom the offence comes.* That is to say, that evil always being evil, the person who, without knowing, serves as an instrument of Divine Justice, whose bad instincts were utilised, commits no less an evil and so deserves punishment. In this manner, an ungrateful child is a punishment or trial for the parents, who are forced to suffer from its attitude. This is because they themselves had been bad children and made their parents suffer. Therefore, they pay the penalty. Nevertheless, the circumstances should not be an excuse for the child's behaviour, who in return will have to pay the penalty through their own children, or in some other manner.

17. *If your hand is the cause of a scandal, cut it off*. This is a very strong statement and it would be absurd for it to be taken literally. Therefore, it should be understood that each one must destroy within themselves everything that might cause a scandal, meaning evil. This must be done by rooting out every impure thought and every tendency towards violence, corruption or depravity. It also means that it is preferable for a person to cut off a hand rather than use it to commit an evil action; or better still, to lose one's sight rather than allow one's eyes to conceive bad thoughts. For those who take the trouble to discover the allegoric meaning of His words, Jesus never said anything that was absurd. Nevertheless, many things cannot be understood without the key to decipher them and this key is offered to us through Spiritism.

INSTRUCTIONS FROM THE SPIRITS

LET LITTLE CHILDREN COME TO ME

18. Christ said: "Let the little children come to me." Profound in their simplicity these words do not contain just a call to children, but also a call to the souls who gravitate in the inferior regions where misfortune knows no hope. Jesus also calls to the infantile intellectuality of the adult, to the weak, to those in slavery, to the depraved and to the wicked. He could teach nothing to the physically infantile, still bound by matter and submitted to the yoke of instinct, as these had not yet reached the superior category of reason or of free will, which is exercised around them and for their benefit.

Jesus wanted humanity to deliver themselves to Him with confidence, in the same way that tiny tots, with their special appeal, win over the hearts of women, who are all mothers. Then He could submit these souls to His tender and mysterious influence. He was the flame that brought light to the darkness, that dawn light that announces the sunrise. He was the initiator of Spiritism, which should attract towards Him not just the children, but all men and women of goodwill. Vigorous action has begun. It is no longer a question of instinctive belief and mechanical obedience; it is necessary for human beings to follow the intelligent law that shows its universality.

Dearly beloved, the time has come in which, when explained, all fallacies will become truths. We shall teach the exact meaning of the parables and show the strong correlation existing between what was and what is now. In truth, I say to you that these great spiritual manifestations will open up the horizons, for here is the messenger that will shine resplendently as the sun upon the mountaintop. – JOHN THE EVANGELIST (Paris, 1863.)

19. Let the little children come to me, for I have the milk that will strengthen the weak. Let all those who are fearful, feeble, or are in need of help and consolation come to me. Let the ignorant come to me, so that I may enlighten them. Let all who suffer come to me, together with the afflicted and the unfortunate. I will teach them the great remedy that will soften their ills, and reveal to them the secret that will cure their wounds! My friends, what is this supreme balsam, that possesses such high virtue that it may be applied to all types of wounds suffered by the heart and heal them? It is love and charity! If you possess this divine flame, why are you afraid? Then every moment of your life, you will say "Dear Father, I pray that your wish be done and not mine. If it is your pleasure to test me through pain and tribulations blessed be it, because I know it is for my own good. If it pleases you Lord, have mercy on this weak creature, giving justifiable happiness to this heart and blessed be You yet again. But do not allow divine love to lie sleeping in my soul; make it rise up unceasingly and present itself at your feet as a witness of my gratitude."

If you have love, then you have the most desirable thing on Earth. You possess a most precious pearl which no occurrence, nor malice of those who hate and persecute, can take away. If you have love, you will have placed your treasure where the worms and rust cannot attack, having extinguished everything capable of defiling the pureness of your soul. Every day you will feel the diminishing weight of matter, and like a bird in the sky which no longer remembers the Earth, you will continually rise up without ceasing until your soul, full of exhilaration, fills itself with the elements of the true life in the bosom of the Lord. - A PROTECTING SPIRIT (Bordeaux, 1861.)

BLESSED ARE THOSE WHOSE EYES ARE CLOSED.[12]

20. My good friends, why did you call me? Was it because you wished that I put my hands upon the unhappy sufferer that is present and cure her? Ah! My God what suffering! She has lost her sight and darkness envelops her. Poor child! Let her pray and wait. I do not know how to perform miracles if God does not wish it. All the cures that I have been able to obtain, that you have been informed about, can only be attributed to He who is our Father. In your afflictions always lift up your eyes to Heaven and say with heart felt sincerity "Heavenly Father, cure me, but cause my sick soul to cure itself before you cure my body. Let my flesh be chastised, if this be necessary, so that my soul may rise up to you with the same whiteness it possessed when You created it." After this prayer, my friends, the Good Lord always listens to you; then you will be given strength, courage and perhaps the cure for which you have asked, in recompense for your abnegation.

---

[12] This communication was given in response to the appeal of a blind person, in whose name the Spirit of J. B. VIANNEY, a parish priest of Ars was evoked.

However, since I am here in this assembly that deals principally with study, I will tell you that those who are deprived of their sight should consider themselves blessed in their atonement. I would remind you that Christ said it was better to pluck out your eye if it were evil, and that it was preferable to cast it into the fire rather than allow it to become the cause of your condemnation. Ah! How many there are in the world who one day, when they are in absolute darkness, will curse the time they saw the light! Oh yes, how happy are those who through atonement find they have been struck in their sight! Then their eyes will not be the cause of offence nor of their downfall. They can live the full life of the soul. They can see more than those whose vision is clear! When God permits that I open the eyelids of some of these sad sufferers and restore their sight, then I say to myself "Dear soul, why do you not wish to know all the delights of the spirit who lives by love and contemplation? Then you would not ask to see images that are less pure and gentle than those you glimpse through your blindness!"

Oh! Blessed are the blind who wish to live with God! More fortunate than you who are here at this moment, they feel happiness; it is tangible to them; they see the souls of men and women, and can rise up with them to the spiritual spheres where they can perceive what even the predestined of the Earth cannot manage to see. Our eyes, when open, are always ready to cause the downfall of the soul; whilst, when shut, they are always ready to help us rise up in the direction of God. Believe me, my good and dear friends, on many occasions blindness is the true light of the heart, whereas sight is frequently the angel of darkness that leads to death.

Now, a few words directed at you, my poor sufferer. Wait and be of good faith! If I were to say, "My child, your eyes will open," how jubilant you would feel. However, who knows if that joy would not be the cause of a great loss! Have faith then in the Lord who gives us happiness and permits sadness. I will do everything for you that I am permitted, but on your side, you must pray, and even more importantly, meditate on all that I have just said.

Before I leave, may all who are here gathered together receive my blessing. - VIANNEY, parish priest of Ars (Paris, 1863.)

21. REMARKS: When an affliction is not a consequence of acts committed in this life, then we must look for the cause in a previous life. Everything that we call a whim of chance is nothing more than the effect of God's justice. He does not inflict wilful punishment but desires that every penalty is in accordance with the misdeed. If in His goodness He has cast a veil over our past actions, He has also pointed out the way by saying, "Who kills by the sword shall perish by the sword." From these words, we should understand that each creature is always punished according to the way in which he or she has sinned. If someone suffers the torment of losing their sight, then it is because their sight was the cause of their downfall. It might also be that this person was the cause of someone else losing their sight, perhaps in consequence of excessive work that had been imposed upon them by the one who has now lost theirs; perhaps also through ill-treatment, lack of care, negligence, etc. In these cases, the person responsible always undergoes the penalty caused by their own actions. On repenting, they may have chosen this very atonement, thereby applying to themselves the words of Jesus: "If your eye is the motive for scandal, then cast it out."

CHAPTER 9

BLESSED ARE THE MEEK AND THE PEACEMAKERS

Insults and violence. - INSTRUCTIONS FROM THE SPIRITS: Affability and mildness. - Patience. - Obedience and resignation. - Anger.

INSULTS AND VIOLENCE

1. Blessed are the meek: for they shall inherit the earth. (MATTHEW, 5:5.)

2. Blessed are the peacemakers: for they will be called children of God. (MATTHEW, 5:9.)

3. You have heard that it was said by them of old time, You shall not kill; and whosoever shall kill shall be in danger of the judgement; but I say to you, That whosoever is angry with his brother without a cause shall be in danger of the judgement: and whosoever shall say to his brother, Raca, shall be in danger of the council; and whosoever shall say, You fool, shall be in danger of hell fire. (MATTHEW, 5:21 & 22.)

4. By these maxims, Jesus makes meekness, moderation, docility, affability and patience the Law. Consequently condemning violence, anger and all discourteous expressions towards others. For example, '*Raca*' was a disdainful expression amongst the Hebrews meaning a *worthless person*, and was accompanied by pronounced spitting and turning the head to one side. At one point Jesus goes so far as to threaten anyone who says to another - *you are insane* - with the fire of hell.

It becomes evident that here as in all circumstances, the intention aggravates or lessens the offence; but why should a simple word become something so grave as to warrant such severe reproof? This is because every offensive word expresses a sentiment that is contrary to the laws of love and charity that preside over all human relationships and between them maintains cordiality and union. By sustaining hate and animosity, we are undermining reciprocated benevolence and fraternity. In short, it is because next to humility before God, charity to your neighbour is the first law of all Christians.

5. What did Jesus mean by the words "Blessed are the meek, for they will inherit the Earth," when He had recommended that people renounce all worldly possessions, after having promised those of Heaven?

While awaiting heavenly riches, humanity has need of the Earth on which to live. Jesus is only recommending that we do not give more importance to the things of this world rather than to the former.

By these words, He wishes to say that until now worldly possessions have been monopolised by those who are violent, to the detriment of the meek and pacific, who frequently lack even the necessities of life, while others have a superfluity. Jesus promises justice will be *done on Earth, as it is in Heaven,* because the meek will be called God's children. When Humanity submits itself to the Law of Love and Charity, then selfishness will cease to exist; the weak and peaceful will no longer be exploited or crushed by the strong and violent. This will be the condition of the Earth when this planet becomes a happy world because it has rid itself of all evil, according to the law of progress and the promise made by Jesus.

INSTRUCTIONS FROM THE SPIRITS

AFFABILITY AND MILDNESS

6. Benevolence towards one's fellow-creatures, that is the result of loving your neighbour, manifests itself in the form of affability and mildness. However, it is not always a good thing to trust in appearances. Education and worldliness can give a person a thin veneer of these qualities. There are many whose feigned good nature is nothing more than an exterior mask, like beautiful clothes hiding interior deformities! The world is full of such people with a smile on their lips, but poison in their hearts. *They are mild as long as nothing irritates them, but they bite at the least provocation.* Their tongues are made of gold when speaking face to face, but change into a poisoned dart when speaking from behind.

Still, in the category of those showing benign countenances, there are those domestic tyrants who make their families and subordinates suffer the weight of their pride and despotism. As if they are trying to get even for any constraints imposed upon them elsewhere. Not daring to use their authority on strangers, who would call them to order, they want at least to be feared by those who cannot resist them. They are proud to be able to say, 'I give the orders here and am obeyed;' but they never think that they could also add, 'And I am detested.'

It is not enough for milk and honey to flow from the lips. If the heart is never associated with these sentiments then there is only hypocrisy. Those whose affability and mildness are not mere pretence are never belied, for they are always the same whether in society or in privacy. Besides, they know that although it is possible to deceive people through appearances, no one can deceive God. - LAZARUS (Paris, 1861.)

PATIENCE

7. Pain is a blessing sent by God to all His elected; so when you suffer do not allow yourself to become afflicted; rather bless the Omnipotent Who, through the pain of this world, has chosen you to receive glory in Heaven.

Be patient! Because this is also a charity and everyone should practice this law as taught by Christ, Who is God's Envoy. Charity given to the poor in the form of alms is the easiest of all. However, there is another kind of charity that is much more laborious and so consequently offers higher merit. That is *to forgive all those placed in your pathway by God to act as instruments for your suffering and to test your patience.*

We know very well that life is difficult; being composed of so many apparently useless, insignificant and valueless things that act as repeated pinpricks and ends up hurting us. However, if on the one hand we carefully observe the duties imposed upon us, and on the other recognise the consolations and compensations received, then we must admit that the blessings are far more numerous than the pains. When our eyes are raised up to Heaven, our burdens appear to be less heavy than when our brow is bowed down to the earth.

Courage, my friends! Christ is your model. He suffered far more than any of you and had nothing to offer penitence for, whereas we must atone for our past and thereby fortify ourselves for the future. So be patient! Be Christians! This word summarises everything. - A FRIENDLY SPIRIT (Havre, 1862.)

OBEDIENCE AND RESIGNATION

8. The Teachings of Jesus constantly teaches obedience and resignation, two virtues that are the companions of mildness and

activity, although human beings wrongly confuse them with denial of sentiment and free will. *Obedience is the consent of reason; resignation is the consent of the heart.* Both are active forces since they carry the burden that has fallen upon them due to foolish revolt. The coward cannot be resigned, any more than the prideful and selfish can be obedient. Jesus was the incarnation of these virtues that were despised by material antiquity. He came to Earth at a time when Roman society was perishing in the failings of corruption. He came so that, even in the bosom of depressed humanity, the triumph of sacrifice and the renouncement of sensuality would shine forth.

Thus, each epoch is marked with the stamp of the virtue or vice it has either to save or to lose. The virtue of your generation is intellectual activity; the vice is moral indifference. I merely use the word 'activity' because a genius may suddenly rise up and discover for themselves the horizons that will be seen by the multitude only at a later date. Whereas activity denotes the reunion of the endeavours of everyone in order to reach a somewhat less brilliant conclusion, but one that will confirm the intellectual elevation of an epoch. Submit yourself then to the impulsion we have come to give your spirits. Obey the great law of progress that is the promise of your generation. Woe to the lazy ones, woe to all those not open to understanding! Woe to them! Because we, who are the guides of Humanity on the march, shall apply the whip and subdue the rebellion by means of the double action of brake and spur. All prideful resistance will have to be overcome sooner or later. However, blessed be all those who are mild, for they will lend yielding ears to these teachings. - LAZARUS (Paris, 1863.)

ANGER

9. Pride induces you to judge yourselves to be more than you are and to repel any comparison that might discredit you. You

consider yourselves to be so far above your fellow brothers and sisters, be this in spirit, in social position or even in personal advantage that even the smallest parallel irritates and annoys you. What happens then? You give way to anger.

Investigate the origin of these outbursts of passing dementia, that makes you resemble a savage, by losing your self-possession and reason; and if you do, then you will almost always be faced with hurt pride. Perchance, is this not pride that has been hurt by a contradiction that makes you repel justifiable observations and angrily reject the wisest counsel? Even impatience originating from contrarieties and often childish ones at that, comes from the importance that each individual gives to their own personality, before which it has been given to understand that everyone should bow down.

In their frenzy, wrathful people hurl themselves at everything, from their own savage nature to lifeless objects, breaking them because they do not obey! Ah! If they could but see themselves at these moments, looking on in cold blood! Either they would be afraid of themselves, or they would think themselves simply ridiculous! Imagine then the impression made on others! Even if it is merely out of self-respect, it behoves them to make an effort to overcome this inclination that only makes them into an object of pity.

If we reflect that anger in no way helps, in fact, it modifies our health even to putting our lives at risk; then we would recognize that we are nothing more than our own victims are. Above all, there is yet another consideration that should restrain us, being that of the unhappiness this kind of behaviour brings to all those around us. If we have a heart, would not this anger be a motive for remorse for having caused those we love to suffer? What a terrible moral weight upon us if, in an excess of fury, we were to practice some act that we would deplore for the rest of our life!

To summarise, anger does not exclude certain qualities of the heart, but it stops us from doing any good and may cause us to practise great evil. This then should be sufficient to induce all human beings to make the necessary effort in order to dominate this trait. Moreover, for those who are Spiritists, there is yet another motive for this solicitation - that of anger being against charity and Christian humility. - A PROTECTING SPIRIT (Bordeaux, 1863.)

10. Because of the false idea that it is not possible for a person to reform their own nature, people judge themselves exempt from even trying to correct their defects. This applies especially to those defects in which the person willingly takes pleasure, or those that would take a great deal of perseverance to eradicate. This is why, for example, an individual who is prone to anger almost always finds excuses for this temperament. Instead of confessing themselves guilty, they accuse their organism and in this manner accuse God for their faults. This is yet one more of the consequences of pride to be found in the midst of our imperfections.

Undoubtedly, there are temperaments that lend themselves more readily than others to violent acts, just as there are muscles that are more flexible than others, so lending themselves better to acts of strength. However, do not believe it is here that the primary cause is to be found, but persuade yourself that a pacific spirit, even when in an ill-tempered body, will always remain pacific. Just as much as a violent spirit, even when occupying a lymphatic body will not be milder, only that the violence will take on another aspect. In this case, the anger would be more concentrated, just as in the first case the anger would be more expansive.

Therefore, it is not the body that gives the anger to those who do not already possess it. Likewise neither does it cause other vices. All virtues and vices are inherent in the spirit. If this were not the case, where would be the merit and responsibility? The person who is bodily deformed can do nothing to remedy this situation because the spirit takes no part in it. However, what can be modified is the actual spirit *when it wants to*, by means of a strong desire. Does not experience show us up to what point the power of desire can take us when we look at the truly miraculous transformations happening all around us every day? Then let us convince ourselves that *humanity only remains bound by vices because it so desires!* Those who really wish to liberate themselves can always achieve this end. If it were not so, then the laws of progress would not be able to exist. – HAHNEMANN (Paris, 1863.)

CHAPTER 10

BLESSED ARE THE MERCIFUL

Forgive others so God may forgive you. - Reconciliation with your adversaries. - The sacrifice most agreeable to God. - The speck and the beam in the eye. - Do not judge others so as not to be judged. He that is without sin let him cast the first stone. - INSTRUCTIONS FROM THE SPIRITS: The pardoning of offences. - Indulgence. - Is it permitted to reprehend others, observe imperfections in others, or divulge the evil in others?

FORGIVE OTHERS SO GOD MAY FORGIVE YOU

1. Blessed are the merciful, for they shall obtain mercy. (MATTHEW, 5:7.)

2. For if you forgive men their trespasses, your heavenly Father will also forgive you: But if you forgive not men their trespasses, neither will your Father forgive your trespasses. (MATTHEW, 6:14 & 15)

3. Moreover, if your brother shall trespass against you, go and tell him his fault between you and him alone: if he shall hear you, you have gained your brother. Then came Peter to him, and said, Lord, how often shall my brother sin against me, and I forgive him? till seven times? Jesus said to him, I say not seven times: but, Until seventy times seven. (MATTHEW, 18:15, 21 & 22)

4. Mercy is a complement to mildness because the person who is not merciful cannot be mild and pacific. Mercy consists of being able to forget and forgive all offence. Hate and rancour denotes a spirit without any elevation or magnanimity. Being able to forget offences is the mark of an elevated soul, which does not perturb itself with the blows it may be dealt. The one is always anxious, of a dark susceptibility and full of bitterness, while the other is calm, full of sweetness and charity.

Woe to those who say they will never forgive! If humanity does not already condemn these people, then God will surely condemn them. What right has a person to demand forgiveness for their own faults if they are unable to forgive those of others? Does not Jesus teach that mercy must have no limits when He says that each one must forgive their brothers and sisters not merely seven times, but seventy times seven?

However, there are two very different ways of forgiving; the first is noble, great, truly generous without any second thoughts, which delicately avoids hurting the self-esteem and susceptibility of the adversary, even when that same adversary has no justification for his or her acts. The second on the other hand is when someone who has been offended, or thinks they have been offended, imposes humiliating conditions on the supposed adversary. So making felt the weight of the pardon that can only cause further irritation instead of calming. Alternatively, where, upon offering a hand to the offended, this is not done with benevolence, but rather with ostentation, so that the person may say to others - look how generous I am! In these circumstances, a sincere reconciliation is quite impossible for either one. No, here there is no generosity, only a form of satisfying pride. In every dispute, the one who shows them self to be more conciliatory, who demonstrates more disinterest, charity and real greatness of soul will always attract sympathy from those who are impartial.

RECONCILIATION WITH YOUR ADVERSARIES

5. Agree with your adversary quickly, while you are in the way with him; or at any time the adversary deliver you to the officer, and you be cast into prison. Truly, I say to you, You shall by no means come out from there, till you have paid the uttermost farthing. (MATTHEW, 5:25 & 26.)

6. In the act of pardoning, just as in the general practice of goodness, there is not only a moral effect but also a material effect. As is already known, death does not liberate us from our enemies; vengeful spirits in the afterlife frequently pursue all those for whom they bear rancour with great hate. From this, we understand the falsity of the proverb, *"The poison dies with the beast"* when it is applied to human beings. The evil spirit waits for the one they do not like to return to a physical body, where he or she is captive, in order to more easily torment, hurt interests or harm affections. The cause of the majority of cases of obsessions lies within this fact, especially those cases that present some gravity, such as subjugation and possession. The person who is either spiritually obsessed or possessed is almost always a victim of vengeance. The motive will be found in their past lives, in which the one who is suffering gave cause for this result. God allows this to happen in order to punish the evil that was originally committed or, if this is not the case, for the lack of indulgence or charity through a refusal to grant a pardon. Consequently, from the point of view of future tranquillity, it is important that each person make amends for all grievances that may have been caused to neighbours and that we pardon all our enemies, thereby eradicating all motives for dissension, as well as all causes for ulterior animosity before death reaches us. In this manner, it is quite possible to make a friend in the next world out of an enemy in this world. At least all those who proceed in this manner put themselves on the right side of the Law. God will not consent to anyone who has pardoned being made to suffer from vengeance. When Jesus recommends that we reconcile ourselves with our adversaries as soon as possible, this is not merely to pacify any discords during the actual existence, but principally to avoid their perpetuation into the future life. Jesus said, *"No one can leave this prison till you have paid the uttermost farthing"* that is to say, not until God's justice has been completely satisfied.

THE SACRIFICE MOST AGREEABLE TO GOD

7. Therefore, if you bring your gift to the altar, and there remember that your brother has something against you; leave there your gift before the altar, and go your way; first be reconciled with your brother, and then come and offer your gift. (MATTHEW, 5:23 & 24.)

8. With the words *"First be reconciled with your brother, then come and offer your gift,"* Jesus teaches that what is most agreeable to God is the sacrifice of our resentments. That before a person asks for pardon they should first have pardoned others and made good any damage caused to their fellow beings. Only then will the offerings be acceptable to God because they will come from a heart expunged of all evil thoughts. Jesus explains this in the material sense of offering gifts because the Jews of those days offered sacrifices, so it was necessary that His words conform to the customs of the time. The true Christian however, does not offer material gifts to God, since all sacrifice has been spiritualised and with this, the precept has gained even more strength. The person offers their soul to God and their soul has to be purified. Thus, *upon entering the temple of God, the person should leave all feelings of hate and animosity outside, including evil thoughts against their fellow beings.* Only in this manner, will the Angels take the prayers and place them at the feet of the eternal Father. This is what Jesus was teaching when He said, "Leave then your gift before the altar and go first and be reconciled with your brother or sister if you wish to be agreeable to the Lord."

THE SPECK AND THE BEAM IN THE EYE.

9. Why do you see the speck that is in your brother's eye, but consider not the plank in your own eye? *Or how will you say to your brother, Let me pull the speck out of your eye; and, behold, a beam is in your own eye? You hypocrite, first cast out the beam*

out of your own eye; and then shall you see clearly to cast out the
speck from your brother's eye. (MATTHEW, 7:3-5.)

10. One of the imperfections of humanity consists in seeing
wrongdoing in others before seeing it in ourselves. In order to be
able to judge ourselves, it would needs be for people to see
themselves intimately reflected as in a mirror, and in some way
consider the reflection as another person, so then be able to ask the
question, "What would I think if I saw someone doing what I do?"
Beyond all doubt, pride is what induces people to disguise all their
moral and physical faults, even from themselves. Such folly is
essentially against charity, seeing that true charity is always
modest, unadorned and indulgent. Prideful charity is a
contradiction, as these two sentiments neutralise each another.
Therefore, how can someone who is sufficiently conceited as to
believe in the importance of their own personality and the
supremacy of their own qualities, be abnegated at the same time?
That is to say, have sufficient self-denial so as to be able to cause
the goodness in others to stand out, knowing that this would
eclipse themselves. Pride, being the father of many vices, is also
the negation of many virtues. It is found to be the base and motive
for almost all human actions. It was because pride is the principal
obstacle to progress that Jesus tried so hard to combat it.

DO NOT JUDGE OTHERS SO AS NOT TO BE JUDGED. LET THE ONE THAT IS WITHOUT SIN CAST THE FIRST STONE

11. Judge not, that you be not judged. For with what judgement
you judge, you shall be judged: and with what measure you mete,
it shall be measured to you again. (MATTHEW, 7:1 & 2.)

12. And the Scribes and Pharisees brought to Him a woman taken
in adultery; and when they had set her in the midst, They said to
Him, Master, this woman was taken in adultery, in the very act.

Now Moses in the law commanded us, that such should be stoned: but what do you say? This they said, tempting Him, that they might have to accuse Him. But Jesus stooped down, and with His finger wrote on the ground, as though He heard them not. So when they continued asking Him, He lifted up Himself, and said to them, he that is without sin among you, let him first cast a stone at her. *And again He stooped down, and wrote on the ground. And they which heard it, being convicted by their own conscience, went out one by one, beginning at the eldest, even to the last: and Jesus was left alone, and the woman standing in the midst.*

When Jesus had lifted up himself, he said to her, Woman, where are your accusers? has no man condemned thee? She said, No man, Lord. And Jesus said to her, Neither do I condemn thee; go, and sin no more. (JOHN, 8:3-11.)

13. With the sentence, *"If any of you are without sin, let them be the first to throw a stone at her"* Jesus makes indulgence the first duty towards others because there is no one who does not need it for themselves. He also teaches that we must never judge others with more severity than we would wish to be judged, nor condemn in others that which we condone in ourselves. Before chastising or condemning someone for a fault, first let us see if that same censure could be applied to us.

Reproach may be launched against a person for two reasons: to suppress evil or to discredit the person whose acts are being criticised. In this last intention, there is absolutely no excuse, because there exists only malice and slander. The first may be laudable and even becomes a duty in certain cases, as good may come from it, and without it the evil in society would never be restrained. Furthermore, is it not the duty of all humankind to help every fellow creature towards progress? Therefore it is important that the principle, "Do not judge others if you have no wish to be judged," should not be taken literally as this could be destructive, whereas the spirit of these words gives life to the concept.

It is not possible that Jesus could have prohibited the overthrowing of evil, seeing that He gives examples of having done just that Himself, in no uncertain terms. Nevertheless, what He wished to say was that the right to censure is to be found in the moral authority of the one who censures. To become guilty of that which one is condemning in another person is to renounce this authority, so depriving oneself of the right to restrain. Furthermore, our inner conscience denies respect and voluntary submission to any person who, having been invested with some kind of authority violates the laws and principles of which they were put in charge. *There is no legitimate authority in the eyes of God but that based on the examples of the goodness it offers.* Likewise, this is what is emphasised by the words of Jesus.

INSTRUCTIONS FROM THE SPIRITS

THE PARDONING OF OFFENCES

14. How many times must I forgive my brother or sister? Not just seven times, but seventy times seven. Here we have the teaching of Jesus that should most strike the intelligence and speak most loudly to our hearts. If these words of mercy were compared with the prayer He taught to His disciples, that prayer so simple, so concise, yet so great in its aspirations, you would always encounter the same thought. Jesus, the pre-eminently just One, replies to Peter with these words, "You must forgive without limit; you must forgive each offence as many times as it is done to you. Your brothers and sisters on Earth must be taught that it is forgetfulness of self that makes a person invulnerable to attack, misbehaviours and insults. Your heart must be mild and humble without measuring out your gentleness; in short, you must do whatever you wish the Celestial Father to do for you. Is He not frequently forgiving you? Have you by any chance counted how

many times His pardon has come down to erase your shortcomings?"

So pay attention to the reply given by Jesus and, just as Peter did, apply it to yourself. Forgive freely, use your indulgence, be charitable and generous, and even be lavish with your love. Give and the Lord will make restitution; forgive and the Lord will forgive you; lower your self and the Lord will raise you up; humble your self and the Lord will take you to sit on His right hand.

Dearly beloved, go forth to study and comment on these words that I have spoken on the part of He, Who, from the heights of celestial splendour is always watching over you. Proceed lovingly in the thankless task that began more than eighteen centuries ago. Forgive your fellow beings, as you would wish them to forgive you. If their acts cause you personal harm, then this is just one more motive for your indulgence, since the merit of forgiveness is in proportion to the seriousness of the wrongdoing. You will gain no merit by overlooking the errors of your fellow beings if they are nothing more than simple scratches.

Spiritists never forget that the pardoning of wrongdoing must not be an empty expression, be this either by word or by action. Since you call yourselves Spiritists, then be so with all fervour. Forgive all evil that has been done to you and think of nothing save one thing: the good that you can do. Those who follow this path must not stray from it even in thought, which is known to God, seeing that each one is responsible for their thoughts. Take care, therefore, to expunge from yourselves all rancorous sentiments. God knows what remains at the bottom of the hearts of each one of His children. *So, happy is he who can sleep at night* saying - I have nothing against my neighbour. - SIMEON (Bordeaux, 1862.)

15. To forgive one's enemies is to ask for forgiveness for oneself. To forgive one's friends is to give them proof of your friendship. To be able to forgive offences is to show yourself better than you were. So then my friends, forgive others in order that God may forgive you. Since if you are hard, demanding and inflexible and use severity even against a small offence, how can you expect God to forget that each day you have an even greater necessity of indulgence? Oh! Woe to those who say, "I will never forgive," for they pronounce their own condemnation! Moreover, if you searched deeper down inside, perhaps you would find that it is yourself who is the aggressor. In the fight that began as a pinprick and ended in rupture, who knows if the first blow was not cast by you, being the one who let escape harsh words of offence or perhaps you did not proceed with all the necessary moderation? Without a doubt, your adversary behaved badly by showing exceeding susceptibility, but this is yet another reason for being indulgent, so as not to allow yourself to become deserving of the tirade that was launched against you. Let us admit, for the moment, that in a given circumstance you were truly offended. Who is able to tell if you would not further poison the matter by means of reprisals, or that you would not cause the situation to degenerate into a grave quarrel when, in fact, the whole matter could easily be forgotten? If the prevention of the consequences of this fact depended on you, and you did nothing to impede them, then you are truly guilty. Finally, let us admit that you do not consider yourself to be deserving of any censure; in this case, your merit would be even greater if you showed yourself to be clement.

Nevertheless, there are two very different ways of forgiving: one being of the lips and the other of the heart. Many people say to their adversary "I forgive you" while inwardly rejoicing at the evil that has returned to them, commenting that they only received what they deserved. How many others say, "I forgive you," hastening to add "But I will never be reconciled, nor do I ever want to see you again in this life!" Is this then forgiveness according to the Gospel? Surely not! True Christian forgiveness is that which casts a veil over the past. Seeing that God is not satisfied with appearances alone, this can be the only kind of forgiveness to be taken into consideration. He listens to the innermost recesses of our hearts, to our most secret thoughts and is never satisfied with mere words of pretence. Complete and absolute forgiveness of all offences is peculiar to great souls, whereas rancour is always a sign of baseness and inferiority. So then, do not forget that true pardon is recognisable much more by its acts than by mere words. - PAUL, the Apostle (Lyon, 1861.)

INDULGENCE

16. Spiritists, today we wish to speak of indulgence, that sweet fraternal sentiment that everyone should harbour towards their fellow beings, but which in fact is so little used.

Indulgence does not see the defects of others, or if it does, it avoids speaking of them or divulging them. On the contrary, it seeks to hide them with the object of becoming the sole possessor of this knowledge, and if malevolence discovers it, then indulgence will always have a ready and plausible excuse. However, we do not mean those excuses that only have the appearance of lessening the failing, while in fact making it more evident, with perfidious intention.

Indulgence will never occupy itself with the evil actions of others unless it is to offer help. Nevertheless, even in this case, it will take care to lessen the fault as much as possible. It will never make shocking observations, nor offer censure, but only give advice and even then usually in a veiled manner. When you criticise, what consequences should be deduced from your words? When you criticise what consequences should be deduced from your words? That you who censures are not guilty of that which is being reproved; so that you may be worth more than the culprit. Oh! Humanity! When will you judge first your own hearts, thoughts and actions, without occupying yourselves with what your brothers and sisters are doing? When will you have stern eyes only for yourselves?

So then, be severe with yourselves, but indulgent with others. Remind yourself of He, who judges in the last instant, who sees the innermost movements of each heart, consequently forgiving many times the failings that you censure or often condemning that which you condone, because He knows the motive behind all actions. Remember also that those who clamour in loud voices for others to be excommunicated, have perhaps themselves committed those very same faults, if not even greater ones.

Therefore my friends, always be indulgent, seeing that indulgence attracts the like, calms and uplifts; whereas inclemency only disanimates and drives away all calm and causes irritation - JOSEPH, a Protecting Spirit. (Bordeaux, 1863.)

17. Always be indulgent with regard to the faults of others whatever these may be. Do not judge with severity any actions but your own. Then the Lord will be indulgent towards you, according to the manner in which you have shown it to others.

Uphold the strong: stimulating them to perseverance. Fortify the weak by showing them the goodness of God, who takes into consideration even the smallest degree of repentance. Show to all the angel of penitence, stretching out white wings over the shortcomings of humanity, veiling them from the eyes of He who cannot tolerate that which is impure. Let all understand the infinite mercy of the Father, never forgetting to say to Him, through thought and above all through actions: "Forgive us our sins as we forgive those who sin against us." Understand well the meaning of these sublime words, wherein not only is the literal sense admirable, but most of all the teachings enclosed therein.

What is it you are asking the Lord for when you implore His pardon? Is it only the oblivion of your offences? Then you would be left with nothing. If God limited Himself to merely forgetting your shortcomings, it is true He would not punish, *but neither would He recompense.* A recompense cannot be offered for good that was not done and even less for evil that has been done, although this evil may have been forgotten. When you ask God to pardon your transgressions, you are in fact asking for the favour of His grace so as not to fall into relapse, to not fail again; together with the necessary strength to be able to turn into other pathways, such as submission and love, to which you should then join repentance and reparation.

When you forgive your fellow beings, do not be content merely to extend a veil of oblivion over the failings, seeing that in most cases this veil is quite transparent in your eyes. Instead, simultaneously sweep away the failings with forgiveness and love. Do for all your brothers and sisters what you would have the Celestial Father do for you. That is to say, substitute anger that only defiles, with love that purifies. Preach as Jesus taught us, by exemplifying active and ceaseless charity. Preach as He did during all the time He remained visible to physical eyes on this planet. Preach as He continues to do unceasingly since He became visible only to the eyes of spirit. Follow His divine Example! Walk in His footsteps, for they will conduct you to a refuge offering rest after the fight. Carry all your crosses as He did, painfully, but with courage and go up to your Calvary upon whose peak you will find glorification - JOHN, Bishop of Bordeaux (1862).

18. Dear friends, be severe with yourselves, but ever indulgent with the weaknesses of others. This is the practice of saintly charity; alas, observed by so few! All have evil tendencies to overcome, defects to correct and bad habits to modify. Everyone has a burden, more or less heavy that must be got rid of in order to

be able to ascend to the summit of the mountain called Progress. Why then have you shown yourself to be so clairvoyant with regard to your neighbour and yet so blind with regard to yourself? When will you cease to see the small speck that troubles your brother's eye and instead, pay attention to the beam in your own eye that is blinding you and causing you to go from one fall to another? Believe what your spiritual brothers are telling you! Every person sufficiently full of pride as to judge themselves superior in matters of virtue and merit are both foolish and guilty; therefore, they will suffer castigation by God on their day of judgement. The true character of charity is always modesty and humility, that consists in not seeing the defects of others, or at least only superficially, but rather in striving to cause their goodness and virtues to predominate. Although the human heart is an abyss of corruption, there too is always the embryo of good sentiments, hidden away in its innermost folds, being the seeds of good sentiments that are in fact the living spark of the spiritual essence.

Spiritism! This blessed Doctrine of consolation! Happy are those who know about it and take profit from the edifying Teachings coming from the Spirits of the Lord! For these people their pathway is illuminated and along their way they are able to read these words that will indicate how it is possible to reach their objective: by practicing charity, charity from the heart, charity to your neighbours and to yourselves. Meaning charity from the heart, charity to your neighbour and to yourself. In short, charity towards every living creature and above all, love for God, because love for God summarises all the obligations and because it is impossible to really love God without practising charity. Therefore He has made it the Law for all creatures. - DUFETRE, Bishop of Nevers (Bordeaux).

IS IT PERMITTED TO REPREHEND OTHERS, OBSERVE IMPERFECTIONS IN OTHERS OR DIVULGE THE EVIL IN OTHERS?

19. *As no one is perfect, does it follow that no one has the right to reprehend his or her neighbour?*

This is certainly not the right conclusion to arrive at, seeing that each one must work for the progress of everyone and above all, especially for those who have been placed in your care. However, for this very reason, it should be done with moderation, in order to obtain a useful end, and not as is so often the case, for the mere pleasure of reviling. In this last case, reprehension would be wickedness; whereas in the first instance, it is a duty demanded by charity that must be accomplished with all possible care. For the rest: the censure that someone makes of another should also be directed at themselves, seeking to find if they too were not deserving of the same reprimand. - SAINT LOUIS (Paris, 1860.)

20. *Is it reprehensible to make note of the imperfections of others when this cannot result in any benefit for them, seeing that it will not be disclosed to them?*

Everything depends on the intention. For sure, it is not forbidden to see evil where it exists. It would be really inconvenient to see only good in all places. This illusion would prejudice progress. The mistake would be in making the observation result in detriment to your neighbour, so discrediting them before general opinion without any need. It would be equally reprehensible to do this simply in order to give vent to a sentiment of spite and the satisfaction of catching others at fault. However, the complete opposite occurs when, on extending a veil over an evil so that the public does not see it, the person who noted the defect observes and studies it in order to discipline him or herself to avoid what has been reproved in another.

Incidentally, is not this observation of benefit to the moralists? How else can human defects be pictured if the models are not first studied? - SAINT LOUIS (Paris, 1860).

21. *Are there cases when it is right to disclose the evil in others?*

This is a very delicate question. In order to be able to reach a conclusion, it is necessary to appeal to a true understanding of charity. If a person's imperfections only cause prejudice to themselves then there can be nothing useful in disclosing these facts. If however, it might cause harm to others, then it is preferable to attend to the interests of the majority. According to the circumstances, it may become a duty to expose hypocrisy and lies, because it is better that one person fall rather than many become their victims. In this case, it is necessary to weight the total sum of the advantages and disadvantages. - SAINT LOUIS (Paris, 1860).

CHAPTER 11

LOVE YOUR NEIGHBOUR AS YOURSELF

The greatest commandment. Do to others, as we would have them do to us.
The parable of the creditors and debtors. - Give to Caesar that which belongs
to Caesar. - INSTRUCTIONS FROM THE SPIRITS: The law of love. - Selfishness. -
Faith and charity. - Charity towards criminals. - Should we risk our life for a
criminal?

THE GREATEST COMMANDMENT

*1. But when the Pharisees had heard that he had put the
Sadducees to silence, they were gathered together. Then one of
them, which was a lawyer, asked him a question, tempting him,
and saying. Master, which is the great commandment in the law?
Jesus said to him, You should love the Lord your God with all
your heart, and with all your soul, and with all your mind. This is
the first and great commandment. And the second is like it, You
should love your neighbour as yourself. On these two
commandments hang all the law and the prophets.* (MATTHEW,
22:34-40.)

2. Therefore all things, whatsoever, you would that men should do
to you, do you even so to them*: for this is the Law and the
Prophets.* (MATTHEW, 7:12.)

*And as you would that men should do to you, do you also to them
likewise.* (LUKE, 6:31.)

*3. Therefore is the kingdom of heaven likened to a certain king,
which would take account of his servants. And when he had begun
to reckon, one was brought to him, which owed him ten thousand
talents. But forasmuch he had not to pay, his lord commanded him
to be sold, and his wife, and children, and all that he had, and
payment to be made. The servant, therefore, fell down and*

worshipped him, saying, Lord, have patience with me, and I will pay you all. Then the lord of that servant was moved with compassion, and loosed him, and forgave him the debt. But the same servant went out, and found one of his fellow servants, which owed him a hundred pence: and laid hands on him, and took him by the throat, saying, Pay what you owe. And his fellow servant fell down at his feet, and besought him, saying, Have patience with me, and I will pay you all. And he would not: but went and cast him into prison, till he should pay the debt. So when his fellow servants saw what was done, they were very sorry, and came and told to their lord all that was done. Then his lord, after he had called him, said to him, Oh you wicked servant, I forgave you all that debt, because you desired me: Shouldn't not you also have had compassion on your fellow servant, even as I had pity on you? And his lord was angry, and delivered him to the tormentors, till he should pay all that was due to him. So likewise shall my heavenly Father do also to you, if you from your hearts forgive not every one his brother their trespasses. (MATTHEW, 18:23-35.)

4. "To love your neighbour as yourself; to do to others as you would have them do to you," expresses the most complete form of charity, because it summarises all of humanities obligations towards their fellow beings. We can find no guide to take as an example that is more guaranteed, in this respect, than that we should do to others what we would have them do to us. What right have we to demand that they behave in any better manner, that they be more benevolent or more devoted to us than we are to them? The practice of these maxims leads to the destruction of selfishness. When they have been adopted as a rule of conduct and as the base of all institutions, then humanity will understand true fraternity, and so make it possible for peace and justice to reign on this planet. There will be no more hate or dissensions, but only union, concordance and mutual benevolence.

GIVE TO CAESAR THAT WHICH BELONGS TO CAESAR

5. Then went the Pharisees, and took council how they might entangle him in his talk. And they sent out to him their disciples with the Herodians, saying, Master, we know that you are true, and teaches the way of God in truth, neither care you for any man: for you regardest not the person of men. Tell us therefore, What do you think? Is it lawful to give tribute to Cesar, or not? But Jesus perceived their wickedness, and said, Why do you temp me, you hypocrites? Show me the tribute money. And they brought him a penny. And he said to them, Whose is this image and superscription? They say to him, Cesar's. Then he said to them, Render therefore to Cesar the things that are Cesar's: and to God the things that are God's. When they heard these words, they marvelled, and left him, and went their way. (MATTHEW, 22:15-22; MARK, 12:13-17.)

6. The question that was asked of Jesus was motivated by the fact that the Jews, who abominated the tribute imposed on them by the Romans, had made the payment of this tribute a religious question. Numerous parties had been set up against this tax. Therefore, this payment constituted a point of irritation amongst them at that time. If this had not been the case, there would have been no point in the question they asked Jesus "Is it licit for us to pay or not pay this tribute to Caesar?" There had been a trap set by this question because according to the reply, those who had set it expected it to go against either the Roman authority or the dissident Jews. But Jesus, "who understood their malice," got round this difficulty and gave them a lesson in justice by saying that to each one should be given what was due to them. (See Introduction, under the sub-title: *The Publicans*.)

7. However, we should not understand the words: "Give to Caesar what belongs to Caesar," in a restrictive or absolute manner. As in everything that Jesus taught, this is a general

principle that has been summarised into a practical and more customary form, taken from a certain circumstance. This principle is the consequence of the other one, in which we should do to others, as we would have them do to us. It condemns every kind of moral or material damage that might be caused to another, as well as all disregard for their interests. It prescribes respect for the rights of each person, as each one desires to be respected. It extends as well to the fulfilment of our obligations towards our family, society and authority, just as much as for individuals in general.

INSTRUCTIONS FROM THE SPIRITS

THE LAW OF LOVE

8. Love summarises the complete Teachings of Jesus, because it is the finest sentiment that exists. At their origin, human beings only have instincts; after some advancement and the onset of corruption, they have sensations; when people become instructed and more purified they develop sentiments. The most delicate apex of sentiment is love, not in the vulgar sense of the word, but that inner sun that condenses and reconciles all aspirations and superhuman revelations at its ardent focal point. The law of love substitutes the personality with the harmonising of all beings; thereby extinguishing social miseries. Blessed is the one who, having surpassed the state of being human, loves with an ample love all suffering fellow beings! Blessed are those who love because they know not the miseries of either body or soul. Their step is light and they live as if transported outside of themselves. When Jesus pronounced that divine word - love, it made the people tremble and thus the martyrs, inebriated with hope, descended into the amphitheatres.

In its turn, Spiritism has come to pronounce the second word in the divine alphabet. Pay attention, because the word '*reincarnation*' lifts up the tombstones from empty graves and triumphing over death, reveals to astonished people its intellectual patrimony. No longer are people conducted to their death, but rather to the conquest of their own being, already becoming elevated and transfigured. Blood has redeemed the Spirit and today the Spirit has to liberate humans from matter.

I have said that in their origin human beings only had instincts. Those in whom instincts predominate are still nearer the starting point than their goal. In order to advance towards this goal, each person must overcome their instincts, that is to say, perfect their sentiments. Instincts are the germination and the embryos of sentiments. They bring progress with them, just as the acorn contains within itself the oak tree, the less advanced creatures are those who, after emerging little by little from their chrysalises, continue to maintain themselves slaves to their instincts. The spirit needs to be cultivated as you would a pasture. All the riches of the future depend on the present labour employed, which will earn much more than earthly goods, for it will offer glorious elevation. Thus, having understood the law of love that joins all creatures, you will seek to find within it the sweetest delights of the soul that are the preludes to celestial happiness. - LAZARUS (Paris, 1862).

9. Love is of a divine essence and everyone, from the first to the last, has a spark of this sacred fire in the bottom of their hearts. It is a many times proven fact that both men and women, however vile, base or criminal, are known to devote ardent affection to living creatures or objects. This sentiment is resistant to every attempt to diminish it and has frequently even been known to reach sublime proportions.

I have purposely said that affection is given to living creatures and some objects, because amongst you are individuals whose hearts are overflowing with love, but who nevertheless expend a wealth of this sentiment upon animals, plants and even material things. These people are a kind of misanthrope who, while complaining to themselves about humanity in general and resisting the natural inclinations of their souls, which is to seek sympathy and affection from those around them, reduce the law of love to the condition of instinct. Nevertheless, no matter what is done, they will not succeed in suffocating the living seed that God deposits within every heart at the moment of creation. This seed will develop and grow, together with morality and intelligence. Although frequently repressed by selfishness, it will become the origin of saintly virtues that will produce sincere and lasting affections, which in turn will help in crossing the rugged and arid pathways of human existence.

There are those who repudiate reincarnation, believing that others will participate in the affections and sympathies of which they are jealous. My poor brothers and sisters! Your affections have made you selfish and your love has become restricted to the intimate circle of your friends and relatives, so that you are indifferent to all others. Well then, so that you may practise the law of love as God intended, it is necessary that you learn step-by-step to love all your fellow beings without distinction. The task will be long and difficult, but it will be fulfilled because God so desires. The law of love is the first and most important precept of the new Teachings, because one day it will destroy all selfishness, under whatever form it may present itself, seeing that apart from personal selfishness there is also that of the family, the clan and nationality. Jesus told us to "Love your neighbour as yourself." Nowadays, what is the limit with regard to your neighbour? Is it the family, the sect, or the nation? No, it is nothing less than the whole of humanity. In the superior spheres and planets, reciprocated love harmonises and directs the advanced Spirits that inhabit them. Your planet, which is shortly destined to make appreciable progress, will see its inhabitants practising this sublime law, which is a reflection of Divinity, in virtue of the social transformation through which it will soon pass.

The effects that the law of love will bring are the moral betterment of the human race and happiness during terrestrial life. The most rebellious and corrupt will reform themselves when they see the resulting benefits stemming from the practise of the precept, "Do not do to others that which you would not wish done to you; on the contrary, do to others all the good that it is within your power to do."

Do not believe then in the sterility and hardening of the human heart. For even against its own will it must give way to true love. It is a magnet that is impossible to resist. Contact with true love revives and fertilises the seed that is latent in every heart. Being a globe of probation and exile, the Earth will then be purified by this sacred fire. Then you will see practised upon its surface the acts of charity, humility, patience, devotion, abnegation, resignation and sacrifice, all of which are the offspring of true love. So, do not tire of listening to the words of John the Evangelist. As perhaps you know, when sickness and old age forced him to stop teaching, he limited himself to simply repeating these gentle words, "My children, you must love one another."

Beloved brethren, make good use of these lessons because although it is difficult to put them into practice, the soul will reap great benefit from them. Believe me when I tell you to love one another and make the sublime effort that I ask of you, then you will soon see the Earth transformed into a Paradise, where the souls of the just may come for repose. - FÉNELON (Bordeaux, 1861.)

10. Esteemed co-disciples, the Spirits who are here present say to you through my intermediary: "Love with all your hearts so that in turn you too may be loved." This thought is so completely just that we find within it everything that can console and alleviate the trials of each day. Better still, by putting this wisdom into practice you will so elevate yourselves above all materiality, that you will become spiritualised even before you leave this earthly body. As the study of spiritual matters has developed your understanding of the future, of one thing you can be sure, you are progressing in the direction of God and will see fulfilled all the promises that correspond to the aspirations of your soul. This is why it is necessary to elevate oneself as high as possible, so we may be able to judge ourselves without the constraint of matter. It is also, why we must never condemn our neighbour without first directing our thoughts to God.

To love, in the most profound sense of the word, is to be loyal, honest, conscientious and do to others what we would have them do to us. It is to search around oneself and search for the inner meaning behind all the pain afflicting your fellow creatures, so as to be better able to offer some relief. In addition, consider the great human family as your own, because at some future date this family will re-encounter itself in other more advanced worlds, together with other spirits who, like you, are also God's children destined to infinite elevation. Thus, you cannot deny your fellow human beings what God has liberally granted you seeing that, on your side, you should be happy that they give you what you need. Therefore, always have a word of comfort and hope for all who suffer so that you may be wholly just and loving.

Believe that the wise saying, "Love greatly so as to be greatly loved", will open up the way. These words are revolutionary and follow a pathway that is sure and invariable. Those of you who listen to them have already made some progress; you are much better than you were a hundred years ago. You have changed so much for your own good, that now you can willingly accept a host of new ideas on liberty and fraternity that before you would have rejected. Moreover, without a doubt in another hundred years or so, you will accept just as easily those ideas which now you are unable to get into your minds.

Today, when the Spiritist Movement has taken such big steps forward, see how quickly the ideas of justice and renovation, which are a constant in the Spiritist Teachings, are largely accepted by the intelligent world. This is due to the fact that these ideas correspond to all that is divine within each one of us. This has come about because we were prepared by a rich and fertile sowing during the last century, when the seeds of great ideas regarding progress were implanted in the bosom of earthly society. Moreover, as everything is linked together under the direction of the Most High, all lessons received and accepted will be contained within the constant universal interchange of love for one's fellow beings. Thanks to Him, all incarnate spirits, being better able to appreciate and judge things, will join hands with those from every corner of this planet. Everyone will come together to understand and love each other, to destroy all injustices and all causes of misunderstandings amongst peoples.

The great concept of renewal through Spiritism, so well presented in *The Spirits' Book*, will produce the prodigious miracles of the forthcoming century and lead to the harmonising of all the material and spiritual interests of Humanity. This will be brought about through a fuller understanding of the maxim: "Love greatly, so as to be greatly loved." - SAMSON, an ex-member of the Spiritist Society of Paris, 1863.

SELFISHNESS

11. Selfishness, that plague of all Humanity, is hindering moral progress and must disappear from the face of the Earth. It has

been reserved for Spiritism to make this planet ascend in the hierarchy of the worlds. Therefore, selfishness is the target at which all believers should point their arms and towards which all strength and courage should be directed. I say 'courage' because this will be greatly needed by each individual if they are to triumph over themselves, rather than triumph over others. So, let each one use all their strength to combat their own selfishness, being certain that this monstrous devourer of all intellects, this offspring of pride, is the cause of all the miseries found in this world. It is a denial of charity and consequently the greatest obstacle to human happiness.

Jesus gave us an example of charity and Pontius Pilate gave us an example of selfishness. While the first, the Just One, was about to traverse the holy stations of His martyrdom, the second was washing his hands and saying, "What does it matter to me!" He even said to the Jews "This is a just man, so why do you want to crucify Him?" Nevertheless, he allowed them to continue to conduct Jesus to His execution.

Due to the antagonism between charity and selfishness, that leprous invasion of the human heart, Christianity has still not completely discharged its entire mission. It is to you, who are the new apostles of the faith, that the superior Spirits are giving guidance. It is upon you that rest the responsibility and the duty of eradicating this evil, so as to give Christianity its full force. This will then allow it to clear the way of all obstacles that impede its progress. Expel selfishness from the Earth so it may ascend in the scale of the worlds, seeing that the time has arrived for Humanity to vest its virile raiments; and for this to happen, it is first necessary that selfishness be expelled from all hearts. - EMMANUEL (Paris, 1861.)

12. If human beings loved one another mutually then charity would be better practised. However, for this to happen it is

necessary to remove the armoured plate that covers your hearts, in order to become sensitive to the sufferings of others. Severity and rigidity kills all good sentiments. Christ never avoided anyone, nor did He repel those who came in search of Him, whoever they might be. He helped the adulterous woman and the criminal, never fearing that His reputation might suffer as a consequence. When will you take Him as your model for all your actions? *If charity reigned on Earth then evil could not prevail; it would fade away in shame; it would hide, seeing that wherever it went it would feel out of place.* Then evil would simply disappear; be quite sure of this!

Begin by giving examples yourself; be charitable to all, without distinction and make an effort not to heed those who look on you with disdain. Leave the task of doing justice to God, to the One who every day in His kingdom separates the wheat from the chaff.

Selfishness is a denial of charity. Moreover, without charity, there will be no rest for human society. I go even further and say there will be no safety. With selfishness and pride, both of which go hand in hand, life will always be a race in which the most cunning will be the winners. It would be a fight of interests in which the most saintly affections would be trodden underfoot, and where not even sacred family ties would be deserving of respect. - PASCAL (Sens, 1862.)

FAITH AND CHARITY

13. My beloved children, but a short while ago I told you that charity without faith is not enough to maintain social order amongst people capable of making them happy. I could have said that charity without faith is not possible. In fact, generous impulses can present themselves even amongst those of no religion at all. Nevertheless, unadorned charity, which can only be practised with abnegation and the constant sacrifice of all selfish

interests, can only be inspired by faith. Nothing but faith can give humanity the courage and perseverance needed to carry the cross of terrestrial life.

Yes, my children, it is useless for a person who is always eager for pleasure to try to delude themselves as to their destiny on Earth. They pretend that they are justified in occupying themselves exclusively with their own pleasure. Beyond doubt, God created us to be happy in eternity; meanwhile, earthly life must serve solely for moral improvement that is more readily obtained with the help of physical organs and the material world. Without taking into account the ordinary vicissitudes of life and the diversities of tastes, the inclinations and the necessities, exercising yourselves in the acts of charity is also a means of improvement. In effect, only by dint of mutual concessions and sacrifices can harmony be preserved between so many different elements.

Nevertheless, you would be right to affirm that humanity was intended to be happy in this world, as long as this was sought not in material pleasures, but in goodness. The history of Christianity tells of martyrs going happily to their execution. Today in your society, there is no longer a need for Christians to face the holocaust of martyrdom or the sacrifice of life, only and exclusively the sacrifice of selfishness, pride and vanity. You will triumph only if you are inspired by charity and sustained by faith. - A PROTECTING SPIRIT (Krakow, 1861.)

CHARITY TOWARDS CRIMINALS

14. True charity constitutes one of the sublime teachings that God has given the world. Complete fraternity should exist amongst all true followers of His teachings. Those who are unfortunate and wretched, by this we mean criminals, should be loved as God's creatures, which they are. Pardon and mercy will

be given to them, just as much as to you, if they repent of all offences committed against His law. Consider yourselves more reprehensible and guiltier than those to whom you deny pardon and commiseration because, as often as not, they do not know God as you do, consequently less will be asked of them than is asked of you.

Do not judge! Oh! Never make a complete judgement, my friends! In as much as the verdict you pronounce will be applied even more severely to yourselves, so you will need indulgence for those sins you so unceasingly incur. Are you ignorant of the fact that there are many actions considered as crimes in the eyes of God, who symbolises pureness, which the world does not deem even as small offences?

True charity does not consist only in giving alms, nor even in the consoling words you may add to your donation. No, this is not the only thing that God demands of you. Sublime charity, as taught by Jesus, also consists of the constant use of benevolence in all things pertaining to your neighbour. This sublime virtue can also be used in your relationships with those to whom the giving of alms would have no utility, but to whom a few words of consolation, encouragement and love would raise them up to the Lord.

We repeat yet again that the time approaches when a great fraternity will reign upon this planet, in which all humanity will obey the laws of Christ. These laws will offer both restraints and hopes, and will conduct all souls to the happy realms. Love one another then, as sons and daughters of the same Father. Never establish differences between those who are unhappy, nor despise any living creature, seeing that God desires everyone to be equal. God permits great criminals to be found amongst you so that they may serve as a lesson. In the near future, when humankind finds itself submitted to the true laws of God, there will no longer be any need for these lessons, *because all impure and rebellious spirits will have been relegated to inferior worlds in accordance with their inclinations.*

Your duty is to help those of whom I have spoken with your prayers; that is true charity. It is not your place to say to a criminal, "You are despicable and should be purged from the face of the Earth. The death penalty is much too good for the likes of you." No! This is not the way to talk! Take note of the model on whom we should base ourselves - Jesus. What would He have said if He found one of those unfortunates at His side? He would have wept over them, considered them to be sick and therefore deserving of pity, and would then have extended a helping hand. In fact, you cannot as yet do the same thing. But at least you can pray for them and help their spirits during the time they still have to pass on Earth. Perhaps they will be touched by repentance if you pray with all your faith. They are our neighbours just as much as the best of humanity. Their souls, having strayed and become rebellious, were created as was your own, to be perfected. Help them then to get out of their quagmire and pray for them. - ELIZABETH OF FRANCE (Havre, 1862.)

SHOULD WE RISK OUR LIFE FOR THAT OF A CRIMINAL?

15. *Someone's life is in danger and in order to save them, another person must put their life at risk. However, it is known that the person in danger is a criminal and that, if they escape, they may commit other crimes. Despite these facts, should someone risk their life in order to save that of the criminal?*

This is a very grave question and can naturally present itself to a Spiritist. I will reply in accordance with my moral progress, since what you wish to know is whether we should expose our life for the sake of a criminal. Devotion is blind; just as enemy soldiers are rescued, so we should also rescue enemies of society or in short, criminals. Do you suppose that in such a case it is only death hurrying to snatch away this unhappy person? Perhaps it is all their past life. Indeed, imagine that in those rapid instants, in which the last breath of life is being swept away, the lost person returns to their past or rather it looms before them. Perchance death is coming too soon and the thought of reincarnation may seem terrible to them. So rush forward to help! Those of you who have been enlightened by the knowledge of the Science of Spiritism, should be the first to offer aid. Snatch this person from their condemnation and who knows but that they, who would have died with blasphemy on their lips, may throw themselves into your arms. In any case, do not stop to ask if they would or would not, just save them, since by this act you are obeying the voice in your heart that tells you, "You can save them, so then do so!" - LAMENNAIS (Paris, 1862.)

CHAPTER 12

LOVE YOUR ENEMIES

Return evil with goodness. - Discarnate enemies. - Whosoever shall smite you on your right cheek, turn to him the other also. - INSTRUCTIONS FROM THE SPIRITS: Vengeance. - Hatred. - Duelling.

RETURN EVIL WITH GOODNESS

1. You have heard that it has been said, You shall love your neighbour, and hate your enemy. But I say to you, Love your enemies, bless them that curse you, do good to them that hate you, and pray for them which despitefully use you, and persecute you; *That you may be the children of your Father which is in heaven: for he makes his sun to rise on the evil and on the good, and sends rain on the just and on the unjust. For if you love them which love you, what reward have you? do not even the Publicans the same? And if you salute your brethren only, what do you more than others? do not even the publicans so? For I say to you, That except your righteousness shall exceed the righteousness of the scribes and the Pharisees, you shall in no case enter into the kingdom of heaven.* (MATTHEW, 5:43-47, 20.)

2. For if you love them which love you, what thank have you? for sinners also love those who love them. And if you do good to them which do good to you, what thank have you? for sinners also do even the same. And if you lend to them of whom you hope to receive, what thank have you? for sinners also lend to sinners, to receive as much again. But love you your enemies, and do good, and lend, hoping for nothing again; *and your reward shall be great, and you shall be the children of the Highest; for he is kind to the unthankful and to the evil. Be you therefore merciful, as your Father also is merciful.* (LUKE, 6:32-36.)

3. If the principle of charity is to love one's neighbours, then to love one's enemies is the most sublime application of this same principle, seeing that the possession of this virtue represents one of the greatest victories that can be achieved against selfishness and pride.

However, there is usually a misunderstanding in relation to the meaning of the word *love* in this situation. When He spoke, Jesus did not mean that each one of us should have the same tenderness for an enemy as would be felt for a brother, sister or friend. Tenderness presupposes confidence; well, no one can deposit confidence in another person knowing that they bear malice; no one can show effusive friendship knowing that the other person is likely to abuse the situation. Between people who have no confidence in each other, there cannot be the same manifestations of sympathy that exist between those who share the same ideas. In short, no one can have the same pleasure when they are with an enemy, as they would feel when in the company of a friend.

The diversity of feelings in these two very different circumstances is the result of a physical law that is the assimilation and repulsion of vibrations. An evil thought produces a vibratory current that causes an unpleasant impression. A good thought encompasses us with a very agreeable emanation. This is the reason for the different sensations that are experienced on the approximation of a friend or an enemy. So then, to love one's enemy cannot signify that there should be no difference between the affection for an enemy and that for a friend. If this precept seems difficult to put into practice, even impossible, this is only because it was falsely understood that Jesus had told us to give both friends and enemies an equal place in our hearts. Seeing that the restrictions of the human language obliges us to use the same term to express different shades of a sentiment, it is then necessary to establish these differences according to the various cases.

Therefore, to love one's enemies does not mean showing affection that would not be within our nature, as contact with an enemy makes our heart beat in an entirely different manner to the way it beats on contact with a friend. Therefore, to love one's enemy means we should not hate, nor bear rancour against them, nor desire vengeance. We should forgive all the evil they have caused, *without hidden thoughts and without conditions.* It also means to not put obstacles in the way of reconciliation and to wish them well, instead of bad things. It is to feel joy, instead of regret, at the good things that may come their way; to help them whenever possible, to abstain *from words or acts* and everything that might prejudice them. Finally, it means to always return goodness for evil *without any intention to humiliate.* Whoever can proceed in this manner fulfils the conditions of the commandment: Love your enemies.

4. To those who are incredulous, loving an enemy is a contra sense. For those to whom the present life is everything, an enemy is someone noxious, who perturbs their rest and from whom, as is thought, only death can bring liberation. This is the reason for desiring vengeance. These people are not interested in forgiving unless it is to satisfy their pride before the world. In certain other cases, the act of pardon seems to them to be a weakness to which they will not stoop. Even if they do not reap vengeance, they will certainly retain rancour and evil desires against the other person.

For the believer, and above all for the Spiritist, the way of looking at this situation is very different, because their vision extends over the past and into the future, between which the present life is nothing more than a point in time. It is known that due to the peculiar destiny of this planet, meetings with evil and perverse people are to be expected. The wickedness to be faced is all part of the ordeals to be supported. From this elevated point of view, vicissitudes are easier to bear, less bitter, whether they originate from other fellow beings or from things. *If they do not complain about their trials, neither should they complain about those who serve as instruments.* If instead of bemoaning, they were to thank God for being put to the test, *they should also thank the hand that offers them the opportunity to demonstrate their patience and resignation.* This idea will naturally dispose them towards forgiveness. They also know that apart from this, the more generous they are the more they become elevated in their own eyes, so putting themselves beyond the reach of their enemies' darts.

The person who occupies an elevated place in this world does not feel offended by the insults of those whom they consider their inferiors. The same happens in the moral world to those who elevate themselves above materialistic Humanity. They understand that hate and rancour only degrade and lower them. In order to be superior to their adversary, their soul must be larger, nobler and more generous than that of their adversary.

DISCARNATE ENEMIES

5. The Spiritist has still other motives for being indulgent towards their enemies. In the first place, they know that evil is not the permanent condition of human beings. This occurs due to a temporary state of imperfection and just as children correct themselves of their defects, so the evil man or woman will one day recognise their errors and gradually become good people.

It is also known that death only relieves them from the material presence of their enemy, because this enemy can continue to pursue them with hate even after leaving the Earth. So that vengeance fails in its objective, as it has the contrary effect of causing even more irritation that is capable of continuing on from one existence to another. It is up to Spiritism to prove through experience and the law which governs relationships, between the visible and invisible worlds, that the expression: *extinguish hate with blood* is radically wrong and that in fact blood only feeds hate even in the after-life. It is therefore up to the Spiritist Teachings to offer a positive reason for this fact, together with a practical motive for forgiveness and for Christ's commandment: *Love your enemies.* There is no heart so perverse that it will refuse, even though reluctantly, to show itself to be sensitive to good behaviour. Through good behaviour, it is possible to take away all pretexts for retaliation and who knows, even make a friend out of an enemy before and after death. Through bad behaviour, a person only succeeds in irritating their enemy, *who then becomes the instrument that God's Justice will use to serve as a punishment for those who are unable to forgive.*

6. It is therefore, always possible to find enemies amongst both incarnates and discarnates. Our enemies in the invisible world manifest themselves and their malice by means of spiritual obsessions and subjugations, as can be frequently seen. These situations represent one kind of trial that just as in all other types of trials helps in the process of advancement. For this reason, the sufferer should accept them with a certain amount of resignation. These happenings are also a consequence of the inferior nature of this globe, for if there were no evil people on this planet, then there would not be any evil spirits around it either. Hence, if we are to be benevolent with our incarnate enemies, we should also treat those of them who are discarnate in a like manner.

In days gone by it was the custom to make bloody sacrifices of innocent victims, in order to appease the hellish gods who were none other than evil spirits. These fiendish gods followed on after the devils, who are the same thing. Spiritism shows us that these devils are merely the souls of perverse men and women, who have not yet disposed of their material instincts and that *no one can succeed in appeasing them, except by sacrificing the hate that exists; that is to say, by being charitable towards them.* This has the effect of not only stopping them in their evil practices, but also of recovering them and bringing them back to the path of goodness, thus contributing to their salvation. In this way, the maxim 'Love your enemies,' is not circumscribed to the Earth ambient and the present life, but rather forms part of the great universal laws of solidarity and fraternity.

WHOEVER SHALL SMITE YOU ON YOUR RIGHT CHEEK TURN TO HIM THE OTHER ALSO

7. You have heard that it has been said, An eye for an eye, and a tooth for a tooth; But I say to you, That you resist not evil; but whosoever shall smite you on your right cheek, turn to him the other also. And if any man will sue you at the law, and take away your coat, let him have your cloak also. And whosoever shall compel you to go a mile, go with him two. Give to him that asks you, and from him that would borrow from you, turn not away. (MATTHEW, 5:38-42.)

8. The prejudices of the world with respect to what is commonly called 'a point of honour' produce the kind of sombre susceptibility that is born of pride and the glorification of one's own personality. This in turn often leads humans to return an injury or offence with another. Those whose moral sense is still embedded in worldly passions take this for justice. That was why the Law of Moses prescribed an 'eye for an eye and a tooth for a tooth' in accordance with the epoch in which he lived. When Christ came, He said, "Return goodness for evil" and added "Do not resist the evil that they wish to do to you. *If someone shall smite you on your cheek, present him the other also.*" To the proud, this teaching seems cowardly because they do not understand that it takes more courage to support an insult than it does to take vengeance. This is always because their vision does not go beyond the present. Should we then take this precept at its face value? No, not more than the other, which tells us to pluck out our eye when it is the cause of offence? If left to its ultimate

consequences, it would mean the condemnation of all restraint, even legal restraint, so leaving an open field for those who are evil, who would find themselves free from any kind of fear. If no breaks were put on their acts of aggression then very quickly the good would become their victims. The very instinct of self-preservation, being one of the Laws of Nature, prevents anyone from offering themselves for assassination.

By enunciating that maxim, Jesus did not mean that self-defence is forbidden, but rather that He *condemned vengeance*. Telling us to offer the other cheek when one has been injured is merely another way of saying we must not repay evil with evil; that a person should humbly accept everything that serves as a means of weakening their pride, because there is greater glory in receiving an offence than in being the offender; in patiently suffering an injustice, than practising it and better to be deceived, than being the deceiver or to be ruined rather than be the one who causes the ruin. It is, at the same time, also the condemnation of all duelling, which in fact is nothing more than a manifestation of pride. Only faith in the future life and the Justice of God, who never allows evil to go unpunished, can give a person the necessary strength to be able to patiently support the blows dealt to either their interests or their self-respect. This is why we are constantly repeating: Look to the future; the more you lift up your thoughts above material life, the less the things of this world will hurt you.

INSTRUCTIONS FROM THE SPIRITS

VENGEANCE

9. Vengeance is one of the last relics of the barbaric customs that tend to disappear from the human race. Like the duel, it is one of the last vestiges of the savage habits under which humanity was

struggling at the outset of the Christian era. This is why vengeance constitutes a sure indication of the backward state of people who lend themselves to it and of the spirits who still inspire them. Accordingly, my friends, this sentiment should never vibrate in the heart of anyone who proclaims to be a Spiritist. You know full well that to avenge oneself is so much against Christ's precept, 'Forgive your enemies', that the person who refuses to forgive not only is not a Spiritist but certainly is not even a Christian. Vengeance is an even more ruinous inspiration as you well know, when its companions are assiduous in falseness and baseness. Indeed, those who deliver themselves to this fatal and blind passion, almost never seek vengeance openly. When they are the stronger, they fall savagely upon those they call the enemy, seeing that the mere presence of these people inflames their spite, anger and hate. However, in most cases they assume a hypocritical attitude, concealing the evil sentiments that animate them deep in their hearts. They take secret pathways, following their unsuspecting enemy in the shadows, awaiting an opportunity to strike without danger to themselves. While hiding from their enemy they constantly spy on them, preparing a hateful trap and when the occasion is propitious, they put the poison in the cup. When their hatred does not reach such extremes, they attack the victim through their honour and affections. Nor do they hesitate in the use of slander and perfidious insinuation ably spread on all sides, that increases along the way. Consequently, when the one who is being persecuted presents themselves in those places where the whispers of the persecutor have passed, they are astonished to receive a cold reception instead of friendly and benevolent faces from those who had previously welcomed them. They are even more surprised when instead of outstretched hands even these are refused. Finally, they feel defeated when even their greatest friends and closest relatives withdraw and avoid them. Ah! The coward who seeks vengeance in this manner is a hundred times more guilty than the one who confronts their enemy and insults them face to face.

So then, let us do away with these primitive customs! Let us dispense with these procedures from bygone days! Every Spiritist who still lays claim to the right to seek vengeance is no longer worthy to take part in the phalanx who holds as their motto: *Without charity, there is no salvation!* But no, I can no longer detain myself on the thought that a member of this great Spiritist family would be capable, in the future, of giving in to the impulse of vengeance, instead of forgiveness. - JULES OLIVIER (Paris, 1862.)

HATRED

10. Love one another and you will be happy. Above all else, take to heart the need to love all those who inspire you with indifference, hate, and scorn. Christ, whom you should consider as your model, gave an example of this kind of devotion. Missionary of Love that He was, He loved so much as to give His very blood and life for Love. It is a painful sacrifice to love those who insult and torment us, but it is exactly this sacrifice that makes you superior to them. If you were to hate them, as they hate you, then you are worth no more than they are. To love them is the Immaculate Host you offer to God on the altar of your hearts that will envelop you in its aroma, as if it were a sweet perfume. If the law of love demands that each one love all their brothers and sisters without distinction, it does not mean that the heart will be protected against evil conduct. On the contrary, it is the most anguishing of trials that I know full well, having experienced this same torture during my last earthly existence. Nevertheless, God is always present and punishes in this life or the next all who violate the law of love. My dear children do not forget that love draws us

near to God and hate drives us away from Him. - FÉNELON (Bordeaux, 1861.)

DUELLING

11. A person is only truly great if, when considering life as a journey that leads to a determined point, they take little heed of the roughness of the way and do not allow their footsteps to turn aside from the straight and narrow path. With their gaze firmly set on the distant point to be reached, it is of no importance to them that briars and thorns threaten to scratch, these do not impede their progress. To devote one's time to avenging an affront is to recoil before life's ordeals and is always a crime in the eyes of God. If you were not beguiled, as indeed you are by your prejudices, you would see duelling as being a supremely ridiculous madness.

It is a crime to commit homicide by duelling, as even your own laws recognise. No one has the right, under any circumstances, to make an attempt against the life of a fellow creature. This is a crime in the eyes of God, who has traced the line of conduct required to be followed. In this case, more than in any other circumstance, you are your own judge. Remember, you will be pardoned only in as much as you are able to pardon others. Through the act of pardoning, you draw near to the Lord, since clemency is akin to strength. As long as one drop of human blood flows upon the Earth, drawn by human hands, the true Kingdom of God, wherein will reign peace and love that will banish animosity, discord and wars forever, will not have been implanted on this planet. When this happens, the word 'duel' will exist in your language only as a distant and vague remembrance of a past that is gone. Then no other antagonism will exist amongst humanity, apart from the noble rivalry of righteousness. - ADOLF, Bishop of Algiers (Marmande, 1861.)

12. No doubt, in certain cases, duelling may constitute a test of physical courage and disdain for life. However, unquestionably it is a proof of moral cowardice, just like suicide. The suicide does not have the courage to face the vicissitudes of life, whereas the duellist cannot support offences. Was it not Christ who said there is more honour and courage in presenting the left check to the person who hit you on the right, than in avenging an offence? Did He not say to Peter, in the Garden of Olives, "Put away your sword because the one who kills with the sword shall also perish by the sword?" In so saying, did He not condemn forever the act of duelling? In fact, my children, what kind of courage comes from a violent disposition, from a bloody and wrathful temperament that bellows at the slightest offence? What greatness can be found in a person who, at the least insult, believes that only blood can repair the damage? Let this person tremble! For, from the bottom of their conscience a voice will persist in saying: "Cain! Cain! What have you done to your fellow being?" They will answer that it was necessary to spill blood in order to save their honour. Then the voice will answer, "In the few minutes that remain to you of your earthly life, you thought only to save your honour before humankind, but you never thought to save it before God!" Poor wretch! How much blood will Christ demand of you for all the violence He has received? Was it not enough that you injured Him with thorns and lances? That you placed upon Him an infamous garment and that in the middle of His atrocious agony, you made Him listen to the mockery and derision that was showered upon Him. How many reparations has He asked of you for your many offences? The last cry of the Shepherd was a supplication to God in favour of His torturers! Oh! Be like Him! Forgive and pray for those who offend you.

Friends, remember the precept 'Love one another.' Then for every blow received through hatred, you will be able to reply with a smile; for every affront you will offer forgiveness. Without a doubt, the world will rise up in fury and treat you like a coward. So, lift your head up high and show you are not afraid to have your brow covered by thorns just as Christ had. That your hand does not wish to be an accomplice to an assassination, authorised by false ideas of honour, that is nevertheless nothing more than pride and self-conceit. When God created humankind, did He bestow the right of life and death one over the other? No, this right was given only to Nature, for the purpose of reconstruction and reorganisation, whereas you are not permitted to dispose even of yourselves. The duellist then, just as the suicide, will be found to be marked by blood when they come before God. For both of these, the Supreme Judge will reserve long and harsh penalties. If this same Judge has threatened all who call their fellow beings by the name of 'Raca', how much more severe will be the punishment for those who reach His presence with the blood of their brothers and sisters on their hands! - SAINT AUGUSTINE (Paris, 1862.)

13. The duel, once called God's Justice, is one of the most barbaric customs persisting in some human societies. What would you say, however, if you saw two adversaries being plunged into boiling water, or being submitted to the contact of red-hot iron in order to put an end to their dispute? The one who is right being the one who best suffers the test? Would you not classify these customs as being unreasonable and senseless? Well, duelling is far worse than all of these because the dextrous duellist commits murder, practised in cold blood with all due premeditation, since they are certain of the efficiency of the blow to be dealt. For the adversary, who is almost sure to succumb by virtue of their weakness and inability, it is suicide committed after cold reflection. I know that on many occasions the person has sought to avoid the consequences of the criminal alternative by placing the responsibility for the act upon chance. Is this not going back, under another name, to the ideas from the Middle Ages of God's

Judgement? We remind you that in those times humanity was infinitely less guilty. Certainly, the use of the words '*God's Judgement*' reveals a very naive faith. However, it was nevertheless some small degree of faith in the Justice of God, Who could never allow the innocent to succumb. Whereas a duel resorts to brute force to such an extent that frequently the one who was offended is the one who succumbs.

Oh, senseless conceit, foolish vanity and insane pride! When will you be substituted by Christian charity, by a love of one's fellow creatures and by humility, all of which were prescribed and exemplified by Christ? This will only happen when human beings cease to be dominated by these monstrous preconceptions that the laws are impotent to repress because it is not enough to prohibit evil. For this to occur it is necessary for the source of goodness and the horror of evil to live jointly in the hearts of all humanity. - A PROTECTING SPIRIT (Bordeaux, 1861.)

14. You frequently ask, "What will people say about me, if I refuse to make the reparation that is being demanded of me, or if I do not complain about those who offend me?" Those of you who are foolish or are backward, will censure you. However, those who have been enlightened by intellectual and moral progress will say that you have proceeded with true wisdom. Let us reflect then for a moment. Due to a word, sometimes said without thinking or a wish to offend coming from one of your fellow beings, your pride is hurt, so you then reply scathingly and there stems a provocation. Before the decisive moment arrives ask yourself if you are behaving like a Christian. What debt will you owe to society if you rob it of one of its members? Think of the remorse of having deprived a woman of her husband, a mother of her child or the children of their mother or father and with this their means of sustenance! For sure, the one who offended owes recompense. Nevertheless, is it not more honourable to give this spontaneously, thus recognising one's errors, rather than to endanger the life of the

one who has the right to complain? As to the one offended, it so happens that sometimes, because they feel gravely injured or that someone dear to them has been insulted, it is not only self-respect that is at stake, but also that their heart has been hurt and is suffering. So apart from it being stupid to risk one's life by throwing yourself against a wretch who is capable of infamy, we ask that if the person dies, does the insult or whatever it was, cease to exist? Is it not true that when blood is spilt it leaves an even deeper impression of a fact that, if false, will fall of its own accord and if true would be better buried in silence? Then nothing more is left than the quenching of thirst for vengeance! Alas! An unhappy satisfaction that usually gives way, even in this life, to pungent remorse! When it is the one that was offended who succumbs, where is the retribution?

When charity finally becomes the general rule of conduct for humanity, all acts and words will be confined to this maxim "Do not do to others that which you would not wish done to yourself." When this happens all cause for dissensions will disappear and with this all duels and wars, which are only duels between nations - FRANÇOIS XAVIER (Bordeaux, 1861).

15. A worldly person, a happy person, because of an offensive word possibly something slight, throws away their life that came from God or throws away the life of a fellow being, which also belongs to God. This person is a hundred times guiltier than the scoundrel who, driven by covetousness and sometimes by necessity, enters into a residence with the intent to rob and kills all those who oppose their intentions. In this case, we are usually dealing with a person of little education having an imperfect notion of good and evil. Whereas as a rule, the duellist belongs to the more cultured class. The one kills with brutality, while the other kills with method and refinement, in view of which society forgives them. I would even add that the duellist is guiltier than the scoundrel who, on giving way to a desire for vengeance, kills

in a moment of exasperation. The duellist, however, does not have the excuse of a frenzy of passion, because between the moment of insult and retribution there has been time for reflection. They act coldly, with premeditation, studying and calculating everything so that they may be more certain of killing their opponent. It is true they also expose their own life, which is what rehabilitates them in the eyes of the public, as they see only an act of courage and disregard for life. But is there any courage on the part of someone who is sure of themselves? The duel, reminiscent of barbarous times in which the right of the strongest was law, will disappear as a result of a better appreciation of what a point of honour really means, and according to the extent that people deposit living faith in a future life. - AUGUSTINE (Bordeaux. 1861).

16. REMARKS: Nowadays duelling is becoming very rare indeed, but if occasionally a painful example still occurs, the number is greatly diminished compared with days gone by. Many years ago, a person could not leave their house without anticipating an encounter and always took the necessary precautions. A characteristic sign of people and their habits in those days was the habitual presence either ostensible or hidden, of arms for both attack and defence. The abolition of this custom will demonstrate the softening of habits. It is interesting to follow this gradation from the epoch in which a gentleman only rode out covered with armour plate, to the times when a sword at the waist was more an ornament or blazon, than a weapon of aggression. Another indication of the modification from those customs is that formerly these combats were held in the middle of a public thoroughfare before a mob; whereas in times that are more recent they were held in secret. Nowadays, death is something that is causing some emotion. But in other times no one took any notice of it. Spiritism will obliterate the last traces of barbarism, by instilling in humanity a sense of charity and fraternity.

CHAPTER 13

DO NOT LET YOUR LEFT HAND KNOW WHAT YOUR RIGHT HAND IS DOING

Do good without ostentation. - Hidden misfortune. - The widow's mite. - Invite the poor and the lame. Give without thought of recompense. - INSTRUCTIONS FROM THE SPIRITS: Material charity and moral charity. - Beneficence. - Compassion. - Orphans. - Beneficence recompensed by ingratitude. - Exclusive benevolence.

DO GOOD WITHOUT OSTENTATION

1. Take heed that you do not your alms before men, to be seen of them; otherwise, you have no reward of your Father that is in heaven. Therefore, when you do your alms, do not sound a trumpet before you, as the hypocrites do in the synagogues and in the streets, that they may have glory of men. Verily I say to you, they have their reward. But when you give alms, let not your left hand know what your right hand does: *That your alms may be in secret: and your Father which sees in secret himself shall reward you openly.* (MATTHEW, 6:1-4.)

2. When he was come down from the mountain, great multitudes followed him. And, behold, there came a leper (1) and worshipped him, saying, Lord, if you wish, you can make me clean. And Jesus put forth his hand, and touched him, saying, I will: be you clean. And immediately his leprosy was cleansed. And Jesus said to him, See you tell no man; *but go your way, show yourself to the priest, and offer the gift that Moses commanded, for a testimony to them.* (MATTHEW, 8:1-4.)

3. There is great merit in doing good without ostentation. However, it is of even greater merit to hide the hand that gives. This is the indisputable mark of great moral superiority, since in

order to regard things from a higher level than the multitude, it is necessary to be able to disregard the present life and identify oneself with the future life. In a word, to place oneself above humanity, to renounce the satisfaction that comes with recognition from fellow beings and await God's approval. Those who prefer the approval of humans prove they put more faith in them than in God and value the present life more than the future life. If they say anything to the contrary, then they act as if they do not believe in what they themselves are saying.

How many there are who only give with the expectancy that the one who has received will shout it to all sides! How many there are who publicly give large sums of money but who, nevertheless, would not give a penny if the fact were to be hidden! This is why Jesus declared "Those who do good ostensibly have already received their recompense." Indeed, those who seek their glorification on Earth through the good they do have already paid themselves. God owes them nothing; the only thing left to receive is punishment for their pride.

Let not your right hand know what your left-hand does is an image that admirably characterises modest beneficence. Nevertheless, if there is true modesty, then there is also false modesty that is a mere imitation. There are certain people who hide the hand that gives, but take great care to leave a small piece showing, while they look about them to see if anyone has seen them trying to hide it. This is shameful, a parody of Christ's maxim! If humans despise prideful benefactors, what then must they be before God? These also have already received their recompense on Earth. They have been seen and they are satisfied by this fact. That is all they will have.

So then, what recompense can there be for a person who causes the benefits they have given to weigh heavily on the shoulders of the receiver and then demands recognition at all costs? What of that person if they make their position felt by extolling the cost of the sacrifice they made for them? Oh! Here there is not even earthly recompense, seeing that this person finds they are even deprived of the pleasing satisfaction of hearing their name blessed. This is the first punishment for their pride, because instead of rising up to Heaven, the tears they dried in benefit of their own pride will fall back upon the heart of the afflicted person and cause it to ulcerate. From the good that was practised there will be no reward because it was deplored and all benefit that is deplored is counterfeit and without value.

Beneficence practised without ostentation is doubly meritorious. Apart from material charity, there is also moral charity, seeing that this protects the susceptibility of the beneficiary, so enabling them to receive a benefit without feeling resentment or a loss of self-esteem. This safeguards human dignity because accepting a job is very different to receiving alms. However, depending on the manner by which it is rendered, converting work into alms can also humiliate the receiver, and there is always pride and evil in humiliating another. True charity is delicate and inventive in disguising a benefit, avoiding even a simple appearance that might cause hurt, given that all moral friction increases suffering originating from necessity. The giver of true charity will always find tender, affectionate words that will place the receiver at ease, especially when they are in the presence of their benefactor, seeing that prideful charity can crush the receiver. Real generosity assumes total sublimation when the benefactor finds a way to invert their positions, thus becoming the one indebted. This then is what is meant by the words "Let not your left hand know what your right hand is doing."

HIDDEN MISFORTUNES

4. During great calamities, charity is filled with emotion and generous impulses are seen on all sides in the repairing of disasters. However, apart from general disasters, there are millions of private catastrophes that go unnoticed, because there are those who lie on beds of suffering without complaining. These discreet and hidden misfortunes are the ones which true generosity knows how to discover, without waiting for those in need to ask for help.

Who is that woman with the distinctive air, simply dressed, although well cared for, who is accompanied by an equally modestly dressed young girl? They enter a sordid-looking house where the woman is obviously well known because they are greeted with respect as they enter. Where is she going? Up to the garret where a mother lies surrounded by her many children. On their arrival, happiness bursts forth upon the thin faces because the woman has come to soothe their pain. She has brought everything they need, tempered with gentle and consoling words that allows her protégés, who are not professional beggars, to accept these benefits without blushing. The father is in hospital and while he is there the mother is unable to provide the necessities of life. By the grace of this good woman, these poor children will no longer feel cold and hungry; they will go to school well-clothed and, for the smaller ones, the mother's breasts that feed them will not go dry. If any member of this family falls sick, this good woman will not refuse the material care they may need. From their house, she will go on to the hospital to take the father some comforts and put his mind at rest as to his family. At the corner of the road, a carriage awaits and inside is a store of everything destined for her various protégés, for one after the other they all receive visits. She never asks what their religion is or what their opinions are, because she considers them her brothers and sisters and children of God, as are all men and women. When she has finished her rounds, she can say to herself, "I have begun my day well." What is her name? Where does she come from? No one knows. To all those unhappy people she has given a name that indicates nothing. Nevertheless, she is the personification of a consoling angel. Each night a host of blessings rise up to the heavens in her name from Catholics, Jews and Protestants alike.

Why such modest clothing? So as not to insult their misery with her luxury. Why does she take her daughter? So that she too may learn how to practise beneficence, for the young girl also wishes to be charitable. However, the mother says to her "What can you give, my daughter, when you have nothing of your own? If I give you something of mine to give away, what merit will that be for you? In that case it is really I who am giving, so what good would that bring you? That would not be just, so when I visit the sick you will help me treat them. To offer care to someone is to give something of yourself. Do you not think that is sufficient to start with? Well then, nothing could be simpler; you can begin by learning how to make useful articles and clothes for the children. In this manner, you will be giving of yourself." When she is a true Christian, this is how a mother should prepare her children to practise those virtues that Christ taught. Is she a Spiritist? What does that matter!

In her own home, she is a woman of the world because her position demands it of her. Those about her know nothing of what she is doing, as she does not wish for any approval other than that which comes from God and her own conscience. However, one day an unexpected circumstance brought one of her protégés to her door, selling hand-made articles. When the woman saw her, she recognised her benefactor. The lady told her "Be silent! – saying to her - *Tell no one*." - Jesus also spoke in this manner.

THE WIDOW'S MITE

5. Jesus sat over against the treasury and beheld how the people cast money into the treasury: and many that were rich cast in much. And there came a certain poor widow, and she threw in two mites, which makes a farthing. And he called to his disciples, and said to them, Verily I say to you, That this poor widow has cast in more, than all they which have cast into the treasury: For all they did cast in of their abundance; but she of her want did cast in all that she had, even all her living. (MARK, 12:41-44; LUKE, 21:1-4.)

6. Many people lament the fact that they are unable to do all the good they would like to do due to lack of financial resources. They would like to be rich in order, so they say, to be able to make good use of those funds. Their intention is no doubt laudable and in some cases even sincere. However, in the vast majority of cases is this desire totally disinterested? Will there not be those who, whilst wishing to do good to others, would also appreciate being able to begin by doing good to themselves? Are there not those who would like to be in a position to offer themselves a few more pleasures or the enjoyment of something superfluous they lack, after which they would be quite ready to offer the poor what is left over? These hidden thoughts, perhaps concealed even from themselves, could nevertheless be found deep in their hearts if they searched. These second thoughts annul all merit for the intention, seeing that true charity thinks of others before it thinks of self. The sublimity of charity would be for each one to seek within their own work the necessary resources they lack to be able to realise their generous intentions, such as by means of employing their strength, intelligence and aptitudes. In so doing, they would be offering the kind of sacrifice most pleasing to the Lord. Unhappily the majority live out their lives dreaming of ways and means of easily and quickly acquiring riches for themselves without any effort. Perhaps by running after foolish fancies like the discovery of buried treasure, or some favourable random

chance, or even the possibility of receiving an unexpected inheritance, etc. What can be said then about those who expect to find spiritual helpers to second their attainment of these objectives? Certainly, they do not know or understand the sacred finalities of Spiritism and even less of the mission of the spirits whom God permits to communicate with incarnate beings. Hence, they are punished by deceptions. (See THE MEDIUM'S BOOK items 294 & 295.)

Those whose intentions are exempt from personal interest must console themselves with the knowledge that it is impossible to do all the good they would wish to do. They should remember the mite of the poor, taken from meagre resources causing deprivation that weighs more on God's scales than the gold of the rich, who give without depriving themselves of anything. The satisfaction of the former would truly be great if they could help all the destitute on a large scale. But if this is denied them, then they must submit to this fact and limit themselves to what is possible. Furthermore, can tears be dried only with money? Should we remain inactive because we have no money? All those who sincerely wish to be of use to their fellow beings can find thousands of ways of helping. If you look for them they will appear, if not in one way then in another, because there is no one who, having full command of their faculties cannot help someone by offering consolation, minimising both physical and moral suffering or by doing something useful. While money may be lacking, do we all not have time, work and hours of repose to spare that we can offer to help others? This too is the alms of the poor, the widow's mite.

INVITE THE POOR AND THE LAME - GIVE WITHOUT THOUGHT OF RECOMPENSE

7. Then said he also to him that bade him, When you make a dinner or a supper, call not your friends, nor your brethren, neither your kinsmen, nor your rich neighbours; lest they also invite you again, and a recompense is made to you. But when you make a feast, call the poor, the maimed, the lame, the blind: And you will be blessed; for they cannot recompense you: for you shall be recompensed at the resurrection of the just. And when one of them that sat at meat with him heard these things, he said to him, Blessed is he that shall eat bread in the kingdom of God. (LUKE, 14:12-15.)

8. Jesus said, "When we give a banquet, do not invite your friends, but instead invite the poor and the maimed instead." In their literal sense, these words appear to be absurd. However, if we understand their spiritual essence they are in fact sublime. It is not possible that Jesus intended us to invite the maimed and the beggars from the streets to unite around our table instead of friends! His language was almost always figurative as the people of those times were not capable of understanding delicate shades of thought. Therefore, it was necessary for Him to use strong words that could produce colourful images. But the essence of His thought is revealed is this sentence, "And you shall be blessed, for they cannot recompense you." This means that we should not do good for a calculated reward, but only for the pleasure to be felt in so doing. Using a striking comparison, Jesus says invite the poor to your feast because you know they cannot recompense you. By the use of the word '*banquet*' we should understand not the actual repast, but a participation in the abundance enjoyed generally.

However, these words can also be applied in a more literal sense. How many people invite to their table only those who, as is said, will honour them or return the invitation? On the other hand, there are others who find satisfaction in receiving friends and relatives less fortunate than themselves. How many amongst you have people like this in your family? In this way, a great service can sometimes be done without it showing. These people put the teachings of Jesus into practice without recruiting the blind and the maimed only if they do so with benevolence, without ostentation and if they know how to dissimulate the benefit by means of sincere cordiality.

INSTRUCTIONS FROM THE SPIRITS

MATERIAL CHARITY AND MORAL CHARITY

9. "Love one another and do to others what we would wish done to us." All that is religion and moral is contained in these two precepts. If they were observed in this world, then everyone would be happy and there would be no more hate or resentment. I go even further and say there would be no more poverty because all the poor people would be fed from the superfluity of the rich. Neither would poor women be seen dragging wretched children along the dark and sombre streets where I lived during my last incarnation.

Those among you who are rich, think on this a while! Help all those who are less fortunate to the best of your abilities. Give, in order that one-day God may recompense the good you have done. So that on leaving your terrestrial body behind, you may encounter a host of grateful spirits who will receive you at the threshold to a happier world.

Oh! If you could but know the joy felt when, on reaching the world beyond, I found those whom I had been given to serve in my last existence!

Therefore, love your neighbours; love them as you would love yourself, because you now know that by repelling even one wretched person it is always possible that perhaps you are sending away a brother or sister, father or mother or friends from other times. If this happens to be the case, imagine your despair when you recognise them again on reaching the spiritual world!

I wish you to understand exactly what *moral charity* really is. It is something that all can practise and that materially speaking *costs nothing*, but which is most difficult to exercise. Moral charity then comprises of giving support to all our fellow beings and is least done in this inferior world where you now find yourselves incarnated. Believe me, there is great merit in keeping quiet while another, perhaps less intelligent, is speaking. This is but one kind of moral charity. To play deaf when mocking words escape the lips of someone accustomed to deride or to ignore the disdainful smiles of those who are receiving you when they quite wrongly suppose themselves to be far above you, constitutes merit. However, in fact, it will quite often be found that in the spiritual world, *the only real life*, these same people are far below you. The merit to be gained in these situations is not due to humility, but to charity, in as much as to ignore bad behaviour is a moral charity.

Nevertheless, this kind of charity must not be allowed to hinder the other kind already mentioned. Therefore, be especially careful never to despise your fellow beings. You must never forget, but always remember everything I have told you; that if you repel a poor or needy person you may perhaps be repelling a spirit who was once dear to you, who temporarily finds him or herself in an inferior position to you. I have found here one of the destitute from Earth whom happily I had been able to help several times and from whom, in my turn, *I must now implore help.*

Remember that Jesus said that we are all brothers and sisters. Always think of this before repelling a beggar or even someone with a contagious disease, like leprosy. Goodbye. Think of those who suffer and pray for them. - SISTER ROSALIE (Paris, 1860.)

10. My dear friends, I have heard many of you asking yourselves "How can I practise charity if I am frequently without the necessities of life?"

My friends, there are thousands of ways of practising charity. You may do this by means of thought, by words or actions and by praying for the unfortunate who have been abandoned and who die without having lived to any purpose. A prayer from your heart will alleviate their suffering. Also, through giving good advice to your daily companions, as well as to those who are desperate. You can say to those for whom privations have caused embitterment, that has led them to blaspheme against God, "I was like you. I too suffered and felt wretched, but I believed in Spiritism and now I am happy." To those who are old who say, "It is useless, now I am at the end of my journey I will die as I have lived." you must tell them, "God shows equal justice to all. Remember the workers of the last hour." To the children who are preparing to succumb to evil temptations you must say, "God is looking at you, my children." Never get tired of repeating these gentle words to them. One day they will germinate in these childlike minds and instead of becoming vagabonds, you will have made real men and women out of them. This too is charity.

Others amongst you may say "Pooh! We are so numerous here on Earth that God cannot possibly see each one of us." Listen carefully, my friends. When you are on the top of a mountain, do you not see the millions of grains of sand that cover it? Well then, that is how God sees you. He allows you your free will, just as He permits the grains of sand to move with the winds that disperse them. Except for one thing, in His infinite mercy, God has put a vigilant spark in the bottom of your hearts that is called your conscience. Listen to it because it will give you good advice. Sometimes you manage to numb it by setting the spirit of evil against it. Then it is silent. Nevertheless, you can be sure that as soon as you begin to have even a shadow of remorse, your poor rejected conscience will again make itself heard. So listen to it, ask it questions, and frequently you will find yourself consoled by the counsel you have received.

My friends, to every new regiment the general always offer a banner. To you, I offer this maxim of Christ as your watchword, "Love one another." Observe this precept, let everyone unite under this banner and you will find happiness and consolation. - A PROTECTING SPIRIT (Lyon, 1860.)

BENEFICENCE

11. Beneficence my friends, in this world gives you happiness of the heart, being the purest and sweetest delight that neither remorse nor indifference can perturb. Oh! If only you could understand something of the greatness and enjoyment which encompasses the generosity of beauteous souls! It is a sentiment that makes people look at each other as they would look at themselves and gladly disrobe in order to clothe a fellow creature in need! If only you could have as your single occupation that of making others happy! What worldly feats can be compared to those celebrated when both men and women, as Divine representatives, have taken happiness to families who have known only bitterness and vicissitudes. They see mortified faces suddenly glow with hope because without any bread these unfortunate parents only heard their children, who were ignorant of the fact that to live is to suffer, crying out unceasingly with clenched fists the words that were as daggers penetrating the maternal hearts, "I'm hungry!" Oh! You must understand then the joyous impressions of those who see happiness born again, where but a moment before there had been nothing but despair. You must understand the obligations that you owe to your brothers and sisters! Go! Go then to meet misfortune! Go and offer help! Offer help especially against hidden miseries that are the most painful of

all! Dearly beloved brethren, go recalling these words of our Saviour, "When you clothe any one of these little ones, remember it is Me that you clothe!"

Charity! That sublime word that synthesises all the virtues, it is you who will conduct all the peoples of the world towards happiness. It is only by practicing the act of charity that infinite delights can be created for each one in the future. Yet even while you remain exiled on Earth, it will be your consolation, a foretaste of the joys to be possessed later, when you find yourselves united in the bosom of the God of love. It was you, divine Virtue, that enabled me to experience the only moments of satisfaction I was to enjoy while on Earth. I hope my incarnate brothers and sisters on this planet will believe these amicable words when I say it is within charity that you must seek peace of heart, contentment of the soul and the remedy for life's afflictions. Oh! When you are on the point of accusing God, first cast your eyes down and you will see all the miseries waiting to be alleviated, the poor children without families, the old without even a friendly hand to close their eyes when death claims them! How much good there is waiting to be done! Oh! Do not complain! On the contrary, offer thanks to God and lavish handfuls of sympathy, understanding and money on all who, disinherited from worldly possessions, languish in suffering and isolation. You will reap sweet happiness in the world and later... Only God knows! - ADOLF, Bishop of Algiers (Bordeaux, 1861.)

12. Be good and charitable, that is the key to Heaven that you hold in your hands. The entirety of eternal happiness is contained in this maxim: Love one another. The soul cannot elevate itself to the high spiritual realms except by devotion to one's fellow creatures; it will not find happiness and consolation except in charitable impulses. Be good and sustain your brothers and sisters; root out that horrible ulcer known as selfishness. In fulfilling this duty, the pathway to eternal happiness will open up before you.

Besides, who amongst you has not yet felt their heart beat with jubilation and inner joy at the narration of an act of wonderful dedication or some truly charitable act? If you only seek the pleasure to be felt from a good deed, then you will remain forever on the pathway to spiritual advancement. Good examples are not wanting; what is rare is simply goodwill. Take note that history keeps pious remembrance of a multitude of good men and women.

Did Christ not tell you everything concerning the virtues of charity and love? Why then do you leave His divine Teaching aside? Why do you close your ears to His divine words and your hearts to His gentle maxims? I wish you would demonstrate more interest and more faith in the reading of the New Testament. However, as you despise this book, considering it to be a compilation of hollow words, a closed letter, this admirable code has been forgotten. All your ills stem from your voluntary abandonment of this résumé of the Divine Laws. Read the scintillating pages of the devotion shown by Jesus and meditate upon them!

Those of you who are strong, prepare yourselves; those who are weak, make your gentleness and faith into your arms. Let us be more persuasive and more constant in the dissemination of your new Teachings. It is only to give you encouragement, to stimulate your zeal and your virtues, that God has given permission for this manifestation. But if you so wished, God's help and your own free-will would be sufficient for all your needs, because spiritual manifestations are only produced for those whose eyes are closed and those with troubled hearts.

Charity is the fundamental virtue that will have to support the entire earthly structure of terrestrial virtues. Without this anchorage, there would be no others. Without charity, there would be no hope of a better life and no interest in moral guidelines. Without charity, there is no faith, because faith is nothing more than pure luminosity that makes a charitable soul become brilliant with light.

In all worlds, charity is the eternal anchor of salvation, the most pure emanation that comes directly from the Creator, part of His own virtue, given by Him to all creatures. How can we despise this supreme generosity? What heart knowing this is so perverse as to suppress and expel this divine sentiment? What child of God is so evil as to rebel against the sweet caress of charity?

I do not presume to speak of what I did, because spirits also have the power of their works and their modesty. Nevertheless, I believe that the work I began during my earthly life is the kind of work that will contribute most to the alleviation of our fellow beings. I frequently see spirits who, having asked, are given the work of continuing my task as their mission in life. I see them, these generous and beloved brothers and sisters, in their pious and divine ministry practising these virtues that I recommend, with a joy that can only be derived from a life of dedication and sacrifice. It is my immeasurable good fortune to see how their condition is honoured, how they are protected and esteemed in the mission they perform. Therefore, fellow beings of good and strong willpower, unite yourselves so that you may continue the work of expanding the diffusion of charity. You will find your reward in the very exercise of this virtue and there are no bounds as to the spiritual happiness that may be felt, even in the present life. So be united, and love one another according to the Teachings of Christ. So be it! - SAINT VINCENT DE PAUL (Paris, 1858.)

13. They call me Charity and I follow the principal path that leads to God. Accompany me, since I am the goal for all to aim at.

This morning I went on my habitual rounds and now I come with great anguish in my heart to say to you: Oh! My friends! How many miseries and tears! So much must be done to dry all those tears and put to rights all those miseries! In vain, I tried to console some of the poor mothers by whispering in their ears, "Courage! There are good souls watching over you and you will not be abandoned, have patience! God exists! He loves you; you are His chosen ones!" They seemed to hear me and turned their startled eyes in my direction. I could read from the appearance of their bodies, that terrible oppressor of the spirit, that they were hungry. Even if my words brought a little serenity to their hearts, it was no comfort for their stomachs. I repeated, "Courage! Courage!" Then one poor mother, still very young and with a small child, held it up with outstretched arms as if asking me for protection for that small creature, who found only insufficient nourishment in those sterile breasts.

Elsewhere, my friends, I saw destitute old people who, being without work, found themselves without shelter becoming victims to all manner of sufferings and hardships. Being ashamed of their misery and never having begged, they found themselves lacking in courage to implore pity from passers-by. With my heart bursting with compassion I, who possess nothing, have turned to begging for them. Therefore, I go from place to place in order to stimulate beneficence and inspire good thoughts in generous and compassionate hearts. This is why I am come here to tell you that hereabouts there are those who are wretched, in whose hovels is no bread, whose stoves are without fuel and whose beds are without blankets. I do not tell you what you must do. I leave this initiative to your kind hearts. If I were to tell you how to proceed, you would gain no credit for your good deeds. I say only that I am Charity and I extend my hands towards you through those of your suffering brothers and sisters.

However, if I ask, I also give and give generously. I am inviting you to a great banquet wherein I will furnish a tree upon which all will be satiated! See how beautiful it is, how full of flowers and fruits! Go! Go! Gather all the fruits of this magnificent tree that is called beneficence. Then, in place of the foliage and fruit you have taken away, I will fasten to it all the good deeds you have practised. Then I will take this tree to God and He will load it again, in as much as beneficence is inexhaustible. Accompany me then, my friends, so that I may count you amongst those who follow my banner! Do not fear, for I will conduct you along the pathway to salvation, for I am *Charity*. - CARITA, martyred in Rome. (Lyon, 1861.)

14. There are various ways of practising charity, which many of you confuse with the giving of alms. However, there is considerable difference between the two. Alms, my friends, are sometimes useful because they can bring alleviation to those who are poor. However, this is almost always humiliating, not only for the giver, but also for the receiver. On the other hand, charity joins the benefactor to the one who is receiving the benefit because it can be disguised in so many ways! It is possible to be charitable even to friends and relations, simply by being indulgent to one another, by mutually forgiving all weaknesses and by taking care not to hurt anyone's self-respect. You, who are Spiritists, can be charitable in the manner in which you behave towards others who think differently from you, by inducing those who are less enlightened to believe without shocking them, without attacking their own convictions. You can also attract them lovingly to our meetings, so they may listen to us and so that we may know how to discover a way into their hearts. All this is just one aspect of charity.

Listen now to what is meant by charity towards the poor, those disinherited of this world, who will be recompensed by God if they are able to accept their miseries without complaint. This depends upon you and the way in which you offer help. You will understand what I mean by the following example.

Several times each week, I go to watch a meeting of women of all ages. For us you know, they are all sisters. What do they do?

They work quickly, very quickly with their agile fingers. I see how radiant are their faces and note how their hearts all beat in unison. What is the purpose of all this work? It is because winter approaches, which will be very hard for those who are poor. During the summer, those busy ants could not put by all the necessary provisions and most of their utensils have been pawned. The needy mothers are anxious and frequently weep thinking of their children who will go cold and hungry during the long winter! Poor unfortunate women, be patient, for God has inspired others wealthier than yourselves, who have joined together to make clothes! One of these days, when the Earth is covered with snow and you are complaining and accusing God of being unjust, which is what you always do and say every time you suffer, then you will see someone appear. The good workers who have established themselves as labourers for the poor will have sent them. Yes, it is for you that they work like that and your complaints will be transformed into blessings because, in the hearts of those who are unhappy, love follows close behind hate.

As these workers need encouragement, communications from the Good Spirits come from all sides. The men folk also take part in this society, bringing their help in the form of readings, which are pleasing to all. As recompense for the enthusiasm of everyone and of certain individuals in particular, we, the spirits, promise to bring these hard-working labourers good customers, who will pay in the form of blessings, that after all is the only currency acceptable in Heaven. We also assure them without fear of contradiction that this currency will never be lacking for any one of these workers. - CARITA (Lyon, 1861.)

15. My dear friends, every day I hear some of those amongst you say, "I am poor, so I cannot offer any charity," and yet each day I see that you lack indulgence towards your fellow beings. You forgive nothing and set yourselves up as very severe judges, without even asking if you would like the same done to you. Is

indulgence not a charity? You, who can do nothing more than offer the charity of indulgence, do at least that, but do it grandly. Referring to material charity, I would like to tell you a story from the other world.

Two men having just died, God was heard to say that while these men had been alive all their good deeds were to be deposited in two separate sacks and that on their death the sacks would be weighed. When each of them reached their last hours, God sent word for them to bring their two sacks. One was crammed full, voluminous and resounding with the metal it contained. The other was so small and thin that it was possible to see through the cloth the few coins it contained. Each man recognised the sack that belonged to him, "This one is mine. I was always poor. Ah! I had almost nothing to give." Nevertheless, what a surprise when they were put on the scales, because the voluminous one became light in weight and the small one showed itself to be heavy; so much so that it raised the first sack high into the air! Then God spoke to the rich man saying, "It is true that you gave much, but you did so from ostentation and to see your name on view in all the temples of pride. Furthermore, in giving you deprived yourself of nothing. Go to the left and be satisfied that the alms you gave count for something, however small." Then God spoke to the poor man saying, "You gave very little, my friend, but each one of your coins that are on the scales, represents a privation for you. Even if you did not distribute alms, you were charitable and the best thing is that you did it naturally, without preoccupying yourself whether it would be put into your account. You were indulgent and did not judge your neighbours; on the contrary, you found excuses for all their actions. Go to the right and you will receive your recompense." - A PROTECTING SPIRIT (Lyon, 1861).

16. Could not the rich and happy woman, who does not have to occupy her time with household duties, dedicate some of the hours of her day to useful work in aid of her fellow beings? Could she

not buy clothes from the money that is left over from her pleasures, for those less fortunate than herself, who shiver with the cold? Could she not make thick warm clothing with her delicate hands, or help a mother-to-be clothe her unborn child? If her own child goes without some ribbons and lace, at least a poor child will have something to keep it warm. By working for the poor and the needy, you are working in the vineyard of the Lord.

And you, a poor labourer, who have nothing superfluous, but being full of love for your fellow brothers and sisters, also wish to give something from the little you have. Give then a few hours of your time, which is the only treasure you possess. Make and sell some of those elegant handicrafts that tempt those who are happy, that you can perhaps make in your evenings. Then you too can play your part in assisting your brothers and sisters in need. Perhaps you will have a few ribbons less, but you will be giving shoes to the barefoot.

And you, women who have vowed your lives to God, continue to work with your undertakings. But take care that these achievements are not for the exclusive adornment of your chapels, to call attention to your abilities and your patience! Work, my daughters, so that the product of your undertakings are destined to help your brothers and sisters before God. The poor are His dearly beloved children; to work for them is to glorify Him. Be unto them the providence that says 'God gives sustenance unto the birds of the sky.' Exchange the gold and silver threads with which you embroider, for food and clothes for those who have none. Do this and your work will be blessed.

All those able to produce should give! Give your talents, inspirations and hearts and God will bless you. Poets and literary people, who are only read by those who are worldly in order to satisfy their leisure, dedicate some of the product of your works to help the needy! Painters, sculptors, artists of all kinds! May you too use intelligence to benefit your fellow beings, for your glory will be no less and some of your sufferings will be avoided.

Everyone can give! Whatever your social standing you will always find something to share with another. From whatever it is that God has bestowed upon you, a part of what He has awarded is owed to those who lack the necessities of life seeing that, in their place, you would wish others to share with you. Perhaps your earthly treasures will be a little less. Nevertheless, your heavenly treasures will likewise be increased. It is there, in Heaven, that you will reap a hundredfold of all that you have sown as benefits to others in this world. - JOHN (Bordeaux, 1861.)

COMPASSION

17. Compassion is the virtue that draws you closer to the angels. It is a sister to charity, which also conducts you to God. Ah! Allow your hearts to be moved by compassion before the spectacle of the miseries and sufferings of your fellow human beings. Your tears will act as a balm on their wounds, and when shed out of sympathy will restore their hope and resignation. Oh! What sweetness is to be felt! Nevertheless, it is true that this same sweetness has a certain bitterness about it because it springs up alongside misery. However, it does not have the acrid flavour of worldly pleasures, nor does it bring with it the pungent deceptions of emptiness that these pleasures leave behind. The enveloping gentle penetration of this sentiment fills the soul with joy. Compassion and pity, when deeply felt, are acts of loving; love is devotion; devotion is the forgetfulness of self and it is this, combined with abnegation in favour of those less fortunate than we are that is the height of virtue. It was that virtue which the Divine Messiah practised throughout His entire life and which He taught in His saintly and sublime teachings. When these teachings are fully restored to their original pureness and when humanity

submits to them, then the world will become a happy place wherein will reign harmony, peace and love.

The most appropriate sentiment for making you progress, by dominating your selfishness and pride, that predisposes the soul towards humility, beneficence and the loving of one another, is compassion! This is the same compassion that moves deep inside when you lay eyes on the suffering of your fellow beings that impels you to extend a helping hand and brings tears of sympathy to your eyes. Accordingly, never stifle this celestial emotion within your heart. Do not proceed as do those who are hard and selfish, who turn aside from the afflicted because the sight of their miseries perturbs their cheerful lives for an instant. Be fearful of remaining indifferent when you could be of help. Tranquillity, bought at the expense of a guilty indifference, is like the tranquillity of the Dead Sea, at the bottom of which lies a vast hidden mass of putrid slime and corruption.

However, compassion is far removed from causing disturbance and inconvenience, of which the selfish person is so afraid. Nevertheless, on contact with the misfortunes and miseries of another person the soul, rebounding upon itself, experiences a natural and profound anguish that beyond doubt vibrates throughout the whole being and causes it to be painfully affected. Nevertheless, the compensation is great when compassion suffices to give courage and hope to an unhappy brother or sister who is moved by a friendly handshake. Whereupon they turn to you affectionately with tear-filled eyes, perhaps from emotion and gratitude, even before they raise these same eyes to Heaven in thanks for having sent someone to console and sustain them in their hour of need. Compassion then, is the melancholic but celestial precursor of charity, being the first of all the virtues that she has as a sister and whose benefits she prepares and ennobles. - MICHAEL (Bordeaux, 1862.)

ORPHANS

18. Brothers and sisters, love the orphans. If you only knew how sad it is to be abandoned, especially in infancy! God permits there to be orphans so that we may be motivated to be their parents. What an act of divine charity it is to protect a creature that has been sadly abandoned, to stop them from being hungry and cold and administer to their soul, so they may not fall prey to vice! When someone offers a helping hand to an abandoned being, they are agreeable to God because they have understood and practised His law. Meditate on the possibility that frequently the child you are helping maybe someone who was very dear to you in a past incarnation. If they were able to recognise you, it would no longer be an act of charity but a simple obligation. In this way my friends, every sufferer is your brother or sister and so has a right to your kindness. However, not the kind of charity that hurts feelings, nor yet the kind of alms that burns the hand that receives it, for unfortunately help is frequently accompanied by bitterness! How many times these sufferers would rather have refused if it were not for the fact of sickness or death being their only other option. So, give with delicacy and together with any benefits you may offer, also give the most precious benefit of all, that of a kindly word, a loving gesture and a friendly smile. Avoid being patronising, which only turns the dagger in the already bleeding heart. Consider that by doing good, you are working for your own benefit as well as for others. – A FAMILY SPIRIT (Paris, 1860.)

BENEFICENCE RECOMPENSED BY INGRATITUDE

19. *What should be thought of those who, having received ingratitude in payment for benefits given, cease to practice goodness, to avoid contact with more people that are ungrateful?*

There is far more selfishness in these people than charity, seeing that they do good only for the purpose of receiving demonstrations of acknowledgement and consequently do not do so disinterestedly. The only act of goodness acceptable to God is the one done with complete disinterest. There is also pride in these people, since those who behave in this manner take pleasure in the humbleness shown by the receivers of the benefits, when they come to lay before them the testimony of their gratitude. Those who seek reward on Earth for the good they have done will not then receive it in Heaven. However, God will esteem all who do not seek their rewards here on Earth.

You should always help the weak, although knowing beforehand that you will receive no thanks for your help. You can always be sure that if the person to whom you did a service forgets, God will take this even more into account than if the beneficiary had paid their debt. *If God permits that sometimes you are paid with ingratitude, this is only to test your perseverance in the practice of goodness.*

Who knows but that a momentarily forgotten benefit will not produce good fruits in the future? You can be sure it is a seed that will germinate with time. Unfortunately, we never see anything but the present! We work for ourselves and never for others. The receiving of benefits will finally soften even the most torpid heart; these may be forgotten in this world, but after having disposed of its outer garment, the spirit who has received will remember this fact and this remembrance will be their punishment. That spirit will deplore its ingratitude and desire to make reparation by paying the debt in a future life, frequently seeking an existence of dedication to its benefactor. In this way, without even suspecting, you will have contributed to the moral advancement of that spirit. You will come to recognise the truth in the words 'a benefit is never lost.' Besides which you will also have worked for yourself, since you will have earned merit for having done good without self-interest and without becoming disanimated by deceptions.

Ah! My friends, if you knew of all the ties that link your present life with those of past existences! If you could see the immense number of relationships that join us, one to the other, for the purpose of mutual progress! Then you would admire even more the wisdom and goodness of the Lord, Who allows us to relive so as to be able, one day, to reach Him. - A PROTECTING GUIDE (Sens, 1862.)

EXCLUSIVE BENEVOLENCE

20. *Is it right to practise beneficence exclusively amongst people of the same opinions, beliefs or political parties?*

No, because it is exactly the idea of sects and parties that must be abolished, for all human beings are brothers and sisters. True Christians only see their human companions as brothers and sisters, never enquiring as to beliefs or opinions before offering help. Would a Christian be obeying the precepts of Jesus Christ, Who tells us to love even our enemies, if they were to repel an unfortunate person just because they professed a different belief? So, always help without asking anyone to give an account of their conscience, because, if they are enemies of religion, this is just the way to make them come to love it, whereas by repelling them you only make them hate religion. - SAINT LOUIS (Paris, 1860.)

CHAPTER 14

HONOUR YOUR FATHER AND YOUR MOTHER

Filial devotion. - Who is my mother and who are my brothers? Corporeal kinship and spiritual kinship. – INSTRUCTIONS FROM THE SPIRITS: Children's ingratitude and family ties.

1. You know the commandments: Do not commit adultery, Do not kill, Do not steal, Do not bear false witness, Defraud not, Honour your father and mother. (MARK, 10:19; LUKE, 18:20; MATTHEW, 19:18 &19.)

2. Honour your father and your mother, that your days may be long upon the land which the Lord your God gives to you. (Decalogue, Exodus, 20:12)

FILIAL DEVOTION

3. The commandment, 'Honour your father and your mother' is an inference from the general laws of charity and love towards our neighbours, seeing that those who do not love their mother and father cannot then love their fellow beings. However, with regard to parents, here the word *honour* contains an extra obligation, which is filial devotion. God wishes to show us that respect, esteem, obedience, caring, submission and deference should be joined to love. All these put together involve an obligation for each person to carry out what is demanded by charity with regard to one's neighbour, which implies an even more rigorous duty towards parents. This duty naturally extends itself to those who take the place of a mother or father and whose merit is much greater because their devotion has nothing of obligation. God will rigorously punish all violations of this commandment.

To honour your mother and father consists in not only showing respect, but also helping them in their needs, offering them rest in their old age and surrounding them with care, just as they did for us during our infancy.

Above all, it is necessary to demonstrate true filial devotion to destitute parents. Do you think this commandment is being kept by those who, believing they are doing a great deal of good, offer only the strictest necessities to their parents, so as to avoid them dying from hunger, while they deprive themselves of nothing? Alternatively, when so as not to leave them unsheltered, they relegate them to the worst rooms in the house, while reserving the best and most comfortable for themselves? The parents are even fortunate when this is not done with ill will, or when they are obliged to pay heavily for the rest of their lives by being forced to do all the domestic cleaning! Is it that old and feeble parents must be servants for their children who are younger and stronger? Did their mother make them pay for her milk when they were babies? Did she count the sleepless nights she had when they were ill or the steps she had to take in order to guarantee they lacked for nothing? No, children do not owe their parents only the strictest necessities; they also owe them, according to their possibilities, all those little extras, like thoughtfulness and loving care, which are nothing more than interest on what they themselves received, being payment of a sacred debt. This then is the only filial devotion that pleases God.

Alas for those who forget what they owe to those who sustained them in their hour of weakness, who, with the giving of a physical life, also gave them moral life and many times imposed upon themselves great privations in order to guarantee the well-being of their children! Woe unto all those who are ungrateful, for they will be punished with ingratitude and abandonment; they will be hurt in their dearest affections, *sometimes even in the present life,* but certainly in a future one, wherein they will suffer themselves what they have made others suffer!

It is true that some parents neglect their duty and are not all they should be to their children. However, it is only God who has the competence to punish, not the children. These are not able to judge because they have perhaps deserved their parents' behaviour. The law of charity demands that evil is paid with goodness and that we be indulgent with the imperfections of others. Moreover, it is required that we should not speak against our neighbour, that we forget and forgive all grievances and that we love even our enemies. Therefore, how much greater must be our obligations when related to our parents! Regarding children in matters relating to their parents, they too should take as a rule of conduct all those principles of Jesus concerning our fellow beings. They must be made aware that all reprehensible behaviour towards strangers is even more reprehensible when related to parents; that what might be only a small offence in the first case, may be considered as a serious crime in the second, because here the offence of lack of charity is joined to that of ingratitude.

4. God said to honour your father and your mother so that you may live a long time in the land that the Lord your God shall give you. Why did He promise earthly life as recompense and not heavenly life? The explanation lies in the words: 'that God shall give you' which, having been omitted in the modern formula of the Decalogue's, has altered the meaning. First, in order to be able to understand clearly, we must go back to the situation and the ideas existing amongst the Hebrews at that time. They still knew nothing of a future life, as they were unable to see anything beyond the physical. They had then to be impressed more by what they saw, than by what they could not see. So God spoke to them in a language well within their reach of understanding, as one would expect to do with a child, to put them into a perspective that could satisfy them. At that time, they were still in the desert; the

land *to be given* by God was the Promised Land and the object of their aspirations. They wished for nothing more and God said that they would live there for a long time. That is to say, they would possess the land for a long time if they kept His commandments.

Now, by the time of the advent of Jesus, they had more advanced ideas. The time had come for them to receive less material nourishment and Jesus Himself began to teach about spiritual life by saying: "My kingdom is not of this world; it is there and not here on Earth that you will receive recompense for all the good you have practised." With these words, the Promised Land ceased to be material and became a spiritual homeland. That is why, when He called their attention to the commandment 'Honour your father and your mother,' it was not this world that is promised, but Heaven. (See chapters 2 & 3.)

WHO IS MY MOTHER AND WHO ARE MY BROTHERS?

5. And the multitude came together again, so that they could not so much as eat bread. And when his friends heard of it, they went out to lay hands on him: for they said, He is beside himself. There came then his brethren and his mother, and, standing without, sent to him, calling him. And the multitude sat about him, and they said to him, Behold, your mother and your brethren without seek for you. And he answered them, saying, Who is my mother, or my brethren? And he looked round about on them which sat about him, and said, Behold my mother and my brethren! For whosoever shall do the will of God, the same is my brother, and my sister, and mother. (MARK, 3:20-21 & 31-35; MATTHEW, 12:46-50.)

6. Some of the words used by Jesus appear to be quite extraordinary when compared with His goodness, kindness and unalterable benevolence. Those who are incredulous never cease to find an argument in this fact, alleging that He contradicted

Himself. However, it is undeniable that His teachings has as its basic principle and foundation stone the Laws of Charity and Love. Well then, is it possible that He would destroy on the one side what He had built on the other? Therefore, we arrive at the following precise conclusion: that if certain propositions made by Jesus are in contradictions to this basic principle, then these words attributed to Him have either been wrongly reproduced, wrongly understood or were never pronounced by Him.

7. Understandably, it causes great amazement that in this passage Jesus showed so much indifference towards His relatives and in a way even repudiated His mother.

With regard to His brothers, we know they did not greatly esteem Him. Being spirits of little evolution, they did not understand His mission; they thought Him to be eccentric in His ways and His teaching did not even touch them, to the extent that not one of them became His disciple. It was said that they shared, at least up to a point, the same preconceptions as His enemies. In short, it is a known fact that whenever He appeared in the family He was received more as a stranger than as a brother. John tells us quite clearly that *they did not believe in Him.* (See John 7:5.)

Concerning His mother, no one can deny the tenderness and affection He devoted to her. However, it is equally our obligation to agree that she did not fully understand her son's mission, since it was noticed that she never followed His teachings, nor did she testify for Him as did John the Baptist. Her predominating feature was maternal solicitude. Nevertheless, to suppose that He denied His mother is not to know His character. Such an idea could not have found refuge in someone who said 'honour your father and your mother.' Then it is necessary to find another meaning for His words, which were usually enveloped in a mist of allegoric form.

Never losing an opportunity to teach, Jesus took advantage of the moment and the arrival of His family to show clearly the difference that exists between bodily kinship and spiritual kinship.

CORPOREAL KINSHIP AND SPIRITUAL KINSHIP

8. Blood ties do not necessarily create bonds between spirits. The body comes from the body, but the spirit does not proceed from the spirit since the spirit already existed before the formation of the body. The parents do not create the spirit of the child; they do nothing more than supply the material wrapping; although it is their duty to help the intellectual and moral development of their child in order to further its progress.

Those incarnated in the same family, especially as close relations, are as often as not, congenial spirits linked by past relationships, which express themselves during their earthly lives by their reciprocated affections. However, it can also happen that they are complete strangers to each other, or they may be distant from each other due to past aversions, which while on Earth are translated into mutual antagonisms that serve as probation. The real family ties are not those of blood then, but those of mutual sympathy and the communion of ideas that hold spirits together before, during and after their incarnations. From this, it follows that two people born of different parents may be more like brothers or sisters, than if they were of the same blood. They can attract each other, search for each other and so feel happy together. Whereas two blood brothers may be repelled by each other, as is frequently seen. This is a moral problem that only Spiritism can resolve through the explanation of the plurality of existences. (See chapter 4, item 13.)

Therefore, we see there are two kinds of families: *the families with spiritual ties and the families with bodily ties*. In the first case, these ties are durable and strengthen with purification, perpetuating in the spiritual worlds by means of the various migrations of the soul. In the second case, the ties are as fragile as the material body, extinguishing with time and in many cases dissolving morally, even in the actual existence. This was what Jesus was trying to make comprehensible when He said to His disciples "Here is my mother and my brothers by spiritual ties, because all those who do the bidding of My Father, who is in Heaven, are my brothers, my sisters and my mother."

The hostility felt by His blood brothers is clearly expressed in this narrative from Saint Mark, when it says that they intended to lay their hands on Jesus, under the pretext that He had *lost His spirit*, or *gone out of His mind*. On being informed of their arrival and knowing the sentiments they harboured against Him it was only natural for Jesus, speaking in spiritual terms, to refer to His disciples as His brothers and sisters. Although His mother was accompanying His brothers, Jesus generalised the teachings, which in no way implies He intended to declare that His mother, according to the physical body, was nothing to Him in spirit nor that she deserved only indifference, as He proved on many occasions.

INSTRUCTIONS FROM THE SPIRITS

CHILDREN'S INGRATITUDE AND FAMILY TIES

9. Ingratitude is one of the most immediate fruits of selfishness and always causes revolt in honest hearts. However, the ingratitude of children towards their parents shows an even more hateful trait of character. It is especially this point of view we are going to consider, so we may analyse the causes and effects of this attitude. In this case, as in all others, Spiritism offers enlightenment on one of the greatest problems of the human heart.

When a spirit leaves the Earth plane, it takes with it all the passions and all the virtues inherent in its nature, going on to improve itself in the spirit world or to remain stationary until it desires to receive enlightenment. Accordingly, many spirits return to the spiritual world full of hate and violence, as well as full of insatiable desires for vengeance. Nevertheless, there are always some amongst them who are more advanced and so able to perceive a faint glimmer of truth, enabling them to appreciate the disastrous consequences of these passions, which in turn induces them to make good resolutions for the future. These spirits understand that in order to reach God there is only one password: *Charity*. However, there can be no charity without being able to forget affronts and insults. Neither can there be any charity if there is no forgiveness or if the heart is filled with hate.

Then, by unprecedented efforts, these spirits manage to observe those they had hated while on Earth. However, on seeing them again, animosity is once more aroused in their hearts, causing revolt at the idea of forgiving them and even more at the thought of any personal renouncement. Above all, they are revolted at the thought of loving those who had destroyed their worldly possessions, their honour or perhaps even their family. Meanwhile, the hearts of these unhappy spirits continue to be disturbed and upset; they hesitate and waver, agitated by contrasting sentiments. If their good resolutions predominate, then they pray to God and implore the Good Spirits to give them strength at this the most decisive moment of their ordeal.

Finally, after years of meditation and prayer, the spirit takes the opportunity of a physical body that is, as yet, merely a project within the family of the one who is detested. This spirit then asks the Spirits designated to transmit orders, for permission to fulfil here on Earth the destiny of that body which is about to be formed. What then will be this spirit's behaviour within the chosen family? That will depend on the greater or less degree of persistence towards the good resolutions made by that spirit. The incessant contact with those it hates constitutes a terrible test, under which it may frequently succumb if its desire to win is not sufficiently strong. In this manner, and according to whether or not the good resolutions predominate, the spirit will be either a friend or enemy to those it was called to live amongst. This is the explanation for the hates and instinctive repulsions often noted between certain children that appear to be inexplicable. In fact, there is nothing in the present life that could have caused such antipathy. In order to find the cause, it would be necessary to look back into the past.

Oh! Spiritists! You must understand the great part that Humanity plays! You must understand that when a body is produced, the soul that incarnates in it has come from space in order to progress. So acquaint yourselves with your duties and put all your love into bringing this soul nearer to God. This is the mission with which you have been entrusted and for which you will receive just recompense if you fulfil your trust faithfully. The care and education given by you will help in its improvement and future well-being. Remember that God will ask of every mother and father: What have you done with the child entrusted to your care? If through any fault of yours it has remained backwards, then as punishment, you will have to watch it amongst the suffering spirits, when it depended on you to help it towards happiness. Then, you yourselves, assailed by remorse, will ask that it be permitted for you to remedy your errors. You will request for yourself and your child another incarnation in which you will surround that spirit with better care and in which, being full of gratitude, this spirit will then reciprocate by loving you.

So then, do not reject the child who repels its mother or who is ungrateful; for it is not mere chance that has made it like that and then it was given to you. An imperfect intuition of the past is revealed by these attitudes and from this, we can deduce that one or the other harbours great hate or has been mortally offended; that one or the other has come to pardon or to atone. Mothers! Embrace the child who causes vexation and say: One of us is guilty! Make yourselves worthy of the Divine enjoyment that God has associated with maternity by teaching your children that they are on Earth in order to perfect themselves, to love and to bless others. Oh! But there are many among you who have actually maintained and developed these innate bad traits, acquired in past lives, due to blameworthy weaknesses or through negligence, instead of eliminating them by means of a good education! Later on, with hearts that are lacerated by the ingratitude of your children, you will begin your atonement, even in this life.

Nevertheless, your task is not as difficult as it may seem. It does not require the wisdom of the world; both an ignorant or wise person may discharge this duty and Spiritism will help you to do just that, by giving you the possibility of knowing the causes of the imperfections in the human heart.

Coming from past existences, these good or evil instincts will manifest themselves from early childhood and it is necessary that parents study them. All badness originates from selfishness and pride. So be on the lookout for the least sign that will reveal the existence of such vices and take care to combat them, without waiting for them to take deep root. Do as the good gardener does: Cut off all defective shoots as soon as they appear on the tree. If you allow selfishness and pride to develop, do not be surprised if later on you are repaid by ingratitude. When parents have done everything possible for the moral advancement of their children, even if they have not been successful, then they have nothing with which to reproach themselves and their consciences may remain tranquil. For the natural anguish resulting from the unproductiveness of their efforts, God reserves a great and immense consolation. This is the *certainty* that it is only a brief delay, that it will be given to them to conclude in another existence the work that has already begun and one day their ungrateful child will recompense them with love. (See chapter 13, item 19.)

God does not give a trial superior to the strength of the person who has asked for it. He only permits those tests that can be fulfilled. Therefore, if this does not happen, it is not for lack of possibilities, but for lack of willpower. In effect, how many there are who instead of resisting their bad tendencies, actually revel in them. It is for these people that are reserved weeping and cries of anguish in future existences. Nevertheless, we should wonder at God's unbounded Goodness because He never shuts the door to repentance. The day will come when the culprit, tired of suffering and their pride finally humbled, will perceive that God is holding out His hands to receive the prodigal child who throws itself at His feet. Now listen well to what I am about to tell you - *the harshest trials are almost always the indication of the end to suffering and to a certain perfecting of the spirit, as long as they are accepted with all thought focused on God.* These are in fact supreme moments during which above all else, it behoves the spirit not to cause failure due to constant complaining, or the fruits of the trial will be lost, so making it necessary to begin again from the beginning. Instead of complaining, thank God for the opportunity He has given you to triumph, so that He may bestow the prize of victory upon you. Then when you leave the vortex of this earthly world, to enter into the world of spirit, you will be acclaimed as a soldier returning triumphant from the fray.

Of all the trials that exist, the hardest to bear are those that affect the heart. A person who is able to support misery and material privation with courage, frequently succumbs under the weight of domestic bitterness, goaded on by the ingratitude of members of the family. Oh, what a terribly pungent anguish this is! Nevertheless, in these circumstances what can more effectively renew moral courage than the knowledge of the causes of the evil? Even if there are protracted lacerations, it is certain that there are no eternal despairs, because it is not possible for God to wish that any one of His creatures suffer indefinitely. What can be more comforting and more animating than the idea that the abbreviation of suffering depends on each effort made to destroy the evil within ourselves, which is the cause of all of our miseries. In order to be able to do this, it is necessary that we do not confine our vision exclusively to this planet, nor to only a single existence. Humanity must lift itself up so that it becomes possible to see the infinity of both the past and the future. When this happens, then God's everlasting justice becomes apparent and you will be able to wait patiently, because all that had previously appeared to be absolute monstrosity on this planet will have become explainable. The various wounds that you have received will appear as mere scratches. In this rapid glance cast over the whole scene, all family ties will present themselves in their true light. You will no longer see only the fragile material ties that join various members of a family together, but also the lasting ties of the spirit that penetrate and consolidate with the process of purification, instead of being broken by the effect of reincarnation.

Families are formed by groupings of spirits who are induced to gather together because of their affinities, moral progress and affections. During their terrestrial migrations, these same spirits seek each other out in order to group themselves as they do in space, so giving origin to united and homogeneous families. If during their peregrinations it so happens they are temporarily separated, then they will meet again later on, happy for the new progress that has been accomplished. As they are not allowed to work exclusively for their own benefit, God permits that less advanced spirits incarnate amongst them in order that these may receive good advice and examples that will help them. Sometimes these spirits cause perturbation in the midst of the others, which serves as both a trial and a task to be fulfilled. Therefore, always receive these perturbed spirits as your brothers and sisters; help them and afterwards, when once again they are in the spiritual world, the family will be able to congratulate itself for having saved an outcast, who in their turn may save others. - SAINT AUGUSTINE (Paris, 1862.)

CHAPTER 15

WITHOUT CHARITY THERE IS NO SALVATION

What the spirit needs in order to be saved. - The parable of the Good Samaritan. - The greatest of the commandments. – The need for charity according to Saint Paul. - Without the Church there is no salvation. - Without truth there is no salvation. - INSTRUCTIONS FROM THE SPIRITS: Without charity there is no salvation.

WHAT THE SPIRIT NEEDS IN ORDER TO BE SAVED - THE PARABLE OF THE GOOD SAMARITAN

1. When the Son of man shall come in his glory, and all the holy angels with him, then shall he sit upon the throne of his glory: And before him shall be gathered all nations: and he shall separate them one from another, as a shepherd divideth his sheep from the goats: and he shall set the sheep on his right hand, but the goats on the left.

Then shall the King say to the them on his right hand, Come, you who are blessed of my Father, inherit the kingdom prepared for you from the foundation of the world: For I was hungry, and you gave me meat: I was thirsty, and you gave me drink: I was a stranger, and you took me in: Naked, and you clothed me: I was sick, and you visited me: I was in prison, and you came to me.

Then shall the righteous answer him, saying, Lord, when did we see you hungry, and fed you? or thirsty, and gave you drink? When did we see you a stranger, and took you in? or naked and clothed you? Or when did we see you sick, or in prison, and came to you? And the King shall answer and say to them, Verily I say to you, Inasmuch you have done it to one of the least of these my brethren, you have done it to me.

Then shall he say also to them on the left hand, Depart from me, you cursed, into everlasting fire, prepared for the devil and his angels: For I was hungered, and you gave me no meat: I was thirsty, and you gave me no drink: I was a stranger, and you took me not in: and you clothed me not: sick, and you visited me not.

Then shall they also answer him, saying, Lord, when saw we you hungered, or thirsty, or a stranger, or naked, or sick, or in prison, and did not minister to you? Then shall he answer them, saying, Verily I say to you, Inasmuch as you did it not to one of the least of these, you did it not to me. And these shall go away into everlasting punishment: but the righteous into life eternal. (MATTHEW, 25:31-46.)

2. And behold, a certain lawyer stood up, and tempted him, saying, Master, what shall I do to inherit eternal life? He said to him, What is written in the law? how do you read this? And answering he said, You shall love the Lord your God with all your heart, and with all your soul, and with all your strength, and with all your mind and your neighbour as yourself. And he said to him, You have answered right; this do and you shall live.

But he, willing to justify himself, said to Jesus, and who is my neighbour? And Jesus answering said, A certain man went down from Jerusalem to Jericho, and fell among thieves, which stripped him of his raiment, and wounded him, and departed, leaving him half dead. And by chance there came down a certain priest that way` and when he saw him, he passed by on the other side. And likewise a Levite, when he was at the place, came and looked on him, and passed by on the other side. But a certain Samaritan, as he journeyed, came where he was: and when he saw him, he had compassion on him. And went to him, and bound up his wounds, pouring in oil and wine, and set him on his own beast, and brought him to an inn, and took care of him. And the next day when he departed, he took out two pence, and gave them to the host, and said to him, Take care of him, and whatsoever you spend more, when I come again, I will repay you.

Which now of these three, think you, was neighbour to him that fell among thieves? And he said, He that shewed mercy on him. Then said Jesus to him, Go, and do likewise. (LUKE, 10:25-37.)

3. All the moral Teachings of Christ are resumed in the need for charity and humility; that is to say, in the two virtues that are contrary to selfishness and pride. In all of His Teaching, Jesus indicates these two virtues as being the ones that lead to eternal happiness. He said that the poor in spirit, that is to say the humble, were blessed because the kingdom of heaven would be theirs; blessed are those who have pure hearts; blessed are the gentle and the peacemakers; blessed are the merciful. He also taught the need to love one's neighbour as oneself, to do to others as we would have them do to us, to love our enemies, to forgive all offences if we wish to receive forgiveness, to do Good without ostentation and to judge ourselves before we judge others. So then, charity and humility are the two things that Jesus never ceased to recommend and for which He stands as an example. He also never ceased to combat pride and selfishness. Nor did He limit Himself to the mere recommending of charity, but put it in very clear and explicit terms as being the only condition for future happiness.

With respect to the description given by Jesus of the Final Judgement, we must separate, as in many other cases, that which is only form or allegory. The people to whom Jesus was speaking, being unable to totally understand spiritual questions, made it necessary for Him to offer them material images that would both shock and impress. Therefore, in order for them to be able to understand what was being said, Jesus was obliged to keep closely to the form of the ideas of those times. Nevertheless, He always reserved for the future the real interpretation of His words and those points that at the time were unable to be clearly explained. But alongside the accessory or figurative parts of this explanation, there is one dominant feature: that of the happiness reserved for the just and the unhappiness awaiting those who are evil.

According to that supreme judgement, what then are the considerations for the sentence? On what grounds will the indictment be based? Does the judge perhaps ask if the person under interrogation has fulfilled this or that formality, if they have more or less observed this or that external practice? No, he will ask but one question, "Has charity been practised?" Then make the pronouncement, "Go to the right all who have helped their brothers and sisters. Go to the left all those who have been unyielding." Is it asked, by chance, what is the orthodoxy of their faith? Is any distinction made between those who believe in this or that manner? No, because Jesus places the Samaritan, considered by some to be a heretic, who practised love towards his fellow creature, above any orthodoxy that lacks charity. So do not consider charity to be merely one of the conditions for salvation. Instead, consider it the only condition. If there were others to be met, then Jesus would have mentioned them. Since He put charity in first place, it is because it implicitly embraces all the other virtues such as humility, kindness, benevolence, indulgence, justice, etc., and because it is the absolute negation of pride and selfishness.

THE GREATEST OF THE COMMANDMENTS

4. But when the Pharisees had heard that he had put the Sadducees to silence, they were gathered together. Then one of them, which was a lawyer, asked him a question, tempting him, and saying, Master, which is the great commandment in law? Jesus said to him, You shall love the Lord your God with all your heart, and with all your soul, and with all your mind. This is the first and great commandment, And the second is like it, Thou shall love your neighbour as yourself. On these two commandments hang all the law and the prophets. (MATTHEW, 22:34-40.)

5. Charity and humility, such is the path to salvation. Selfishness and pride are the paths to ruin. This principle is

formulated on the following precise terms, "Love your God with all your soul and your neighbour as yourself; *all the law and the prophets are contained in these two commandments.*" And so there would be no mistake in the understanding of the meaning of the love for God and for our neighbour, He then added, "And there is a second commandment, similar to the first." This means that it is not possible to love God without loving your neighbour, or to love your neighbour without loving God. Straightaway, all that you do against your neighbour, you also do against God. Therefore, it is not possible to love God without practising charity towards one's neighbour. All of humanity's obligations are resumed in the maxim: *without charity there is no salvation.*

THE NEED FOR CHARITY ACCORDING TO SAINT PAUL

6. Thou I speak with the tongues of men and angels, and have not charity, I am become as sounding brass, or a tinkling cymbal. And though I have the gift of prophecy, and understand all mysteries, and all knowledge, and though I have all faith, so that I could remove mountains, and have not charity, I am nothing. And though I bestow all my goods to feed the poor, and though I give my body to be burned, and have not charity, it profits me nothing.

Charity suffers long, and is kind; charity envies not; charity boasts not of itself, is not puffed up. Does not behave itself unseemly (badly), seeks not her own interests, is not easily provoked, thinks no evil; Rejoices not in iniquity, but rejoices in the truth; Bears all things, believes all things, hopes for all things, endures all things. And now remains faith, hope and charity, these three; but the greatest of these is charity. (SAINT PAUL, I Corinthians, 13:1-7 & 13.)

7. Saint Paul profoundly understood this great truth, which says: 'When I have learned the language of the Angels; when I have the gift of prophecy, when I can penetrate all the mysteries;

when I have all the faith that is possible, even to the point of transporting mountains, if I do not have charity, then I am nothing. Within these three virtues: faith, hope and charity, the most superior of these is charity.' In this manner and without any possible doubt, Paul places charity even above faith. This is because charity is within the reach of everybody, from the ignorant to the wise person, from the rich to the poor; it is also quite independent of any particular belief.

He does even more: he defines true charity by showing it as being not only beneficence, but also a collective of all the qualities of the heart in terms of goodness and benevolence towards all of our fellow beings.

WITHOUT THE CHURCH THERE IS NO SALVATION - WITHOUT TRUTH THERE IS NO SALVATION

8. The maxim - *without charity there is no salvation* - stands upon a universal principle and opens the door to supreme happiness for all of God's children. Whereas the dogma - *without the church there is no salvation* – does not rest upon a fundamental faith in God and the immortality of the soul that is a belief common to all religions, *but on a special faith, on particular dogmas* that are exclusive and absolute. Far from uniting God's children, it separates them. Instead of inciting them to love their brothers and sisters it feeds upon and sanctions the irritations between various sectarians of different cults, who reciprocally consider each other to be eternally damned, despite the fact that these same sectarians may be relations or friends. Therefore, by despising the great law of equality in the presence of the tomb, it separates people one from another, even in the area of repose. Whereas the maxim - *without charity there is no salvation* - consecrates the principle of equality before God and the freedom of conscience. By taking this as a norm, all men and women

become brothers and sisters, whatever their way of worshipping the Creator, they hold up their hands and pray for each other. However, with the dogma - *without the church there is no salvation* - they excommunicate and persecute each other reciprocally, living as enemies. The father does not ask after his son or the son after his father, nor a friend after his friend, since they consider themselves mutually condemned without possible remission. Therefore, it is a dogma that is essentially against the teaching of Christ and the Evangelic Laws.

9. *Without truth there is no salvation* is equal to *without the church there is no salvation*, being equally exclusive, since there is no one sect existing that does not claim to hold the privilege of truth. Which person can boast of being in possession of all the truth when our sphere of knowledge is constantly enlarging and ideas are being rectified every day? The absolute truth is the patrimony of only the most elevated category of Spirits. Earthly humanity cannot allege the possession of it because it is not given to earthly humanity to know everything. It is only permissible to aspire to relative truth, which is proportionate to the level of progress. If God had made the possession of truth an express and absolute condition for future happiness, He would have pronounced a verdict of general condemnation. Whereas charity, even in its most ample form, may be practised by all. Spiritism, in accordance with the Gospel, admits the possibility of salvation for every person, independent of any beliefs, granted that God's laws are observed. It does not say that *without Spiritism there is no salvation*, just as it does not intend to teach all the truth as yet. Nor does it say that *without truth there is no salvation* because this maxim, instead of uniting, would only separate and perpetuate antagonisms.

INSTRUCTIONS FROM THE SPIRITS

WITHOUT CHARITY THERE IS NO SALVATION

10. My children, within the sentence: *Without charity there is no salvation*, is enclosed the destiny of humanity, both here on Earth and in Heaven. Because on Earth, beneath the shadow of this banner all may live in peace; in Heaven because those who have practised it will find grace in God's eyes. This phrase is the celestial beacon, the luminous column, which will guide humanity in life's desert, putting all on the right pathway to the Promised Land. It shines in Heaven as a saintly halo on the brows of the chosen ones. On Earth, it is engraved in the hearts of those to whom Jesus said, "Go to the right and receive the blessing of My Father." You will recognise them by the aroma of charity that spreads around them. Nothing can indicate with more exactitude, nor summarise so well humanity's obligations than this divine maxim. Spiritism could not prove its origin better than present it as its rule, because it is a reflection of the purest Christianity. Humanity will never go astray if it takes this as its guide. Therefore, my dear friends, dedicate yourselves to understanding the deep meaning behind these words and the consequences of their application. Then discover for yourselves all the many ways in which they may be applied. Submit all your activities to be administered by charity and your conscience will respond. Not only will it cause you to avoid practising evil, but it will also make you practise goodness, in as much as a dormant virtue is not enough; it is necessary to possess an active virtue. Therefore, in order to do Good there is always the need for the action of willpower, whereas in order to avoid practising evil it is sufficient to be inert or unconcerned.

Friends, give thanks to God for having permitted you to enjoy the enlightenment of Spiritism. Not that those who possess this enlightenment are the only ones who will be saved, but because it helps you to understand the Teachings of Christ, so making you into better Christians. Therefore, make every effort so that your fellow beings, when observing you, are induced to recognise that the true Spiritist and the true Christian are one and the same. Seeing that all those who practise charity are the disciples of Jesus, without putting any embargo on whatever sect they may follow. - PAUL, the Apostle. (Paris, 1860.)

CHAPTER 16

IT IS NOT POSSIBLE TO SERVE BOTH GOD AND MAMMON

The salvation of the rich. - Preserve yourself from avarice. - Jesus in the house of Zacchaeus. - The parable of the bad rich man. - The parable of the talents. - The providential utility of riches. Trials of riches and misery. - The inequality of riches. - INSTRUCTIONS FROM THE SPIRITS: True property. - The application of riches. - Detachment from earthly possessions. - Transmission of riches.

THE SALVATION OF THE RICH

1. No servant can serve two masters: for either he will hate the one, and love the other; or else he will become attached to the one, and despise the other. You cannot serve both God and Mammon. (LUKE, 16:13.)

2. And a man came to Jesus and said, Good Master, what good thing shall I do, that I may have eternal life? And He said to him, Why callest me good? there is none good but One, that is God. but if you want to enter into life, keep the commandments. He said to him, Which? Jesus said, Do no murder, do not commit adultery, do not steal, do not give false testimony, honour your father and mother, and love your neighbour as yourself.

The young man said to him, All these things have I kept from my youth up: what lack I yet? Jesus said to him, If you wish to be perfect, go and sell what you have, and give to the poor, and you will have treasure in Heaven: and come and follow me.

But when the young man heard that saying, he went away sorrowful: for he had great possessions. Then said Jesus to His disciples, verily I say to you, that a rich man shall hardly enter into the kingdom of heaven. And again I say to you, It is easier for a camel to go through the eye of a needle, than for a rich man to enter into the Kingdom of God.[13] (MATTHEW, 19:16-24. This same text is also repeated by LUKE, 18:18-25, & by MARK, 10:17-25.)

PRESERVE YOURSELF FROM AVARICE

3. And one of the company said to him, Master, speak to my brother, that he divide the inheritance with me. And he said to him, Man, who made me judge or a divider over you? And he said to them, Take heed, and beware of covetousness; for a man's life consists not in the abundance of the things which he possesses. And he spoke a parable to them, saying, The ground of a certain rich man brought forth plentifully: And he thought within himself, saying, What shall I do, because I have no room where to bestow my fruits? And he said, This will I do: I will pull down my barns, and build greater; and there will I bestow all my fruits and my goods. And I will say to my soul, Soul, you have much goods laid up for many years; take your ease, eat drink and be merry. But God said to him, you fool, this night your soul shall be required of you: then whose shall those things be, which you have provided? So is he that lays up treasure for himself, and is not rich towards God. (LUKE, 12:13-21.)

JESUS IN THE HOUSE OF ZACCHAEUS

4. And Jesus entered and passed through Jericho. And, behold, there was a man named Zacchaeus, which was the chief among the publicans, and he was rich. And he sought to see Jesus who he was: and he could not for the press, because he was little of stature. And he ran before, and climbed up into a sycamore tree to see him: for he was to pass that way. And when Jesus came to the

---

[13] In the Hebrew language there exists the same word meaning both a camel and a cord. In the translation of the Bible the first meaning was quoted, but it is possible that Jesus used the other meaning, namely a cord. This would at least appear to be more normal.

place, he looked up, and saw him, and said to him, Zacchaeus, make haste, and come down; for to day I must abide at your house. And he made haste, and came down, and received him joyfully. And when they saw it, they all murmured, saying, That he was gone to be a guest with a man that is a sinner. (See the 'INTRODUCTION', under the heading - PUBLICANS.)

And Zacchaeus stood, and said to the Lord; Behold, Lord, the half of my goods I give to the poor; and if I have taken any thing from any man by false accusation, I restore him fourfold. And Jesus said to him, This day is salvation come to this house, forsomuch as he also is a son of Abraham. For the Son of man is come to seek and to save that which was lost. And Zacchaeus stood before Jesus and said, "Look, Lord, I will give half of my goods to the poor; and if I have taken anything from any man by false accusation, I will restore him fourfold. And Jesus said to him, This day salvation is come to this house, for this man is also a son of Abraham. For the Son of Man is come to seek and to save that which was lost. (LUKE, 19:1-10.)

THE PARABLE OF THE BAD RICH MAN

5. There was a certain rich man, who was clothed in purple and fine linen, and lived sumptuously every day. And there was a beggar named Lazarus, who was laid at his gate, covered with sores, desiring to be fed with the crumbs, which fell from the rich man's table: moreover the dogs came and licked his sores. And it came to pass, that the beggar died, and was carried by the angels to be beside Abraham. The rich man also died, and was buried; And in hell, and he lifted up his eyes, being in torments, and saw Abraham afar off, and Lazarus in his bosom. And he cried and said, 'Father Abraham, have mercy on me, and send Lazarus, that he may dip the tip of his finger in water and cool my tongue, for I am tormented in this flame.

But Abraham said, 'My son, remember that you in your lifetime received your good things, and likewise Lazarus evil things: but now he is comforted and you are tormented.'

And beside all this, between us and you there is a great gulf fixed, so that they which would pass from hence to you cannot; neither can they pass to us, that would come from thence.

Then he said, I pray you therefore, father, that you would send him to my father's house: for I have five brethren; that he may testify to them, so they will not also come into this place of torment. Abraham said to him, They have Moses and the prophets, let them hear them. And he said, No, father Abraham; but if one went to them from the dead they will repent. And he said to him, If they do not hear Moses and the prophets, neither will they be persuaded, though one rose from the dead. (LUKE, 16:19-31.)

THE PARABLE OF THE TALENTS

6. For the kingdom of heaven is as a man travelling into a far country, who called his own servants, and delivered into them his goods. And unto one he gave five talents, to another two, and to another one; to every man according to his several abilities; and straightway took his journey. Then he that had received the five talents went and traded with the same, and made them other five talents. And likewise he that had received two, he also gained another two. But he that had received one went and digged in the earth, and hid his lord's money. After a long time the lord of those servants returned and reckoned with them. And so he that had received five talents came and brought other five talents, saying, Lord, you delivered to me five talents: behold, I have gained beside them five talents more. His lord said to him, Well done, you good and faithful servant: you have been faithful over a few things, so I will make you ruler over many things: enter into the joy of your lord. He also that had received two talents came and said, Lord, you delivered to me two talents. I have gained two other talents besides them. His lord said to him, Well done, good and faithful servant; You have been faithful over a few things, so I will make you ruler over many things: enter into the joy of your lord. Then he which had received the one talent came and said, Lord, I knew that you are a hard man, reaping where you have not sown, and gathering where you have not scattered seed. And I was afraid, and went and hid your talent in the earth: lo, here you have that is yours. His lord answered and said to him, You wicked and slothful servant! You knew that I reap where I sowed not, and gathered where I have not scattered seed: You should therefore have put my money to the exchangers, and then at my coming I should have received mine own with interest. Take therefore the talent from him and give it to him who has ten talents. For to everyone that has shall be given, and he shall have abundance: but from him that has not, shall be taken away even what he has. And cast the unprofitable servant into outer darkness: there shall be weeping and gnashing of teeth.' (MATTHEW, 25:14-30.)

THE PROVIDENTIAL UTILITY OF RICHES - TRIALS OF RICHES AND MISERY

7. If riches were meant to constitute an absolute obstacle to salvation for all who possess them, as might be inferred from certain words supposedly uttered by Jesus, when these are interpreted in a literal fashion instead of in their spiritual meaning, then God, who conceded them, would have placed an instrument of ruination in the hands of certain people against which they could not appeal. But this idea is quite repugnant to all reason. However, it is beyond doubt that from the destruction it causes, the temptations it provokes and the fascination it holds, we may deduce that riches constitute a very dangerous trial, even more dangerous than that of misery. It is the greatest provoker of pride, selfishness and sensuality. It is the strongest tie that holds humans to Earth and distracts them from thoughts of Heaven. On many occasions, it produces such a state of dizziness that those who go from misery to wealth completely forget their first condition. They

also quickly forget those who had shared this state with them, even those who had helped them and become insensitive, selfish and futile people. Nevertheless, from the fact that riches make the journey difficult, it does not follow that it becomes impossible. Nor that it cannot become a means of salvation for those who know how to utilise it, just as certain poisons may restore health when employed in the correct quantities and used with discernment.

Jesus told the young man who inquired how he could obtain eternal life, that he should dispose of all his worldly goods and follow Him. However, this did not mean that Jesus was establishing an absolute principle that everyone should get rid of everything they possess, nor that this is the only price to be paid for salvation. It was meant to show that *attachment to worldly goods* was an obstacle to salvation. The young man in this case had judged himself to be released from further struggle because he had observed certain commandments and therefore he refused the idea of abandoning all the worldly goods he possessed. His desire to obtain eternal life did not run to the extreme of acquiring it through this sacrifice.

What Jesus proposed to him was a decisive test destined to uncover the depths of his thoughts. Beyond doubt, he could be a perfectly honest person in the eyes of the world, never causing harm to anyone, never cursing his neighbours, never being vain, futile or prideful and always honouring his mother and father. Still he did not possess true charity, because his virtues did not go as far as abnegation. This is what Jesus wished to demonstrate by applying the principle: Without charity there is no salvation.

In the strict acceptance of these words, the result would be the abolition of riches due to their being detrimental to future happiness and the cause of a great deal of the evil on Earth. For the rest, it would be the condemnation of all work as being the means of gain. This would be an absurd consequence that would only convey humankind back to a primitive existence and be in complete contradiction to the Law of Progress which is one of God's laws.

If riches were the cause of much evil, if they aggravate so many evil passions, if they really provoked so many crimes, it is not the riches themselves that we should blame, but humankind who misuses them as it does all of God's gifts. It is through ill usage that humanity constantly turns what could be most useful into something pernicious. This is a consequence of the inferior state of earthly life. If riches could only produce wrongdoing and mischief, then God would not have placed them upon Earth. It is up to humanity to make them produce Good and even if they are not a direct element of moral progress, then beyond doubt they are a powerful element in intellectual progress.

Indeed, all humanity has the mission of working for the material betterment of this planet. It is up to everyone to reclaim it, to make it salubrious and to make arrangements so that one day the planet may receive all the population that its area can and should contain. To be able to feed this larger population, it will become imperative to increase production. If the production of one country is insufficient, then it will be brought in from outside. This is why relationships between nations become a vital requirement; but in order to accomplish this it also becomes necessary to destroy all the obstacles that separate these countries, so that intercommunication can be rapid. For this work, which has already taken centuries to accomplish, it has been essential to extract materials from the very entrails of the Earth. Science was sought for the means of executing these tasks with more speed and safety. In order to accomplish this there is need for resources; this necessity then brought about the creation of riches, just as it had provoked the discovery of science. These activities also imposed the need to amplify and develop intelligence, which until that time had been used primarily for the satisfaction of material necessities. Moreover, it will be the same intelligence that will later help humanity understand all the great moral truths. Seeing that riches are the primary means of executing these tasks, without which there would be no more great works, no activity, no stimulation or research, it is with good reason that riches are considered as an element of progress.

THE INEQUALITY OF RICHES

8. The inequality of riches is one of the problems that humanity will go on trying to resolve without success, as long as only the present life is considered. The first question that presents itself is this: why are we all not equally rich? For the simple reason *we are not all equally intelligent, active and industrious enough to acquire it, nor sober and provident enough to keep it.* Besides, it is a mathematically demonstrable fact that riches, if equally divided, would give a minimum and insufficient portion to each one. Thus, supposing this division was actually made, in a short time this equilibrium would be undone by the diversity of characters and aptitudes. Also, supposing it to be possible and lasting, each one would have merely sufficient to live on, resulting in the annihilation of all great works, that contribute towards progress and the well being of humanity. Finally, if it were conceded that each person was given the indispensable, then there would no longer be any incentive to impel people to make great discoveries or to found useful enterprises. Therefore, if God has concentrated riches in certain places, it is because from there it can be poured out in sufficient quantities, according to needs.

Having accepted this fact, we then ask why God has conceded riches to people who are incapable of making them bear fruit for the good of all. Here we have yet another proof of the wisdom and goodness of God. By giving Humanity free will, He wishes that the position of being able to distinguish right from wrong be reached through individual experience and that the practice of Good be solely the result of effort and choice. Humans should not be fatally led towards either Goodness or evil, thus turning them into passive and irresponsible instruments, as are animals. Wealth is a means of being able to test one's morality. However, as it is also a powerful means of action towards progress, God does not wish it to remain unproductive over long periods of time, so *He unceasingly displaces it.* Each one possesses it eventually, so that they may drill themselves in utilising it and demonstrate what uses they have learnt to put it to. Nevertheless, it is materially impossible for all to possess it at the same time, as it happens that if everyone had riches, then no one would work, which would result in the improvement of the planet being compromised. *Each one then has a turn in possessing it.* In this manner, those who do not have it today, have already had it or will have it at some future time. Likewise, those who have it now, perhaps will not have it tomorrow. There are rich and poor because God, being just, prescribes work to each one in turn. For those who are suffering poverty, it is a test of patience and resignation; for others riches are a test in charity and abnegation.

It is with good reason that the very bad use to which some people put their riches are to be deplored, as are the ignoble passions provoked by their greed. This makes us ask if God is just to give riches to such persons. It is certain that if human beings had only one life to live, nothing could justify such a division of worldly wealth. However, if we keep in sight not only the present life, but also the assemblage of existences, we would see that everything is justly balanced. From this point of view, the poor person lacks a motive with which to accuse providence, just as they have no motive to be envious of the rich who, in their turn also lack a motive to glorify themselves for what they possess. On the other hand, if the application of riches is abused, it will not be by means of decrees or sumptuary laws that the wrongdoing will be remedied. The laws can temporarily change the exterior, but it cannot succeed in changing the heart. Hence, these laws would be of fleeting duration and would then be followed by more unrestrained reactions. The origin of evil lies in pride and selfishness; therefore, all manner of abuses will cease when the Law of Charity governs humanity.

INSTRUCTIONS FROM THE SPIRITS

TRUE PROPERTY

9. The only true property that human beings can own is that which may be taken with them on leaving this world. What is found on arrival on Earth and that which is left behind on parting, is enjoyed only while staying incarnate. Therefore, as humanity is forced to abandon all worldly possessions, it can be inferred that it has no real ownership of riches, only their temporary usage. What then constitutes true property? Nothing that is for the use of the body, but everything that is for the use of the soul: intelligence, knowledge and moral qualities. This is what we bring and take with us, that no one can take away from us, being far more use in the next world than in this one. It is up to each person to be richer on departure than they were on arrival in this world, seeing that their future position will depend solely on what qualities have been gained in the present life. When someone travels to a distant country, they take as part of their luggage only those things that will be useful to them in that place; they do not worry about the things that will be of no use. Proceed in a like manner in relation to your future life and provide yourselves with all that can be of use to you there.

The traveller who arrives at a hostel is only given a good room if they are able to pay for it. Those who have very little resources are forced to make do with something less agreeable. When they have nothing that belongs to them, they must sleep on straw. The same applies to a person on, arrival in the world of the Spirits, for *it will depend entirely on what they own as to where they will go.* Nor will payment be made in terms of gold. No one will be asked what they had had on Earth, or what position they had occupied, nor even if they were a pauper or a prince. Instead, they will be asked, "What have you brought with you?" No possessions or titles will be evaluated, only the total sum of virtues possessed. Well now, looked at from this aspect, it is possible that the simple worker will be far richer than the prince. In vain may the latter allege that before leaving the Earth their entrance into the next world was paid for in gold. The only reply being: No one may buy a place here; it must be conquered by means of doing Good to others. Earthly money may buy land, houses or palaces, but in our world, everything is paid for by means of the qualities of the soul. Are you rich in these qualities? Then you are welcome and may go to one of the high places where all kinds of happiness awaits. However, if you are poor in these qualities then you must go to the low places, where you will be treated according to what you possess. - PASCAL (Geneva, 1860.)

10. Earthly goods belong to God, Who distributes them in accordance with His wishes. Humans are nothing more than the usufructuary, a relatively honest and intelligent administrator of these properties. They belong so little to the individual person, that God frequently annuls all such provisions, so that the riches escape from even those who considered themselves to hold the best entitlement.

You would say perhaps, this is understandable when related to inherited property, but not to that acquired by work. Undoubtedly, if there were such a thing as legitimate riches, then it would apply to the latter, when honestly gained. However, *a property is only legitimately acquired when during its acquisition there has been no harm done to anyone.* An account will have to be given right down to the last cent of all ill-gotten gains, that is to say gains that may have injured someone. From the fact that a person may owe the acquiring of riches to themselves, does it follow that upon dying any advantage may be gained from this circumstance? Are not the precautions they may have taken to transfer these riches to descendants frequently useless? If God does not desire them to be transmitted, then nothing can prevail against His wishes. Can someone use and abuse what they own during their lifetime without needing to give an account? No. On permitting the acquisition, it is to be supposed that God had in mind to recompense the person during the actual existence for their effort, courage and perseverance. If however, it was used exclusively for the satisfaction of their senses or their pride; or if they became the cause of failure in their hands, it would have been better not to have received them, seeing that what is gained on the one hand is lost on the other, so annulling all merit for the work. On leaving the Earth, God will say that the recompense has already been received. - M. A PROTECTING SPIRIT (Brussels, 1861.)

THE APPLICATION OF RICHES

11. It is not possible to serve both God and Mammon. Those of you who are dominated by the love of gold, who would sell your very souls in order to possess treasure, do not forget this reminder, because these things permit you to elevate yourselves above other men and women, so allowing you to enjoy passions that make you their slaves. No, it is not possible to serve both God and Mammon! So then, if you feel your soul to be dominated by the lust of the flesh, make haste to rid yourself of this yoke that tyrannises you, in as much as God, who is just and strict, will say to you, "What did you do with the property I entrusted to you, unfaithful steward? This powerful motive for good works has been used exclusively for your own personal satisfaction!"

What then is the best way to employ riches? If you look for the answer in the words "Love one another", you will find the solution, for here lies the secret of the best way to employ riches. Those who love their neighbour already have a line of action delineated for them in these words; because the application that most pleases God is charity. Not that cold and selfish charity that consists in distributing only that which is superfluous from their golden existence, but rather that charity full of love, that seeks out misfortune and helps raise it up without causing humiliation. You, who are rich, give what you have in excess! But do even more, give something of what is necessary to you, because what you consider necessary is, in reality, also superfluous, but give wisely. Do not reject those who weep because you may be afraid of being duped, but find the underlying cause of the matter. In the first place, seek to alleviate; secondly seek information and then see if the possibility of work, counselling or even offering affection, would not be more efficient than the mere giving of alms. Spread all around you with affluence, your love for God, for work and for your neighbour. Place your riches on a secure base, being that of good works, and you will be guaranteed great profit. The riches of intelligence should serve you just as do those of wealth. Therefore, disperse around you the benefits of education and scatter the treasure of your love over your brothers and sisters that they may bear fruits. - CHEVERUS (Bordeaux, 1861.)

12. When I consider the brevity of life, I am painfully impressed by the incessant preoccupation placed on material well being, that has become the main objective in life. Whereas you place so little significance and give so little time and often none, to your moral perfectioning. Nevertheless, this is what is essential and what counts towards eternity. From the amount of effort put into material welfare it would appear we are dealing with a question of the utmost importance for humanity. When in reality it will be found that in the majority of cases, this same work is

nothing other than an attempt to satisfy exaggerated needs and vanities or is a surrender to excesses. What grief, sorrow and torments you cause yourselves! What sleepless nights, just to increase what is often a more than sufficient wealth! At the height of blindness, it is not infrequent to see those whose immoderate love of wealth and pleasures allows them to be subjected to arduous and tiring work; while they boast of the life of sacrifice and merit they lead, as if they were working for others and not for themselves! What fools you are! Do you really believe that the care and effort expended will be taken into consideration when, on the one hand, you are motivated by selfishness, cupidity and pride and on the other hand you neglect your future and the duties that fraternal solidarity imposes on all who reap the advantages that society has to offer? You have thought only of your physical bodies! Your own well being and pleasures have been the exclusive object of your selfish solicitude. For the sake of the body that perishes, you have despised the spirit that will live forever. This is why that spoiled and flattered lord becomes your tyrant; it dominates your spirit, thus making you its slave. Can this possibly be the objective for which God granted you life? - A PROTECTING SPIRIT (Krakow, 1861.)

13. Seeing that humans are both administrators and trustees for the wealth that is placed in their hands by God, it will therefore be indispensable to render a strict account of the uses it has been put to, by virtue of their free will. Bad usage consists of it being used exclusively for personal satisfaction; good usage, on the contrary, is whenever this results in benefit to others. Each person's merit is in the degree of sacrifice they impose upon themselves. Beneficence is just one way of employing riches; it can be used to alleviate misery, appease hunger and offer shelter and warmth to those who have none. Nevertheless, an equally imperious obligation that is also very noteworthy, is that of preventing misery. This, above all else, is the mission of the great fortunes; a

mission to be fulfilled through the many kinds of work for which it can be used. Neither does the good resulting from these works cease to exist because those who work in this manner take legitimate benefit from it; seeing that it develops intelligence and ennobles the dignity of humankind by allowing the satisfaction of being able to say that they earn their means of sustenance; whereas the receiving of alms only humiliates and degrades. Riches, that are concentrated in one hand, should be like a spring of running water that spreads fertility and well-being wherever it goes. Oh you who are wealthy! Employ your riches according to the wishes of God, Who would be the first to quench your thirst at this blessed spring! Even in this present life, you could reap unequalled happiness for the soul, instead of the material pleasures of selfishness that only produce a sensation of emptiness in the heart. Your name would be blessed on Earth and when you leave it, the Lord our God would say to you as was said in the parable of the talents, "Good and faithful servant, enter into the happiness of your God." In this parable the servant who buried the money that was entrusted to him, represents those who are miserly and in whose hands riches remain unproductive. Meanwhile, if Jesus spoke principally of alms it was because in those days, in the country where He lived, the kinds of work in the arts and industry where riches could be usefully employed were not yet known. So then, to all who are able to give, be it much or little, I would say this: give money only when necessary, but as often as possible convert it into wages, so that the person who receives is not ashamed. - FÉNELON (Algiers, 1860.)

DETACHMENT FROM EARTHLY POSSESSIONS

14. My brothers, sisters and friends, I am come to offer you my contribution to help you advance fearlessly along the pathway to improvement into which you are entering. We are all indebted one to the other. Therefore, it is only possible to achieve regeneration

by means of a sincere and fraternal union between Spirits and incarnate beings.

Attachment to earthly possessions constitutes one of the strongest obstacles to both moral and spiritual advancement. Through this attachment, all faculties for loving are destroyed, as they are only devoted to material things. Let us be honest with each other: do riches bring unmixed happiness? When your safes are full of money, is there not still an emptiness in your hearts? At the bottom of this basket of flowers is there not a viper? I understand the satisfaction that is experienced and quite justifiably so, when by means of honourable and assiduous work a fortune has been gained. Nevertheless, from this same satisfaction, that is very natural and has God's approval, to the attachment that absorbs all other sentiments and paralyses the impulses felt by the heart, there is a large gap. As large as the distance that separates exaggerated extravagance from that of sordid covetousness, two vices between which God has placed charity, that saintly and cleansing virtue that teaches the rich person to give without ostentation, so that the poor may receive without being debased.

Whether the fortune has come to you from your family, or whether you have earned it by working, there is something you should never forget, which is that everything proceeds from God and everything refers us to Him. Nothing belongs to you on this Earth, not even your own physical body. Death strips you of it even as it does of all earthly possessions. You are merely trustees and not the owners, so do not delude yourselves. God has only lent these things to you and they must be returned. What is more, they have been lent to you under the condition that at least the surplus should go to those who lack what is necessary.

One of your friends lends you a certain sum of money. However lacking in honesty you may be, you make a point of scrupulously restituting what was lent and are grateful to that person. Well then, this is the exact position of all who are rich. God is the Celestial Friend who lends you riches, wishing nothing more for Himself than love and recognition for the loan. However, He does demand that in turn the rich person gives to the poor who, just as much as they, are His sons and daughters.

Ardent and demented greed are aroused in your hearts by the possessions that God has entrusted to you. Have you ever stopped to think that when you allow yourselves to become immoderately attached to a perishable fortune, which is just as transitory as yourselves, that one day you will have to account to God for what was done with what came from Him? Have you forgotten that through riches you assume a sacred mission to administer charity here on Earth, to be its intelligent distributors? Hence, when what was entrusted to you is used only for your own benefit, does it not follow that you are unfaithful trustees? What then will be the result of this voluntary forgetfulness of duty? Inflexible and inexhaustible death will tear away the veil under which you have been hiding, so forcing you to give an account to Him Who has been forgotten and Who, at that moment stands before you as Judge.

It is useless to try to delude yourselves while on Earth by covering up, under the name of virtue, what is usually nothing more than selfishness. It is useless to call that which is only greed and cupidity by the name of economy and foresight, or to call that which is only prodigality for your own advantage, by the name of generosity. For example, a father abstains from practising charity, economises and accumulates wealth so that, as he puts it, he may leave his children the greatest possible amount of property in order to avoid their ever-knowing misery. This is very just and fatherly, I agree, and no one can censure him for this. However, is it always the only motive behind his action? Does he not frequently feel bound by his own conscience to justify this personal attachment for earthly possessions, both in his own eyes and those of the world? Even if paternal love were the only motive, is that reason enough to forget his brothers and sisters before God? When he has a surplus, will he leave his children in misery if they have a little less? In this manner, is he not giving them a lesson in selfishness and hardening their hearts? Will it not cause their love for their neighbours to wither away? Mothers and fathers, you are labouring under a grave error if you believe this is the way to gain affection from your children. By teaching them to be selfish with others, you are only teaching them to be selfish with you too.

It is common to hear it said, from someone who has worked very hard and accumulated wealth with the sweat of their brow, that the value of money is better appreciated when it has been worked for. This is very true. Well then! The person who declares they know the full value of money should practise charity; their merit will then be greater than the one who, being born to abundance, is ignorant of toil and work. Also, if this same person, who remembers their own sufferings and endeavours, is selfish and unmerciful to the poor they will be more guilty than the other, since the more each one knows for themselves the hidden pains of misery, the greater tendency there should be to help others.

Unhappily, in people who possess riches there is always a sentiment as strong as their attachment for the riches: that is pride. Not infrequently, the newly rich can be heard making someone, who asked for assistance, dizzy with tales of their success and abilities; instead of helping them they end by saying, "Do as I did." According to this prideful person's way of thinking, God's goodness does not even enter into the matter of their having obtained the riches. The merit for having obtained them is theirs alone. Their pride has blinded their eyes and deafened their ears. Despite their intelligence and aptitudes, they still do not understand that with only one word God can cast them.

The squandering of riches is not a demonstration of detachment from earthly possessions, it is merely carelessness and indifference. As trustees of these possessions, human beings have no right to dissipate them, neither have they the right to confiscate them for their own benefit. Extravagance is not generosity; rather it is frequently a type of selfishness. Someone who spends money by the handful in order to satisfy a fantasy, will perhaps not give even a penny to someone in need. Detachment from worldly possessions consists in appreciating them according to their just value. This means in knowing how to make use of them for the benefit of others and not exclusively in self-benefit, in not sacrificing all interest in a future life for them and in being able to lose them without a murmur in case it pleases God to take them away. If due to unforeseeable circumstances, you become as Job, then say as he did: "Lord, You have given and You have taken away. Let Your Will be done." This is true detachment. Above all else be submissive and trust He, Who, having given and taken away, may once again restitute what was taken. Resist desanimation and desperation with all your courage, as these paralyse your strength. When God causes you to suffer a blow, never forget that alongside the most painful trial He always places a consolation. Above all, ponder the point that there are possessions infinitely more precious than those to be found on Earth and this thought will help you towards detachment. The less attachment you have for something means the less sensitive you will be to its loss. The person who holds on to earthly possessions is like a child, who sees only the moment. Whereas the one who is able to detach themselves is like an adult, who sees the more important things in life because they understand the prophetic words of the Saviour: "My kingdom is not of this world."

The Lord orders no one to dispose of what they possess, since this would condemn them to voluntary pauperism, seeing that this would turn them into social encumbrances. To proceed in this manner is to misunderstand the true meaning of detachment from worldly possessions. In fact, this is a selfishness of another kind, because it means that the individuals exempt themselves from the responsibility that riches have placed on all who possess them. God gives riches to those He considers apt to administer them for the benefit of others. The rich person is given a mission that can be beautified by him and be personally profitable. To reject riches when God has bestowed them is to renounce the benefits of the goodness it can do, when administered with good judgement. By knowing how to do without them, when you do not have them, knowing how to employ them usefully when you receive them, and by knowing how to sacrifice them when necessary, you are proceeding according to God's wishes. Well then, let those into whose hands has come what in the world is called a goodly fortune, say: "My Lord, you have entrusted me with a new mission; give me the strength to fulfil it according to your wishes."

My friends, here you have what I wished to teach about detachment from worldly possession. I would summarise what I have written by saying: Know how to be content with only a little. If you are poor, do not envy the rich, because riches are not necessarily happiness. If you are rich, then do not forget that these riches at your disposal are only entrusted to you; that you will have to justify the use to which you put them, just as you would have to give an account of an investment for which you are responsible. Do not be an unfaithful trustee, utilising it only for the satisfaction of your own pride and sensuality. Do not think you have the right to dispose of a loan as if it were a gift, exclusively for your own benefit. If you do not know how to make restitution then you do not have the right of request. Remember that the person who gives to the poor is settling a debt contracted with God. - LACORDAIRE (Constantine, 1863.)

TRANSMISSION OF RICHES

15. *Does the principle, according to which human beings are merely trustees of a fortune that God has permitted them to enjoy during their lifetime, take away the right to transmit it to their descendants?*

After their death a person has a perfect right to transmit what they enjoyed during their lifetime, because the effect of this right is always subordinate to the Will of God, Who can, when He deems fit, prevent those descendants from enjoying what was transferred to them. This is the reason why many apparently solid fortunes collapse. A person's wish then becomes impotent when they desire to maintain their fortune in the hands of descendants. However, this does not take away the right to transfer the loan received from God, seeing that God can always take it away when He judges it opportune. – SAINT LOUIS. (Paris, 1860.)

CHAPTER 17

BE PERFECT

CHARACTERISTICS OF PERFECTION

1. But I say to you, Love your enemies, bless those who curse you, do good to those who hate you, and pray for them that despitefully use you, and persecute you. For if you love them which love you, what reward have you? Do not even the Publicans the same? And if you salute your brethren only, what do you more than others? Do not even the Publicans? So be you therefore perfect, as your Father that is in Heaven is perfect. (MATTHEW, 5:44 & 46-48.)

2. Since God possesses infinite perfection in all things, the proposition, "Be perfect as your Celestial Father is perfect," if taken literally would presuppose the possibility of attaining absolute perfection. If it were given to humans to be as perfect as their Creator, then they would become His equal, which is inadmissible, but the people to whom Jesus spoke did not understand this nuance, which caused Him to limit Himself to the presentation of a model and tell them that they must strive to reach it.

Those words then must be understood in the sense of relative perfection, that which humanity is capable of achieving and that most nearly approaches the Divinity. What does this perfection consist of? Jesus said, "In loving one's enemies, in doing Good to those who hate us, in praying for those who persecute us." In this way, He shows that the essence of perfection is Charity in its most ample form because it implies the practice of all the other virtues.

In fact, by observing the results of all the vices and even of simple defects, it can be recognised that there is not one that does not more or less disfigure the sentiment of charity. This is because all of them have their beginnings in selfishness and pride, which are the negation of it. This is due to the fact that everything that over-stimulates our self-esteem destroys, or at least weakens, the elements of true charity which are: benevolence, indulgence, abnegation and devotion. Love for one's fellow creatures, when extended to a love for one's enemies, cannot be allied to any defect that is against charity. Therefore, for this reason, it is always an indication of a greater or lesser moral superiority. From this, it follows that the degree of perfection is in direct relation to the extent of this love. It was for this reason that Jesus, after having given His Disciples the rules of charity and all that they contain of what is most sublime, then said to them, "Be perfect, as your Celestial Father is perfect."

THE GOOD PERSON

3. The truly good person is one who complies with the laws of justice, love and charity in their highest degree of purity. If they examine their conscience concerning their own actions they will ask themselves if they have violated those laws, or if they have practised any evil and if they have done all the Good *that was possible.* Yet again, they will ask themselves if they have voluntarily disregarded any occasion to be useful, or if anyone has any complaint to make against them, and finally if they have done to others everything that they would wish done to themselves.

They deposit their faith in God, in His goodness, in His justice and His wisdom. They know that without His permission nothing can happen. Therefore, they submit themselves to His will in all things.

They have faith in the future, which is the reason to put spiritual possessions before those of a temporary nature.

They know that all the vicissitudes of life, all pain and all deceptions are trials or atonements and accept them without murmuring.

Possessing the sentiments of charity and love for their neighbours, they do Good for the sake of goodness, without waiting for payment of any kind. They repay evil with goodness, take up the defence of the weak against the strong and always sacrifice their own interests in the name of justice.

These people encounter satisfaction in the benefits they are able to spread, the service they are able to render, the happiness they promote, the tears they are able to dry and the consolation they offer to those who are afflicted. Their first impulse is always to think of others before thinking of themselves and to look after those interests before looking after their own interests. On the other hand, the selfish person always calculates the benefits and losses arising from any generous action.

The Good person is always Good, humane and benevolent with everyone, without distinction *as to race or creed*, because they see all men and women as brothers and sisters.

They respect all sincere convictions in others and never launch reprobation against those who think otherwise.

In all life's circumstances, they are guided by a desire to be charitable. This is because they know that those who prejudice others with evil words, injure them with their pride, disregard their susceptibilities, or do not draw back at the thought of causing suffering or a contrariety, however small, especially when it could be avoided, lack the sense of obligation to love one's neighbour and therefore do not deserve the clemency of the Lord.

They do not harbour rancour or hatred, nor yet desire vengeance. Instead, they follow the example of Jesus by forgiving and forgetting all offences, only remembering the benefits received, because they know that we ourselves will only be forgiven in as much as we are able to forgive others.

They are indulgent with the weaknesses of others because they know that they also need indulgence, remembering that Christ said, "Let the one who is without sin cast the first stone."

They do not take pleasure in looking for defects in others, nor in calling attention to them. If necessity obliges them to do so, then they always try to look for the good qualities so as to lessen the bad ones.

Good people study their own imperfections and work unceasingly to combat them, using all their strength so that tomorrow they will be able to say they are just a little better than they were the day before.

They never try to emphasise the importance of their own spirit or their talents at the expense of others. On the contrary, they take every opportunity to highlight in others whatever these people may have that is useful and positive.

They are not conceited about their riches or of any personal advantage, knowing that everything that has been given to them may be taken away. They use, but do not abuse, the possessions that have been conceded to them, because they are only a depository, for which they will be required to give a full account. They know that the most detrimental employment these riches can be put to, is the satisfaction of their own passions.

If then, by social order, a person has been placed in a position of command over their fellow beings, they treat them with kindness and benevolence, because before God all men and women are equal. They use their authority to lift up the morale of these people and never crush them with their pride. Likewise, they avoid everything that might make a subordinate position painful.

On the part of those who are subordinate, let it be understood that the duties that go with this position should be clearly appreciated and conscientiously fulfilled. (See chapter 17 - item 9.)

Finally, a good person is always one who respects the rights of their fellow beings as assured by the laws of nature, in the same way they would wish their own to be respected.

These are not all the qualities that distinguish a good person, but anyone who tries hard to possess those that we have just mentioned, are already travelling along the pathway that leads to all the others.

GOOD SPIRITISTS

4. Spiritism, when thoroughly understood and above all when deeply and sincerely felt, leads to the results already expounded that characterise a true Spiritist just as much as a true Christian, for they are one and the same. Spiritism does not institute any new morals; it only makes it easier for everyone to understand and practice Christ's morals by giving an unshakable and enlightened faith to those who are in doubt or who waver.

Meanwhile, many of those who believe in the spiritual manifestations do not understand their consequences or the far-reaching moral effects; or if they do understand, they do not apply them to themselves. To what is this attributed? Is it due to some failing in the clarity of the Teachings? No, seeing it contains no allegories or forms that could lead to false interpretations. Clarity is its very essence and this is its strength because it touches human intelligence directly. There is no mystery and those who are initiated are not in possession of any secrets hidden from ordinary people.

So then, is it indispensable to possess outstanding intelligence in order to understand? No, in as much as there are people of notable capacities who do not understand, whereas there are many of ordinary intelligence, even young people, who grasp the meaning of even the most delicate points with remarkable precision. This proves that the so-called *material* part of Science only requires eyes to be able to observe. The *essential* part demands a certain degree of sensitivity that can be called *maturity in the moral sense*; a maturity that is independent of age or level of education, that in a special sense is inherent to the development of the incarnate soul.

In some people, material ties are still too strong for them to be able to release themselves from earthly things. A kind of mist surrounding them does not allow them to have a vision of the Infinite, resulting in the fact of them not being able to break away from old tendencies or habits because they cannot see that there exists something better than what they already have. They believe in spirits as a simple fact. However, this modifies none or very few of their instinctive tendencies. In a word, they perceive nothing more than a small ray of light insufficient to guide them or offer profound aspirations that would make it possible for them to overcome their inclinations. The phenomenon touches them more than the morality, that seems to be hackneyed and monotonous. They ask only that the spirits unceasingly initiate new mysteries, without asking themselves if they have become worthy of penetrating the hidden secrets of the Creator. These then are the imperfect spirits, some of whom have remained stationary in time or have turned away from the faith held by companions, due to their having drawn back before the necessity of self-reform. Perhaps they have kept sympathy with those who share the same weaknesses or prejudices. Nevertheless, the acceptance of the fundamental principles of the Teachings is the first step, from which it will be easier for them to take the second step in another existence.

The person who can justifiably be classified as a true and sincere Spiritist is to be found on a superior level of moral progress. The spirit of this person almost completely dominates their physical body, so giving them a clearer perception of the future. The principles of the Teachings, that leave many untouched, cause them to feel deep inner vibrations. In short, *their heart is moved* and this is what makes their faith unshakeable. It is like a musician who is touched by just a few chords, whereas another person hears only sounds. *The true Spiritist, can be recognised by their moral transformation and by the efforts they employ in order to dominate their bad instincts.* While one is content with a limited horizon, the other, who understands that better things exist, makes every effort towards their spiritual progress and always manages to do this, when their desire is strong and true.

THE PARABLE OF THE SOWER

5. That same day went Jesus out of the house and sat by the sea side. And great multitudes gathered about Him, so that He went into a ship, and sat: and the whole multitude stood on the shore. And He spoke many things to them in parables, saying, Behold, a sower went forth to sow: And when he sowed, some seeds fell by the way side, and the fowls came and devoured them. Some fell upon stony places, where they had not much earth: and forthwith they sprang up, because they had no deepness of earth: And when the sun was up, they were scorched; and because they had no roots, they withered away. And some fell among thorns, and the thorns sprang up, and choked them. But others fell into good ground, and brought forth fruit, some a hundredfold, some

sixtyfold, some thirtyfold. Who has ears to hear, let him hear.
(MATTHEW, 13:1-9.)

*Hear you therefore the parable of the sower. When any one hears
the word of the kingdom, and understands it not, then the wicked
one comes and snatches away that which was sown in his heart.
This is he which received seed by the way side. But he that
received the seed into stony places, the same is he that heard the
word, and straight way with joy received it: Yet has he not in
himself, but stays only for a while: for when tribulation or
persecution arises because of the word, by and by he is offended.
He also that received seed among the thorns is he that hears the
word: and the care of this world, and the deceitfulness of riches
chokes the word, and he becomes unfruitful. But he that received
seed into good ground is he that hears the word, and understands
it; which also bears fruit, and brings forth some a hundred times,
some sixty, some thirty.* (MATTHEW, 13:18-23.)

6. The Parable of the Sower truly represents the various ways in
which we may make use of the teachings from the New
Testament. There are so many people for whom these teachings
are nothing more than dead words that can be compared to seeds
that fall on stony ground and produce no fruits at all.

This parable brings us a no less justifiable application of the
different categories of Spiritists. Do we not find symbolised in it
those who are only attracted to material phenomena, from which
they are unable to learn anything because they only see it as an
object of curiosity? Does it not show us those who seek the
brilliance of spirit communication merely to interest themselves as
long as it satisfies their imagination and who, after listening to the
messages, continue to be just as cold and indifferent as they were
before? Then there are those who consider the advice very good
and admire it, but only apply it to others and never to themselves.
Finally, there are those for whom the Teachings are as seeds that
fall on good soil and produce fruits.

INSTRUCTIONS FROM THE SPIRITS

DUTY

7. Duty is the moral obligation of each person, firstly to themselves and then immediately afterwards to others. Duty is the law of life. It is encountered in the smallest details as well as in the most elevated acts. Now, I wish to speak only of moral duty and not of that duty which refers to the professions.

Within the order of sentiments, duty is very difficult to fulfil because it finds itself in antagonism with the seductions of interests and of the heart. Its victories have no witnesses and its failures suffer no repressions. The intimate duty of human beings is left to their free will. The pressure of their conscience, this guardian of interior integrity, alerts and sustains people, but shows itself frequently impotent against the deceptions of passion. The duty of the heart, when faithfully observed, elevates people, but how can we define it with exactitude? Where does duty begin? Where does it end? *Duty begins exactly at the point where the happiness or tranquillity of our neighbour is threatened and therefore terminates at the limit we would not wish to be passed in relation to ourselves.*

God has created all human beings equal in relation to pain; whether small or great, ignorant or educated; everyone suffers from the same motives, so that each one may judge in clear conscience the evil that can be done. With regard to goodness in its infinite variety of expressions, the criterion is not the same. *Equality in the face of suffering is God's sublime providence. He desires that none of His children, instructed through their common experiences, should practise evil with the excuse of not knowing its effects.*

Duty is a practical summary of all moral speculations; it is the bravery of the soul that faces the anguishes of battle. It is austere and mild, ready to adapt itself to the most diverse complications while maintaining inflexibility before temptations. *The person who fulfils their duty loves God more than their fellow beings and loves their fellow beings more than themselves.* They are at the same time judge and slave in their own cause.

Duty is the most beautiful laurel of reason and is born of it as a child is born of its mother. Human beings should love duty, not because it protects them from the evils of life, from which humanity cannot escape, but because it transmits vigour to the soul necessary for its development.

Duty grows and irradiates under a constantly more elevated form in each of the superior stages of human existence. A person's moral obligations towards God never cease. They must reflect the eternal virtues that do not accept imperfect outlines because He wishes the grandeur of His work to always be resplendent in His own eyes. - LAZARUS (Paris, 1863.)

VIRTUE

8. At its highest level, virtue is a combination of all those essential qualities that constitute a good person. Namely to be good, charitable, hard working, sober and modest. Unfortunately, these virtues are usually accompanied by slight moral failures that tarnish and weaken them. The person who calls attention to their virtues is not virtuous because they lack the principle quality that is modesty; but they possess the vice in greatest opposition to modesty that is pride. A virtue that is really deserving of this name does not like to exhibit itself. We must pay attention in order to be aware of its presence; it hides in the shadows and runs away from public admiration. Saint Vincent de Paul was virtuous. The dignified curate of Ars was virtuous, as are a great many others

who are little known in this world, but are known to God. All of these good people were ignorant of the fact that they were virtuous. They allowed themselves to be carried along by their saintly inspirations, practising goodness with absolute disinterestedness and complete forgetfulness of self.

It is to this virtue well understood and practised that I call you, my children; it is to this really Christian and spiritual virtue that I invite you to commit yourselves. Remove from your hearts the sentiments of pride, vanity and self-love that always tarnish the most beautiful of these qualities. Do not imitate those people who offer themselves as models, who blow their own trumpets about their own qualities for all who are tolerant enough to listen. This ostentatious virtue usually hides a mass of wickedness and hateful weaknesses.

In principle, people who exalt themselves, who erect statues to their own virtues by this very fact annul all the merits they might effectively have had. Furthermore, what can be said of those whose only value is in appearing to be what they are not? You must clearly understand that whoever does something good, has a feeling of intimate satisfaction in the bottom of their hearts. However, from the moment that satisfaction is exteriorised to provoke praise it degenerates into self-love.

Oh, all of you whom the Spiritist faith has reanimated and warmed with its rays, who knows just how far away from perfection humanity finds itself, you will never deliver yourselves over to this failing! Virtue is a blessing that I desire for all sincere Spiritists, but with this warning: It is better to have fewer virtues and to be modest, than to have many virtues and be proud. It was because of pride that various groupings of humanities throughout the ages have successively lost themselves. It will be through humility that they will one day redeem themselves. - FRANÇOIS-NICOLAS-MADELEINE (Paris, 1863.)

THOSE WHO ARE SUPERIOR AND
THOSE WHO ARE INFERIOR

9. Just like riches, authority is delegated; and those who have received it will be required to give an account of what they have done with it. Do not believe that it has been given for the futile pleasure of command, nor even less as a right or property, as is falsely thought by the majority of powerful people on Earth. Besides, God is constantly proving that it is neither the one nor the other, since He takes it away whenever it pleases Him. If it were a privilege inherent to the person who exercised it, it would be inalienable. However, no one can say that something belongs to them when it may be taken away without their consent. God confers authority with the title of *mission* or test as He sees fit and takes it back in the same manner.

Whoever is a trustee of authority, whatever its extent may be, from the master over his servants to a sovereign over his peoples, it must never be forgotten that such people have souls in their charge. They will have to answer for both the good and bad directives given to those subordinates. The misdemeanours they may commit and the vices to which they may succumb in consequence of the directives received, or the *bad examples* they are given will all revert to those in command. Just as in the same way the fruits of the solicitudes offered in conducting these subordinates towards goodness, will also revert to those in authority. Every person on Earth has either a small or a great mission and whatever form it may take, it is always given towards goodness. Therefore, to turn it away from its purpose is to fail in the execution of the task.

Just as God asks those who are rich, "What was done with the fortune you had in your hands that should have been a source for spreading fruitfulness all around you?" He will also inquire of those who have some authority, "What have you done with your authority? What evils have you avoided? What progress have you made? If I gave you subordinates, it was not so that you could turn them into slaves for your desires or docile instruments for your whims or your greed. I made you strong and entrusted to you those who were weak, so that you could protect them and help them to climb up towards me."

The superior person, who keeps Christ's words, despises none of their subordinates. They know that social distinctions do not exist before God. Spiritism teaches us that if these people are obeying that superior person today, perhaps they had already given that person orders in the past, or may give them in the future. Then that superior person will be treated in the same manner as when they were under them.

If the superior has duties to be fulfilled, the subaltern also has duties on their side that are no less sacred. If this person is also a Spiritist, their conscience will tell them, in no uncertain terms, that they are not exempt from fulfilling these duties, even when their superior does not fulfil theirs. This is because they know that you do not repay evil with evil and that the failings of some do not authorise others to fail likewise. If they suffer in their position, they will comment that beyond doubt they deserve it because perhaps they had abused the authority they had been given at some other time, so now they are feeling the disadvantages they had made others suffer. If they are obliged to support this situation, for lack of a better one, then Spiritism teaches them to be resigned; as a test in humility that is necessary for their advancement. Their beliefs guide them in their conduct, leading them to proceed as they would like their subordinates to behave, if they were the superiors. For this reason, they are more scrupulous in the fulfilment of their obligations as they come to understand that all negligence in the work that has been confided to them, would cause a loss to the one who pays them and to whom they owe their time and effort. In a word, this person is guided by their sense of duty that their faith has instilled in them and the certainty that all turning aside from the straight and narrow pathway will be a debt incurred, that sooner or later must be repaid. - FRANÇOIS-NICOLAS-MADELEINE. Cardinal MORLOT (Paris, 1863.)

THE WORLDLY PERSON

10. A sentiment of pity should always animate the hearts of those who gather together under the eye of the Lord, imploring the assistance of the Good Spirits. Therefore, purify your hearts! Do not allow yourselves to be perturbed by futile and mundane thoughts. Lift up your spirits towards those you are calling to so they, having encountered favourable dispositions in you, may launch a profusion of seeds that should germinate in all hearts and produce the fruits of charity and justice.

Do not think, however, that in constantly urging you to pray and meditate we wish you to lead the life of a mystic, or that you should maintain yourselves outside the laws of the society in which you are condemned to reside. No. You must dwell with the people of your time in the manner in which they live. Sacrifice necessities and even the frivolities of the day, but sacrifice them with a pure sentiment that can sanctify them.

You are called upon to be in contact with spirits of diverse natures and opposite characters; do not enter into conflict with any with whom you may find yourself. Always be happy and content, with the happiness that comes from a clear conscience and the contentment of one who will inherit Heaven and is counting the days until they receive their inheritance.

Virtue does not consist in having a severe and gloomy appearance, or in repelling the pleasures that the human condition permits. It is sufficient to refer all your acts to God, who gave you your life. It is enough that at the commencement and at the end of each task, you lift up your thoughts to the Creator, asking Him with a heartfelt impulse for His protection in order to execute the work, or His blessing on its termination. On doing anything at all, take your thoughts up to that Supreme Source. Do nothing without first thinking of God, so that this thought may come to purify and sanctify your acts.

Perfection, as Christ said, can only to be found in the practice of unlimited charity, since the duties of charity cover all social positions, from the lowliest to the most elevated. The person who lives a life of isolation by choice will have no means of exercising charity. It is only by being in contact with one's fellow creatures, in painful battle, that we are able to find occasion to practise it. People who live in isolation are therefore entirely deprived of the most powerful means of perfecting themselves. In only having to think of oneself, life becomes that of a selfish person. (See chapter 5 - item 26.)

However, do not imagine that in order to be in constant contact with us and live under the watchful eye of God, you must wear a hair shirt and cover yourselves with ashes. No, no, and yet again no! Be happy within the picture of human needs, but in this happiness never allow a thought or an act that could offend God, or cause a shadow to fall upon the face of those who love you or direct you. God is love and He blesses all who sanctify their own. - A PROTECTING SPIRIT (Bordeaux, 1863.)

LOOK AFTER BOTH BODY AND SPIRIT

11. Does spiritual perfection depend on the mortification of the body? In order to resolve this question, I will base myself on elementary principles and begin by demonstrating the need to take care of the body which, according to the alternatives of health and sickness, has a very important influence upon the soul because we must consider it a prisoner of the flesh. In order that this prisoner

can live, move and even have an illusion of liberty, the body must be sound, of good disposition and vigorous. Let us then make a comparison. Let us suppose that both are in perfect condition; what then should be done to maintain the balance between their aptitudes and their necessities that are so very different? A battle seems to be inevitable between these two and it is not easy to find the secret of how to reach a balance.

In this case, two systems are confronting each other. That of the ascetics who wish to bring down the body, and that of the materialist who wishes to diminish the soul. Resulting in two forms of violence, each one almost as foolish as the other. Alongside these two enormous groupings, look at the indifferent multitudes that are without either conviction or passion, who love with tepidness and are economic with their pleasure. Where then is wisdom? Where then is the science of living? Nowhere at all! This great problem would have remained unsolved if Spiritism had not come to help the researchers and demonstrate to them the relationship that exists between the body and the soul, and to tell them that as they are both reciprocally necessary, it is indispensable that both are looked after.

So then, love your soul and also look after your body, which is the instrument of the soul. To pay no attention to these needs that Nature itself indicates, is to ignore God's Laws. Do not castigate your body due to failings that your free will can induce you to commit and for which it is just as responsible as is the badly driven vehicle for the accidents it causes. Perchance, will you be more perfect if by tormenting your body you do not become less selfish, less prideful and more charitable towards your neighbours? No, perfection is not to be found in this manner, but exclusively in the reformation to which you submit your spirit. Discipline it, subjugate it and mortify it. This is the way to make it more docile to God's will and is the one and only way that leads to perfection - GEORGES, A PROTECTING SPIRIT. (Paris, 1863.)

CHAPTER 18

MANY ARE CALLED, BUT FEW ARE CHOSEN

The parable of the wedding feast. - The narrow door - Not all who say, "Lord! Lord!" will enter into the kingdom of Heaven. - Much will be asked of the one who has received much. - INSTRUCTIONS FROM THE SPIRITS: To those who have will be given more. - Christians are recognised by their works.

THE PARABLE OF THE WEDDING FEAST

1. And Jesus answered and spoke to them again by parables, and said, The kingdom of heaven is like a certain king, which made a marriage for his son, And sent forth his servants to call them that were bidden to the wedding: and they would not come. Again he sent forth other servants, saying, Tell them which are bidden, Behold, I have prepared my dinner: my oxen and my fatlings, are killed, and all things are ready: come to the marriage. But they made light of it, and went their ways, one to his farm, another to his merchandise; And the remnant took his servants, and ill-treated them spitefully, and slew them. But when the king heard thereof, he was angry: and he sent forth his armies, and destroyed those murderers, and burned up their city.

Then said he to his servants, The wedding is ready, but they which were bidden were not worthy. Go you therefore into the highways, and as many as you can find, invite them to the marriage. So the servants went out into the highways, and gathered together as many as they found, both good and bad: and the wedding was furnished with guests.

When the king came in to see the guests, he saw there a man which had not on a wedding garment: And he said to him, Friend, how come you in hither not having a wedding garment? And he was speechless. Then said the king to the servants, Bind him hand

and foot, and take him away, and cast him into outer darkness;
there will be weeping and gnashing of teeth. For many are called,
but few are chosen. (MATTHEW, 22:1-14.)

2. Those who are incredulous laugh at this parable that seems to them to be childishly ingenuous, because they are unable to understand there could be so many difficulties in going to participate in a wedding feast. Even more so, that the guests would resist the invitation to such a point as to massacre those who had been sent to invite them by the master of the house. "Parables" say the incredulous, "beyond doubt are figurative, but nevertheless it is not necessary to ultra-pass the limits of plausibility."

The same may be said about allegories or ingenious fables if their respective outer coverings are not removed to find their hidden meaning. Jesus composed His allegories from the most common of everyday occurrences and customs and then adapted these to the characters of the people to whom He spoke. The vast majority of these allegories had as their objective the penetration into the minds of the masses the idea of a spiritual life. Many appear to be unintelligible merely because those who listen do not look at them from this point of view.

In this parable, Jesus compares the kingdom of heaven to a feast, where everything is happiness and good fortune. When referring to the first guests to be invited He alludes to the Hebrews, who were the earliest peoples to be called by God to know His law. Those sent by the king are the prophets who came to advise them to follow the road of true happiness. However, their words were barely listened to and their warnings were disregarded; many were massacred, like those in the parable. The guests who declined the invitation with excuses of having to look after their pastures and their businesses symbolise those worldly people who, being absorbed in terrestrial matters, remain indifferent to the things of heaven.

It was the common belief amongst the Jews of those times that their nation had to achieve supremacy over all other nations. In effect, was it not God who had promised Abraham that his posterity would cover the face of the Earth? However, as always, they paid attention only to form and not to the substance, believing it meant actual material domination.

Before the coming of Christ all peoples, with the exception of the Hebrew's, were idol worshippers and polytheistics. If a few people, superior to the vast majority, conceived the idea of a unique God that idea remained only as a personal belief. Nowhere was it received as a fundamental idea, except perhaps by a few initiates who hid their knowledge under a veil of mystery, impenetrable to the masses. The Hebrew's were the first to publicly practise monotheism and it was to them that God transmitted His Law. Firstly through Moses and later through Jesus. From this tiny focal point, the light that was destined to spread throughout the whole world went forth to triumph over paganism and to give Abraham a *spiritual* posterity "as numerous as the stars that fill the skies." Nevertheless, having completely abandoned idol worship, the Jews scorned the moral law and persisted in the practice of an external cult that was easier. Evil came to a head and the nation was destroyed, enslaved and divided into sects; incredulity had reached even the sanctuary. It was at this point that Jesus appeared, having been sent to call them to keep the Law and to open up the new horizons of a future life. Having been the first to be invited to the great banquet of universal faith, they rejected the words of the Celestial Messiah and sacrificed Him. In this manner, they lost the rewards that should have been reaped from their own initiatives.

However, it would be unjust to accuse the entire population for this state of affairs. The responsibility rests primarily with the Pharisees and Sadducees, who sacrificed the nation through the pride and fanaticism of some and the incredulity of others.

Therefore, it is these above all the rest, whom Jesus identified among those guests who refused to appear at the wedding feast. He then added that on seeing their refusal, the master of the house told his servants to go out into the highways and gather all those they could find, good and bad alike. In this manner Jesus was saying that the Word would be preached to all the other peoples, pagans and idol worshippers and that these on accepting it would be admitted to the feast in place of the initial guests.

Nevertheless, it is not enough to be invited; it is not enough to say you are a Christian or to sit at the table in order to take part in the celestial banquet. Before all else, it is essential as an express condition, to be clothed in the nuptial tunic; that is to say, to be pure of heart and comply with the spirit of the Law. However, although all the law is contained in the words *'without charity there is no salvation,'* amongst all those who hear the divine Word there are so few who keep it and make good use of it! So few become worthy to enter into the kingdom of heaven! This is why Jesus said: *"Many are called, but few are chosen."*

THE NARROW DOOR

3. Enter you in at the strait gate: for wide is the gate, and broad is the way, that leads to destruction, and many there are which go through there. Because strait is the gate, and narrow is the way, which leads to life, and few there are that find it. (MATTHEW, 7:13-14.)

4. Then one said to Him, Lord, are there few that be saved? And he said to them, Strive to enter in at the strait gate: for many, I say to you, will seek to enter in, and will not be able. When once the master of the house is risen up, and shut the door, and you begin to stand without, and to knock at the door, saying, Lord, Lord, open to us; and He will answer and say to you, I know you not whence you are come from: Then shall you begin to say, We have eaten and drunk in Your presence, and You have taught in our streets. But He will say, I tell you, I know you not, or from whence come; depart from me, all you workers of iniquity. There will be weeping and gnashing of teeth, when you shall see Abraham, and Isaac, and Jacob, and all the prophets, in the Kingdom of God, and you yourselves thrust out. And they shall come from the east, and from the west, and from the north, and from the south, and shall sit down at the feast in the Kingdom of God. And, behold, there are last which shall be first, and there are first which shall be last. (LUKE, 13:23-30.)

5. Wide is the door to damnation, because evil passions are numerous and the vast majority follow this pathway. That of salvation is narrow, because each person is obliged to exert great control over themselves in order to dominate their evil tendencies, if they wish to pass through and this is something that few are resigned enough to do. It complements the maxim 'Many are called, but few are chosen.'

This then is the present situation of Earth's population, because as the Earth is a world of atonement, evil is the predominating factor. When the planet has been transformed, then the pathway to goodness will be the one most frequently followed. Therefore, these words should be understood in a relative manner and not as an absolute. If this were to be the permanent state of humanity then God would have condemned the great majority of His creatures to damnation, which is an inadmissible supposition since we recognise that God is all justice and all kindness.

What crimes have human beings committed to deserve such an unhappy state of affairs, in the present and in the future? Why is everything here on Earth so degraded, if the soul has had no previous existence? Why are there so many obstacles placed before each one? Why is the gateway so narrow as to allow only a few to enter, if the destiny of the soul is permanently determined immediately after death? With only one existence, humans would always be at odds with themselves and with God's justice.

However, with the pre-existence of the soul and the plurality of worlds, the horizons spread out and enlightenment comes to even the most obscure points of faith. Then the present and the future become linked to the past, so it is possible to understand the depth, truth and wisdom of the maxims of Christ.

NOT ALL WHO SAY, "LORD! LORD!" WILL ENTER INTO THE KINGDOM OF HEAVEN

6. Not every one that says to me, "Lord, Lord," will enter into the kingdom of heaven; but he that does the will of my Father, which is in Heaven. Many will say to me on that day, Lord, Lord, did we not prophesied in your name? and in Your name have cast out devils? and in Your name done many wonderful works? And then will I profess to them, I never knew you: depart from me, you that work iniquity. (MATTHEW, 7:21-23.)

7. Therefore whoever hears these sayings of mine, and does them, I will liken him to a wise man, which built his house upon a rock, and the rain descended, and the floods came, and the winds blew, and beat upon the house; and it fell not: for it was founded upon a rock. And everyone that hears these sayings of mine, and does them not, shall be likened to a foolish man, who built his house upon sand: And the rain descended, and the floods came, and the winds blew, and beat upon the house and it fell: and great was the fall of it. (MATTHEW, 7:24-27, and similarly in LUKE, 6:46-49.)

8. Whosoever, therefore, shall break one of these least commandments, and shall teach men so, he shall be called the least in the kingdom of heaven: but whosoever shall do and teach them, the same shall be called great in the kingdom of heaven. (MATTHEW, 5:19.)

9. All who recognise the mission of Jesus say, "Lord! Lord!" But of what use is it to call Him 'Teacher' or 'Lord' when you do not follow His precepts? Are they Christians then, those who honour Him with exterior acts of devotion, while at the same time

yielding to pride, selfishness, greed and all the passions? Are they then His disciples, those who pass their days in prayer, yet show themselves no better, nor more charitable, nor more indulgent towards their fellow beings? No, seeing that just as the Pharisees they have a prayer on their lips but not in their hearts. They can impress people with their manner, but not God. In vain they can say to Jesus, "Lord! Do we not prophesy, that is to say, do we not teach in Your name? Do we not expel demons in Your name? Do we not eat and drink with You?" Nevertheless, He will reply to them saying, "I know not who you are; go away from me, you who commit iniquity, you who deny by your acts what you say with your lips; who slander your neighbour, who rob widows and commit adultery. Go away from me, you whose hearts distil hate and bile, who spill the blood of your brothers and sisters in My name; who cause tears to flow instead of drying them. For you there will be weeping and gnashing of teeth, seeing that God's Kingdom is for those who are gentle, humble and charitable. Do not expect to bend God's justice by the multiplicity of your words or by the amount of your kneeling. The only pathway that is open, wherein you may find grace in His sight, is by the sincere practice of the law of love and charity."

These words of Jesus are eternal, because they are the truth. They constitute not only a safe conduct to celestial life, but also a pledge of peace, tranquillity and the stability of earthly things. This is why all human institutions, be they political, social or religious that rely on these words will always remain steadfast as the house built upon a rock. Human beings will retain them because in them will be found happiness. However, those who violate these words will be as the house built upon sand, which the wind of renewal and the river of progress will sweep away.

MUCH WILL BE ASKED OF THE ONE WHO HAS RECEIVED MUCH

10. And that servant, who knew his lord's will, and prepare not himself, neither did according to his will, shall be beaten with many stripes. But he that knew not, and did commit things worthy of stripes, shall be beaten with few stripes. For to whomsoever much is given, of him they will ask the more. (LUKE, 12:47 & 48.)

11. And Jesus said, For judgement I am come into this world, that they, which see not, might see; and that they which see might be made blind. And some of the Pharisees which were with him heard these words, and said to him, Are we blind also? Jesus said to them, If you were blind, you should have no sin: but now you say, We see; therefore your sin remains. (JOHN, 9:39-41.)

12. These maxims find their application especially in the teachings of the Spirits. Whoever knows Christ's precepts, but does not keep them are certainly guilty. Although the Gospel that contains them is only taught within Christian denominations, even amongst these there are many who do not read them! Even amongst those who do read them, there are many who do not understand them! The result of this is that the words of Jesus remain lost to the majority of humanity.

When teaching, the Spirits reproduce these maxims in many varied formats. In developing and commenting on them, so as to bring them within the understanding of all, they have the particularity of never being circumscribed. Every person, be they learned or illiterate, believer or incredulous, Christian or not, is able to receive them, because the Spirits communicate in all places. No one who receives them, either directly or through an intermediary, can allege ignorance; neither can they excuse themselves through lack of instruction, nor because of allegorical obscurity. Therefore, those who do not take advantage of these maxims to better themselves; who admire them only as something curious or interesting, without allowing their hearts to be touched; who do not become less futile, less prideful, less selfish, less attached to material things or who become no better towards their neighbour, will be all the more guilty in proportion to the number of ways open to them to acquire knowledge of the truth.

Mediums that receive good communications are even more censurable if they continue to persist in evil, because they frequently write their own condemnation. In addition, if it were not for their being so blinded by pride, they would recognise that the Spirits are actually speaking to them. Instead of taking the lessons they receive, or those they read about written by others for themselves, their only preoccupation is in applying these lessons to others. In this manner, they confirm these words of Jesus, "You see the speck in the eye of your neighbour, but do not see the beam that is in yours." (See chapter 10 - item 9.)

In the sentence, "If you had been blind, you would not have sinned," Jesus wished to show that culpability is according to how enlightened a person may or may not be. Thus, the Pharisees, who maintained the pretence of being the most enlightened peoples of their nation, showed themselves to be guiltier before God than those who were ignorant. The same applies today.

Much will be asked of Spiritists, because they have received much; on the other hand, to those who have taken every advantage of their learning, much will be given. Therefore, the first thought of all sincere Spiritists should be to find out if, in the counselling received from the Spirits, there is not something that applies to them.

Spiritism will multiply the number of those who are *called*; likewise, through growing faith the proportion of those who are *chosen* will also be multiplied.

INSTRUCTIONS FROM THE SPIRITS

TO THOSE WHO HAVE WILL BE GIVEN MORE

13. And the disciples came, and said to him, Why do you speak to them in parables? He answered and said to them, Because it is given to you to know the mysteries of the kingdom of heaven, but to them it is not given. For whosoever has, to him shall be given, and he shall have more abundance: but whosoever has not, from him shall be taken away even that he has. Therefore speak I to them in parables: because they seeing see not: and hearing they hear not, neither do they understand. And in them is fulfilled the prophecy of Esaias, which says, By hearing you shall hear, and shall not understand; and seeing you shall see, and shall not perceive. (MATTHEW, 13:10-14.)

14. And He said to them, Take care what you hear: with what measure you use, it will be measured to you: and to you that hear shall more be given. From he that has, to him shall be given: and he that has not, from him shall be taken that which he has. (MARK, 4:24 & 25.)

15. "It shall be given to who already has, and to who has not it shall be taken away." Let us meditate on these great teachings that have so often seemed paradoxical. Those who have received signify those who understand the meaning of the divine Word. They have received it solely because they have tried to be worthy of it and because the Lord, in His merciful love, animates the efforts of those who are inclined towards goodness. By their unceasing perseverance, their efforts attract the blessings of God that act like a magnet calling to itself progressive betterment. It is these copious blessings that make them strong enough to scale the sacred mountain on whose pinnacle is found rest after labour.

"It will be taken from the one that has nothing or has very little." This is to be understood as a figurative antithesis. God does not retract the good He has conceded. Blind and deaf humanity! Use your intelligence and your hearts; see with the eyes of your spirit; listen by means of your soul and do not interpret so coarsely and unjustly the words of He, Who makes the justice of God shine resplendently before your eyes. It is not God who takes away from the one who has but little, but that spirit itself who, by being wasteful and careless, does not know how to conserve, increase and bring to fulfilment the mite which had been given to that heart.

The one who does not cultivate the field, which the labour of their father had gained with his work and left for their inheritance, will see it covered with weeds and parasites. Is it then their father who took away the harvest they did not prepare? If through lack of care they allowed the seedlings destined to produce the crop to wither, is it the father they should accuse for their having produced nothing? No, certainly not! Instead of accusing the one who had done all the preparing and criticise their donation, they should complain to the real author of their miseries. Then with repentance and a desire to be industrious, they should put themselves to work courageously to reclaim the soil by sheer willpower. They should dig deeply, with the help of repentance and hope and confidently sow good seeds that they have separated from the bad, watering them with love and charity. Then God, the God of love and charity, will give to those who have already received. They will see their efforts crowned with success and one grain will produce a hundred and another a thousand. Courage, workers! Take up your harrows and your ploughs; work with your hearts; tear out the weeds; sow the good seed that the Lord has given and the dew of love will cause the fruits of charity to grow. - A FRIENDLY SPIRIT. (Bordeaux, 1862.)

CHRISTIANS ARE RECOGNISED BY THEIR WORKS

16. "Not all of those who say: Lord! Lord! will enter into Heaven, but only those who do the Will of my Father, who is in Heaven."

Listen to these words of the Master, all those who reject the Spiritist Teachings as the work of the devil. Open your ears because the moment to listen has arrived.

Is it sufficient to be working for the Master, to be His faithful servant? Is it enough to say 'I am a Christian' for anyone to be a follower of Christ? Search for the true Christians and you will recognise them by their works. "A good tree cannot give forth bad fruits or a bad tree good fruits." "Every tree that does not give forth good fruits will be cut down and cast into the fire." These are the words of the Master. Disciples of Christ understand them well! What kind of fruits should be given by the tree of Christianity that is a mighty tree, whose leafy branches cover part of the world with shade, but does not yet cover all who should gather round it? The fruits of the Tree of Life are the fruits of life, of hope and of faith. Christianity, as it has done for many centuries, continues to preach these divine virtues. It uses all its strength to distribute its fruits, but so few pick them! The Tree is always good, but the gardeners are bad. They have tried to mould it to their own ideas, to prune it in accordance to their necessities. They have cut it, diminished it and mutilated it. Its sterile branches do not produce bad fruits, because they produce nothing anymore. The thirsty travellers, who stops under its branches looking for the fruits of hope that are capable of restoring strength and courage, sees only bare branches foretelling a coming storm. In vain they seek for the fruits of life, from the Tree of Life. Only dry leaves fall at their feet because the hands of humanity have so tampered with it that it has become scorched.

My dearly beloved, open then your hearts and ears. Cultivate the Tree of Life, whose fruits give eternal life. The One who planted it incites you to treat it with love, and even yet you will see it give an abundance of its divine fruits. Conserve it just as it was when Christ gave it to you. Do not mutilate it; it wants to cast its immense shade over the Universe, so do not cut its branches. Its tasty fruits will fall abundantly to satiate the hungry travellers who wishes to reach the end of their journey. Do not gather these fruits in order to keep them and then leave them to rot, so they are of no use to anyone. "Many are called, but few are chosen." There are those who monopolize the Bread of Life, just as there are those who monopolize material bread; do not be one of them. The Tree that gives good fruit must give to everyone. Go then and seek those who are hungry, lead them under the leafy branches of the Tree of Life and share with them the shelter it offers. "You cannot collect grapes from amongst the thorns." My friends, turn away from those who call to you in order to show you the thorns of the way; instead, follow those who will lead you under the shade of the Tree of Life.

The Divine Saviour, the just par excellence spoke, and His words will never die, "Not all who say: Lord! Lord! will enter into the kingdom of heaven, but only those who do the Will of my Father who is in heaven."

May the Lord of blessings bless you; may the God of Light illuminate you; may the Tree of Life offer you abundant fruits! Believe and pray. – SIMEON. (Bordeaux, 1863.)

CHAPTER 19

FAITH TRANSPORTS MOUNTAINS

The power of faith. - Religious faith. The state of unshakeable faith. - The parable of the withered fig tree. - INSTRUCTIONS FROM THE SPIRITS: Faith, the mother of hope and charity. - Divine faith and human faith.

THE POWER OF FAITH

1. And when they were come to the multitude, there came to him a certain man, kneeling down to him, saying, Lord, have mercy on my son for he is a lunatic, and sore vexed: for many times he falls into the fire, and many times into the water. And I brought him to your disciples, and they could not cure him. Then Jesus answered and said, O faithless and perverse generation, how long shall I be with you? how long shall I suffer you? bring him here to me. And Jesus rebuked the devil; and he departed out of him: and the child was cured from that very hour. Then came the disciples to Jesus in private and said, Why could we not cast him out? And Jesus said to them, Because of your unbelief: for verily I say to you, If you have faith the size of mustard seed, you shall say to this mountain, Remove from here to there; and it will remove*; and nothing shall be impossible for you.* (MATTHEW, 17:14-20.)

2. In considering ourselves, it is certain that confidence in our own strength gives us the capacity to carry out material things, that we would not be able to do if we doubted ourselves. However, here we wish to deal exclusively with the moral sense of these words. The mountains that faith can transport are the difficulties, the resistances, the ill will; in fact, all those things that humans have to face, even when we refer to the best things. The prejudices, routines, material interests, selfishness, the blindness of fanaticism and prideful passions are but a few of the mountains

that block the way of those who work for the progress of Humanity. Robust faith gives perseverance, energy and resources that allow us to overcome these obstacles, be they large or small. Wavering faith only results in uncertainty and is the kind of hesitancy that our adversaries take advantage of; this kind of faith does not even try to find a means to win because it does not believe in the possibility of victory.

3. Another acceptation of the term gives us to understand that faith is the confidence we have in the realisation of something, the certainty of attaining a specific end. It gives us a kind of lucidness that permits us to know in our minds the goal we wish to reach and the means of getting there. So those who have faith go forward in a manner of speaking, with absolute security. In either of these cases, faith can give rise to the realisation of great things.

Faith that is real and sincere is always calm; it permits a patience that knows how to wait, because having its foundation in intelligence and an understanding of life, it is certain of reaching the objective it aspires to. Vacillating faith feels its own weakness; when its interest is aroused, it becomes frenzied and thinks it can supply the force it lacks by using violence. Calmness during the struggle is always a sign of strength and confidence, whereas on the contrary violence denotes weakness and self-doubt.

4. It behoves us not to confuse faith with presumption. True faith is linked to humility; those who have it deposit more confidence in God than in themselves, as they know they are but simple instruments of Divine Purpose and can do nothing without God. This is the reason why the Good Spirits come to their aid. Presumption is more pride than faith, and pride is always punished sooner or later by the deceptions and frustrations inflicted upon it.

5. The power of faith receives a direct and special magnetic application; through its intermediary, the person acts under the influence of these fluids, being universal agents, modifying their

qualities and giving them, in a manner of speaking, irresistible impulsion. From this, it follows that whoever joins a normally great fluidic power to that of ardent faith can, solely by the strength of their willpower directed towards goodness, operate those singular phenomena of healing and other occurrences known in olden times as miracles. This is because they are nothing more than the consequences of a Law of Nature. This is the reason for Jesus saying to His apostles that if they did not cure it was because they had no faith.

RELIGIOUS FAITH. THE STATE OF UNSHAKABLE FAITH

6. From the religious point of view, faith consists of a belief in the special dogmas that constitute the various religions. All of them have their articles of faith. From this aspect, faith may be either *blind* or *rationalised*. Blind faith examines nothing and accepts without verification both truth and falsehood, and at each step clashes with evidence and reason. Taken to the extreme, it produces *fanaticism*. While sitting upon error, sooner or later it collapses. The only faith that is based on truth guarantees the future because it has nothing to fear from the progress of enlightenment, seeing that *what is true in obscurity is also true in daylight.* Each religion claims to have possession of the exclusive truth. *However, for someone to proclaim blind faith on a point of belief is to confess themselves impotent to demonstrate that they are right.*

7. It is commonly said that *faith cannot be prescribed*, from which many people declare it is not their fault if they have no faith. Beyond doubt, faith cannot be prescribed, and what is even more certain, *it cannot be imposed.* No, it cannot be prescribed but only acquired, and there is no one who is prevented from possessing it, even amongst those who are most refractory. We are

speaking of basic spiritual truths and not of any particular belief. It is not the part of faith to seek these people out, but they themselves who should go and seek faith, and if they search with sincerity, they are bound to find it. You can be sure that those who say, "There is nothing I should like more than to believe, but I cannot," only say this with their lips and not with their hearts, seeing that while they are saying it they close their ears. However, the proof is all around them, so why do they refuse to see? On the part of some it is indifference; of others the fear of being forced to change their habits. Nevertheless, in the majority, there is pride that refuses to recognise the existence of a superior force, because they would then have to bow down before it.

In certain people faith appears to be inborn, a spark being enough to cause it to unfold. This ease of assimilation of spiritual truths is an evident sign of previous progress. On the contrary, in others, there is a difficulty of assimilation that is a no less evident sign of their backward natures. The first already believe and understand, having brought with them on being reborn the intuition of what they know. Their education is complete. The second still has everything to learn; their education is still to come. Nevertheless, come it will, and if it is not completed in this existence then it will be in another.

The resistance of the unbeliever, we must agree, is usually due less to himself than to the manner in which things have been put to him. Faith needs a base, one that gives a complete understanding of what we are asked to accept. In order to believe it is not enough *to see*, but above all else, it is necessary to *understand*. Blind faith is no longer of this century, so much so, that it is exactly blind dogmatic faith that produces the greatest number of unbelievers today, because it tries to impose itself, demanding the abdication of the most precious prerogatives of humankind, which are rationalisation and free-will. It is principally against this kind of faith that the unbeliever rebels, so showing that it is true to say faith cannot be prescribed. Due to the non-acceptance of any proofs, blind faith leaves the spirit with a feeling of emptiness that gives birth to doubt. Rationalised faith, when based on facts and logic, leaves no doubts. Then the person believes because they are certain, and no one can be certain unless they understand. This is why they are unshakeable because *unshakeable faith is that which can stand face to face with reason in all epochs of humanity.*

This is the result to which Spiritism conducts us, as long as it does not encounter systematic and preconceived opposition, so triumphing against incredulity.

THE PARABLE OF THE WITHERED FIG TREE

8. And on the morrow as they were come from Bethany, he was hungry: and seeing a fig tree afar off having leaves, he came, if perhaps he might find any thing thereon: and when he came to it, he found nothing but leaves; for the time of figs was not yet. And Jesus answered and said to it, No man eat fruit of thee hereafter for ever. And his disciples heard it. And in the morning, as they passed by, they saw the fig tree dried up from the roots. And Peter calling to remembrance said to him, Master, behold, the fig tree which you cursed is withered away. And Jesus answering said to them, "Have faith in God. For truly I say to you, That whosoever shall say to this mountain, Be you removed, and be you cast into the sea; and shall not doubt in his heart, but shall believe that those things which he says shall come to pass, he shall have whatsoever he says. (MARK, 11:12-14 & 20-23.)

9. The fig tree that dried-up is a symbol of those people appearing to have a tendency towards goodness, but who in reality produce nothing worthwhile. They are like the preachers who show more brilliance than substance. Whose words have a superficial varnish to them in order to please the ear, but which on close examination reveal nothing substantial for the heart, and

after having listened to them we ask ourselves of what benefit they have been.

It also symbolizes all those who can be useful but are not; of all utopias, empty orders and doctrines without solid bases. What is most lacking in the majority of cases is true faith, productive faith, the kind of faith that moves the fibers of the heart, in a word, the faith that moves mountains. These people are as trees covered in leaves but devoid of fruit. This is why Jesus condemns them to sterility, for the day will come when they will find themselves dry, even to the roots. This is to say that all orders and doctrines, which have produced no good for Humanity, will be reduced to nothing. That all people who are deliberately purposeless or idle, because they have not put into action the resources they have brought with them, will be treated as the fig tree that dried up.

10. Mediums are the interpreters of the Spirits; supplying the physical organs through which they may transmit their instructions. Here is the reason why they are endowed with faculties for this purpose. In these present days of social renewal, they have a very special incumbency. They are like trees that are destined to supply spiritual sustenance to their brothers and sisters. Their numbers multiply so there may be an abundance of nutriment. They are everywhere, in all countries, in all social classes, amongst rich and poor, great and small, so that no place may be without them to demonstrate to humans that *all are called*. However, if they turn away from the providential objective for which this precious faculty was conceded; if they employ it for futile or prejudicial things; if they put it to the service of mundane interests; if the fruits are bad instead of being good; if they refuse to utilise it for the benefit of others; if they take no benefit from it for themselves, thereby becoming better people, then they are like the sterile fig tree. God will take away the gift that has become useless in their hands, that seed from which they did not know

how to bring forth fruit, and will allow them to fall into the hands of evil Spirits.

INSTRUCTIONS FROM THE SPIRITS

FAITH, THE MOTHER OF HOPE AND CHARITY

11. In order to be profitable, faith must be active; it must not become benumbed. Mother of all the virtues that lead to God, it has a duty to attentively keep watch over the development of all of its children.

Hope and charity are the consequences of faith; these three virtues form an inseparable trinity. Is it not faith that helps us to have hope in the realisation of God's promises? If there were no faith what would there be to hope for? Is it not faith that gives love? If you do not have faith, what would be your worth and what quality would your love have?

Faith, that divine inspiration from God that awakens all those noble instincts that lead humans towards goodness, is the base of all regeneration. Therefore, it is necessary that this base be strong and durable, as even the smallest doubt will cause it to tremble, and what then of the edifice constructed upon it. Consequently, this edifice must be raised upon immovable foundations. Your faith must be stronger than the sophisms and mockery of the incredulous, seeing that faith which cannot stand up to ridicule is not true faith.

Sincere faith is gripping and contagious; it communicates itself to those who have none or who do not even desire it. It finds persuasive words that touch the soul, whereas apparent faith only uses high-sounding words that leave those who listen cold and indifferent. Preach through the firmness of your hope, so they may see the confidence that fortifies and puts you in condition to confront all life's vicissitudes.

So then, have faith with all that it contains of beauty and goodness, with its pureness and rationality. Do not accept a faith that cannot be substantiated. Love God knowing why you love Him. Believe in His promises knowing why you believe in them. Follow our counsel convinced of the end to which we direct you, and the ways by which we take you in order to achieve it. Believe and wait, without losing heart; miracles are the works of faith. - JOSEPH, A PROTECTING SPIRIT (Bordeaux, 1862.)

DIVINE FAITH AND HUMAN FAITH

12. In human beings, faith is the inherent sentiment of their future destiny. It is the source, in a latent state, of the consciousness they have of the immense faculties implanted in their inner-self, that it is their duty to make blossom forth and grow by the action of their will.

Until now, faith has not been understood, except from the religious sense because Christ extolled it as a powerful lever and because He has been seen only as the head of a religion. But Christ, who performed material miracles, demonstrated through these same miracles, what humans can do when they have faith; that is to say when they have the will to wish and the certainty that such willpower can obtain results. By following the example of Jesus, the apostles also obtained miracles. Well then, what were these miracles except natural causes that were unknown by humans at that time? But today have mostly been explained and will be completely understood through the study of Spiritism and magnetism.

Faith is both human and divine according to how people apply their faculties to satisfy their earthly needs or for their heavenly and future aspirations.   Individuals of genius, who launch themselves upon accomplishments of some great enterprise, triumph if they have faith, because they feel within themselves they can and must reach it. This certainty of accomplishment provides them with immense power. The morally good person who, believing in their heavenly future, wishing to fill their life with noble and beautiful actions and being sure of the happiness that awaits them, draws the necessary strength from their faith, thereby accomplishing miracles of charity, devotion and selflessness. Finally, there are no evil tendencies that cannot be overcome with faith.

Magnetism is one of the greatest proofs of the power of faith put into action. It is through faith that magnetism heals and produces remarkable phenomena that previously were regarded as miracles.

We repeat: Faith is both *human and divine*. If all incarnates were fully convinced of the forces they bring within themselves, and if they wanted to utilize their will power to put it to serve these forces, they would be able to accomplish that which, till today, are still called prodigies, but which nevertheless are nothing more than the development of human faculties. - A PROTECTING SPIRIT. (Paris, 1863.)

CHAPTER 20

WORKERS OF THE LAST HOUR

INSTRUCTIONS FROM THE SPIRITS: The last shall be the first. - The mission of the Spiritists. - The workers of the Lord.

1. For the kingdom of heaven is like a man who is a householder, which went out early in the morning to hire labourers for his vineyard. And when he had agreed with the labourers for a penny a day, he sent them into his vineyard. And he went out about the third hour, and saw others standing idle in the marketplace. And said to them: Go you also into the vineyard, and whatever is right I will give you. And they went their way. Again he went out about the sixth and ninth hour, and did likewise. And about the eleventh hour he went out, and found others standing idle, and said to them, 'Why do you stand here all day idle?' They said to him, Because no man has hired us. He said to them, 'Go also into the vineyard, and whatsoever is right, that shall you receive.

So when the evening came, the lord of the vineyard said to his steward, 'Call the labourers, and give them their hire, beginning from the last to the first. And when they came that were hired about the eleventh hour, they received every man a penny. But when the first came, they supposed that they should have received more; and they likewise received every man a penny. And when they had received it, they murmured against the good man of the house, Saying, 'These last have worked but one hour, and you have made them equal to us, which have borne the burden and the heat of the day.'

But he answered one of them and said, Friend, I do you no wrong: did you not agree with me for a penny? Take what yours is and go your way. I will give to this last, even as to you. Is it not lawful for me to do what I will with my own? Is your eye evil, because I am good?

So the last shall be first, and the first last: for many are called but few chosen. (MATTHEW, 20:1-16. See also the Parable of the Wedding Feast, Chapter 18, item 1.)

INSTRUCTIONS FROM THE SPIRITS

THE LAST SHALL BE THE FIRST

2. The worker of the last hour has a right to his wages; nevertheless, it is important that his lateness is not due to either laziness or reluctance, but to the fact that, although willing to work, he had been patiently waiting for someone to employ him. He has a right to his wages because since dawn, he has waited anxiously for someone who would finally offer work; he was hard working, it was only that he lacked the opportunity.

However, if he had refused to work at any time during the day, or if he had said, "Wait a while, rest is very agreeable to me; when the last hour sounds then I will think about the day's wages. What need have I to be bothered by an employer I have no regard for and do not even know? The later the better." This person, my friends, would not have received the wages of a worker, but of laziness.

What would you say then of someone who, instead of remaining inactive, utilized those hours destined for the day's labour to practice culpable acts? Who blasphemed against God, spilt the blood of their brothers and sisters, launched perturbation amongst families and ruined those who trusted in him by abusing their innocence. Someone who, in short, satiated themselves with all the ignominies of human nature? What would become of this person? Is it enough for them to say at the last hour: Sir, I have used my time badly. Take me on till the end of the day so I do some work, although it will be very little of what was my share and give me the wages of a good worker? No, no! The Master would say, "I have no work for you at present. You squandered away your time; you forgot what you had learnt; you can no longer work in my vineyard. Consequently, you must recommence your learning and when you are better disposed come again to me and I will throw open my vast fields to you, where you may work at any time of the day."

Good Spiritists, my dearly beloved, you are all workers of the last hour. The one who says, "I began work at dawn and will only finish at nightfall," is very conceited. All of you came when you were called - some a little earlier, some a little later - to this incarnation whose shackles you now carry. For how many centuries has the Lord called you to His vineyard without you wishing to enter it? Here is the moment to pocket your wages, so put to good use the time that is left and never forget that your existence, however long it may appear to be, is nothing but a fleeting moment in the immensity of time that forms eternity. - CONSTANTINE, A PROTECTING SPIRIT (Bordeaux, 1863.)

3. Jesus liked the simplicity of symbols and in His virile language, the workers who arrived at the first hour were the prophets. Moses and all the initiates, who have marked the steps of progress that continued to be signposted throughout the ages by the apostles, the martyrs, the founders of the Church, the wise men, the philosophers and finally by the Spiritists. These, who are the last to come, were announced and prophesied from the dawn of the advent of the Messiah and they will receive the same recompense or, I should say, a larger recompense. Being the last to arrive, Spiritists take advantage of all the intellectual labours of their predecessors, because humans must inherit from humans and because human work and the subsequent results are collective: God blesses solidarity. Moreover, many who relive today, or who will relive tomorrow, are terminating work begun previously. More than one patriarch, more than one prophet, more than one

disciple of Christ is to be found amongst these; nevertheless, more enlightened, more advanced, working now not at the base but at the summit of the edifice. These then will receive wages according to the value of the undertaking.

The beautiful teaching of reincarnation is perpetual and needs spiritual affiliation. A spirit, when called upon to give an account of its earthly mandate, sees for itself the continuity of an interrupted task that is always resumed. It sees, feels and intuitively grasps the thoughts of its predecessors. It begins the lesson anew matured by experience, to advance yet further. All of them, the workers of the first and last hours, with their eyes fully open to the profound justice of God, murmur no more, they simply adore.

This is but one of the real meanings of this parable that holds, just as do all those given by Jesus when speaking to the people, the rudiments of the future. It also shows us, in all forms and from all aspects, the revelation of the magnificent unity that harmonises all things in the Universe, and the solidarity that joins all present beings to the past and to the future. - HENRI HEINE (Paris, 1863.)

THE MISSION OF THE SPIRITISTS

4. Do you not already hear the noise of the tempest that will sweep away the Old World and destroy all the iniquities of this planet? Ah, praise the Lord, all those who have put their faith in His sovereign justice. Who, as new apostles of the belief revealed by the superior prophetical voices, go forth to preach the new teachings of *reincarnation* and the elevation of spirits, according to whether they have fulfilled their missions well or badly and how they supported their terrestrial trials.

Forget your fears! The tongues of fire are above your heads. Oh, true adepts of Spiritism; you are God's chosen ones! Go forth and preach the Divine Word. The time has come when you should sacrifice your habits, your work and your futile occupations to its dissemination. Go forth and preach! The elevated Spirits are with you. You will most certainly speak to those who do not wish to hear the Voice of God, because this Voice calls them unceasingly to abnegation. You will preach disinterestedness to those who are avaricious, abstinence to the dissolute, gentleness to domestic tyrants and despots! Lost words, I know, but it does not matter. It is necessary that you irrigate the land to be sown with the sweat of your labour, seeing that it will not come to fruit or produce except under the repeated blows of the evangelical hoe and plough. Go forth and preach!

Yes, all of you, men and women of good faith, who are conscious of your inferiority before the many worlds scattered in infinite space! Launch yourselves into the crusade against injustice and iniquity. Go forth and ostracise the worship of the golden calf, which spreads more and more each day. Go forth because God guides you! Simple and ignorant humanity, your tongues will be freed and you will speak as no orator speaks. Go forth then and preach, for those of the population who are heedful will happily take in your words of consolation, fraternity, hope and peace.

What matter the ambushes rigged against you along the way! Only wolves fall into wolf traps, since the Shepherd will know how to defend His sheep from the sacrificial butchers.

Go forth those who, great before God and more blessed than Saint Thomas, believe without demanding to see and accept the fact of mediumship even when they have not managed to obtain it for themselves. Go then, for the Spirit of God is guiding you.

March forward, magnificent phalanx of faith! Before you, the great battalions of unbelievers will dissipate, just as does the morning dew at the first rays of the sun.

"Faith is the virtue that moves mountains," said Jesus. However, heavier than the greatest mountain are the impurities and all the vices that derive from them, which lie deposited in the hearts of all Humanity. So then, depart full of courage to remove this mountain of iniquities that future generations should know as a legend, in the same way that you know only very imperfectly of the times that preceded pagan civilisation.

Yes, moral and philosophical upheavals will be produced at all points of the globe, as the hour approaches when the Divine Light will spread itself over both worlds.

Go forth then and take the Divine words to the great who will despise them, to the learned who will demand proof and to the humble and simple people who will accept them. It will be principally amongst these last, who are martyrs to work, that earthly trial, that you will find faith and fervour. Go then, for these people will receive the saintly consolations that you have to offer with hymns of gratitude and praise to the Lord. Moreover, bowing down before Him, they will offer up thanks for the afflictions they are destined to suffer here upon the Earth.

Gather together your courage and decision and go forward like an imposing phalanx! Set to work! The plough is ready, the soil awaits; now is the time to work!

Go forth and thank God for the glorious task He has entrusted to you! However, be watchful because amongst those who are called to Spiritism, many will loose their way! Therefore, pay attention to the pathway and always seek the truth.

A question – *If amongst those called to Spiritism many will go astray, by what signs may we recognise those who are on the good path?*

Reply - You will recognise them by the principles of true charity they will teach and practice. You will recognise them by the number of afflicted they console, by the love for their neighbours and their abnegation and personal disinterestedness. Finally, you will recognise them by the victories achieved from the application of these principles, because God wishes His Laws to triumph. Those who follow His Laws are the chosen ones who will prevail. But He will destroy those who falsify the spirit of these Laws to satisfy their own vanity and ambition. - ERASTUS - the medium's Guardian Angel. (Paris, 1863.)

THE WORKERS OF THE LORD

5. The time approaches when those things that have been announced for the transformation of Humanity will be fulfilled. All those who have worked in the field of the Lord with disinterest and no other motive than charity will be blessed! Their days of work will be paid a hundred times more than was expected. Blessed are those who have said to their fellow beings, "Brothers and sisters, let us work together and unite our efforts so that when the Lord arrives He will find His work finished." For the Lord will say to them, "Come unto me, you who have been good servants, you who knew how to silence your rivalries and discords, so that no harm should come to the work!" But woe to those who, through their dissensions, have held back the time of the harvest, because the tempest will come and they will be taken away in the turbulence! They will cry, "Have mercy! Have mercy!" However, the Lord will say to them, "How can you implore mercy when you had none for your fellow men and women, refusing to offer them a helping hand and trampling on the weak instead of upholding them? How can you beseech mercy when you sought your recompense in earthly pleasures and the satisfaction of your pride? You have already received your recompense, just as you wished. There is nothing more you can ask for; the celestial rewards are for those who have not looked for earthly compensations."

At this moment, God is preparing a census of His faithful servants. He has already taken note of those whose devotion is only apparent, so that they may not usurp the wages of the courageous servants. This is because those who do not draw back from the task are the ones to whom He entrusted the most difficult positions in the great work of regeneration by means of Spiritism. These words will be fulfilled, "The first shall be the last and the last shall be the first in the kingdom of heaven." - THE SPIRIT OF TRUTH (Paris, 1862.)

CHAPTER 21

THERE WILL BE FALSE CHRISTS AND FALSE PROPHETS

A tree is known by its fruits. - The mission of the prophets. - The prodigies of the false prophets. - Do not believe all the spirits. - INSTRUCTIONS FROM THE SPIRITS: The false prophets. - Characteristics of the true prophet. - The false prophets from the spiritual world. - Jeremiah and the false prophets.

A TREE IS KNOWN BY ITS FRUITS

1. For a good tree brings not forth corrupt fruit: neither does a corrupt tree bring forth good fruit. For every tree is known by his own fruit. For of thorns people do not gather figs, nor of a bramble bush do they gather grapes. A good man out of the good treasure of his heart brings forth that which is good; and an evil man out of the evil treasure of his heart brings forth that which is evil: for of the abundance of the heart his mouth speaks. (LUKE, 6:43-45)

2. Beware of false prophets, *which come to you in sheep's clothing, but inwardly they are ravening wolves. You shall know them by their fruits.* Do men gather grapes of thorns, or figs of thistles? *Even so every good tree brings forth good fruit: but a corrupt tree brings forth evil fruit.* A good tree cannot bring forth evil fruit, neither can a corrupt tree bring forth good fruit. *Every tree that does not bring forth good fruit is cut down, and cast into the fire. Wherefore by their fruits you will know them."* (MATTHEW, 7:15-20.)

3. Take heed that no one deceives you. For many will come in my name, saying, 'I am Christ': and shall deceive many.

And many false prophets shall rise, and shall deceive many. And because iniquity shall abound, the love of many shall grow cold. But he that shall endure unto the end, the same shall be saved.

Then if anyone shall say to you, "Lo, here is Christ, or there He is!" believe it not. For there shall arise false Christ's, and false prophets, and shall show great signs *and wonders: insomuch that, if it were possible, they shall deceive the very elect.* (MATTHEW, 24:4, 5, 11-13, 23 & 24. Also, found in MARK, 13:5, 6, 21 & 22.)

THE MISSION OF THE PROPHETS

4. The gift of revealing the future is generally attributed to the prophets so that the words *prophecy* and *prediction* have become synonymous. In the evangelical sense, the word *prophet* has a much wider significance. This name is given to all those sent by God with the mission to instruct humankind and to reveal both that which is hidden and the mysteries of spiritual life. Therefore, a person may be a prophet without making any predictions. This was the idea understood by the Jews at the time of Jesus. This is why when they took Him before the high priest Caiaphas, the scribes and elders who were there spat upon Him, and hit Him with their fists saying, "Christ, prophesy to us and tell us who hit you." Nevertheless, it has happened that there have been prophets who could see into the future, either through intuition or through providential revelations, so they could transmit these warnings to humans. Due to the fact of these predictions having been fulfilled, the gift of predicting the future came to be considered one of the attributes of being a prophet.

THE PRODIGIES OF THE FALSE PROPHETS

5. "For there will arise false Christ's and false prophets, and they will perform great prodigies and amazing things so that, if this were possible, they should deceive even the very elect." These

words give us the true meaning of the term prodigy. In theological interpretation, prodigies and miracles are exceptional phenomena outside the Laws of Nature. As the Laws of Nature are the *exclusive* work of God, beyond all doubt He can annul them if He so pleases. Nevertheless, simple good sense tells us that it is not possible that He would give those who are perverse and inferior, power equal to His own, nor even less the right to undo what He Himself has done. Jesus would never have sanctioned such a principle. Moreover, according to the sense attributed to these words, if the spirit of evil had the power to perform prodigies such as these, then even those who were chosen would be deceived. Then the result of being able to do what God does would mean that prodigies and miracles would not be the exclusive privilege of God's messengers, which would prove nothing. There would then be no means of distinguishing the miracles of the saints from those of the devil. Therefore, it is necessary that we look for a more rational meaning to these words.

To the ignorant masses, all phenomena whose cause is unknown are thought of as supernatural, marvellous or miraculous. Once the cause is found, it is recognised that the phenomenon, however extraordinary, is nothing more than the application of one of the Laws of Nature. In this manner, the circle of supernatural facts becomes restricted as scientific knowledge widens. Humans in all epochs have exploited certain knowledge they possess for the sake of ambition, self-interest and a desire to dominate; seeking the prestige of possessing supposedly superhuman powers or to lay claim to divine missions. These then are the false christs and false prophets. The diffusion of knowledge in these matters will annihilate their credibility, resulting in diminishing their numbers in proportion to the rate at which humanity enlightens itself. The fact of being able to perform what some like to call prodigies in no way constitutes a sign of a divine mission, seeing that it may result from acquired knowledge within the reach of everyone, or from special organic faculties that either the worthy or ignoble are able to possess. The true prophets are recognisable by characteristics that are more serious and exclusively moral.

DO NOT BELIEVE ALL THE SPIRITS

6. "Beloved, do not believe every spirit, *but test the spirits whether they are come from God: because many false prophets are gone out into the world."* (JOHN, 1st Epistle, chap. 4:1)

7. Far from sanctioning the false christs and false prophets - as some people take pleasure in saying - spiritual phenomena comes, on the contrary, to deal them a deathblow. Do not ask Spiritism for prodigies or miracles, since it formally declares it does not perform them. In the same manner that physics, chemistry, astronomy and geology reveal the laws of the material world, so Spiritism reveals other previously unknown laws that govern the relationships existing between the physical and spiritual worlds, laws that just as much as those of science are Laws of Nature. By giving an explanation for certain types of phenomena, that until now had remained inexplicable, it destroys all that remains of the miraculous. Consequently, those who feel tempted to exploit these phenomena for personal gain, by pretending to be messengers from God, will not be allowed to abuse the credulity of the public for long, but will be quickly unmasked. Moreover, as has already been said, these phenomena alone prove nothing. Its moral effects prove every mission, and not everyone can produce these. One of the results of the development of the Spiritist science is that through research into the causes of certain of these manifestations, many mysteries are explained. Only those who prefer darkness rather than light have every interest in combating this progress. But the truth is like the sun that dissipates even the densest fog.

Spiritism also reveals another far more dangerous aspect of false christs and false prophets, that is to be found not amongst incarnates, but amongst the discarnates. These are the deceiving, hypocritical, prideful and falsely wise spirits, who on passing from Earth into their spiritual wanderings, have adopted venerated names as masks under which to hide, in order to facilitate the acceptance of the most strange and absurd ideas. Before mediumistic relationships were understood, they acted less conspicuously, by means of inspiration, unconscious mediumship either heard or spoken. There is a considerable number of communicants who in various epochs, and above all in recent times, have presented themselves as some of the old prophets, as Christ, as the Virgin Mary and even God. John warns against these spirits by saying "Beloved, believe not every spirit, but test the spirits whether they are from God, because many false prophets are gone out into the world." Spiritism offers us the means of testing them when it shows us the characteristics by which we may recognise the Good Spirits, who *are always moral, never material.*[14] It is particularly to the manner by which the Good may be distinguished from the bad that these words of Jesus may be applied. "It is by the fruits that you know the quality of the tree. A bad tree cannot produce good fruits." Spirits are judged by the quality of their works, just as a tree is judged by its fruits.

INSTRUCTIONS FROM THE SPIRITS

THE FALSE PROPHETS

8. Where it is said, "Christ is here," do not go. On the contrary, be on guard because the false prophets there will be numerous. Do

---

[14] See the manner by which Spirits can be identified in THE MEDIUM'S BOOK - second part, chapter 24 and subsequent chapters.

you not see that the leaves of the fig tree are fading? Do you not see that its multiple shoots are awaiting the time of coming into flower? Did not Jesus say to you: know the tree by its fruits? Then if the fruit is bitter you already know that the tree is evil; however, if the fruits are sweet and healthy you can say that nothing pure can come from a rotten stump.

My brethren, this then is how you should judge; you should examine the works. Signs of such a mission should accompany those who say they are invested with divine powers. That is to say, they should possess to the highest degree all the eternal Christian virtues that are charity, love, tolerance and goodness, that will conciliate all hearts. If in support of their works they also present the equivalent acts, then you may say: These really are true messengers of God.

Nevertheless, be mistrustful of honeyed words; be mistrustful of the Scribes and Pharisees who pray in public places clothed in long tunics. Mistrust all those who lay claim to a monopoly of the truth!

No, no, Christ is not amongst these, seeing that those He sends to propagate His sacred Teachings and regenerate His people will, above all, follow His example by being gentle and humble of heart. Those who have to save humanity that is running towards damnation will, by their examples and counselling, be essentially modest and humble. Run away from all who show even an atom of pride, as you would run away from an infectious disease that is apt to contaminate everything it touches. Remember that *every person bears the stamp on their brow, and even more especially in their actions, of their spiritual progress or their decadence.*

Therefore, my beloved children go forth and advance, without ulterior thoughts or hidden thoughts, along the blessed route that you have accepted. Go forth, always go forth without fear; turn aside with great care from all that may impede your march towards the eternal objective. Travellers, it is only for a while longer that you will be in the shadows and suffer the pains of atonement if you open your heart to these sweet Teachings, which will reveal to you the Eternal Laws and satisfy every aspiration of your soul with regard to the unknown. You may already give embodiment to the fleeting sylph you see passing by in your dreams and which, being short-lived, only enchants your spirit, without touching your heart. My beloved ones, now death has disappeared to give place to the radiant angel you know, the angel of re-encounter and reunion! Now, having faithfully fulfilled the task placed upon you by the Creator, you have nothing more to fear from His justice, since He is the Father and always forgives those of His children who have strayed when they cry out for mercy. Accordingly, continue to advance unceasingly! Let your slogan be progress, continuous progress in all things until finally you reach the happy termination of your journey, where you will find awaiting all who have proceeded. - LOUIS (Bordeaux, 1861.)

CHARACTERISTICS OF THE TRUE PROPHET

9. *Mistrust the false prophets.* This recommendation is useful in all epochs, but above all in times of transition, such as now when a transformation of humanity is occurring, because a multitude of those who are ambitious and scheming will promote themselves as reformers and messiahs. We should be on guard against these impostors and it is the duty of all honest people to unmask them. You may well ask how they can be identified. Here then are their characteristics:

The command of an army is only entrusted to a capable general who is capable of leading it. Do you believe that God is less prudent than human beings? You may be sure that He only consigns important missions to those He knows are capable of fulfilling them, seeing that great missions are heavy burdens that crush those who are lacking in sufficient strength to carry them. In all things the teacher must know more than the disciple. In order to lead humanity to advance, both morally and intellectually, we must have people of superior intelligence and morality. This is why Spirits who are already advanced, having passed their tests in other existences, are always chosen for these missions, because if they were not superior to the ambient in which they are required to act, their effect would be nullified.

Having said that, we must conclude that the true missionary of God must justify their mission through superiority, virtues, greatness, results and by the moralising influence of their work. We may also take into consideration yet another consequence that if, due to their character, their virtues or their intelligence, they show themselves to be less than the part they purport to represent, or the personality whose name they have opted to represent, then they are nothing more than storytellers of low character, who cannot even imitate their chosen model.

Another consideration is that, in the greater part, true missionaries of God are ignorant of the fact. They fulfil the mission to which they were called by the strength of character they possess, seconded by occult forces that inspire and direct them, even against their will, but without premeditation. In a word - *the true prophet is revealed by their actions and is discovered by others, whereas the false prophets declare themselves as messengers of God.* The first is humble and modest; the second is full of pride, speaks with arrogance and as do all those who lie, appear to always be afraid of not being believed.

Some of these impostors have already been seen passing themselves off as apostles of Christ, others as Christ Himself and to the disgrace of all humanity, they have encountered those sufficiently credulous as to believe in their baseness. However, a simple pondering is enough to open the eyes of even the most blind in this matter. That is to say, that if Christ were to reincarnate on Earth, He would come with all His power and all His virtues; unless one admits that He had degenerated, which would be absurd. Well, in the same manner, if we were to take away even one of God's attributes, we would no longer have God. So likewise, if we take away even one of Christ's virtues, we would no longer have Christ. The question is, do those who purport to be Christ have all of His virtues? Observe them, scrutinise their ideas and actions. You will recognise that apart from anything else, they lack the distinctive qualities of Christ that are charity and humility, while abounding in all those that Christ does not possess, such as covetousness and pride. Furthermore, take note that at this moment in various countries, there are many supposed Christs, just as there are many Elijah's, Saint Johns or Saint Peters and clearly it is impossible for them all to be true. You may be sure they are only creatures who exploit the credulity of others and who find it convenient to live at the expense of those who listen to them.

So then, mistrust the false prophets, especially at a time of renewal such as the present, because there will be many impostors who say they are from God. They try to satisfy their vanity here on Earth, but a terrible justice will befall them, of that you may be sure. - ERASTUS (Paris 1862.)

THE FALSE PROPHETS FROM THE SPIRITUAL WORLD

10. False prophets are not found solely amongst incarnates. They are also to be found in even greater numbers amongst the prideful spirits who, by appearing to be all love and charity, sow disunion and hold back the work of emancipating humanity by infiltrating their absurd doctrines, after having gained a medium's acceptance of them. In order to fascinate those they desire to

delude, to give more weight to their theories, they appropriate without scruples those names that humankind pronounces only with great respect.

These Spirits scatter a tumult of antagonism amongst groups, impelling them to isolate themselves from all others and to look upon each other with suspicion. This situation alone is enough to unmask them, since by so proceeding they are the first to offer a clear denial of who they claim to be. Blind therefore are those who allow themselves to fall for so great a hoax.

However, there are many other ways by which they may be recognised. Spirits of this particular category to which they say they belong, have to be not only very good, but also eminently rational. Well then, put all their doctrines to the test of reason and good sense, and then see what you have left. You will agree with me that every time a spirit indicates things of an utopian, childish, impracticable or ridiculous nature; or formulates a dogma that the most rudimentary notions of science contradict, as a solution for the problems of Humanity; or as a means of achieving their transformation, then these ideas can only come from a very ignorant or lying spirit.

On the other hand, you may be sure that if an individual does not always appreciate the truth, it is appreciated by the good sense of the masses, which constitutes yet one more criterion. If two principles contradict each other, we can find the measure of value inherent in both by verifying which of the two generates a greater echo and sympathy. *Apart from the fact that it would be illogical to admit to oneself that any doctrine, whose number of adepts progressively diminishes, is more truthful than that of another whose followers continually increase.* In desiring that the truth reach everyone, God has not confined it to a narrow circle, but has made it appear in all places, so that the light shines in all places alongside the darkness.

Do not hesitate, even for a moment, in repelling all those spirits who present themselves as exclusive counsellors, preaching separation and isolation. They are usually vain and mediocre spirits, who seek to impose upon and dictate to weak and credulous people by lavishing exaggerated praise upon them, with the aim of fascinating them and thus hold them under their domination. Generally, these kind of spirits, who are eager for power, continue to look for victims to tyrannise even after death. In general, *mistrust all communications that have a mystical and singular character or those that prescribe eccentric acts and ceremonies.* In all of these cases, there is always a legitimate motive for suspicion.

Equally, you may be sure that when a truth is to be revealed to humankind it is, by way of saying, instantly communicated to all serious groups who have at their disposal serious mediums, not only to one group at the exclusion of all others. No mediums are perfect if they became obsessed, and there is manifest obsession when they are accustomed to receive communication from only one specific spirit, however elevated that spirit pretends to be. Consequently, every medium or any group who believes they are privileged because of the communications they alone obtain, especially when they are subject to practices bordering on superstition, will undoubtedly find themselves caught up in a well-characterised situation of spiritual obsession. Above all, this will surely be the situation when the dominating spirit communicator swaggers under a name which both incarnates and discarnates alike honour and respect, and would not normally allow reputations to be compromised in this manner.

It is incontestable that, by submitting all the facts, phenomena and communications received from spirits to the crucible of reason, it becomes easy to reject the errors and absurdities. A single medium may become fascinated or a single group deluded, but a strict control from other groups, from acquired science, the elevated quality of the directors of groups, the quality of the communications received by the principal mediums, together with logic and, whenever possible, the verification of authenticity of the most serious spirit communicators, it is possible to quickly render justice to all falsehoods and trickery from any band of astutely mystifying or evil spirits. - ERASTUS, a disciple of Saint Paul (Paris, 1862.)

(See the Introduction – item 2 headed *The Universal Verification of the Teachings of the Spirits*. Also, consult THE MEDIUMS' BOOK by Allan Kardec, Second Part - Chapter 23 - *OBSESSION*.)

JEREMIAH AND THE FALSE PROPHETS

11. This is what the Lord of Hosts said, "Do not listen to the words of the prophets that are prophesying to you; they make you vain: They speak a vision of their own heart, and not out of the mouth of the Lord. They say also to them that despise me, 'The Lord said,' you will have peace; And they say to every one that walks after the imagination of his own heart, 'No evil will come to you.' For who has stood in the council of the Lord, and has perceived and heard his word? Who has marked his word, and heard it? I have not sent these prophets, yet they run: I have not spoken to them, yet they prophesied. I have heard what the prophets say who prophesy lies in my name, saying, 'I have dreamed! I have dreamed!' How long shall this be in the hearts of the prophets that prophecy lies? Yes, they are prophets of the deceit of their own heart. And when this people, or a prophet, or a priest, shall ask you, saying, What is the burden of the Lord? You shall then say to them, What burden? I will even forsake you said the Lord." (JEREMIAH, 23:16 – 18; 21; 25 & 26; 33)

My friends, I wish to talk to you about this passage from the prophet Jeremiah. Speaking through him, God had said, "It is the vision of their own hearts that makes them speak." These words clearly indicate that already in those times the charlatans and the impassioned abused the gift of prophecy and exploited it. They consequently abused the simple and almost blind faith of the people by predicting, *for money*, good and agreeable things. This kind of fraud was very widespread within the Jewish nation. Therefore, it is easy to understand that the poor people, in their ignorance, had no possible means of distinguishing the good from the bad. They were always more or less duped by the pseudo-prophets, who were nothing more than impostors and fanatics. There is nothing more significant than these words, "I have not sent these prophets yet they run, I have not spoken to them yet they prophesy."

Further on it says, "I heard these prophets who prophesy lies in My Name, saying, 'I have dreamed! I have dreamed!'" This is one of the ways they used to explain the confidences they were supposedly given. The masses, being credulous, did not think to dispute the truth of these dreams and visions. They thought it quite natural and frequently invited these 'prophets' to speak.

After the words of the prophet, listen to the wise counsel of the Apostle John, when he said, "Do not believe all the spirits. First, test them to see if they come from God." This is because among those who are invisible there are also those who take pleasure in deluding, if they have the chance. The deluded ones are, as we can see, the mediums who do not take the necessary precautions. Beyond all doubt, it is unquestionably one of the greatest obstacles against which many fail, especially when they are new to Spiritism. For them, it is a test from which they will be able to extricate themselves only by using much prudence. Therefore, before anything else, learn to distinguish the Good Spirits from the bad spirits so that you, in your turn, may not become a false prophet. - LUOZ, a Protecting Spirit (Carlsruhe, 1861.)

CHAPTER 22

DO NOT SEPARATE WHAT GOD HAS UNITED

The indissolubility of marriage. - Divorce.

THE INDISSOLUBILITY OF MARRIAGE

1. The Pharisees also came to him, tempting Him, and saying to him, Is it lawful for a man to put away his wife for every cause? And he answered and said to them, Have you not read, that he which made them at the beginning, made them male and female, And said, For this cause shall a man leave father and mother, and shall cleave to his wife: and the two of them will be one flesh? Wherefore they are no more two, but one flesh. What therefore God has joined together, let no man separate. They say to him, Why did Moses then command to give a written divorcement, and to put her away? He said to them, Moses because of the hardness of your hearts suffered you to put away your wives: but from the beginning it was not so. And I say to you, Whosoever shall put away his wife, except it is for adultery, and marries another, commits adultery: and whoever marries her which is put away does commit adultery. (MATTHEW, 19:3-9.)

2. The only things that are immutable are those that stem from God. Everything that is the work of humans is subject to change. The Laws of Nature are the same at all times and in all countries. Human laws change according to the times, places and intellectual progress. In marriage, what is of a Divine Order is the union of the sexes, so that the substitution of those who die may be put into effect. However, the conditions that regulate this union are so human in design that in the whole world there are not, even in Christendom, two countries where these laws are exactly identical, and none where in the course of time they do not suffer changes.

The result of this is that according to civil law, what is legitimate in one country at a certain time is considered to be adultery in another country and at another time. This is because civil law has as its objective the regulation of the interests of families, interests that vary according to customs and local necessities. In this manner for example, in certain countries a religious marriage is the only legitimate one; in others, it is also necessary to have a civil marriage and finally, there are yet other places where a civil marriage is sufficient on its own.

3. But in the union of the sexes, apart from the divine physical law common to all living creatures, there is another Divine Law, which is immutable, as are all of God's laws, one that is exclusively moral, which is the Law of Love. God wishes all beings to unite themselves not only through the ties of the flesh but also through those of the soul. This is so that the mutual affection of the spouses is transmitted to the offspring, and that it should be two and not just one to love them, look after them and help them to progress. Is the law of love taken into consideration in ordinary conditions within marriage? Not in the least. The mutual sentiments of two beings who are attracted one to the other through reciprocated sentiments are not consulted, seeing that in the majority of cases this sentiment is severed. What is looked for is not the satisfaction of the heart, but that of pride, vanity and cupidity; in a word, all material interests. When everything goes well according to these interests, it is said to be a marriage of convenience; when the pockets are well lined, it is said that the spouses are equally harmonised and should be very happy.

However, no civil laws or the obligations that these laws determine can replace the law of love. If this law does not preside over the union, it frequently happens that *those who were forcibly united separate themselves*. The oath that was sworn at the foot of the altar, when pronounced as a banal formula, then becomes a perjury. It is for this reason that we have unhappy marriages, which end up becoming criminal. This is a double disgrace that could have been avoided if, on establishing the conditions for that marriage the law of love, that is the only law sanctioning the union in the eyes of God, had not been abstracted. When God said, "And they two shall be one flesh," and when Jesus said, "What God has joined together let no man put apart," these words should be understood as a reference to the union according to God's immutable law and not according to the mutable laws of humanity.

4. So then, is civil law superfluous? Should we go back to matrimony according to Nature? Certainly not! Civil law has the object of regulating social relationships and family interests in accordance with the requirements of civilisation. Therefore, it is useful and necessary, but variable. It should be provident, because civilized people cannot live as savages. However, there is nothing, absolutely nothing, that prevents it being an inference of God's law. All obstacles against the execution of this Divine Law stem from prejudices and not from civil law. These prejudices, even if they are still alive, have lost much of their predominance amongst the enlightened peoples of this world. They will gradually disappear with moral progress, which in fact will open the eyes of humankind to countless evils, to failings and even to crimes that result from unions that had been contracted purely on the basis of material interest. One-day people will ask if it is really more humane, more charitable and more moral to join together two beings when they are unable to live together or to restore their liberty; or whether the prospect of an indissoluble prison will increase the number of irregular unions.

DIVORCE

5. Divorce is a human law whose objective is to legally separate those who are in fact already separated. It is not against God's law since it only reforms what humans have done and is only

applicable in cases in which Divine Law was not taken into account. If it were contrary to God's law, then the Church would be forced to consider as betrayers of a trust, those of its heads who, by their own authority and in the name of religion, have imposed it on more than one occasion. In these cases, divorce would have been a double betrayal of a trust, because it only had worldly interests in view and not the satisfaction of the law of love.

However, even Jesus did not sanction the absolute indissolubility of marriage when he said, "It was because of the hardness of your hearts that Moses permitted you to repudiate your women." This signifies that ever since the time of Moses, when mutual affection was not the only motive for matrimony, separation could become necessary. Nevertheless, he added that: "In the beginning, it was not like this," meaning that at the origin of humanity, when people had not yet been perverted by pride and selfishness but lived according to God's laws, the unions were based on sympathy and not ambition or vanity. Therefore, there was no desire to repudiate.

Jesus goes even further to specify a case in which repudiation can happen, being that of adultery. Well, adultery cannot exist where there is sincere reciprocated affection. It is true that He prohibited a man to marry a repudiated woman. But here we must take into consideration the customs and character of the people in those times, when the Mosaic Law prescribed stoning to death. When wishing to abolish one barbaric custom, it was necessary to find a substitute penalty, that was found in the disgrace that would come from the prohibition of a second marriage. It was to a certain extent one civil law being substituted by another. Nevertheless, like all laws of this nature, it would pass through the test of time.

CHAPTER 23

STRANGE MORAL

Whosoever does not hate their father and mother. - Abandon father, mother and children. - Leave to the dead the care of burying their dead. - I have not come to bring peace, but dissension.

WHOSOEVER DOES NOT HATE THEIR FATHER AND MOTHER

1. And there went great multitudes with him: and he turned and said to them, If any man come to me, and hate not his father, and mother, and wife, and children, and brethren, and yes, his own life also, he cannot be my disciple. And whosoever does not carry his cross, and come after me, cannot be my disciple. So likewise, whosoever he be of you that forsakes not all that he has, he cannot be my disciple." (LUKE, 14:25-27 &33.)

2. He that loves father or mother more than me is not worthy of me: and he that loves son or daughter more than me is not worthy of me. (MATTHEW, 10:37.)

3. Although very rare, certain words attributed to Christ, make a singular contrast to his habitual manner of speaking, so much so that we instinctively repel their literal sense without causing the sublimity of His Teachings to suffer damage. Written after His death, since none of the Evangelists wrote while He was alive, it is licit to believe that in cases like these the depths of His thoughts were not well expressed. In addition, which is no less possible, the original sense while having been passed from one language to another has consequently suffered some alteration. It is sufficient that a small error committed only the once, for those who copy it

continue to repeat it, as frequently happens in the relating of historical facts.

The term *hates* in this phrase from Luke: *if any man comes to me and hates not his father and his mother and wife and children* – should be understood by the light of this hypothesis. It would not occur to anyone to attribute these words to Jesus. So then, it would be superfluous to discuss it or even less to try to justify it. For this, it would be necessary first to know if He had actually pronounced these words and if He had, whether, in the idiom in which they had been expressed, the word in question had the same meaning as it does in our language. In this passage from John, "He who *hates* his life, in this world, will conserve himself for the eternal life," there is no doubt that Jesus did not attach the same meaning to these words as we do.

The Hebraic language was not rich in expressions and contained many words that had varied meanings. Such a one, for example, is that used in Genesis to describe the phases of creation. It also served simultaneously to express a given period of time and the period of a day. Later on, from this situation came the translation into the term *a day* and the belief that the world was created in a period that lasted six times twenty-four hours. Another was the word used to designate both *camel* and a *rope* since the ropes were made from camel hair. This is why they translated the word into the term '*camel*' in the allegory of the eye of the needle. (See Luke, Chapter 16:2)[15]

Furthermore, it behoves us to pay attention to the customs and character of the various peoples, that have a very great influence over the particular nature of their language. Without this knowledge, the true meaning of certain words frequently escapes us. The same term when passed from one language to another may gain either more or less strength according to the idea it provokes. In one it may involve insult and blasphemy, while in another it may totally lack importance. Even in the same language, some words lose their value and meaning with time. For this reason, a rigorously literal translation does not always express the exact thought, so in order to maintain this exactitude, it is sometimes necessary to use other equivalent words rather than corresponding terms or even use paraphrases.

These comments will be found especially applicable in the interpretation of the blessed Scriptures and in particular those of the Gospels. If the nature of the environment in which Jesus lived is not taken into account we shall be exposed to misunderstandings as to the meaning of certain expressions and certain facts, because of the habit we have of likening others to ourselves. In any case, it behoves us to divest the term *hate* of its

---

[15] *Non odit* in Latin, *Kaï or miseï* in Greek do not mean *hate*, but rather *to love less*. What the Greek verb *miseïn* indicates is expressed even better by the Hebrew verb, which would have been used by Jesus. This verb does not only signify *hate*, but also *to love less, to not love as much as*, or *to not love the same as someone else*. In the Syrian dialect, which it is said was used more frequently by Jesus; this meaning is even better accentuated. It is in this sense that GENESIS (Chapter 29:30 & 31) says: "And Jacob loved Raquel more than Lia, and Jehovah seeing that Lia was hated..." It is evident that the true meaning here is that she was *loved less*. This is how it should be translated. In many other passages in Hebrew and, above all in Syrian, the same verb is used in the sense of *to not love as much as another*, which makes it contradictory to translate it into *hate*, this having another clearly defined meaning. The text of Matthew, however, puts the matter quite clearly.   (Note by M. Pezzani.)

modern meaning, as this is contrary to the true message of the Teachings of Jesus. (See also chapter 14, item 5 and subsequent items.)

ABANDON FATHER, MOTHER AND CHILDREN

4. "And everyone that has forsaken their houses, or brothers or sisters, or father, or mother, or wife, or children, or lands for my sake, shall receive a hundred times as much and shall inherit everlasting life." (MATTHEW, 19:29.)

5. Then Peter said, "See, we have left all and followed You." And he said to them, "Truly, I say to you, There is no man that has left house, or parents, or brethren, or wife, or children, for the kingdom of God's sake. Who shall not receive vastly more in this present life, and in the world to come life everlasting." (LUKE, 18:28-30.)

6. And another also said, "Lord, I will follow you; but let me first go home and say them farewell, which are at home at my house." And Jesus said to him, No man, having put his hand to the plough, and looking back, is fit for the kingdom of God. (LUKE, 9:61 & 62.)

Without arguing about words, we should look for the thought behind them, which is evidently, "that the interests of the future life should take precedence over all other interests and human considerations," because this thought is in accordance with the essence of the Teachings as taught by Jesus, whereas the idea of renouncing one's family would be a frank denial of these Teachings.

Moreover, do we not have these maxims in mind when we consider the sacrifice of our interests and family affections for those of our homeland? Do we, by chance, censure those who leave parents, brothers and sisters, wives and children in order to fight for their country? On the contrary, do they not gain in merit for having given up homes and families in order to fulfil their duty? This then is because there are some duties that are greater than others. Does not the law impose that the daughter leaves her parents in order to follow her husband? The world is full of thousands of cases in which painful separation is necessary. Nevertheless, affections are not broken because of this. These temporary separations do not diminish either the respect or the solicitude that children owe to their parents, nor the affection of these parents for their children. Therefore, we see that even if we take these words literally, with the exception of the word *hate*, they would not be any contradiction to the commandment that prescribes that every person should honour their mother and father. Nor even a contradiction of parental affections and certainly not if they were understood in their spiritual meaning. These words then had the finality of showing through overstatement how imperious is the duty of occupying oneself with the future life. Besides, they would have been less shocking for a people in an epoch in which, because of their customs, family ties were not as strong as they are within a society that is morally more advanced. These ties, always weak in primitive peoples, fortify themselves with the development of sensitivity and a sense of morality. Separation is necessary for progress because without it families and races would become degenerate if there were no intermingling of different strains. This is a Law of Nature and is as much in the interest of moral progress as it is for physical progress.

Here things are considered purely from the earthly point of view. Spiritism makes us look higher, by showing us that the true ties of affection are not of the flesh, but of the spirit and that these ties do not break with separation, or even through the death of the physical body. In fact, they become more robust in the spiritual life by means of the cleansing of the spirit. This knowledge is a consoling truth from which great strength can be gained by all humans to help them bear the vicissitudes of life. (See chapter 4, item 18 and chapter 14, item 8.)

LEAVE TO THE DEAD THE CARE OF BURYING THEIR DEAD

7. And he said to another Follow me. But he said, Lord, allow me first to go and bury my father. Jesus said to him, Let the dead bury their dead, but go you and preach the kingdom of God. (LUKE, 9:59 & 60.)

8. What can the words 'Let the dead bury their dead' mean? The previous considerations show primarily that in the circumstances in which they were spoken, they could not have contained a censure for the person that considered it a devotional duty of children to bury their father. Therefore, we have a more profound meaning here that can only be perceived with a more complete knowledge of spiritual life.

Life in the spiritual world is in effect the real life, the normal life of a spirit. Terrestrial existence, being transitory and passing, is a kind of death when compared to the splendours and activity of the spiritual life. The body is nothing more than a gross covering that temporarily clothes the spirit. It is a true fetter that secures it to the soil and from which the spirit feels happy to be liberated. The respect given to the dead is not inspired by matter but is due to the remembrance that the absent spirit imbues. It is similar to someone who bestows an object that belonged to them and which they handled, that is kept as a remembrance by those who had affection for the person. This is what the person could not understand. So Jesus taught that person by saying: Do not worry about the body, but think first of the spirit; go and teach about God's Kingdom; go and tell humanity that their homeland is not to be found upon the Earth but in Heaven, because true life only exists there.

I HAVE NOT COME TO BRING PEACE, BUT
DISSENSION

9. Think not that I have come to bring peace on Earth. I came not to send peace, but a sword. For I am come to set a man at variance against his father, and the daughter against her mother, and the daughter-in-law against her mother-in-law. And a man's enemies will be those of his own household. (MATTHEW, 10:34-36.)

10. "I am come to send fire on the Earth: and what will I, if it be already kindled? But I have a baptism to be baptised with; and how am I anxious till it be accomplished! Do you suppose I am come to give peace to the Earth? I tell you No; but rather division: for from henceforth there shall be five in one house, divided, three against two, and two against three. The father shall be divided against the son, and the son against the father: the mother against the daughter, and the daughter against the mother; the mother in law against her daughter in law, and the daughter in law against her mother in law." (LUKE, 12:49-53.)

11. Could it really be possible that Jesus, the personification of gentleness and goodness, who never ceases to preach the need to love our neighbours, could have said, "I come not to bring peace, but the sword; to separate the son from the father, the husband from his wife? I am come to set fire to the Earth and am in a hurry for this to happen?" Are not these words in flagrant contradiction to his Teachings? Is it not blasphemy to attribute to Him the language of a bloody and devastating conqueror? No, there is no blasphemy nor contradiction in these words because it was He who pronounced them and they are a testimony to His great wisdom. It is only that they are a little ambiguous and the form does not express the thought with exactitude, thus giving rise to misunderstanding as to their true meaning. Taken literally, they have a tendency to transform His mission that was all peaceful, into one of perturbation and discord, which is absurd and good

sense repels this, seeing that Jesus could not contradict Himself. (See chapter 19, item 6)

12. Every new idea inevitably encounters opposition and there is not one that is implanted without a fight. Well, in these cases the resistance is always in proportion to the importance of the *foreseen* results because the greater these are, the more numerous are the interests that are affected. If it is notoriously false, if it is taken as inconsequential, then no one becomes alarmed. Everyone lets it go, being certain that it lacks vitality. However, if it is true, if it is placed on a solid base, if it appears to have a future, then a secret presentiment alerts its antagonists to the fact that it constitutes a danger for them and to the order of things to whose maintenance they are pledged. Then they throw themselves against it and its adepts.

Therefore, we can measure the importance and the results of a new idea by the amount of emotion its appearance causes, by the violence of the opposition it provokes, as well as by the degree and persistence of the anger of its adversaries.

13. Jesus came to proclaim Teachings that would undermine the very base of the abuses upon which the Pharisees, the Scribes and the Priests all lived. Accordingly, they sacrificed Him, believing that by killing the man they would kill the idea. Nevertheless, this idea survived because it was the truth. It has augmented itself because it corresponds to God's design. Although born in a small and obscure hamlet in Judaea, it went and planted its standard in the very capital of the pagan world. This was right in the face of its fiercest enemies, who had the greatest interest in combating it because it was subverting century old beliefs to which they were attached, much more for personal interest than from conviction. Terrible battles awaited there for the Apostles and the victims were innumerable. However, the idea always grew and triumphed because, being the truth, it rose above those that had proceeded.

14. It is worth noting that Christianity sprang up when Paganism had already entered into a decline and was struggling against the light of reason. It was practised only as a matter of form as faith had disappeared; only personal interest sustained it. Now those who are moved by interest are persistent and never give way to evidence. They become more and more irritated as the counter-arguments become more decisive and demonstrate more clearly their beliefs. These people know very well they are wrong, but this does not deter them, as true faith is not yet a part of their soul. What they most fear is the light that will give sight to those who are blind. The errors are to their advantage, so they hold on to them and defend them.

Did not Socrates also teach a doctrine very similar to that of Christ? Why then did it not prevail amongst one of the most intelligent peoples on the planet at that time? This was because the time was not yet ripe. He sowed on land that had not been ploughed. Paganism was still not worn out. Christ received His mission at the propitious moment. It is true that a great deal was still lacking for humanity of that epoch to enable them to reach the level of Christian ideas. Nevertheless, there was a general aptitude amongst them that permitted the assimilation of this knowledge because of the beginning of a sense of emptiness that the common beliefs did nothing to fill. Socrates and Plato opened up the way and prepared the spirits of the people. (See the INTRODUCTION, item 4, *SOCRATES & PLATO, the forerunners of Christian ideas and of Spiritism.*)

15. Unfortunately, the adepts of the new Teachings were unable to agree as to the interpretation of the words of Jesus, whose meaning was frequently hidden by allegory and figures of speech. Because of this, numerous sects were quick to flourish, each claiming to possess the exclusive truth and even eighteen centuries have not been sufficient for them to come to an agreement. However, they forgot the most important of the divine precepts

that Jesus placed as the cornerstone of His edifice as an express condition for salvation. These are charity, fraternity and love for one's neighbour. Whereupon, these sects launched curses at each other and cast themselves one upon the other, the strongest crushing the weakest, drowning themselves in blood and annihilating themselves by torture and fire. After having conquered Paganism, these Christians, who had been the persecuted, became the persecutors. Fire and steel were used to implant the Cross of the Shepherd, despite its being unblemished in both worlds. It is a confirmed fact that religious wars have been the cruellest and produced more victims than all the political wars put together. In no other warfare are so many acts of atrocity or barbarism practised.

Is this the fault of Christ's Teachings? Clearly not, as it formally condemns all violence. Did Jesus ever tell His disciples to go out and kill or commit massacres or burn those who did not believe? No! On the contrary, He always said that all peoples are brothers and sisters, that God is supremely merciful, that we must love our neighbours and our enemies and do Good to those who persecute us. He also said, "All those who kill by the sword would perish by the sword." Therefore, the responsibility does not lie with the Teachings of Jesus, but rather with those who have falsely interpreted it and turned it into an instrument for the satisfaction of their own passions. It belongs to those people who have despised the words "My Kingdom is not of this world."

In His profound wisdom, Jesus had foreseen what would happen, but these things were inevitable because they are inherent in the inferior nature of Humanity that cannot be transformed suddenly. It was necessary for Christianity to go through this long and cruel test during all these centuries in order to show its strength; seeing that despite all the evil committed in its name it has remained pure and uncontaminated. This has never been disputed. The blame has always fallen upon those who have abused it. At every act of intolerance, it has always been said that if Christianity had been better understood and more widely practised this would never have happened.

16. When Jesus declared, "Think not that I am come to bring peace on Earth, but division," His thought behind this statement was as follows: "Do not believe that My Teachings will be established pacifically; they will bring bloody battles wherein My name will be used as a pretext because Humanity will not have understood Me or will not have wanted to understand. Brothers and sisters, separated by their respective beliefs, will unsheathe their swords one against the other and division will reign within the breast of families whose members do not share the same beliefs. I have come to launch fire upon the Earth to purge it of errors and prejudices, just as you put fire to a field in order to destroy the weeds. I am in a hurry for the fire to start so the purification may be that much quicker, seeing that truth will come forth triumphantly from this conflict. War will be succeeded by peace, hate between two parties by universal brotherhood and the darkness of fanaticism by the clarity of enlightened faith. Then when the field is prepared, I will send a Comforter, the Spirit of Truth that will re-establish all things. This is to say that by understanding the meaning of My words the more enlightened people will finally comprehend and so put an end to the killing of brother-by-brother and sister-by-sister, which has disunited all the children of the same Father. Finally then, being tired of combat that has brought no result, only desolation and perturbation even into the hearts of families, people will recognise where their true interests lie in relation to this world and the next. They will see on which side are to be found the friends or enemies of their tranquillity. Then all will put themselves under the same banner which is that of charity and all things will re-establish themselves on Earth in accordance with truth and the principles which I have taught."

17. Spiritism has come at the appointed time to realise the promises made by Christ. However, this cannot be done without first destroying all abuse. Just as happened with Jesus, Spiritism is faced with pride, selfishness, ambition, greed and blind fanaticism that when taken to their last defences, will try to block the pathway causing hindrance and persecutions. Therefore, it too has to do battle. However, the time of battles and bloody outrages is passing, so that those to be suffered from now on will be of a moral nature and even these are nearing the end. The first lasted for centuries, but these will last but a few years. Because instead of breaking forth in only one place at a time, the light will now shine from all points of the globe and will quickly open the eyes of those who are still blind.

18. These words of Jesus should be understood as referring to the wrath that His Teachings would provoke, the momentary conflicts that it will create, to the fights it will have to endure before it is established, just as happened to the Hebrews before they entered into the Promised Land. Neither should it be understood as inferring a predetermined design on His part to sow disorder and conflict. Evil comes from human beings, never from Jesus. He was like the doctor who comes to cure, but whose medicine provokes a beneficial crisis in those who are sick.

CHAPTER 24

DO NOT HIDE THE LIGHT UNDER A BUSHEL

The light under a bushel. Why Jesus spoke in parables. - Do not keep company with the Gentiles. - The healthy do not need a doctor. - The courage of faith. - Carry your cross. He who will save his life, shall lose it.

THE LIGHT UNDER A BUSHEL - WHY JESUS SPOKE IN PARABLES

1. Neither do men light a candle, and put it under a bushel, but on a candlestick; and it gives light to all that are in the house. (MATTHEW, 5:15.)

2. No man when he has lighted a candle, covers it with a vessel, or puts it under a bed; but sets it on a candlestick, that they which enter in may see the light. For nothing is secret, that shall not be made manifest; neither anything hid, that shall not be known and made public. (LUKE, 8:16 & 17.)

3. And the disciples came, and said to him, Why do you speak to them in parables? He answered and said to them, Because it is given to you to know the mysteries of the kingdom of heaven, but to them it is not given. Therefore speak I to them in parables: because they seeing, see not; and hearing they hear not, neither do they understand. And in them is fulfilled the prophecy of Esaias, which said, By hearing you shall hear, and shall not understand; and seeing you shall see, and shall not perceive. For this people's heart is waxed gross, and their ears are dull of hearing, and their eyes they have closed; lest at any time they should see with their eyes, and hear with their ears, and should understand with their heart, and should be convinced, and I should heal them. (MATTHEW, 13:10-11; 13-15)

4. It appears strange to hear Jesus say that the light should not be covered up when He constantly hid the meaning of His words under the veil of allegories, that are not understood by everyone. However, He explains this when He tells His disciples that He speaks in parables because the people are not ready to understand certain things, "They see, they listen, but do not understand. Therefore, it would be useless to tell them everything at this time. Nevertheless, I have told you, because it has been given to you to understand these mysteries." So He treated the people as you would children whose ideas had not yet developed. In this manner, we come to comprehend the real meaning of the words, "Neither do we light a candle and then put it under a bushel, but on a candlestick so that it gives light to all that are in the house." This sentence does not mean that we should reveal all things, without due consideration as to the convenience of this revelation. All teaching should be proportional according to the intelligence of those to be taught, because there are certain people for whom a too brilliant light would only blind, without enlightening them in any way.

The same thing can happen to humanity in general, as can happen to an individual. The generations have their infancy, their youth and their maturity. Each thing must come at the right moment; seeds when sown out of season will not germinate. However, what prudence holds back momentarily, sooner or later will be discovered. When the correct degree of development has been reached people will seek the living light for themselves as they feel obscurity weighing upon them. God has given humans intelligence to understand and to be guided amongst the things of the Earth and of Heaven, therefore, people will seek to rationalise their faith. It is at this point that we must not put the candle under a bushel, *seeing that without the light of reason faith becomes weak.* (See chapter 19, item 7.)

5. Then if Providence, in its wise precaution, only reveals the truth gradually, it is always obvious that these truths are only disclosed in proportion as Humanity shows itself sufficiently mature to receive them. Providence holds them in reserve and not under a bushel. However, as human beings enter into possession of maturity, they almost always hide them from the masses with the intention of dominating the people. These are the ones who truly place the candle under a bushel. This is why every religion has its mysteries whose examination is prohibited. However, as these religions began to become outdated, so science and intelligence have advanced and broken through the veil of mystery. Having become adult, the masses wished to penetrate to the bottom of these matters and remove from their faith that which was contrary to their observations.

Absolute mysteries cannot exist. Jesus was right when He said that there was no secret that would not come to be known. Everything that is hidden will be discovered one day. What people still do not comprehend will be revealed in succession in more advanced worlds, when they have reached purification. Here on Earth they still find themselves in a thick fog.

6. We ask ourselves what advantage can be gained from these multitude of parables whose meaning remains hidden. It must be noted that Jesus only expressed Himself in parables in matters that were rather abstract in the Teachings. But having declared that humility and charity to one's neighbour were the basic conditions for salvation, everything He said in this respect is completely clear, explicit and without any ambiguities. This is as it should be because this is a rule of conduct, a rule that everyone has to comprehend in order to observe. This was the essential point for the ignorant masses to whom He said only, "This is what you need to do in order to reach Heaven." On other matters, He only disclosed His thoughts to His disciples. This was because they were more advanced both morally and intellectually, so that Jesus

could initiate them in the knowledge of more abstract truths. This is also why He said, *'to those who already have, even more will be given.'* (See chapter 18, item 15.)

Nevertheless, even with the apostles, He was not precise on many points, the complete understanding in these areas being reserved for later times. It was these multiple parts that caused so many diverse interpretations, until science on the one hand and Spiritism on the other, revealed the new Laws of Nature so making the real meaning perceptible.

7. Today, Spiritism projects its light over an immense number of obscure points. However, it does not do this without due consideration. When the Spirits give their Teachings, they conduct themselves with admirable prudence. They consider gradually, one by one, the various known parts of the Teachings, leaving other parts to be revealed only when it would be opportune to bring them forth from obscurity. If they had presented the complete Teachings right from the first moment, fewer people would have shown themselves disposed to accept them. Those who were not prepared would have become frightened by them, so that consequently the dissemination would have suffered. If the Spirits have still not told everything outright, it is not because there are mysteries within the Teachings that only the privileged few may penetrate; nor is it because they have hidden the candle under a bushel, but because each piece of knowledge must come at the most opportune moment. This gives time for each idea to mature and spread before presenting another and *for events to prepare the way for the acceptance of new ideas.*

DO NOT KEEP COMPANY WITH THE GENTILES

8. These twelve Jesus sent out, and commanded them, saying, "Go not into the way of the Gentiles and into any city of the Samaritans go not: but go rather to the lost sheep of the house of

Israel. And as you go, preach, saying, saying, The kingdom of heaven is at hand." (MATTHEW, 10:5-7.)

9. On many occasions, Jesus shows us that His vision was not confined just to the Jewish people but rather embraced all Humanity. Moreover, if He told His apostles not to go to the Pagans, it was not that He disdained conversing with them. This would not have been at all charitable. Rather it was that the Jews, who already believed in one God and were waiting for a Messiah, were already prepared through the Laws of Moses and the Prophets to accept His Word. With the Pagans, where even the base was lacking, there would have been everything to do and the apostles were not yet sufficiently enlightened for so difficult a task. This is why He said to them, "Go rather to the lost sheep of Israel," that is to say, go and sow in lands that are already cleared. Jesus knew that the conversion of the Gentiles would happen at a later date. Indeed, later on, the apostles did go to plant a cross in the very heart of Paganism.

10. These words can also be applied to the adepts and disseminators of Spiritism. The systematically incredulous, the obstinate mockers and the profit-seeking adversaries are today what the Gentiles were to the apostles. So to follow their example, go first to make converts amongst those of goodwill, those who desire enlightenment, where a fertile seed may be found and where there are many. Do not waste time with those who do not want to see or hear, where they resist even more out of pride and the greater importance that is put on their conversion. It is better to open the eyes of a hundred blind people, who wish to see clearly, than of only one person who takes pleasure in darkness. By proceeding in this manner it is possible to increase in greater numbers those who will uphold the cause. Leaving some people undisturbed is not a case of showing indifference, but simply good sense. The time will come when they will have been persuaded by public opinion and by hearing the same information being

constantly repeated all around them. Then they will think they have accepted the ideas voluntarily, by their own impulse and not under pressure from others. Furthermore, ideas are similar to seeds, they cannot germinate before the appropriate time or in land that has not been previously prepared. Therefore, it is better to wait for the right time and first cultivate those that are starting to germinate, in order that the later germinating ones do not abort by virtue of a too intensive cultivation.

At the time of Jesus and because of the narrow-minded and materialistic ideas in vogue, everything was localised and circumscribed. The house of Israel was but a small nation; the Gentiles being other small nations around them. Today ideas have been universalised and spiritualised. The new light is the privilege of no particular nation; no barriers exist for it; the focus point is in all places and all humans are brothers and sisters. The Gentiles are no longer a people but an opinion that is accepted in all places and over which truth will triumph little by little, just as Christianity triumphed over Paganism. These opinions are no longer combated with weapons of war, but with the force of ideas.

THE HEALTHY DO NOT NEED A DOCTOR

11. And it came to pass, as Jesus sat at dinner in the house, behold, many Publicans and sinners came and sat down with Him and His disciples. And when the Pharisees saw it, they said to His disciples, Why does your Master eat with Publicans and sinners? But when Jesus heard that, He said to them, They that be whole need not a physician, but they that are sick. (MATTHEW, 9:10-12.)

12. Jesus addressed Himself most especially to those who were poor and deprived, as they had the greatest need for consolation; and also the blind, who were humble and of good faith, because they asked Him to enlighten them. He did not address Himself to those who were proud or who believed they had all the knowledge

they needed and wished for no more. (See the INTRODUCTION: items entitled *PUBLICANS* and *THE TAX COLLECTORS.*)

These words and many others, find their most fitting application within Spiritism. There are those who are sometimes surprised that mediumship is given to people of little worth and capable of its misuse. They say that it seems that such a precious faculty should be given exclusively to those who are most deserving of it.

Before anything else, let us say that mediumship stems from a certain organic predisposition and therefore anyone may be gifted with this ability, in the same way that we are gifted to see, hear and speak. Moreover, there is nothing that people cannot abuse by means of their free will. If God had only conceded speech, for example to those incapable of speaking ill, then there would be more dumb people than those able to speak. God has given human beings various faculties together with the liberty to use them. However, He also punishes those who abuse them.

If the possibility of communicating with spirits had only been given to the most worthy, who would dare to make such a claim? Furthermore, where is the boundary between worthiness and unworthiness? Mediumship is conferred without distinction so that the Spirits can bring enlightenment to all walks of life, to all classes of people, to rich and poor alike, to those who are honest so they may be fortified in their goodness and also to the corrupt so they may be corrected. Are these not the sick who need a doctor? Why then would God, Who does not wish for the death of sinners, deprive them of the help that can pull them out of the mire? The Good Spirits come to their help and the personal advice that is received is of a nature that will impress them in a manner more striking than if it had been received indirectly. God, in His goodness, wishing to spare them the work of having to go out and get help from afar, puts the light straight into their hands. Are they not even more guilty for failing to notice this fact? Can they excuse themselves by claiming ignorance, when their own condemnation has been written, seen, heard and spoken by themselves? If they do not take advantage of this, then they will be punished by means of the loss or perversion of the faculty that was bestowed. In this case, evil spirits will take hold, obsessing and deceiving them. Nevertheless, this will not lessen the receiving of real afflictions with which God punishes His unworthy servants whose hearts are hardened by pride and selfishness.

Mediumship does not necessarily imply habitual relations with Superior Spirits. It is merely *an aptitude* to serve as an instrument, which may be more or less useful to spirits in general. So then, a good medium is not one who communicates with ease, but one who is agreeable to the Good Spirits and who is helped only by them. It is solely in this sense that the excellence of moral qualities becomes the all-powerful influence in mediumship.

THE COURAGE OF FAITH

13. Whosoever, therefore, shall confess me before men, him will I confess also before my Father which is in heaven. But whosoever shall deny me before men, him will I also deny before my Father which is in Heaven. (MATTHEW, 10:32 & 33.)

14. For whosoever shall be ashamed of me and of my words, of him shall the Son of Man be ashamed, when He shall come in His own glory, and that of His Father's, and of the holy angels. (LUKE, 9:26.)

15. To have the courage of one's belief has always been held in great esteem by humankind because there is merit in facing dangers, persecutions, contradictions and even simple sarcasm, to which all those who openly proclaim their ideas are almost always exposed, especially when those ideas are not to the general liking. Here as in everything, the merit is in proportion to the

circumstances and the importance of the result. There is always a weakness in drawing back from the consequences entailed by opinions and in denying them. However, there are some cases in which this constitutes an act of cowardice as great as the one committed by fleeing from the moment of battle.

Jesus denounced this kind of cowardice from the particular point of view of His Teachings by saying that if anyone were ashamed of His words then He too would be ashamed of them. That He would disown the person who repudiated Him and would only acknowledge before the Father, Who is in Heaven, those who publicly acknowledge Him. In other words, *those who are afraid to confess themselves to be disciples of truth are not worthy to be admitted into the kingdom of truth.* In this way they will lose the advantages of their faith, because it is a selfish faith that they keep for themselves, hiding it for fear of the prejudice they may come to suffer in the world. Meanwhile, those who put truth above all material interests and openly proclaim it are working both for their own future and for that of others.

16. This is how it will be for the followers of Spiritism because the Teaching they profess is nothing more than the development and application of the Gospel. Christ's words were also directed at them. They plant on Earth what will be harvested in the spiritual world and it is there that they will gather the fruits of their courage and weakness.

CARRY YOUR CROSS - HE WHO WILL SAVE HIS LIFE SHALL LOSE IT

17. Blessed are you, when men hate you, when they separate you from their company, and reproach you, and cast out your name as evil, for the Son of Man's sake. Rejoice on that day, and leap for joy: for, behold, your reward is great in heaven: for in the like manner did their fathers to the prophets. (LUKE, 6:22 & 23.)

18. And when He had called the people to Him, with His disciples also, He said to them, "Whosoever shall come after me, let him deny himself, and take up his cross, and follow me. For whosoever shall save his life, shall lose it: but whosoever shall lose his life for my sake and the Gospel's, the same shall save it." For what shall it profit a man if he shall gain the whole world, and lose his own soul? (MARK, 8:34-36. Also LUKE, 9:23-25; MATTHEW, 10:39; JOHN 12:24 & 25.)

19. Jesus said, "Rejoice when people hate and persecute you for My sake, seeing that you will be rewarded in Heaven." These words should be understood in the following manner: Consider yourself blessed when there are fellow beings who, by their ill-will towards you, give you the opportunity to prove the sincerity of your faith, seeing that the evil they do to you will only result in your benefit. Lament their blindness and do not curse them.

Then He added, "Take up your cross, all those who wish to follow Me." By which He meant that you must courageously support the trials and tribulations that your faith may bring about. Whereas any person who wishes to save their life and their property by renouncing Christ will lose all the advantages of Heaven. While those who lose everything in this world, even their life for the sake of truth, these will receive a prize for courage, perseverance and abnegation in the future life. Meanwhile, to those who have sacrificed the heavenly benefits for earthly pleasures, God will say, "You have already received your recompense."

CHAPTER 25

SEEK AND YOU WILL FIND

Help yourself, then Heaven will come to your aid. - Behold the fowls of the
air. – Do not worry about possessing gold.

HELP YOURSELF, THEN HEAVEN WILL COME TO YOUR AID

1. Ask and it shall be given you; seek, and you shall find*; knock,
and it shall be opened to you: For everyone that asks receives;
and he that seeks finds; and to him that knocks it shall be opened.*

*Or what man is there of you, whom if his son ask bread, will he
give him a stone? Or if he ask a fish, will he give him a serpent? If
you then, being evil, know how to give good gifts to your children,
how much more shall your Father which is in Heaven, give good
things to them that ask Him?* (MATTHEW, 7:7-11.)

2. From an earthly point of view the maxim '*Seek and you will
find*', is the same as that other one '*Help yourself and the heavens
will come to your aid*'. This is the base of the *Law of Work* and
consequently the *Law of Progress,* since progress is the child of
work, seeing that this puts into action the forces of intelligence.

During humankind's infancy, people only used their intelligence
for seeking food as a means of protection against the climate and
for defending themselves from their enemies. However, God has
given them something more than He gave to animals, which is *an
incessant desire to better themselves.* It is this desire that impels
them to seek out the best ways of improving their position in life,
which duly leads them to make discoveries, to invent things and to
perfect the sciences, because it is science that gives them what
they lack. Through their research, their intelligence heightens and

their morals gradually become purified. The needs of the body give way to those of the spirit. After material nourishment, humans need spiritual nourishment. This is how they pass from savagery to a state of civilisation.

However, the amount of progress achieved by each person during a single lifetime is very small indeed, in most cases even imperceptible. How then could humanity progress without pre-existence and the *re-existence* of the soul? If the souls who daily leave the Earth were never to return, then humanity would be constantly renewing itself with primitive elements, having everything still to do and learn. There would then be no reason why humans should be more advanced today than they were during the first epochs of the world because at each birth all intellectual work would have to recommence. On the other hand, by returning with the degree of progress realised and acquiring something more each time, the soul then gradually passes from the barbaric state to that of *materialistic civilisation* and then on to one of *moral civilisation.* (See chapter 4, item 17.)

3. If God had exempted humans from bodily work, their limbs would have withered. If He had exempted them from intellectual work, then their spirit would have remained in a state of infancy or mere animal instinct. This is why He made work a necessity by saying: *Seek and you will find; work and you will produce.* In this way you are the product of your own work; you receive the merit of it and the recompense in accordance with what you have done.

4. It is by virtue of this principle that the Spirits do not help in sparing humans beings the work of research, by bringing them discoveries and inventions prepared and ready for use. Nor in such a way that they would have nothing to do, except accept what was put into their hands, without any inconvenience whatsoever, not even to bend down and pick it up nor yet to think about it. If things were like that, then the laziest could enrich themselves and

the most ignorant could become wise at the cost of no effort and both would have merits attributed to them for things they had not done. No, *the Spirits do not come to exempt humanity from the Law of Work, but to show them the goal to be reached and the pathway that leads there, by saying: walk and you will get there.* You will find stones under your feet; look and then move them away. We will give you the necessary strength if you care to utilise it. (See THE MEDIUMS' BOOK, (1) chapter 26, item 291 onwards.)

5. From the moral point of view, these words of Jesus signify: ask for the light that will show the way and it will be given; ask for strength to resist evil and you will receive it; ask for the assistance of the Good Spirits and they will come to guide you just as did the Angel of Tobias. Ask for good counsel and it will never be refused; knock on our door and it will be open to you; but ask with sincerity, faith, fervour and confidence; present yourself humbly and not with arrogance, without which you will be abandoned to your own strengths and you will fall as a just punishment for your pride.

This then is the meaning of the words: Seek and you will find; knock and it will be opened.

BEHOLD THE FOWLS OF THE AIR

6. *Lay not up for yourselves treasures upon earth, where moth and rust do corrupt, and where thieves break through and steal: But lay up for yourselves treasures in Heaven, where neither moth nor rust do corrupt, and where thieves do not break through nor steal. For where your treasure is, there will your heart be also.*

Therefore I say unto you, Take no thought for your life, what you shall eat, or what you shall drink: nor yet for your body, what you shall put on. Is not the life more than meat, and the body more than clothing?

Behold the fowls of the air: for they sow not, neither do they reap, nor gather into barns; yet your heavenly Father feeds them. Are you not much better than they? Which of you by taking thought can add one cubit to his stature?

And why take thought for clothes? Consider the lilies of the field, how they grow; they do not work, neither do they spin, And yet I say to you, That even Solomon in all his glory was not arrayed like one of these. Wherefore, if God so clothe the grass of the field, which today is, and tomorrow is cast into the oven, shall he not much more clothe you, Oh you of little faith!

Therefore, take no thought, saying, What shall we eat? or, What shall we drink? or Wherewithal shall we be clothed? (For after all these things do the Gentiles seek;) for your heavenly Father knows that you have need of all these things.

But seek first the kingdom of God, and His righteousness: and all these things shall be added unto you. Take therefore no thought for tomorrow: for tomorrow shall take thought for the things of itself. Sufficient unto the day is the evil thereof. (MATTHEW, 6:19-21 & 25-34.)

7. In a literal translation, these words would be a denial of all providence of all work and consequently of all progress. With this kind of principle, humanity would be limited to waiting passively, while all physical and intellectual strengths remained inactive. If such were the normal conditions on Earth then human beings would never have left the primitive state. If this condition were to become law today then it would only remain to live in total idleness. This could not have been the thought of Jesus, since this would be a contradiction of what He had said on other occasions and it would also contradict the Laws of Nature. God created humans without clothes or shelter, but He gave them intelligence so as to be able to make them. (See chapter 14, item 6 & chapter 25, item 2.)

Therefore, these words must not be seen as anything more than the poetical allegory of Providence that never abandons those who put their confidence in it, but wishes that all work in their turn. If Providence does not always come in the form of material help, then it inspires those ideas from which is found the means of getting out of difficulty. (See chapter 27, item 8.)

God understands our necessities and provides for them when it is necessary. Nevertheless, humans are insatiable in their desires and do not always know how to be content with what they have. Possessing what is necessary is not enough for them; they want what is superfluous. Then Providence leaves them to themselves. Many times they become unhappy through their own fault and for having paid no attention to the voice of their conscience which had warned them. In these cases the Lord lets them suffer the consequences, so it may serve as a lesson for the future. (See chapter 5, item 4.)

8. The Earth will produce sufficient to feed all of its inhabitants, when people discover how to administer the benefits that it offers, according to the Laws of Justice, Charity and Love for one's neighbour. When fraternity reigns amongst all peoples, as it does amongst the provinces of any country, then the momentary superfluity of the one will overcome the insufficiency of another and everyone will have what is necessary. Then the rich person will consider themselves as someone who possesses a great number of seeds; if they scatter them, they will produce a thousand fold for that person and enough for others as well. However, if they eat all the seeds by themselves, or waste them or allow the surplus they left to be lost, nothing will have been produced and there will not be enough for everyone. If they hoard the seeds in their barns, then the maggots will devour them. This is why Jesus said, "Do not accumulate treasures on Earth because they are perishable; but accumulate them in Heaven where they are eternal." In other words, do not give material possessions more

importance than the spiritual ones and know how to sacrifice the former for the latter. (See chapter 16, item 7 onwards.)

Charity and fraternity cannot be decreed by law. If they are not in the heart, then selfishness will always stifle them. It is up to Spiritism to see that they penetrate the heart.

DO NOT WORRY ABOUT POSSESSING GOLD

9. Provide neither gold, nor silver, nor brass in your purses. Nor script for your journey, neither two coats, neither shoes, nor yet staves: for the worker is worthy of his meat.

10. And into whatsoever city or town you shall enter, enquire who in it is worthy; and there abide till you leave. And when you go into a house, salute it. And if the house be worthy, let your peace come upon it: but if it be not worthy, let your peace return to you. And whosoever shall not receive you, nor hear your words, when you depart out of that house or city, shake off the dust of your feet. Truly I say to you, It shall be more tolerable for the land of Sodom and Gomorrah in the day of judgement, than for that city. (MATTHEW, 10:9-15.)

11. These words that Jesus directed to His apostles when He sent them to announce the Good News for the first time were nothing unusual in those days. They were in accordance with the patriarchal customs of the Orient, where the traveller was always made welcome in the tent. But then in those days travellers were very rare indeed. Among modern peoples, the development of travel has created new customs. Very distant lands, where the great movement has not yet penetrated, are the only places to conserve the customs of ancient times. If Jesus were to return today, He could no longer tell his apostles to put themselves on the road without provisions.

Apart from their actual meaning, these words hold a very profound moral sense. In proffering them, Jesus was teaching His disciples to have confidence in Providence. What is more, by having nothing, they could not cause covetousness amongst those who received them. This was the way to distinguish those who were selfish from those who were charitable. This is why He told them to "Find out who is worthy to put you up," or rather who is sufficiently generous to clothe a traveller who has nothing with which to pay. These are the people who will be worthy to receive your words and who will be recognisable by their charity.

With regard to those who cared neither to receive them nor to listen to them, did He tell His disciples that they should curse them, that they should impose the teachings upon them or that they should use violence and force to convert them? No, He simply told them to go away and seek others who were willing to listen.

Today Spiritism says the same thing to its followers. Do not violate any consciences. Do not force anyone to leave their faith in order to adopt yours. Do not excommunicate those who do not think as you do. Welcome all who come to join you and leave in peace all those who are repelled by your ideas. Remind yourselves of the words of Christ. In other times the heavens were taken over by violence, but today they are taken over by mildness. (See chapter 4, items 10 & 11.)

CHAPTER 26

FREELY YOU HAVE RECEIVED, FREELY GIVE

The gift of healing. - Paid prayers. - The moneychangers expelled from the Temple. - Gratuitous mediumship.

THE GIFT OF HEALING

1. "Heal the sick, cleanse the lepers, raise the dead, cast out devils: freely you have received, freely give." (MATTHEW, 10:8.)

2. Jesus told His disciples "Give for free what has been received gratuitously." With this recommendation, He prescribes that no one should be charged for something for which nothing had been paid. Now, what the disciples had received gratuitously was the faculty of healing those who were sick and that of casting out devils, that is to say evil spirits. God had given them this faculty gratis for the alleviation of those who suffer and as a means of propagating the faith. Then Jesus recommended that they should not turn this into an object of commercialisation, neither speculation nor a means of livelihood.

PAID PRAYERS

3. Then in the audience of all the people he said to his disciples, Beware of the Scribes, which desire to walk in long robes, and love greetings in the markets, and the highest seats in the synagogues, and the chief rooms at feasts. Which devour widow's houses, and for a show make long prayers: the same shall receive greater damnation. (LUKE, 20:45-47); also MARK, 12:38-40 and MATTHEW, 23:14.)

4. Jesus also said, Do not charge for your prayers, nor do as the Scribes who 'on the pretext of long prayers, *devoured the homes of widows,* that is to say, they took possession of their fortunes. A prayer is an act of charity, an ecstasy of the heart. To charge someone for the prayers we direct to God in their name is to transform oneself into a paid intermediary. Then prayer becomes a mere formula whose price is in proportion to the length of time it lasts. Moreover, only one of the following can be true: either God measures or does not measure His blessings by the number of words used in a prayer. If words are necessary in large numbers, why then are so few said or even none, for those who cannot pay? This is a lack of charity. If one word is sufficient then an excess of words is useless. How then can we charge for prayers? This would be a corrupt practice.

God does not sell His benefits; He concedes them. How then can someone who is not even an agent, who cannot guarantee results, charge for a request that may produce no results? It is not possible that God could make an act of clemency, kindness and justice, requested from His infinite mercy, subject to the payment of a sum of money and that if the sum were not paid or was insufficient, then the justice, kindness and clemency would be withdrawn. Reason, good sense and logic tell us it is impossible that God, Who is absolute perfection, would delegate to imperfect beings the right to establish a price for His justice. God's Justice is like the Sun: it exists for all, rich and poor alike. Just as it is considered immoral to trade with the favours of any earthly sovereign, could it then be licit to commercialise those of the Sovereign of the Universe?

Paid prayers present yet another inconvenience, which is that the one who buys them judges themselves in most cases to be relieved from the need to pray. They consider themselves exonerated since they gave their money. We know that Spirits are touched by the fervour of the thoughts of those who are interested in them, but what fervour can be felt by one who arranges a third party to pray for them on payment of money? What kind of fervour has this third party when they delegate the task to another and that one to yet another and so on? Does this not reduce the effectiveness of prayer to the value of a particular currency?

THE MONEYCHANGERS EXPELLED FROM THE TEMPLE

5. *"And they come to Jerusalem: and Jesus went into the temple, and began to cast out them that sold and bought in the temple, and overthrew the tables of the moneychangers, and the seats of them that sold doves; and would not suffer that any man should carry any vessel through the temple. And He taught, saying to them, is it not written: My house shall be called of all nations the house of prayer? but you have made it a den of thieves. And the scribes and chief priests heard it, and sought how they might destroy him: for they feared him, because all the people were astonished at his doctrine."* (MARK, 11:15-18; and MATTHEW, 21:12 & 13.)

6. Jesus expelled the merchants from the temple. With this act, He condemned the trading of sacred things *in any form whatsoever*. God does not sell His blessings, nor His pardon or the right of entrance into the kingdom of heaven. Therefore, no one has the right to stipulate a price for such things.

GRATUITOUS MEDIUMSHIP

7. Modern Mediums - since the apostles also possessed mediumship - have equally received this faculty gratis from God: this being interpreters of the Spirits for the instruction of humankind, to show them the pathway of goodness and conducting them along by means of faith and not to sell words that do not belong to them, seeing that they are not fruits of their

conception, of their research or of their personal work. God wants the light to reach everyone. He does not want the poorest to be disinherited of it so they can say: they have no faith because they could not afford to pay for it; or that they did not have the consolation of receiving encouragement and testimony of affection from those they weep for, because they are too poor. This is why mediumship is not a privilege and is to be found in all places. To make someone pay for it is to turn it away from its providential objective.

8. Those who understand the conditions in which Good Spirits communicate and the feeling of repugnance they have towards everything that shows selfish interest, know how little it takes to drive them away. These people could never accept that Superior Spirits are at the disposal of the first who comes along and evokes them at so much per session. Simple good sense rejects such an idea. Would it not also be a profanity to evoke for money those we respect or those who are dear to us? Beyond doubt, communications can be obtained in this manner, but who can guarantee their sincerity? Spirits of a frivolous, deceitful, mocking nature and all the bank of inferior spirits, who are not at all scrupulous, always come running ready to reply to whatever is asked, with no regard for the truth. Those who desire serious communications should, before all else, ask with seriousness and following this should inform themselves of the nature of the sympathies the medium may have with the beings from the spirit world. Therefore, the first conditions necessary to attract the benevolence of the Good Spirits are humility, devotion, abnegation and total disinterest, *both moral and material.*

9. Besides the moral question, an effective consideration also presents itself that is no less important. This refers to the actual nature of the faculty itself. Serious mediumship cannot be and never ever will be a profession. Not just because it would be morally discredited and rapidly become mere fortune telling, but

because there is a material obstacle in opposition. Mediumship is a faculty that is unstable, elusive and variable, whose permanency no one can count upon. It is a very uncertain source for anyone wishing to exploit it and it can fail at the moment it is most needed. A talent acquired by study and work is another matter and it is for this very reason a skill that can be legitimately used to advantage. However, mediumship is neither an art nor a skill; therefore, it cannot become a profession. It only exists through the co-operation of spirits. If they are absent, there is no mediumship. The aptitude can exist, but the exercise of it would be annulled. In addition, there is not a single medium in the world who can guarantee obtaining a spiritual phenomenon at any given moment. So then, to exploit mediumship is to make use of something that does not belong to that person. To state the contrary is to deceive the person being charged. What is more, it is not *they themselves* whom the exploiter commands, but rather the concourse of spirits, the souls of the dead, whose co-operation they put a price on. This idea causes instinctive repugnance. It was because of the trafficking and the exploitation by charlatans that degenerated into abuse, together with ignorance, incredulity and superstition that motivated Moses to prohibit it. Modern Spiritism, understanding the serious nature of this question, has completely discredited its exploitation, so elevating this faculty to the category of a mission. (See THE MEDIUMS' BOOK, 2nd part, chapter 28 and HEAVEN AND HELL, 1st part, chapter 11.)

10. Mediumship is something sacred, which should be practised in a saintly and religious manner, and if there is one type of mediumship that requires this condition even more absolutely than others do, it is that of healing.[16] Doctors give the fruits of their

---

[16] In Spiritism the word HEALING is understood to mean restorative work carried out by Good Spirits using someone, possibly a medium, as their instrument or channel. (Translator's note.)

study, which were often gained at the cost of painful sacrifices. Magnetisers give their own fluids, sometimes even their health. A price can be put upon these. However, a curing medium retransmits healing fluids from the Good Spirits. Consequently, they have no right to sell them. Jesus and His apostles, although poor, did not charge for the cures they obtained.

Therefore, those who lack the necessary means of financial support can seek funds wherever they like, excepting within mediumship; only dedicating their spare time to this work, after material needs have been satisfied. The Spirits will take into consideration all devotion and sacrifices; whereas they will turn away from any person who expects to turn them into a springboard from where they can gain fame or fortune.

CHAPTER 27

ASK AND IT SHALL BE GIVEN

The quality of prayers. - The effectiveness of prayer. - The act of prayer. Transmission of thought. - Intelligible prayers. - Prayers for suffering spirits and the dead. - INSTRUCTIONS FROM THE SPIRITS: How to pray. - Happiness can be found through prayer.

THE QUALITY OF PRAYERS

1. And when you pray, you shall not be as the hypocrites are: for they love to pray standing in the synagogues and in the corners of the streets, that they may be seen of men. Truly I say to you, They have received their reward. But you, when you pray, enter into your room, and when you have shut the door, pray to your Father which is in secret: and your Father which sees in secret shall reward you openly.

But when you pray, use not vain repetitions, as the heathen do: for they think that they shall be heard for their much speaking. Be not you therefore like them: for your Father knows what things you have need of, before you ask him. (MATTHEW, 6:5-8.)

2. And when you stand praying, forgive, if you have anything against any: that your Father also which is in Heaven may forgive you your trespasses. But if you do not forgive, neither will your Father which is in heaven forgive your trespasses. (MARK, 11:25 & 26.)

3. And he spoke this parable to certain which trusted in themselves that they were righteous, and despised others: some that believed themselves to be righteous and so despised others: Two men went up into the temple to pray. the one a Pharisee and the other a Publican. The Pharisee stood and prayed to himself, God, I thank you that I am not as other men are, possess. And the

Publican, standing far off, would not lift up so much as his eyes to heaven, but beat upon his breast, saying, God be merciful to me a sinner! I tell you, this man went down to his house justified rather than the other: for every one that exalts himself shall be abased; and he that humbled himself shall be exalted. (LUKE, 18:9-14.)

4. Jesus clearly defined the quality of prayer. He said that when you pray you should not make yourself conspicuous, but rather pray in secret. Do not prolong your prayers because it is not by the multiplicity of the words that you will be heard, but by their sincerity. Before praying, if you have anything against another, forgive them, seeing that prayer is not pleasing to God if it does not come from a heart cleansed of all sentiments that are contrary to charity. Finally, pray with humility, as did the publican, and not with pride as did the Pharisee. Look at your defects, not at your qualities and if you compare yourself to others, look for what is bad in yourself. (See Chapter 10, items 7 & 8.)

THE EFFECTIVENESS OF PRAYER

5. Therefore I say to you, what things so ever you desire, when you pray, believe that you will receive them, and you will have them. (MARK 11:24.)

6. There are those who contest the effectiveness of prayer, because as God knows all our needs, it is useless to enumerate them to Him. Those who think this, then add that seeing everything in the Universe is linked together by eternal laws our petitions cannot change God's decrees.

Beyond all doubt, there are natural and immutable laws that cannot be annulled at the caprice of each individual, but from this fact to the belief that all circumstances in life are submitted to fatality is a long step indeed. If it were like that, then humankind would be mere passive instruments without free will or initiative. In this hypothesis, it would only remain for people to bow down their heads in submission before all occurrences, without making any effort to avoid them or try to ward off dangers. God did not grant reason and intelligence to human beings for them not to use them, willpower not to desire things, or activity for people to remain inactive. As everyone is free to act one way or the other, for themselves and towards others, the consequences depend on what each one does or does not do. By each one's initiative, there are events that forcibly escape fatality and yet do not destroy the harmony of the universal laws, just as the quickening or slowing down of the pendulum of a clock does not annul the law of movement upon which the mechanism is based. God then can accede to certain petitions without destroying the immunity of those laws that govern the whole, as consent is always dependent on His will.

7. From the maxim: "Whatever you ask for through prayer will be granted," it would be illogical to conclude that one can receive just by asking and unjust to accuse Providence if a request made is not conceded, because it is known what is best for our own good. This is what happens to a prudent father, who refuses to give his son certain things that would be against his own interests. Generally, human beings only see the present moment. Meanwhile, if the suffering is useful to our future happiness, then God will let us suffer, just as a surgeon allows the patient to suffer an operation that will cure him.

What God will grant if we direct ourselves to Him with confidence, is courage, patience and resignation. What He will also grant are the means of resolving situations with the help of ideas suggested to us by Good Spirits at God's instigation, whereby we retain the merit for the decisions taken. God helps all those who help themselves according to the maxim, "Help yourself and the heavens will come to your aid." Nevertheless, He does not help those who wait for outside assistance without using their own faculties. However, in most cases what people desire is to be helped by miracles without using any effort of their own. (See Chapter 25, item 1 and following items.)

8. Let us take an example. Someone is lost in a desert. Thirst is torturing them terribly. Fainting, the person falls to the ground. They ask God to help them and wait. No angels will come to give them water. However, what does happen is that a Good Spirit suggests the idea of picking themselves up and taking one of the paths to be seen in front of them. By pure mechanical movement, uniting what is left of their strength the person gets up and discovers not far away a stream. On sighting this, they gain courage. If the person has faith, they exclaim, "Thank you, dear God, for the idea you inspired and for the strength you gave me." If they are without any faith, they will say, "What a good idea *I had*. How *lucky* I was to take the right-hand path and not the one on the left! Chance sometimes serves one admirably! I must *congratulate myself* for *my* courage and for not being defeated!"

Nevertheless, you may ask why the Good Spirit did not say clearly: "Follow that path and you will find what you need." Why did this Spirit not show itself, guide them and sustain them in their lack of animation? In that way, the person would have been convinced of the intervention of Providence. Firstly, to teach them that people must help themselves and make use of their strength. Secondly, because that person doubted His existence. God put the confidence the person had in Him to the test, as well as testing their submission to His will. This person was in the situation of a child, who falls down and because someone is with them starts to cry and waits to be picked up. If the same child saw no one they would make the effort and get up by themselves.

If the Angel who accompanied Tobias had said, "I am sent by God to guide you on your journey and preserve you from all danger," then Tobias could claim no merit. In entrusting himself to his companion he would not even have had to think. This is why the Angel only made himself known after the return.

THE ACT OF PRAYER - TRANSMISSION OF THOUGHT

9. Prayer is an invocation. It is by means of thought that human beings enter into communication with the being to whom they direct themselves. This may be for the purpose of asking for something, giving thanks or as a glorification. We may pray for ourselves or for others, for the living or for the dead. Those spirits who are charged with the execution of His will hear prayers addressed to God. All those addressed to Good Spirits are referred to God. When someone prays to beings other than God, these serve as mediators or intercessors because nothing can happen without God's wishes.

10. Spiritism makes the act of prayer understandable by explaining how thought is transmitted, either when the Spirit to whom we are praying comes to our aid or when our thoughts rise up to this being. In order to understand what happens in this circumstance, it is necessary to consider all incarnate and discarnate beings as immersed in the Universal Cosmic Fluid which occupies space, just as we on Earth are immersed in the atmosphere of this planet. This fluid receives an impulse from the will; this is the vehicle for thought, just as air is the vehicle for sound, with the difference that the vibrations of air are circumscribed, whereas those of the Universal Cosmic Fluid extend infinitely. So when a thought is directed at someone, either on Earth or in space, from an incarnate to a discarnate being, or vice-versa, a fluidic current is established between them that transmits the thought from one to the other just as air transmits sound.

The energy contained in this current remains proportional to the force behind the thought and the desire. This then is how Good

Spirits can hear the prayers directed to them wherever they may be. It is also how Spirits communicate amongst themselves, how they transmit their inspirations to us, and how contacts between incarnates are established at a distance.

This explanation has in mind principally those people who do not understand the utility of completely mystical prayer. It is not meant to seemingly materialise prayer, but rather to make its effect intelligible by showing it can have direct and effective results. However, this does not make it any less subordinate to God's wishes; He is the Supreme Judge of all things and it is only through His wishes that the action of prayer can become effective.

11. It is through prayer that humans obtain the assistance of the Good Spirits, who come to sustain them in their good resolutions and inspire wholesome ideas. In this manner, they acquire the necessary moral strength to be able to surmount difficulties and come back to the straight and narrow path, should they at any time stray from it. By these means, they can also turn away the evil they attract through their faults. For example, a person loses their health due to excesses and so leads a life of suffering until the termination of their days. Has this person the right to complain if they do not obtain the cure they so desired? No, because they could have found the strength to resist temptation, through the act of prayer.

12. The evils of life can be divided into two parts, one being those that cannot be avoided and the other being the tribulations of which they themselves are the principal cause, due to carelessness and excesses. (See chapter 5, item 4.) Then we would see that the number in the second group far exceeds those in the first. Therefore, it is evident that humans are the author of the greater part of their own afflictions and that these could be avoided if they always behaved with prudence and wisdom.

It is no less certain that these miseries are the result of our infractions against God's Law and that if we duly observed these Laws we would be completely happy. If we did not exceed the limit of what is necessary for the satisfaction of our needs, we would not have the sicknesses that are provoked as consequences of these excesses. Neither would we experience the vicissitudes that derive from them. If we put a limit on our ambitions, we would not have to fear ruin. If we did not desire to raise ourselves higher than we are able, we would not have to be afraid of falling. If we practised the Law of Charity we would not slander, be jealous or envious and we would avoid arguments and fights. If we did no evil to anyone, we would not need to fear revenge, etc.

Let us admit that humans can do nothing with respect to other ills and that any amount of prayer is useless in ridding us of them. However, would it not mean a great deal to have the possibility of exempting ourselves from those ills that stem from our own behaviour? Here it is easy to conceive the action played by prayer, which aims at attracting wholesome inspirations from the Good Spirits and in asking them for strength to resist our bad thoughts, whose realisation could be disastrous for us. In this case, *what prayers do is not remove the wrong from us, but turn us away from our bad thoughts that cause us harm. Although prayer does not prevent the fulfilling of God's laws, nor does it suspend the course of the Laws of Nature, it stops us from infringing these laws by guiding our free will.* However, within these hidden influences our free will is maintained. Therefore, each person finds themselves in the position of someone who requests good counselling and then puts them into practice; but always maintaining the liberty to follow them or not. God desires it to be like this, so that people can have the responsibility for their actions, thereby leaving them merit for their choice between good and evil. This is what humans can always be sure of obtaining if they ask fervently. This is the kind of situation where, above all, the words "Ask and it shall be given" can be applied.

Could not the effects of prayer, even when reduced to these proportions, bring immense results? It has been reserved for Spiritism to prove its action through the revelation of the relationship existing between the physical and spiritual worlds. However, its effects are not limited just to these results.

All spirits recommend that we pray. To renounce prayer is to ignore the benevolence of God and to reject for oneself His assistance and for others the good that can be done.

13. On attending to any request that may be addressed to Him, God frequently has in mind to recompense the intention, devotion and faith of the one who prays. This is why the prayers of a good person have greater merit in God's eyes and are always more effective. The corrupt and evil person cannot pray with the same fervour and confidence that can only come from a sentiment of true piety. From a selfish heart or one who prays only from the lips, there come only words, but never a charitable impulse that is what gives force to prayer. This is so clearly understood that instinctively, when requesting a prayer from someone else, preference is given to a person we feel is agreeable to God, because their prayer will be more readily heard.

14. As prayer exercises a type of magnetic action, it could be supposed that its effect would depend on fluidic power. However, this is not so. To be precise, spirits exercise this action on humans to overcome any insufficiency in those who pray, either by direct influence *in His name,* or by giving the person momentarily an exceptional force when they judge them deserving of this grace, or when it can be useful to them.

The person who does not consider themselves sufficiently good as to exercise a wholesome influence, should not refrain from praying for the good of another because of a mistaken belief of being unworthy to be heard. The consciousness of their own inferiority constitutes a test in humility, which is always pleasing to God. Who then takes into account the charitable intention that animated that person. Fervour and confidence in God are the first steps in the return to goodness, for which the Good Spirits feel blessed in being able to offer stimulation. Prayer is repelled only from *the prideful, who deposit faith in their own power and merits, believing it possible to superimpose themselves upon the Will of the Eternal Father.*

15. The power of prayer lies in the thought and does not depend on words, the place or the moment in which it is proffered. Therefore, it is possible to pray in all places, at any time, alone or with others. The influence of a place or time is only felt according to the circumstances that favour the meditation. *Communal prayer has a more powerful action when all who are praying join together in a heartfelt thought and envisage the same objective,* since it is as if many beseeched together in one voice. However, it will do no good for a large number of people to gather together for prayer, if each one acts in isolation, on their own account. A hundred people can pray selfishly, whereas two or three joined by the same aspirations, praying like true brothers and sisters in Christ, will give more power to their prayer than would the hundred selfish people. (See chapter 28, items 4 & 5.)

INTELLIGIBLE PRAYERS

16. *Therefore, if I know not the meaning of the voice, I shall be to him that speaks a barbarian, and he that speaks shall be a barbarian to me.* For if I pray in an unknown tongue, *my spirit prays, but my understanding is unfruitful. Else when you shall bless with the spirit, how shall he that occupies the room of the unlearned say Amen at your giving of thanks,* seeing he does not understand what you are saying? *For you are truly giving thanks*

well, but the other is not uplifted. (PAUL, I Corinthians, 14:11, 14, 16 & 17.)

17. Prayer only has value through the thought to which it is united. Therefore, it is impossible to join any thought to something that is not understood, since what is not understood cannot touch the heart. For the great majority of human beings prayers that are said in an unknown language are nothing more than a conglomeration of words that say nothing to the spirit. In order for prayer to touch, it is necessary for each word to awaken an idea and when the words are not understood they are unable to do this. It would be merely a simple formula, whose virtue depended on the greater or lesser number of times it was repeated. Many pray from duty, others from obedience to habit; this is why they judge themselves to be exonerated from their duty after having prayed a determined prayer a sufficient number of times, in a certain order. God reads what passes deep in our hearts. He scrutinises our thoughts and our sincerity. Therefore, in judging Him to be more sensitive to the format rather than the depth, is to discredit Him. (See chapter 28, item 2.)

PRAYERS FOR SUFFERING SPIRITS AND THE DEAD

18. Suffering spirits ask for prayers and these are useful to them, because on recognising that someone thinks of them they feel comforted and less unhappy. However, prayer has a more direct action on them by reanimating them and instilling in them a desire to elevate themselves through repentance or by making amends and can turn them away from bad thoughts. It is in this sense that prayers cannot only alleviate, but can also shorten their suffering. (See HEAVEN & HELL, the second part – Examples.)

19. Some people do not accept the offering of prayers for the dead, as according to their belief, the soul has only two alternatives - to be saved or to be eternally condemned to suffering

- which would result in prayer being useless in either case. Without discussing the merits of this belief, let us admit for a moment the reality of eternal unpardonable penitence, which our prayers are impotent to interrupt. We ask if, even in this hypothesis, it would be logical, charitable or Christian to refuse prayer for the reprobate. However impotent these might be in liberating them, would these prayers not be a demonstration of pity, capable of softening their suffering? On Earth, when a person is condemned to perpetual prison, even if there was not a minimum chance of obtaining a pardon, is it forbidden for a charitable person to help alleviate the weight of the sentence through prayer? When an incurable disease attacks someone, there being no hope of a cure, should we abandon the person without offering some kind of relief? Remind yourselves that amongst the wicked you may find someone who has been dear to you, perhaps a friend, a father or a mother, a son or a daughter. Then ask yourself if, because of your belief that there is no possibility of a pardon, would you refuse a glass of water to mitigate their thirst? Or a balsam that would heal their wounds? Would you not do for them what you would do for one condemned to the galleys? Would you not give them proof of your love and console them? No, this idea would not be Christian. A belief that hardens the heart cannot conform to the existence of a God Who, amongst many duties, puts that of loving one's neighbour in first place.

The non-existence of eternal punishment does not imply a denial of temporary penalty, given that it is not possible for God in His justice to confound good with evil. In this case, to deny the efficiency of prayer would be to deny the efficacy of consolation, encouragement and good advice. This would be equal to denying the strength we absorb from the moral assistance received from those who wish us well.

20. Others base their ideas on a more misleading reason: that of the immutability of Divine decree. God, they say, cannot modify

His decisions just when asked by one of His creatures, because if this were so then nothing on Earth would have stability. Therefore, humans cannot ask God for anything; it only rests for humankind to submit and adore Him.

In this idea, there is a false interpretation of the principle of the immutability of Divine Law or, better still, an ignorance of this Law with regard to future penalties. This Law is revealed by the Spirits of the Lord at this time, now that humanity is sufficiently mature to understand what, within the faith, conforms to or is contrary to the Divine attributes.

According to the doctrine of the absolute eternity of all punishment, the remorse and repentance of the culprit are not taken into account. All desire to better oneself is useless, for they are condemned to remain eternally evil. However, if they were condemned for a determined period of time, then the punishment would cease when that time had expired. But who can say that by then their sentiments have improved? Who can say, as shown by many who have been condemned on Earth, that on leaving prison they will no longer be as bad as before? In the first case, it would be keeping a person under the pain of punishment after they had become good; in the second, it would be the granting of amnesty to one who continues to be guilty. God's law is more provident than that; being always just, impartial and merciful, it places no fixed duration for punishment, whatever the case may be. This law can be resumed in the following manner:

21. Human beings always suffer the consequences of their errors. There is no infraction of God's Laws that does not have its punishment.

The severity of the penalty is proportional to the gravity of the offence.

The duration of the penalty for an error *is indeterminate, being subordinate to the repentance of the culprit and their return to goodness*; the penalty lasts as long as the evil. It will be perpetual if the persistence in doing evil is also perpetual; it is of short duration if repentance comes quickly.

From the moment the culprit cries for mercy, God listens and sends hope. However, the simple fact of remorse for the evil done is not enough; it is necessary that reparation is made. This then is why the guilty party is submitted to new tests wherein they can, by their own will, do Good in reparation for the evil that was done.

In this manner, humans are constantly choosing their own destiny. They may shorten their anguish, or prolong it indefinitely. Happiness or unhappiness depends on their will to do Good.

This is the Law, the *immutable* Law that conforms to the goodness and justice of God.

In this manner, the guilty and unhappy spirit can always save itself because God's Law establishes the condition by which this becomes possible. What the spirit is lacking in most cases is the willpower, the strength and the courage. Nevertheless, through our prayers, we can inspire this willpower. We can uphold the sufferer and encourage them and through our counselling we can give them the enlightenment they lack. *Thus instead of asking God to annul His law, we turn ourselves into instruments for the execution of His Law of Love and Charity.* In this manner, He allows us to participate, so giving us proof of His infinite charity. (See HEAVEN & HELL, 1st part, chapters: 4, 7 & 8.)

INSTRUCTIONS FROM THE SPIRITS

HOW TO PRAY

22. The first duty of all human beings, the first act that should mark the return to activity each day, is prayer. Most people pray, but only a very few really know how to pray! Of what importance to God are sentences that are mechanically linked together from habit, a duty to perform that weighs as heavily as any other duty?

The prayers of a Christian, of a *Spiritist,* or of whatever cult, must be made as soon as the spirit returns to the physical body. They should be raised up to the feet of the Divine Majesty with humility and profundity, in an impulse of gratitude for all the many benefits received until that day; for the night just past during which it was permitted, although without knowing, to get close to friends and guides so as to be able to absorb new strength and more perseverance through this contact. You should lift yourself up humbly to the feet of the Lord, to offer up your weaknesses, plead for help, indulgence and mercy. This prayer should be profound because it is your soul that should raise itself up to the Creator and in doing so, it should become transfigured, as was Jesus on the mount when He showed the radiant splendour of His hope and love.

Your prayer should include a request for His blessings upon those things you need, but let it be for things you *really* need. Therefore, it is useless to ask the Lord to shorten your tests and trials, or to give you happiness and riches. Preferably, ask for more precious items, such as patience, resignation and faith. Do not say, as many do, "It is not worth praying because God does not answer my prayers." In most cases, what do you ask Him for? Have you ever remembered to ask Him to help you with your own moral betterment? Oh no! Seldom have you done this. What you most remember to ask for is *success in all your Earthly projects* and then you complain that God does not bother about anyone and that if He did there would not be so many injustices! How foolish! How ungrateful! If you search deep into your conscience you would almost always find the motive for your suffering. So then, before all else: ask that you may become a better person and you will see that you are showered with consolations and blessings. (See chapter 5, item 4)

You should pray constantly, without any need to seek your chapel or fall on your knees in public. Daily prayer is the fulfilment of your duty, without any exception of any kind whatsoever. Is it not an act of love towards God when you help your brothers and sisters in any moral or physical need? It is an act of gratitude to lift up your thoughts to Him, when something happy occurs, when you avoid an accident or even when some simple triviality grazes your soul. So do not forget to say, *"Blessed be my Father in Heaven!"* Is it not an act of contrition to humble yourself before the Supreme Judge when you feel yourself weakening? Even though it is only by means of a fleeting thought, so as to say, *"Forgive me, Father, for I have sinned (from pride, selfishness or lack of charity); give me the strength not to fail again and courage to make reparation for my fault!"*

This is quite apart from regular morning and evening prayer and those for sacred days. As you see, prayer can be for all moments without interrupting your activities. On the contrary, in this manner it sanctifies them. You can be sure that just one of these thoughts, if sent from the heart, is listened to by our Celestial Father, even more so than those long repetitious prayers said out of habit and almost always without any determined motive behind them, *only because the habitual hour is calling you mechanically.* – V. MONOD. (Bordeaux, 1862.)

HAPPINESS CAN BE FOUND THROUGH PRAYER

23. Come-hither all those who wish to believe! The Celestial Spirits are come to announce great things! My children, God is opening up His treasures to distribute them for our benefit. Oh, incredulous humanity! If only you knew what a great benefit faith is to our hearts and how it induces the soul to repentance and prayer! Prayer! Ah! How touching are the words that fall from the lips of one who prays! Prayer is the Divine Dew that lessens the excessive heat of our passions. Favourite daughter of faith, it leads us along the pathway that takes us to God. In moments of reclusion and solitude, you will find yourselves together with the Lord. For you, the mysteries disappear because He reveals them to you. Apostles of thought, life is meant for you. Your soul liberates itself from matter and launches itself into the infinite and etheric worlds that poor humanity does not know.

March forward! Press on along the path of prayer and you will hear the voices of the Angels! What harmony! We no longer hear the confused noises and strident sounds of the Earth; only the sound of the lyres of the Archangels, the soft and gentle voices of the Seraphim that is more delicate than the morning breeze that plays among the foliage of the woodlands. Amongst what delights you will walk! Your earthly language cannot express such bliss; so quickly does it enter into all your pores, so alive and refreshing is the spring from which you are able to drink through prayer! Sweet voices and inebriating perfumes are what the soul hears and breathes when you launch yourself into prayer, into those unknown and inhabited spheres! All aspirations are divine when liberated from carnal desires. You too can pray, as did Jesus, while carrying His Cross from Golgotha to Calvary. So take up your burden and you will feel sweet emotions that will pass through your soul, even though you bear the weight of some infamous cross. He was going to die in order to live the Celestial Life in the House of His Father. - SAINT AUGUSTINE. (Paris, 1861.)

CHAPTER 28

A COLLECTION OF SPIRITIST PRAYERS

PREAMBLE

1. The Spirits have always said, "The form means nothing but the thought is everything. Say your prayers in accordance with your convictions and in the manner which is most agreeable to you, since a good thought is worth more than numerous words which do not touch the heart."

The Spirits do not prescribe an absolute formula for prayers. When they do it is merely to help us form our ideas and above all, to call our attention to certain principles of the Spiritist Teachings. On the other hand, perhaps it is to offer guidance to those who find it difficult to express their ideas, because there are some who believe they have not prayed properly if they have not been able to formulate their thoughts well.

The collection of prayers contained in this chapter is a selection of some that the Spirits have dictated on several occasions. Beyond doubt, they could have dictated other prayers, in different terms, appropriate to various ideas and special cases. Nevertheless, the style is of little importance if the thought is essentially the same. The object of prayer is to elevate our soul to God. The diversity of forms should not establish any difference between those who believe in Him and even less between the adepts of Spiritism, because God accepts all of them when they are sincere.

Therefore, you should not think of this collection of prayers as absolute formulas, but rather as a varied selection of those received from the Spirits. It is a way of applying the moral principles as taught by Christ that have been developed in this book; a complement to their writings based on our duties before God and our neighbour, in which we are again reminded of all the principles of the Spiritist Teachings.

Spiritism recognises the prayers of all cults as being good, as long as they come from the heart and not just from the lips. It does not impose them, nor does it condemn them. God is far too great, according to the Spiritist Teachings, to consider repelling a voice that implores or which sings His praises, just because it is not done in this or that manner. *Anyone who wants to launch anathema against any prayers that are not within their own formulas will prove they know nothing of the greatness of God.* To believe that He has some kind of attachment to a certain formula is to attribute to Him the smallness and the passions of humanity.

According to Saint Paul, one of the essential conditions of prayer (See chapter 27, item 16) is that it be understandable, so as to move our spirit. For this to happen it is not enough that it be said in a language understood by the person who is praying; since there are prayers spoken in everyday language that say little more to our thoughts than they would in a foreign language. For this reason, they do not touch our hearts.   The over abundance of words and the mysticism of the language frequently suffocate the few ideas they may contain.

The principal quality of a prayer is clarity. It should be simple and concise, without useless phraseology or an excess of adjectives, which are nothing more than decoration. Each word should be of value in expressing an idea and in touching a fibre of the soul. In short, *it should cause you to reflect.* This is the only way in which it can reach its objective, since in any other manner it is *nothing but a noise.* However, in most cases it can be seen with what distraction and inconstancy they are said. We see lips that move, but by the expression on the faces and by the sound of the voices, we can verify that it is only mechanical, a solely exterior act, to which the soul remains indifferent.

The prayers in this collection are divided into five categories, as follows: 1) General Prayers. 2) Prayers for oneself. 3) Prayers for the living. 4) Prayers for the dead. 5) Special prayers for the sick and the spiritually obsessed.

With the objective of calling special attention to the aims of the various prayers and making their meaning more comprehensive, they are preceded by preliminary comments explaining the motives behind each one, entitled *Preface*.

1 - GENERAL PRAYERS

THE LORD'S PRAYER

2. PREFACE. - The Spirits recommended that we begin this anthology with the Lord's Prayer, not simply as a prayer, but also as a symbol. Of all the prayers, this one is considered the most important because it came from Jesus Himself (See Matthew, 6:9-13.) and because it can substitute all others, according to the intention and the thoughts that are joined to it. It is the most concisely perfect model, a truly sublime work of art in its simplicity. With effect, in its much-reduced form, it manages to summarise all of duties of humans before God, before ourselves and before our neighbour. It includes a mark of faith, an act of adoration and submission, a request for those things necessary to terrestrial life and the principle of charity. Whoever says this prayer for another asks for them what they would ask for themselves.

Nevertheless, because of its shortness, the deep meaning of some of its words escapes most people. This is usually because they say them without thinking of the meaning of each of the phrases. They say them just like a mechanical formula, whose efficiency is proportional to the number of times it is repeated. This number is usually cabalistic: *three, seven or nine*, in view of the ancient superstitious belief in the power of numbers and of their practical use in magic.

In order to fill the void often felt by the shortness of this prayer, the Spirits have recommended and helped us to add a commentary to each of the phrases that increase their meaning and shows the best way to make use of each one. In accordance with individual circumstances and the time at your disposal at any given moment, you can say the Lord's Prayer in its *simple* form or in the more *developed* way.

3. PRAYER:

(1) Our Father in heaven, hallowed be Your name!

Lord, we believe in you, because everything about us reveals Your goodness and Your power. The harmony of the Universe is proof of wisdom, prudence and a foresight that surpasses all human faculties. The Name of a Being Who is supremely great and wise is written on all the works of Creation, from the humble grass and the smallest insect up to the stars and planets in space. On all sides, we see proof of a paternal solicitude. Blind then is the person who does not recognise Your works. Prideful is the one who does not worship You, and ungrateful is the one who does not give thanks to You.

(2) May Your kingdom come!

Lord, you gave humanity laws full of wisdom, which would make them happy if only they observed them. With these laws, justice and peace could be established and all could help each other instead of causing mutual harm as they do. The strong should uphold the weak instead of crushing them. The evils that are born of abuses and excesses of all kinds could be avoided. All the miseries of this world stem from the violation of Your laws, because there is not one infraction that does not bring its fatal consequences.

You gave the animals an instinct that traces the limits of their necessities and to which they respond mechanically. However, to humanity as well as instinct, You also gave intelligence and reason. Still more, You gave the liberty to keep or to violate those of Your laws that concern each one personally, or rather the faculty to choose between good and evil, so that we have the merit and the responsibility for our actions.

No one can protest ignorance of Your laws, because in Your paternal providence You desired that they be recorded in the consciousness of each one, without distinction as to cults or nationality. In this manner, those who violate them do so because they despise You.

The day will come when according to Your promise all will practise these laws. Then incredulity will have disappeared; all will recognise in You the Supreme Lord of all things and the reign of Your laws will herald Your reign here on Earth.

Lord, deign to hasten the accession of Your reign by giving Humanity the necessary enlightenment that will conduct them along the pathway of truth!

(3) May Your will be done on Earth as it is in heaven!

If submission is the duty of a son towards his father, of the inferior towards his superior, how much greater is that of a being towards their Creator! By the words: 'Your will be done, Lord,' it is for us to observe Your laws and to submit ourselves without lamentations to all Your divine designs. Humankind will become submissive when they understand You are the source of all wisdom and that without You we can do nothing. Then they will do Your bidding on Earth as do Your elected ones in Heaven.

(4) Give us this day our daily bread!

Give us the necessary food for the maintenance of our physical strength and give us spiritual nourishment for the development of our spirits.

The animals find their pastures, but humans depend on their own activities and their mental resources to produce their food because You gave them freedom.

You have said "You will earn your bread by the sweat of your brow," and with these words You made work an obligation. That makes us exercise our intelligence in the search for the means to provide our necessities and to attend to our well-being: some by their material work, others by their intellectual work. Without work, humanity would remain stationary and could not aspire to the happiness of the Superior Spirits.

Please help those of goodwill, who depend on You for what is necessary; but not, however, those who take pleasure in being lazy and like to receive all things without any effort, nor those who seek superfluity. (See chapter 25.)

How many succumb through their own fault, through negligence, through being improvident, through ambition, or through not being content with what You have given them! These are the authors of their own misfortune and do not have the right to complain, since they are punished according to the manner in which they have sinned. Nevertheless, You will not abandon even these, because You are infinitely merciful and will extend a providential hand to them, if they return to You with sincerity, like the prodigal son. (See chapter 5, item 4.)

Before lamenting our bad luck, we ask ourselves if it is not our own fault at each misfortune that befalls us; we try to verify if we could have avoided it. We repeat to ourselves that God has given us intelligence to be able to resolve every difficult situation and that we must put this intelligence to good use.

Seeing that humans are subject to the law of labour here on Earth, give us the courage and the strength to fulfil this law. Give us also prudence and moderation so that we may not lose its fruits.

Give us our daily bread Lord, or rather the means of acquiring our necessities through work, because no one has the right to ask for superfluity.

If we are unable to work, we will have confidence in Your divine providence.

If it is within Your design to test us with great privation, despite our efforts, we accept this as a just expiation for the faults that we have committed in this life or in a previous one. We know that You are just, and that there are no undeserved penalties since You never punish without a motive.

Dear Lord, preserve us from envying those who have what we have not, or those who have superfluous things at their disposal, when we are wanting in what is necessary. Forgive them, Lord, if they forget the law of charity and love towards one's neighbour, which You taught. (See chapter 16, item 8.)

Withdraw also from our spirit any idea of denying the existence of Your justice, when we see evil prosper and the unhappiness that sometimes befalls a good person. Thanks to this new enlightenment given to us, we know that Your justice never fails, nor does it make exceptions. The material prosperity of an evil person is as fragile as their bodily existence and they will experience terrible reverses; whereas life will be eternal bliss for those who suffer with resignation. (See chapter 5, items 7, 9, 12 & 18.)

(5) Forgive our sins, as we forgive those who sin against us. - Forgive our offences, as we forgive those who offend us.

Lord, each one of our infractions against Your laws is an offence committed against You. It is a debt contracted, which sooner or later will have to be paid. We implore Your infinite mercy, subject to our promise to employ every effort not to incur further debts.

You made charity an express law for everyone; but charity does not only consist of helping our fellow beings in their needs, but also in forgetting and forgiving offences. With what right do we demand Your indulgence, if we lack charity towards those who have given us motive for complaint?

Lord, give us the strength to stifle within ourselves all resentment, hate and rancour. *Do not let death surprise us with a desire for vengeance in our hearts.* If You approve of our being taken from this world today, help us to be able to present ourselves completely cleansed of animosity, just like Christ, Whose last words were in favour of His tormentors. (See chap. 10.)

The persecutions that those who are evil inflict upon us constitute part of our earthly tests. We should accept them without a murmur, as we should accept all tests without cursing those who, by their wrongdoing, open a pathway to eternal happiness for us. Because You told us through the intermediary of Jesus that "Blessed be those who suffer for the sake of justice!" Consequently, blessed is the hand that injures or humiliates us, because the mortifications of the body strengthen our soul, and we shall then be raised up from our humiliations. (See chapter 12, item 4.)

Blessed be Your name Lord, because You have taught us that our destiny is not irrevocably fixed after death. We will find in other existences the means by which we may make atonement and repay all our past debts. Thus, we will be able to realise in a new life, all those things to help our progress that we were unable to do in this one. (See chap. 4; chap. 5, item 5.)

In this manner, all the apparent irregularities of life are finally explained. The light is cast over our past and our future, as a brilliant sign of Your supreme justice and of Your infinite goodness.

(6) Lead us not into temptation, but deliver us from all evil.[17]

Lord, give us the necessary strength to resist all suggestions coming from the evil spirits, who will try to divert us from the path of goodness by inspiring us with evil thoughts.

Nevertheless, we too are imperfect spirits incarnated on Earth to expiate our sins and better ourselves. The cause of evil lies deep within our own souls, and the evil Spirits do nothing more than take advantage of our inferior tendencies to tempt us.

Each imperfection is an open door to their influences; whereas they become powerless and give up any attempt against perfect beings. Everything we do to send them away will be useless, as long as we do not put up a decided and unbreakable decision to practice goodness, together with a total renunciation of all evil. Therefore, it is against ourselves that our efforts must be directed. Then the evil spirits will leave us naturally, since evil attracts them; whereas goodness repels them. (See further on in this chapter: Prayers for the obsessed.)

Lord, uphold us in our weaknesses; inspire us through the voices of our Guardian Angels and the Good Spirits with a desire to correct our imperfections, so that we may prevent access to our soul by evil Spirits. (See further on, item 11.)

---

[17] There are some translations of the Bible that say: *do not induce us to temptation* (et nos inducas in tentationem). This sentence gives us to understand that temptation stems from God, Who voluntarily impels people towards evil. This is a blasphemous idea that puts God on an equal basis with Satan. Therefore, it could not have been in the mind of Jesus. Actually, it is in accordance with the popular idea that exists about the part played by Devils. (See HEAVEN & HELL, 1st part, chapter 9 - THE DEVILS.)

Evil is not Your work Lord, because the source of all goodness cannot engender any badness. It is we ourselves who create it when we infringe Your laws, and through the ill use we make of the liberty You concede us. When humanity has learned to keep Your laws, then evil will disappear from Earth; just as it has already disappeared from more advanced worlds.

Evil does not constitute a fatal necessity for anybody and only appears to be irresistible to those who take pleasure in it. Therefore, if we have a desire to practise evil, we can also have a desire to practise goodness. For this reason, dear God, we beg Your assistance and that of the Good Spirits so we may resist temptation.

(7) So be it!

Dear God, may the realisation of our desires be pleasing to You and may we bow down before Your infinite wisdom. In all things that we are unable to understand, may Your blessed will be done and not ours, since You only desire our improvement and know what is best for us.

We offer You this prayer, dear Lord, not only for ourselves, but also for all suffering creatures, both incarnate and discarnate, for our friends and our enemies, for all those who ask for our help and especially for X... (*Name*). We beseech Your mercy and blessings for all.

NOTE: Here you can offer thanks to God for all that has been conceded to you and formulate any requests you may have, either for yourself or for others. (See further on, prayers Nos. 26 & 27.)

SPIRITIST MEETINGS

4. "For where two or three are gathered together in my name, there am I in the midst of them." (MATTHEW, 18:20.)

5. PREFACE - In order to be gathered together in the name of Jesus, our material presence alone is not enough. It is also indispensable to be assembled in the spiritual sense, by means of a communion of intentions and thoughts towards goodness. In this way, Jesus, that is to say either He or those Pure Spirits, who are His representatives, will be found in your midst. Spiritism enables us to understand the way the spirits can be among us. This is by means of their fluidic or spiritual body; and if they should make themselves visible, they do so with an appearance that allows us to recognise them. The more elevated in the spiritual hierarchy the greater is their power of radiation, so that on possessing the gift of ubiquity, they may be present in various places simultaneously. In order to achieve this it requires merely the emission of a thought.

With these words, Jesus wished to show the effect of union and fraternity. It is not the greater or lesser number of people that attract the Spirits, but the sentiment of charity, which animates them reciprocally. If it depended on numbers, He would have said some ten or twenty instead of two or three people. For this purpose, two people are enough. However, if these two people pray separately, even if they direct themselves to Jesus, there will be no communion of thought between them, especially if they are not motivated by a mutual sentiment of benevolence. If they are animated by mutual prejudice, hate, jealous or envy, then the fluidic currents of their thoughts will repel each other, instead of uniting them in a harmonious impulse of sympathy. *Then they will not be united in the name of Jesus.* In that case, Jesus will only be the pretext for that meeting and not the true motive. (See chapter 27, item 9.)

This does not mean to say that Jesus will not listen to just one person. However, if He did not say "I will attend anyone who calls me" it is because He demands, above all else, the love for one's neighbour, from which it is possible to give greater proof in a group than in isolation, and because all personalised sentiment denies it. It follows then, that in a large meeting, if two or three people joined themselves through their hearts in a sentiment of true charity, while all the others remained isolated concentrating their ideas on selfish and worldly things, Jesus would be with the first group and not with the rest. It is not then the simultaneity of the words, the songs or the exterior acts, that constitute the gathering together in the name of Jesus. Rather it is the communion of thoughts according to the true spirit of charity, of which He is the personification. (See chap. 10, items 7 & 8, and chap. 27, items 2 & 4.)

This should be the character of all serious Spiritist meetings, in which the assistance of the Good Spirits is earnestly desired.

6. PRAYER (*For the commencement of a meeting.*) - We beseech You, O Lord God, the All Powerful, to send us the Good Spirits to help us and take away all those who may induce us towards error; give us the necessary light so that we may distinguish truth from falsity.

Equally, remove the evil Spirits, either incarnate or discarnate, who may try to launch discord amongst us, and so turn us away from charity and love for our neighbours. If some of these Spirits try to enter our ambient, do not allow them access to any of our hearts.

Good Spirits, who see fit to come to teach us, make us yielding to their counselling; turn us away from all thoughts of selfishness, pride, jealousy or envy. Inspire us to be indulgent and benevolent towards our fellow beings, be they friends or enemies, present or absent. In short, through the sentiments with which we are animated, make us recognise your beneficial influence.

To the mediums You choose as transmitters of Your Teaching, give them awareness of their mandate and the seriousness of the act they are about to practise, so they may fulfil this task with the necessary dedication and meditation.

If at our meeting, there are any people present driven by sentiments other than those of goodness, open their eyes to the light and forgive them Lord, as we forgive them, for any evil intentions they may harbour.

We ask especially that the Spirit of X..., *(Name)* who is our spiritual Guide, may be present and watch over us.

7. PRAYER *(For the closing of a meeting.)* - We give thanks to the Good Spirits who came to communicate with us. We implore them to help us put into practise the instructions they have given and that on leaving this ambient, they may help us to feel strengthened for the practise of goodness and love towards our fellow beings.

We also desire that Your teachings help all those Spirits who are suffering, ignorant or corrupt, who have participated in our meeting and for whom we implore God's mercy.

FOR THE MEDIUMS

8. *"In the last days God says, 'I will pour out my Spirit on all people. Your sons and daughters will prophesy, young men will see visions, your old men will dream dreams. Even on my servants, both men and women, I will pour out my Spirit in those days, and they will prophesy."* (Acts, 2: 17 & 18.)

9. PREFACE - God wishes that the light shines for everyone and that the voices of the Spirits penetrate to all parts so that all may obtain proof of immortality. It is with this objective in mind that the Spirits manifest themselves in all parts of the Globe, and that mediumship is revealing itself in people of all ages and all conditions, in men and in women, in children and in old people. This is one of the signs that the predicted times have arrived.

In order to know the things of the visible world and discover the secrets of material Nature, God has given humans bodily vision, the senses and special instruments. With a telescope their eyes reach into the vastness of space, with the microscope they discover the world of infinite minuteness. To be able to penetrate the invisible world He has given them the faculty of mediumship.

Mediums are the interpreters who have undertaken to transmit to all human beings the teachings of the Spirits; or rather, they are the material instruments that the Spirits avail themselves of, so as to be able to express themselves intelligently to human beings. They fulfil a sacred mission, seeing that the aim is to open up the horizons of eternal life.

The Spirits come to instruct humans as to their destiny, so that they may be led towards the path of goodness, and not to save them from material work, which must be fulfilled in this world for their advancement; not for the furthering of their ambition and covetousness. This is something that must be clearly understood by mediums so that they will not make bad use of their faculty. Those who fully understand the seriousness of the mandate with which they have been entrusted will carry out this duty religiously. Their conscience will condemn them if by any sacrilegious act they transform themselves into a distraction or amusement, *for themselves or for others*, those faculties that were given to them for a serious purpose, which is that of placing them in communication with Beings from beyond the grave.

As interpreters of the Spirit's Teachings, mediums should play a very important part in the moral transformation that is in progress. The services they are able to offer will be in accordance with the correctness of the guidance they have given to their faculty, because those who follow an incorrect pathway cause more harm than good to Spiritism. More than one person will delay their progress due to the unfortunate impression these mediums produce. Therefore, all mediums will have to give an account of the use to which they put their faculty, which was given to them for the purpose of doing Good to their fellow beings.

The medium who desires to be constantly helped by Good Spirits will have to work hard towards self-betterment. Those who wish their faculty to grow and be enriched, must therefore enrich themselves morally and abstain from all that can turn them aside from its providential purpose.

If sometimes Good Spirits make use of an imperfect medium, it is in order to give Good advice, with which they try to make them take the road to goodness. If, however, they meet hardened hearts and their advice is not listened to they will leave and the field will then be open for the evil Spirits. (See chap. 24, items 11 & 12.)

Experience has proved that for those who do not take advantage of the advice received from the Good Spirits, communications that initially showed some brilliance will, little by little, degenerate and finally fall into error, either in the wording or by becoming ridiculous, which are incontestable signs of the retreat of the Good Spirits.

To obtain the assistance of the Good Spirits and to remove lying and frivolous ones, must be the aim to which all serious mediums should join forces. Without which mediumship becomes a sterile faculty, even capable of causing detriment to the one that possesses it, since it can degenerate into a dangerous obsession or attachment.

Any medium who understands their duty and is not proud of a faculty that does not belong to them, seeing that it may be taken away, will always attribute the good things they receive to God. If their communications receive praise, they will not become vain because they know that they are independent of their personal merit. They will give thanks to God for having allowed the Good

Spirits to manifest through their intermediary. If there is occasion for criticism, they are never offended because the communications are not their own work. On the contrary, they recognise in their inner selves that they were not able to be good instruments and do not possess all the necessary qualities that would obstruct interference from backward sprits. Therefore, take care to acquire these qualities and implore, by means of prayer, that your strength does not fail.

10. PRAYER -Almighty God, permit the Good Spirits to come and help me in the communication that is being solicited. Protect me from the presumption of judging myself to be safe from evil Spirits; from the pride that may induce me to err with respect to the value of what I receive; from all sentiments that are the opposite of charity towards other mediums. If I fall into error, inspire someone to alert me of this fact. Give me the humility that will enable me to accept any deserved criticism and to recognise that the advice the Good Spirits wish to give through me is not only addressed to others, but primarily to me.

If I become proud of the faculty whose bestowal You approved or if I am tempted to abuse it in whatever form, I ask You to take it back rather than it is permitted to stray from its providential objective that is for the good of all and also my own moral betterment.

2 - PRAYERS FOR ONESELF.

TO ONE'S GUARDIAN ANGELS AND PROTECTING SPIRITS

11. PREFACE - From the moment of birth, everyone has a Good Spirit linked to them who constantly protects. At our side, this Spirit carries out the mission of a father to his child, which is that

of conducting us along the path to goodness and progress throughout the various tests of life. It feels happy when we respond to its solicitude and suffers when it sees us succumb.

Its name is not important because it is not known on Earth. So then, we call it by the name of Guardian Angel or our Good Spirit. We could also call it under the name of one of the superior Spirits with whom we feel a special sympathy.

Apart from this Guardian Angel, who is always a Superior Spirit, we have other Spirit protectors, who although slightly less elevated, are just as good and generous. These are the Spirits of friends or relatives, even people we have not known in the present life. They help us with their advice and quite often intervene in the happenings of our life.

Sympathetic Spirits are those who are linked to us through certain similarities of taste and tendency. They may be either good or evil, according to the nature of our inclinations that have attracted them towards us.

The seductive spirits endeavour to turn us aside from the path of goodness by suggesting bad thoughts to us. They take advantage of our weaknesses, as if these were so many open doors that give them access to our soul. Some of them hold on to us as if we were their prey, but *they withdraw when they recognise themselves impotent to fight against our will.*

God has given us a principal and superior guide as our Guardian Angel and family Spirits as secondary guides. However, it is a mistake to believe that we *inevitably* have a evil element at our side to counter-balance the good influences we receive. Evil spirits seek us *voluntarily* as long as they can dominate us due to our weaknesses or our negligence in following the inspirations from the Good Spirits. Therefore, it is we ourselves that attract them. The result is we are never without the assistance of Good

Sprits, but the withdrawal of the evil spirits depends entirely on ourselves. Due to their imperfections, human beings are the primary cause of all the miseries that afflict them, and are frequently their own evil spirit. (See chapter 5, item 4.)

A prayer to Guardian Angels and protecting Spirits should have as its objective the solicitation of their intercession with God, to ask for strength to resist evil suggestions and help in all of life's necessities.

12. PRAYER - Wise and benevolent Spirits, messengers of God, whose mission is to help human beings and conduct them towards goodness. Uphold me in life's tests, give me the strength to suffer without complaining; turn away from me all evil thoughts and do not allow me to give access to any bad spirits who may try to induce me to evil. Clarify my conscience with respect to my defects, and take away the veil of pride from my eyes, which can prevent my seeing them and admitting them to myself.

Most especially to X... (*Name*), my Guardian Angel, who watches over me, and all the rest of the protecting Spirits who take an interest in me, I beg you to help me to become worthy of your protection. You know my needs; may they be attended to, according to the Will of God.

13. PRAYER (*Another one*) - Dear God, allow the Good Spirits who accompany me to help me when I am in difficulty and uphold me when I falter. Lord, may they inspire me with faith, hope and charity. May they be a point of support, an inspiration and a testimony of Your mercy. In short, may I always encounter in them the strength that I lack for the tests of life, the strength to resist all evil suggestions, the faith that saves and the love that consoles.

14. PRAYER (*Another one*) - Beloved Spirits and Guardian Angels, who God in His infinite mercy has permitted to assist

humanity, be my protector during all of life's tests! Give me the necessary strength, courage and resignation. Inspire me towards all that is good, and restrain me from the downward incline to evil. May your sweet influences fill my soul, so helping me to feel that a devoted friend, who can see my suffering and who participates in all my joys, is by my side.

Moreover, you, my Good Angel, never abandon me because I need all of your protection to be able to support with faith and love the tests that God has sent me.

TO TURN AWAY THE EVIL SPIRITS

15. "Woe to you, Scribes and Pharisees, you hypocrites! For you make clean the outside of the cup and the dish, but inside they are full of greed and self-indulgence. Blind Pharisee! First cleanse the inside of the cup and dish, and then the outside will be clean. Woe to you, Scribes and Pharisees, you hypocrites! For you are like whitewashed tombs, which appear beautiful on the outside, but on the inside are full of dead people's bones, and everything unclean. In the same way, on the outside you appear to other people as righteous, but on the inside you are full of hypocrisy and wickedness." (MATTHEW, 23:25-28.)

16. PREFACE - Evil spirits are only found where they can satisfy their perversity. In order to turn them away it is not enough to ask them to go, nor even to order them to go. It is imperative that people eliminate from within themselves that which is attracting them. Evil spirits discover the ulcers of the soul, the same way that flies discover those of the body. In this manner then, as you would cleanse a wound in order to avoid maggots, cleanse also your soul of all its impurities, to avoid the proximity of evil spirits. We live in a world that teems with these spirits, so the good qualities in the heart do not always make them abandon their attempts on us. Nevertheless, these qualities give us strength to resist them.

17. PRAYER - In the name of God the All Powerful, may the evil Spirits turn away from me and may the Good Spirits defend me from them!

Wicked spirits, who inspire vile thoughts in people; deceiving and lying spirits, who delude people; mocking spirits, who amuse yourselves with human incredulity, I repel you with all the strength within my soul and close my ears to your suggestions. Nevertheless, I also implore that God's mercy be upon you.

Good Spirits, who undertook to accompany me, give me the necessary strength to resist the influence of evil spirits and the necessary enlightenment so as not to become a victim of their intrigues. Safeguard me from pride and presumption, turn aside all thoughts of jealousy, hate, badness, and all sentiments contrary to charity from my heart, which are all as open doors to the evil spirits.

TO ASK FOR A DEFECT TO BE CORRECTED

18. PREFACE - Our bad instincts result from the imperfections of our spirit and not from our physical organism. If this were not so then human beings would be exempt from all responsibility. Our betterment depends on ourselves, because every person who has all his or her faculties has always the liberty to do or not to do. To practice what is good the only requirement is will power. (See chap. 15, item 10 and chap. 19, item 12.)

19. PRAYER - Dear Lord, You gave me the necessary intelligence to be able to distinguish right from wrong. Thus, on recognizing something to be wrong, I am guilty if I do not struggle to resist the temptation.

Preserve me from pride, which can prevent me from perceiving my defects and from evil spirits, who can incite me to continue in doing wrong.

Amongst my imperfections I recognize that I am specially inclined to ..., if I am unable to resist, it is because I have already acquired the habit of giving in to it.

You did not create me guilty because You are just, but with equal aptitude for good or for evil. If I have preferred the evil road, it was because of my free will. But for the same reason that I had the liberty to do wrong, I also have the liberty to do Good and therefore to change my pathway.

My present defects are the remains of the imperfections I brought from my past existences. This is my original sin, from which I may liberate myself through the action of my free will with help from the Good Spirits.

Good Spirits who protect me, and above all you, my Guardian Angel, give me the strength to resist evil suggestions and so be victorious in this battle.

These defects are the barriers that separate us from God, and each defect surmounted is a step further along the pathway of progress, which will draw me nearer to Him.

The Lord, in His infinite mercy, thought fit to concede me this present life so that it would serve for my advancement. Good Spirits help me to take advantage of this opportunity so that I may not lose it. When it pleases God to remove me from it, help me to leave it in a better condition than on entering. (See chap. 5, item 5 & chap. 17, item 3.)

TO ASK FOR STRENGTH TO RESIST TEMPTATION

20. PREFACE - Every bad thought can have two origins: our own spiritual imperfection or the action of a harmful influence. In the last case, we have the indication of a weakness that exposes us to these influences, and it is for this reason that our soul is imperfect. The one who fails cannot offer as an excuse the

influence of a strange spirit, seeing that *this spirit would not have led them into wrongdoing if they were inaccessible to seduction.*

When we have a bad thought, we can suppose it was an evil spirit that suggested the evil. But we have complete liberty to accede or resist, just as if we were facing a living person. At the same time, we should make a mental picture of our Guardian Angel, or protecting Spirit, who from its side combats within us the bad influences, and anxiously *awaits the decision we are going to make.* Our hesitation in acting upon the evil suggestions is due to the voice of our Good Spirit, who makes it heard through our conscience.

One recognises a thought is bad when it draws away from charity, which is the base of all true morality; or when it comes based on pride, vanity and selfishness; or when its realisation may cause harm to another person. In short, when we are induced by our thoughts to do to others what we would not like someone to do to us. (See chap. 28, item 15 & chap. 15 item 10.)

21. PRAYER - All-Powerful Lord, do not let me succumb to the temptation to fall into error! Benevolent Spirits who protect me, turn this bad thought away from me and give me the strength to resist this evil. If I succumb, then I will deserve to expiate my failing in this same life and in the next, because I am free to make my choice.

THANKSGIVING FOR A VICTORY OVER TEMPTATION

22. PREFACE - Those who resist temptation owe this fact to the assistance given by the Good Spirits, whose voice they listened to. So, you should thank God and you're Guardian Angel for their help.

23. PRAYER - Dear God, I thank You for having permitted me to be victorious in the battle that I sustained against evil. Allow this victory to give me strength to resist new temptations.

And you, my Guardian Angel, receive my thanks for the assistance you gave. Allow that my submission to your counsel makes me worthy to receive your protection once again.

TO ASK FOR ADVICE

24. PREFACE - When we are unsure about something we have to do, before anything else we should ask ourselves the following questions:

1. Will what I am hesitating about cause harm to anyone?

2. Will it be useful to anyone?

3. If someone did this to me, would I be pleased?

If what we think of doing is of interest only to ourselves, then it is permissible to weigh the personal advantages or disadvantages that might arise.

If it concerns others and if, in doing Good for one person, it redounds in badness for another, it is also equally necessary to weigh the advantages and disadvantages before deciding whether to act or refrain.

Finally, even when dealing with the best things it is necessary to consider the opportunity and the circumstances being offered. In as much as something that is good in itself can give bad results when put into the wrong hands, or if it is not directed with prudence and circumspection. Before putting it into effect, it is best to consult our strength of will and the possible means of execution.

In any case, we can always solicit the assistance of our Protecting Spirits, remembering this wise maxim: *When in doubt, do nothing.* (See chap. 28, item 38.)

25. PRAYER - In the name of God the All-Powerful, in my uncertainty, I call upon the Good Spirits who protect me, to inspire me to make the best decisions. Lead my thoughts always towards goodness and protect me from the influences of those who tempt me to stray.

AFFLICTIONS OF LIFE

26. PREFACE - We can ask God for earthly favours and He will concede them to us when they have a serious purpose. However, seeing that we judge their utility from our own point of view and as immediate necessities, we do not always recognise the bad side of what we ask for. God, Who can see things in a better perspective and only desires the best for us, may refuse what we request. Just as a father would refuse his child what he knew would be prejudicial for him. If what we request is refused, we should not be disappointed. On the contrary, we should think that to be deprived of our wish is a test or expiation, and that our recompense will be in proportion to the degree of resignation we show. (See chap. 27, item 6 & chap. 2, items 5-7.)

27. PRAYER -God Omnipotent, Who sees all our miseries, please deign to hear the supplication we direct to You at this moment. If my request is inconsiderate, forgive me. If it is just and convenient, according to the way You see things, may the Good Spirits who execute Your wishes come to my aid and help me to realise my request.

Whichever way it may be, Lord, let Your will be done! If my request is not answered, it will be because it is Your wish that I am tested, and I submit without complaint. Help me not to become disanimated and that neither my faith nor my resignation be shaken. (Then formulate your request.)

THANKSGIVING FOR OBTAINING A FAVOUR

28. PREFACE - We should not consider as happy events only those that are of great importance. Frequently, things that are apparently insignificant are those that most influence our destiny. People easily forget the goodness received, preferring to remember only the afflictions. If we were to register day-by-day the many benefits we receive, without even having asked for them, we would be greatly surprised to perceive there are so very many that we have swept from our minds and would feel ashamed of our ingratitude.

On lifting up our soul to God each night, we should remember in our innermost self the many favours that He has granted us during the day and offer thanks for them. But most especially, at the moment we receive the effects of His goodness and protection, we should spontaneously bear witness to our gratitude. For this, it is enough that we direct a thought attributing the benefit to Him, without even interrupting our work.

Benefits from God are not limited to material things. We should also thank Him for the ideas and happy inspirations we receive. Whereas the selfish person attributes all of these things to their own personal merits, and the incredulous person to mere chance, the one who has faith renders thanks to God and the Good Spirits. Long sentences are not necessary for this purpose. *"Thank you, dear God, for the inspiration of that good thought"*, says more than a long prayer. The spontaneous impulse that made us attribute to God the good that had happened, bears witness of an act of thanksgiving and humility, which will attract the sympathy of the Good Spirits. (See chap. 27, items 7 & 8.)

29. PRAYER - Beloved Lord of infinite goodness, may Your name be blessed for the benefits conceded to me! I would be unworthy if I were to attribute these happenings to mere chance or to my own merit.

Good Spirits, who execute God's wishes, I thank you and most especially my Guardian Angel. Turn away from me all idea of being proud of what I have received and help me to make use of it exclusively for the Good. Most of all, I thank …

AN ACT OF SUBMISSION AND RESIGNATION

30. PREFACE - When we are suffering an affliction, if we look for the cause, we will frequently find it in our own imprudence, thoughtlessness or in some past action. In these cases, we have to attribute the suffering to ourselves. If the cause of an affliction cannot be found to stem in any way from our own actions, then we are dealing with a test in this life, or atonement for an error committed in a previous one. In this case, by the nature of the expiation we can know the nature of the error, as we are always punished in the same manner as our sin. (See chap. 5, items 4, 6 & subsequent items.)

In general, we can only see the evil that is present in our afflictions. We do not see the favourable consequences they may have later on. Goodness is frequently the outcome of a past evil, just as the cure for illness results from the painful methods used to obtain it. In any case, we must submit to the will of God and courageously support the tribulations of life if we want them to count in our favour. These words of Christ could then be applied to us: "Blessed are those who suffer". (See chap. 5, item 18.)

31. PRAYER - Dear Lord, Your justice is supreme. Therefore, all suffering in this world must have a just cause and be of use. I accept the affliction which I am undergoing, or which I have just

suffered, as atonement for my past errors and as a test for the future. Good Spirits who protect me, give me the necessary strength to support this without complaining. Help me to look at it as a providential warning; may it enrich my experience, reduce my pride, and diminish my ambition, stupid vanity and selfishness. In short, may it contribute to my progress.

32. PRAYER *(Another one.)* - Dear God, I feel the need to ask You for the necessary strength to support the test that You have sent me. Allow my spirit to be enlightened, with the necessary understanding, so that I can appreciate the full extent of a love that afflicts because it desires to save. Dear God I submit myself with resignation, but I am so weak I fear I will succumb if you do not uphold me. Do not abandon me, Lord, because without You I am nothing.

33. PRAYER *(Another one.)* - I lift up my eyes to You, Eternal Father, and feel fortified. You are my strength! Dear Lord, do not abandon me! I am crushed under the weight of my iniquities! Help me! You know the weakness of my flesh! Please, do not cease to watch over me!

I am being devoured by an ardent thirst! Make the spring of living water burst forth to quench this thirst. May my lips open only to sing Your praises and not to complain about my afflictions! I am weak; Lord, but Your love will sustain me.

Eternal Father, only You are great, only You are the reason and the purpose of my life! Blessed be Your Name even if You make me suffer, because You are the Lord and I am an unfaithful servant. I bow down before You without complaint because only You are great, only You are the aim of all our lives!

WHEN IN IMMINENT DANGER

34. PREFACE - Through the dangers we face, God reminds us of our weaknesses, and the fragility of our existence. He shows us that our life is in His hands, and that it is held only by a thread, which may break when we least expect it to happen. From this point of view, privilege does not exist for anyone because the same alternatives are to be found for both great and small alike.

If we look at the nature and the consequences of danger, we will see in most cases that these consequences, if they are verified, will have been a punishment for a misdeed or *for an unfulfilled duty.*

35. PRAYER - Almighty God, and you who are my Guardian Angel, help me! If I must succumb, may God's Will be done. If I am to be saved, may the rest of my life be given to repay the evil I have done, for which I am truly repentant.

THANKSGIVING FOR HAVING ESCAPED A DANGER

36. PREFACE - By the danger we have been through, God shows us that from one moment to another we may be called to give account for the way in which we have utilised our present life. This is to alert us to the fact that we should examine ourselves and mend our ways.

37. PRAYER - Dear God! Dear Guardian Angel! I thank you for the help I received during the danger that threatened me. May this danger be a warning to me and enlighten me with respect to my errors that have brought me this peril. I understand, Lord, that my life is in Your hands and that You may take it away when You see fit. Inspire me then, through the Good Spirits who protect me, with the idea of how best to take advantage of the time You grant to me in this world!

Guardian Angel! Uphold me in my decision to correct my faults and to do all the good that is within my power, so that I may arrive in the spiritual world with fewer imperfections, whenever it pleases God to call me!

AT BEDTIME

38. PREFACE - The body reposes during sleep, but the spirit needs no repose. While the physical senses are in a torpid state, the soul partly frees itself from the body and enters into the enjoyment of its spiritual faculties. Sleep has been given to human beings to enable them to repair both their organic and moral strengths. While the body recuperates the spent energies that have been used during the waking state, the spirit fortifies itself amongst other spirits. From all it sees, all it perceives, and from the advice it is given, it takes the ideas that occur to it afterwards, in the form of intuitions. This is the temporary return of the exile to its true world, a moment of liberty that is conceded to the prisoner.

However, as sometimes happens with a perverse prisoner, the spirit does not always take advantage of these moments of liberty for the purpose of progress. If it has bad instincts, instead of seeking the company of the Good Spirits, it seeks out those who are like itself and visits places where it may give vent to its tendencies.

So then, the person who is convinced of this fact will lift up their thoughts to God before they go to sleep. They will ask for advice from the Good Spirits and from all whose memory is dear to them, so they may go to join them for the brief moments of liberty conceded to them. On awakening, they feel fortified against evil and are more courageous when faced with adversities.

39. PRAYER - Lord, for a few short instants my soul will be together with other spirits. May the Good Spirits come and give me counsel. Guardian Angel, please help me to keep a lasting and beneficial impression of this encounter on awakening!

ON SENSING APPROACHING DEATH

40. PREFACE - During our lifetime having had faith in the future, together with the elevation of our thoughts towards our future destiny, helps in the process of a rapid liberation of the spirit, because this weakens the links that tie it to the material body. So much so that quite frequently, even before the physical body has expired, the soul has already launched itself into the great immensity, because it is impatient to be free. On the contrary, the person who has concentrated on all that is material finds these ties more difficult to break and *the separation more painful and difficult*, and upon awakening in the after-life they are full of anxiety and perturbation.

41. PRAYER - Dear God, I believe in You and Your infinite kindness. Therefore, I cannot believe that You have given human beings intelligence that allows us to gain knowledge of You and an aspiration for the future, just to plunge us into nothingness.

I believe that my body is only a perishable covering for my soul and that when I cease to live, I will awaken in the world of the spirits.

Almighty God, I feel the ties that hold my soul to my body are breaking and that in a short while I will have to account for the use I have put to the life that I am about to leave.

I will experience the consequences of the good and the bad I have practised. There will be no possibility of illusions, no subterfuge. My past will unfold before me and I will be judged according to my works.

I will take nothing of earthly possessions with me such as honours, riches, satisfactions of vanity or pride; in short, everything that belongs to the body will remain in this world. Even the smallest particle of these things will not accompany me, nor would they be of any use to me in the spiritual world. I will take only what belongs to my soul, that is the good and bad qualities I possess, to be weighed on the balance of strict justice. I know that the judgement will be even more severe according to the number of times I refused the opportunities that were given to me to practise good, in proportion to the position I held on Earth. (See chap. 16, item 9.)

Merciful God, may the sincerity of my repentance enable it to reach You! May You see fit to cast Your cloak of indulgence over me!

If You see fit to prolong my present existence, may I utilise that time to make good, as far as I am able, all the evil that I have done. But if my hour has come, I take with me the consoling thought that I will be permitted to redeem myself by means of new tests, so that one day I may deserve the happiness of the elected ones.

If it is not given to me to enjoy such perfect happiness immediately, known only to those who are pre-eminently just, I know I am not denied hope eternally. Eventually I will reach my goal, according to the amount of effort I make.

I know that the Good Spirits and my Guardian Angel are near and will receive me; soon I shall see them, just as they see me. I know too, that *if I deserve it*, I will meet again all those I have loved here on Earth, and that those I leave behind will later come to join me. One day we shall all be united forever and, until that time comes, I will be able to visit them.

I know too, that I will re-encounter those I have offended. May they forgive me for whatever they have to reproach me for, such as my pride, my hardness and my injustices, so that their presence will not overwhelm me with shame!

I forgive all those who have either done or tried to do me harm; I hold no rancour against them and beg You, dear God, to forgive them.

Lord, give me strength to leave all the material pleasures of this world without regret. They are as nothing compared to the healthy and pure delights of the world into which I am about to enter. Where for those who are just, there are no more torments or miseries. Only the guilty suffer, but even these always have the consolation of hope.

To you Good Spirits, and you my Guardian Angel, I implore you not to allow me to fail at this supreme moment. If I should waver, then cause the Divine Light to shine in my eyes, so my faith may be reanimated.

NOTE: See Item 5 - Prayers for the sick and obsessed. (Further on.)

3 - PRAYERS FOR OTHERS

FOR SOMEONE WHO IS AFFLICTED

42. PREFACE - If it is in the interest of the afflicted person to continue their test or trial, then any request made will not shorten it. However, it would be a lack of charity to abandon this person, alleging that our prayers would not be heard. Apart from this, even if the test is not interrupted, they may obtain some degree of consolation that will lessen their suffering. What is really useful for someone who is suffering a test, is courage and resignation. Without these, whatever they are going through will bring them no

results, resulting in their having to go through it all again. Therefore, with this objective in mind we should be asking the Good Spirits to help them, by lifting their morale through counselling and encouragement, or even by helping them in a material way, if this is possible. In such cases, prayer can have a decisive effect by directing a fluidic current towards them with the intention of fortifying their morale. (See chap. 5, items 5 & 27; chap. 27, item 6 & 10.)

43. PRAYER - Dear God of infinite goodness, may it please You to soften the bitter situation in which X... (*Name*) is in, if this is according to Your will.

Good Spirits, in the name of Almighty God, I beseech you to help X... (*Name)* in their affliction. If it is not in their interest to be spared this suffering, make them understand that it is necessary for their progress. Give X... (*Name)* confidence in God and the future, which will make them less bitter. Also, give them strength so that they do not give in to despair, which will make them lose the fruits of this suffering and make their future even more painful. Conduct my thoughts to ... (N*ame*) to help them maintain their courage.

AN ACT OF THANKSGIVING FOR A BENEFIT CONCEDED TO SOMEONE ELSE

44. PREFACE - Those who are not dominated by selfishness will rejoice over the Good that comes to their neighbour, even if they did not make a solicitation by means of prayer.

45. PRAYER - Dear God, thank You for the happiness conceded to X... (*Name*). Good Spirits, help them to see that this benefit is the consequence of God's goodness. If the Good received constitutes a test, please inspire this person with thoughts of how

to make the best use of it and not become conceited, so it does not rebound to their detriment in the future.

And you, the Good Spirit who protects me and desires my happiness, turn aside from me all sentiments of jealousy or envy.

FOR OUR ENEMIES AND THOSE WHO WISH US ILL

46. PREFACE - Jesus said, "Love even your enemies". This maxim shows all that is most sublime in Christian charity. But in saying this, Jesus did not mean we should have the same tenderness for an enemy as we have for a friend. With these words, He teaches us to pardon offences, to pardon all evil done to us and to repay all evil with goodness. Apart from the worth that this conduct has in God's eyes, it also serves to show people the nature of true superiority. (See chap. 12, items 3 & 4.)

47. PRAYER - Dear God, forgive X... (*Name*) the evil they have done and still desire to do to me, as I wish You to forgive me for any offences I have committed against this person. If You placed this person in my pathway as a trail, let Your Will be done.

Turn me away, dear Lord, from the idea of cursing them and any other wicked sentiments against them. Never allow me to rejoice at any misfortune that may beset them, so that I may not blemish my soul with thoughts that are not worthy of a Christian.

Lord, may Your mercy extend to him/her and induce him/her to harbour better sentiments towards me!

Good Spirits induce me to forget all evil and remember only the Good. May neither hate, rancour, nor the desire to pay back evil with evil enter into my heart, since sentiments of hate and vengeance belong to bad Spirits, be they incarnate or discarnate! On the contrary, may I be prepared to extend a friendly hand to this person, so repaying evil with goodness and helping them, if this is within my reach.

In order to prove the sincerity of my words, I beg You to give me the opportunity to be useful to this person. But above all, dear God, prevent me from doing this out of pride and ostentation, oppressing them with humiliating generosity that would only cause me to lose the fruits of my action. Because in that case, I would deserve the words of Christ when He said, "*You have already received your recompense.*" (See chap. 13, items 1 & subsequent.)

THANKSGIVING FOR A BLESSING GIVEN TO OUR ENEMIES

48. PREFACE - To not desire evil towards your enemies is to be only partly charitable. True charity consists in wishing them well and in feeling happy about the good that comes to them. (See chap. 12, items 7 & 8.)

49. PRAYER - Dear God, in Your justice you saw fit to make X... (*Name*) happy, and on his/her behalf I thank You, despite the evil he/she has done or tried to do to me. If he/she seeks to use this benefit to humiliate me, I accept this as a test of my capacity to be charitable.

Good Spirits who protect me, do not let me feel grievous because of this. Turn away from me all jealousy and envy, which only degrades. On the contrary, inspire me with the generosity that elevates. Humiliation comes from evil and not from goodness, and we know that eventually justice will be done to each one according to their works.

FOR THE ENEMIES OF SPIRITISM

50. Blessed are those who hunger and thirst for righteousness: for they will be filled.

Blessed are those who are persecuted because of righteousness, for theirs is the kingdom of heaven. Blessed are you when people insult you, and persecute you and falsely say all manner of evil against you, because of me. Rejoice and be exceedingly glad, for great is your reward in heaven, because they also persecuted the prophets sent before you. (MATTHEW, 5:6 & 10-12.)

Do not be afraid of those who kill the body but cannot kill the soul. Rather, be afraid of those who can loose both soul and body in hell. (MATTHEW, 10:28.)

51. PREFACE - Of all the liberties, the most inviolable is that of thought, which includes the liberty of conscience. To cast a curse against those who do not think as we do, is to demand that liberty for ourselves but refuse it to others. This is a violation of the first commandment of Jesus, which is that of charity and love towards one's neighbour. To persecute others for the beliefs they profess is to attack the most sacred right of human beings, which is to believe whatever they want and to worship God as they see fit. To compel others to practise exterior acts similar to those we ourselves practise is to show that we are more attached to the form than the essence and to appearances rather than conviction. Forced renouncement will never produce faith. It can only make hypocrites. It is an abuse of material power, which does not prove the truth. *Truth is sure of itself; it convinces and does not persecute, because there is no need.*

Spiritism is an opinion, a belief; even if it were a religion, why should its adepts not have the liberty to call themselves Spiritists, as do Catholics, Jews and Protestants or the participants of this or that philosophical doctrine, of this or that economic order? A belief is either true or false. If it is false, it will fall by itself, seeing that error cannot stand up against truth when intelligences are enlightened. If it is true then persecution cannot make it become false.

Persecution is the baptism of all new ideas that are great and just. It grows with the development and importance of the idea. The fury and wrath of its enemies are in direct proportion to the fear it instils in them. This is the reason why Christianity was persecuted in the past and why Spiritism is today. However, with the difference that the former was persecuted by the pagans and the latter by Christians. It is true that the time of bloody persecutions is now past; nevertheless, if today they no longer kill the body, then they torture the soul; attacking it even in its most intimate sentiments, in its most dearest affections. Families are divided, exciting mothers against daughters, wives against husbands. Even physical violence is not absent, the body being attacked through the lack of material necessities by taking people away from their means of livelihood, thereby attacking the believer through hunger. (See chap. 23, items & subsequent.)

Spiritists, do not be upset by the blows that are hurled at you. They are the proof that you have the truth. If this were not so, they would leave you in peace and not attack you. It is a test of your faith, since it is through your courage, resignation and perseverance that God will recognise you as being one of His faithful servants. He is even now making note, to be able to give to each one the part that rests with them according to their works.

Following the example of the first Christians, carry your cross with dignity. Believe in the words of Christ when He said, "Blessed are those who suffer persecution for the love of justice, for theirs is the kingdom of heaven. Do not be afraid of those who kill the body, for they cannot kill the soul." He also said, "Love your enemies; do Good to those who do evil to you and pray for those who persecute you." Show yourselves to be His true disciples and that His teachings are all Good by doing what He said and did.

The persecutions will not last for long. Wait with patience for the coming of the dawn, since the morning star is already appearing on the horizon. (See chap. 24, items 13 & subsequent.)

52. PRAYER - Almighty God, You have said to us through the lips of Jesus, Your Messiah, "Blessed are those who suffer persecution for the love of justice; forgive your enemies; pray for those who persecute you." In addition, He gave us an example of this by praying for His tormentors.

Following this example, dear God, we beg Your mercy for those who despise Your most sacred precepts, which are the only ones capable of bringing peace to this world and the next. As Christ said, we also say "Forgive them, Father, for they know not what they do."

Give us strength to support with patience and resignation their mockery, insults, slander and persecutions, as a test of our faith and humility. Free us from all ideas of reprisal, seeing that the hour of justice comes to all, and we await it submitting ourselves to Your holy Will.

PRAYER FOR A CHILD THAT HAS JUST BEEN BORN

53. PREFACE - Only after passing through the tests that are offered by physical life, can spirits reach perfection. Those who are in an errant state await God's permission to return to an existence which can offer them progress, either by the expiation of their faults, by means of the vicissitudes to which they will be subjected, or by the undertaking of a mission that will benefit humanity. Their advancement and future happiness will be in proportion to the manner in which they employ the time given to them on Earth. The duty of guiding their first steps and of leading them towards goodness is up to their parents, who will have to give an account to God for the degree of fulfilment they gave to

this mandate. It was to help them that God made paternal and filial love a Law of Nature, a law that can never be transgressed with impunity.

54. PRAYER *(To be said by the parents.)* - Dear Spirit, who has incarnated in the body of our child, we bid you welcome. We thank You, Almighty God, for the blessing of this child.

We know that this is a trust You have deposited in us and for which one-day we will have to give an account. If he/she belongs to the new generation of spirits who are to inhabit the Earth, we thank you Lord for this blessing! If it is an imperfect spirit, it is our duty to help him/her progress towards goodness by means of counselling and good examples. If he/she falls prey to evil through our fault, we shall be responsible for this, seeing that we will have failed in our mission.

Lord, uphold us in this task and give us the necessary strength and willpower to be able to fulfil it to the best of our ability. If this child has come to test us, may Your will be done, Lord!

Good Spirits, who have watched over this birth and will accompany this child during the course of his/her new existence, do not abandon him/her. Turn away from him/her all the evil spirits who will try to tempt him/her into badness. Give this being strength to resist all their suggestions, and courage to suffer with patience and resignation the tests that await here on Earth. (See chap. 14, item 9.)

55. PRAYER *(Another one.)* - Dear God, You have entrusted me with the destiny of one of Your spirits; therefore, Lord, make me worthy of this task. Grant me Your protection and illuminate my intelligence, so that I may perceive right from the beginning the tendencies of this child it is my duty to prepare for ascension to Your peace.

56. PRAYER *(Another one.)* - God of infinite goodness, since You have seen fit to permit the spirit of this child to come once again, to undergo earthy trials destined to make it progress, give it enlightenment enough so that it may learn to know You, love You and worship You. Through Your omnipotence may this soul regenerate itself from the source of Your Divine Teachings. That, under the protection of its Guardian Angel, its intelligence may develop, amplify and lead it to aspire to move closer to You. May the science of Spiritism be a brilliant light that illuminates it throughout the many choices of life. Finally, may it learn to appreciate the full extent of Your love, which puts us to the test so that we may purify ourselves.

Lord, cast a paternal eye over this family to which You have entrusted this soul, so that it may learn to understand the importance of its mission. May the seeds of goodness within this child germinate until such time as, by its own aspirations, it elevates itself to You.

O Lord, may it please You to answer this humble prayer, in the name of and by the worthiness of He who said, "Let the little children come to me, because the kingdom of heaven is for those who resemble them."

FOR ONE WHO AGONIZES

57. PREFACE - Agonising is the prelude to the separation of the soul from the body. It can be said that at this moment the person has one foot on Earth and the other in the next world. Sometimes this phase is painful for those who are deeply attached to worldly things, who live more for the possessions of this world than those of the next, or whose conscience is agitated by regrets and remorse. On the other hand, for those whose thoughts seek the infinite and who are able to disengage themselves from matter, it is less difficult to break the links that tie them to the Earth and

there is nothing of pain in these last moments. Only a thin thread links their physical body to their soul, while in the first case there are thick roots that hold them prisoner. In every case, prayer exercises a powerful action in the work of separation. (See HEAVEN & HELL - 2nd part, Chap. 1 – "The Passing.")

58. PRAYER - Merciful and Omnipotent God, here is a soul who is about to leave its terrestrial covering in order to return to the spiritual world, which is the real homeland. May it be given to them to make this passing in peace and may You extend Your mercy to them.

Good Spirits, who have accompanied this person on Earth, do not abandon them at this supreme moment. Give them strength to support the last sufferings that they need to pass through in this world, for the good of their future advancement. Inspire them to use any last glimmerings of intelligence or any fleeting awareness they may have, to the consecration of repentance for any faults.

Allow my thoughts to act in such a way to help them achieve this separation with less difficulty, and may this soul take the consolation of hope with it at the moment of departure from this Earth.

4 - PRAYERS FOR THOSE NO LONGER ON EARTH

FOR SOMEONE WHO HAS JUST DIED

59. PREFACE - Prayers for those who have just left the Earth are not for the exclusive purpose of showing our sympathy. They also have the effect of helping to release them from their Earthly ties, and in this manner shorten the period of perturbation which frequently follows the separation, so allowing a more peaceful awakening on the other side. Nevertheless, in this case, as in all

other circumstances, the efficacy depends on the sincerity of the thought, and not on the quantity of words offered with more or less solemnity, in which very frequently the heart does not participate.

Prayers that truly come from the heart encounter a resonance in the spirit to whom they are directed, whose ideas are still in a state of confusion; as if they were friendly voices come to awaken them from sleep. (See chap. 27, item 10.)

60. PRAYER - Almighty God, may Your mercy be shown to the soul of X... (*name*), whom You have just called back from Earth. We beg and implore that the trials suffered here may be counted in their favour and that our prayers may soften and shorten the penalties still to be suffered in the spiritual form!

Good Spirits, who came to fetch this soul, and most especially their Guardian Angel, help them to free themselves from matter. Give them light and a consciousness of themselves so that they may quickly leave the state of perturbation, inherent in the passing from the body back to the spiritual life. Inspire repentance in their spirit for all errors and faults committed and a desire to obtain permission to remedy them, to quicken their advancement in the direction of the life of those who are eternally blessed.

Moreover, you X... (*name*), who have just entered into the world of the sprits, we wish to say that despite this fact, you are still with us; you hear and see us, since you have merely left the perishable physical body, which will quickly be reduced to dust.

You have left the gross envelope that is subject to vicissitudes and death, now retaining only your etheric body that is imperishable and inaccessible to material suffering. If you no longer live through a physical body, you live instead through your spirit, and the spiritual life is free from those miseries that afflict humanity.

You no longer have over your eyes the veil that hides the splendours of the future existence. Now you may contemplate new marvels, while we remain bathed in darkness.

You may travel through space and visit the worlds with all liberty, while we still painfully drag ourselves about here on Earth, prisoners in our material bodies that are like heavy armour.

Infinite horizons stretch before you, and on seeing their grandeur you will understand the vanity of terrestrial desires, worldly aspirations and the futility of the so-called joys to which humankind delivers itself.

For humanity, death is nothing more than a separation from matter, lasting but a few instants. From this place of exile in which we continue to live according to the Will of God, with the duties we still have to fulfil in this world, we will continue to follow you in thought until the moment when it is permitted for us to join you once again, just as now you are reunited with those who preceded you.

We cannot go to where you are, but you may come to us. Then come to those who love you; help them in life's trials and watch over those who are dear to you. Protect them as much as you are able; lessen the bitterness of your absence by suggesting to them the thought that now you are happier and that one day, for certain, we will again be reunited in a better world.

In the place where you are now, all earthly resentments should be extinguished. You must hold yourself inaccessible to them now, for the sake of your future happiness! Therefore, forgive all those who may have behaved badly towards you, just as those against whom mistakes were committed now forgive you.

NOTE - To this prayer, which applies to everyone, can be added some special words according to the intimate circumstances of the family, the relationship to the deceased with the one who is praying or the social position of the departed.

When dealing with a child, Spiritism teaches us that we are not referring to a spirit that had been recently created, but to one that had already lived other lives and might even be well advanced. If this last existence has been a short one, then it is because it was needed to complete a test or trial, or as a test for the parents. (See Chap. 5, item 21.)

61. PRAYER[18] *(Another one.)* - All-Powerful Lord, may Your mercy extend over all those brothers and sisters who have just left the Earth! May Your light shine upon them! Remove them from darkness! Open their eyes and ears! May the Good Spirits surround them and let them hear Your words of hope and peace!

Lord, even though we are not worthy, we implore Your merciful indulgence for X... (name) recently recalled from exile. Make their return that of a prodigal son/daughter. Forget, dear Lord, the faults they may have committed and remember only the good they have done. We know Your justice is immutable, but Your love is immense. We beseech You therefore, to attenuate Your justice through the fountain of goodness that emanates from You!

May the light shine brightly before your eyes, dear X... (*name*) who has just left the Earth! May the Good Spirits come to be near you, to surround you and help you to break your earthly chains! Now you can understand and see the grandeur of God. So submit yourself without complaint to His justice; moreover, never despair of His mercy. My dear brother/sister may a profound examination of your past open the doors to the future, by making you understand the errors you have left behind, as well as the work that

---

[18] This prayer was dictated to a medium from Bordeaux at the moment when an unknown funeral procession was passing by their residence.

waits, so you may remedy them! May God forgive you and may the Good Spirits uphold and animate you! Your brothers and sisters on Earth will pray for you, and ask that you pray for them.

THOSE FOR WHOM WE HAVE AFFECTION

62. PREFACE - The idea of nothingness is very terrible! Those who believe that the voice of a friend who weeps for someone is lost in a vacuum, without encountering the least sign of response are to be pitied! Those who think everything dies with the body can never have known a pure and saintly affection. They believe that the being, who enlightened their world with vast intelligence, is a mere combination of matter that is extinguished forever, just as a flame. That, of a dearly loved person such as a father, mother or adored child, nothing remains but a handful of dust that the wind will inevitably disperse.

How can anyone who has a heart remain indifferent to this idea? Why are they not frozen with terror at the thought of absolute annihilation? How can they not even show a wish that this was untrue? Has not reason been sufficient for them to be able to dissipate their doubts? Well then, Spiritism has come to dispel all uncertainty as to the future, by means of the material proof of survival of the soul and the existence of beings in the beyond that it gives! This is happening to such an extent, that on all sides these proofs are being received with joy. Confidence is reborn, because humans now know that terrestrial existence is only a brief passage leading to a better life, that work done in this world is not lost and that really true affections are not destroyed beyond hope. (See chap. 4, item 18 & chap. 5, item 21.)

63. PRAYER - Dear Lord, may You deign to favourably receive this prayer in the name of X... (*name*). Help them perceive the divine lights that will make their pathway to eternal happiness

easier. Permit the Good Spirits to take them my words and thoughts.

You, who were so dear to me in this world, listen to my voice that calls to offer anew my pledge of affection. God allowed you to be liberated before me and I cannot complain about this without being selfish, because this would be equal to a wish that you be still subject to the sufferings of physical life. So wait with resignation for the moment of our reunion in this happier world, where you have preceded me.

I know that this separation is only temporary, and that however long it may appear to be, its duration is nothing compared to the blessed eternity that God has promised to His chosen ones. May His Goodness preserve me from doing whatever it might be that could delay this longed for moment, so that I may be saved from the pain of not encountering you when I leave my earthly captivity.

Oh, how sweet and consoling is the certainty that there is nothing between us but a material veil that hides you from my sight! That you can even be here at my side, hear me speaking as of old, or perhaps even better than then; that you do not forget me as I do not forget you; that our thoughts are constantly intermingling and your thoughts accompany me and uphold me.

May the peace of the Lord be with you.

FOR SUFFERING SOULS WHO ASK FOR PRAYERS

64. PREFACE - To understand the relief that prayer can give to suffering spirits, it is necessary to remember by what manner this is achieved, as has been previously explained. (See chap. 27, items 9, 18 & subsequent.) Those who are convinced of this fact will be able to pray with greater fervour because of the certainty that they do not do so in vain.

65. PRAYER - God of clemency and mercy, may Your goodness extend to all the spirits we have recommended to You in our prayers, especially the spirit of X... (*name*).

Good Spirits, whose only occupation is to do Good, intercede together with me for their relief. Make a ray of hope shine before their eyes and enlighten them as to the imperfections that maintain them distant from the homes of the blessed. Open their hearts to repentance and the desire to cleanse themselves, so they may accelerate their advancement. Make them understand it is by their own efforts that they may shorten the duration of their trials.

May God, in all His goodness, give them the necessary strength to persevere with their Good resolutions!

May these words, infused with benevolence, soften their trials, so showing them that there are those on Earth who sympathise and wish them happiness.

66. PRAYER *(Another.)* - We ask, Lord, that You shower the blessing of Your love and mercy on all who suffer, be they wandering spirits or incarnates. Have pity for their weaknesses. You made us fallible, but gave us the capacity to resist evil and conquer it. May Your mercy extend to all those who are not able to resist their evil tendencies and continue to drag themselves along evil pathways. May the Good Spirits surround them. May Your light shine in their eyes, so that attracted by the life-giving warmth of this light, they may come to prostrate themselves at Your feet, humbly, repentant and submissive.

Merciful Father, we also ask for those of our brothers and sisters who have not had the strength to resist their earthly trials. Lord, You gave us a burden to carry, to be laid only at Your feet. However, our weaknesses are great and our courage fails us sometimes during the course of the journey. Have pity on those indolent servants who have abandoned the work before the time.

May Your justice spare them and allow the Good Spirits to take them some relief, consolation and hope for the future. The prospect of pardon strengthens the soul; Lord, show this pardon to those guilty ones who are in despair and thus, being upheld by this hope, allow them to absorb enough strength from the actual immensity of their failings and sufferings so they may be able to redeem the past and prepare themselves for the conquest of the future.

FOR AN ENEMY WHO HAS DIED

67. PREFACE - Charity towards our enemies should accompany them into the Beyond. We need to understand that the evil they did was a test for us, which would be useful to our state of advancement, if we knew how to take advantage of it. It could have been even more beneficial to us than purely material afflictions, by the fact of our having had the opportunity of combining together courage, resignation, charity and the forgetting of offences. (See chap. 10, item 6, & chap. 12, items 5 & 6.)

68. PRAYER - Lord, it pleased You to call the soul of X... (*name*) before You called me. I forgive him/her the evil he/she did and the bad intentions nurtured towards me. May he /she repent for it now that he/she is no longer under the illusions of this world.

Dear God, may Your mercy descend upon X... (*name*), and turn away from me any idea I might have of rejoicing at their death. If I am in debt towards them for any reason, may they forgive me, as I forgive those misdemeanours committed against me.

FOR A CRIMINAL

69. PREFACE - If the efficiency of prayer were proportional to its length, then the longest ones would be reserved for the guiltiest,

because they are in more need than those who have lived saintly lives. To refuse prayer for criminals is to lack charity towards them and to be unaware of the mercy of God. To believe they would be useless because they have committed this or that grave crime would be to prejudge the Almighty's justice. (See chap. 11, item 14.)

70. PRAYER - Lord, God of Mercy, do not repudiate this criminal who has just left this Earth! Human justice has condemned this person, but this does not exempt them from Your justice, if their heart has not been touched by remorse.

Take away the blindfold that hides the gravity of their faults! May their repentance deserve Your kindly treatment and soften the sufferings of their soul. Perhaps our prayers and the intercession of the Good Spirits can also help and offer them hope and consolation. Inspire in them the wish to make amends for their actions in another existence, and give them strength so as not to succumb under the new struggles they will undertake!

Lord, have pity on this person!

FOR A SUICIDE

71. PREFACE - A person never has the right to dispose of their own life, since only God can retrieve them from captivity on Earth, when He judges it opportune. Nevertheless, Divine justice may soften the rigours in accordance with the circumstances; however, reserving all severity towards the person who wished to evade the trials of life. The suicide is like a prisoner who escapes from prison before they have served their sentence who, when recaptured, is treated with greater severity. The same happens with a suicide who imagines they are escaping from the miseries of the moment, only to plunge into even greater misfortunes. (See chap. 5, item 14 onwards.)

72. PRAYER - We know, Lord, the destiny that awaits those who violate Your law, by voluntarily abbreviating their days. Nevertheless, we also know that Your mercy is infinite. So please condescend to extend this mercy to the soul of X... (*name*). May our prayers and Your commiseration lessen the harshness of the sufferings they are experiencing for not having had the courage to await the end of their trials.

Good Spirits, whose mission it is to help those who are wretched, take this spirit under your protection; inspire them to regret the error committed. May your assistance give them strength to support with greater resignation the new trials through which X... (*name*) will now have to pass in order to make reparation. Turn this person away from the evil spirits, capable of once again impelling them towards that same act and so prolonging their suffering by making them lose the fruits of future expiations.

We also direct ourselves to you, whose unhappiness is the motive for our prayers, to offer a wish that our commiseration may diminish the bitterness and help to create within you the hope for a better future. Your future lies in your hands, believe in the goodness of God, Whose bosom opens to accept all repentance and only remains closed to hardened hearts.

FOR REPENTANT SPIRITS

73. PREFACE - It would be unjust to include in the category of evil spirits the suffering and repentant ones who ask for prayers. They may have been bad; nevertheless, they no longer are, since they recognised the error of their ways and deplore them; now they are only unhappy. Some of them have even begun to enjoy relative happiness.

74. PRAYER - God of Mercy, who accepts the sincere repentance of the sinner, be they incarnate or discarnate, here is a spirit who took pleasure in evil, but who now recognises its errors and is entering into the Good pathway. Condescend, Lord, to receive it like a prodigal child and forgive it.

Good Spirits, whose voices this person did not listen to, from now on they are wishing to hear; permit them to glimpse the happiness of the elected ones of the Lord, so that they may persist in their desire to purify themselves in order to be able to reach You. Uphold them in all their Good intentions and give them the necessary strength to resist their bad instincts.

To the repentant spirit of X... (*name*) we offer our congratulations for the inner changes that you have made and we thank the Good Spirits who have helped you to do this.

If you previously took pleasure in evil, it was because you did not understand how sweet the enjoyment of doing Good is; also because you felt too lowly to be able to manage to change. Nevertheless, from the moment you placed your first step on the path of Goodness a new light shone in your eyes. Then you began to enjoy an unknown happiness and hope entered your heart. This is because God always hears the prayer of a sinner who repents; He never spurns anyone who seeks His help.

To be once again completely within God's grace, you must apply yourself from now on to not only never again committing evil, but to doing Good and above all else, to repair the evil that you have done. Then you will satisfy God's justice; each Good action you practise will wash away one of your past mistakes.

The first step has been taken; so now, as you continue to advance along this pathway the easier and more agreeable it will become. Persevere then, so one day you will have the glory of being counted amongst the Good and happy Spirits.

FOR HARDENED SPIRITS

75. PREFACE - Bad spirits are those who have not yet been touched by repentance, who take pleasure in evil and feel no remorse. They are insensitive to reprimands, repel prayer and frequently blaspheme against God's name. They are the hardened souls, who after death seek vengeance upon incarnates for the suffering they had endured. They persecute all those they had hated during their life, by either spiritually obsessing them or by exercising all kinds of harmful influences over them. (See chap. 10, item 6, and chap. 12, items 5 & 6.)

There are two distinct categories of perverse spirits: those who are plainly evil and those who are hypocrites. It is infinitely easier to bring the first back to goodness than the second. The first, more often than not, have brutal and coarse natures, just as is seen in human beings. They practise evil more from instinct than from calculation and do not seek to appear better than they are. However, there is in them a latent germ that needs to open up, which is usually achieved by means of perseverance, firm benevolence, counselling, reasoning and prayer. It has been noticed that in 'automatic-writing' these spirits have difficulty in writing the name of God, which is a sign of an instinctive fear, an intimate voice of conscience that tells them they are unworthy. It is at this point they are ready to convert themselves and we can be optimistic for them; we only need to find the vulnerable point in their hearts.

Hypocritical spirits are almost always very intelligent. However, they do not have a grain of sensitivity in their hearts; nothing touches them. They only simulate good sentiments to gain confidences. They are happy when they encounter those who are foolish enough to accept them as saintly spirits, because then they can control them as they wish. The name of God, far from inspiring the least tremor of fear, serves them as a mask to cover their vileness. In both the invisible and visible worlds, the hypocrites are the most dangerous, because they act in the shadows, without anyone suspecting. They appear to have faith, but it is only apparent and never sincere.

76. PRAYER - Lord, may it please You to cast a kindly glance over the imperfect spirits who find themselves in the obscurity of ignorance and so do not know You, especially the spirit of X... (*name*).

Good Spirits, help us to make this person understand that by inducing people towards evil, by spiritually obsessing them and tormenting them, they only prolong their own sufferings. Make the example of the happiness You enjoy into an encouragement for them.

Dear spirit, who still takes pleasure in the practise of evil, listen to the prayer we offer for you; it should convince you we only wish to help you, although you do us harm.

You are unhappy, because it is not possible to be happy while practising evil. So why do you remain in suffering when the possibility of avoiding it depends on yourself? Look at the Good Spirits surrounding you at this moment and see how blessed they are! Would it not be more agreeable for you to enjoy the same happiness?

You say that for you this is impossible; but nothing is impossible for the one who truly desires something. God gave you, as He did all His creatures, the liberty to choose between good or evil, happiness or wretchedness; no one is condemned to practise evil. Just as you have the will to do evil, you may also find the will to do the Good and so be happy.

Cast your eyes back towards God. Direct your thoughts for an instant to Him and a ray of divine light will illuminate you. Say these simple words together with us: *Dear God, I repent, forgive me!* Try to repent and do the Good instead of doing evil things, and you will soon see His mercy descending upon you and an indescribable feeling of well-being will substitute the anguish you are experiencing.

Once you have taken the first step along the pathway to Goodness the rest will be easy to follow. You will understand then what a long period of happiness you have lost through your own fault. Nevertheless, a radiant future full of hope will open before you and make you forget your miserable past, full of perturbation and moral tortures, which would be a hell for you if they were to last for eternity. The day will come when these tortures will be such that you will desire to make them cease at any price. Nevertheless, the longer you leave it the more difficult this will be.

Do not believe that you will always remain in your present state; no, this is impossible. You have two prospects before you: to suffer even more than you have suffered until now, or to be blessed as are the Good Spirits who surround you. The first is inevitable if you persist in being obstinate, when a simple effort on your part would be sufficient to take you out of the bad situation in which you find yourself. Therefore, hurry, seeing that each day you delay is a lost day of happiness!

Good Spirits, permit these words to echo in the mind of this backward soul, so they may be helped to approach God. We ask this in the name of Jesus Christ, Who has such great power over evil spirits.

5 - PRAYERS FOR THE SICK AND THE OBSESSED

FOR THOSE WHO ARE SICK

77. PREFACE - Sicknesses belongs to the tests and vicissitudes of earthly life. It is inherent in the grossness of our material nature and in the inferiority of the world we inhabit. Passions and excesses of all kinds create unhealthy conditions in our organism that are sometimes transmitted by heredity. In worlds that are more advanced in both their physical and moral aspects, the human organism being more purified and less material, is no longer subject to the same infirmities, and the body is not secretly undermined by the corrosives of passions (See chap. 3, item 9). We must therefore resign ourselves to the consequences of the ambient in which our inferiority places us, until we deserve to pass on to a higher plane. However, while we are waiting, this does not prevent us from doing whatever we can to improve our present situation. But if despite our best efforts we do not manage this, then Spiritism teaches us to support our passing miseries with resignation.

If God had not wished that in certain cases bodily sufferings be dissipated and softened, He would not have put the possibility of cure within our reach. His solicitude in this respect, being in conformity with the instinct of self-preservation, indicates that it is our duty to seek out these means and apply them.

Apart from ordinary medication elaborated by Science, magnetism allows us to know the power of fluidic action and Spiritism reveals another powerful force in *the mediumship of healing* and the influence of prayer. (See chap. 26 - on healing mediumship.)

78. PRAYER *(To be said by the sick person)* - Lord, You are all justice. The sickness You saw fit to send me must be deserved, because You never impose suffering without just cause. Therefore, I entrust my cure to Your infinite mercy. If it pleases You to restore my health, may Your Name be blessed! If on the contrary it is necessary for me to suffer more, may You be blessed just the same. I submit without complaint to Your wise purpose, since what You do can only be for the Good of Your creatures.

Dear God, let this infirmity be a timely warning to me that will cause me to meditate upon myself. I accept it as an expiation for my past, as a test of my faith and a submission to Your blessed will. (See prayer in item No. 40.)

79. PRAYER *(For the sick person)* - Dear God, Your designs are impenetrable and in Your wisdom, You have sent this affliction to X... *(name)*. I implore You Lord, to cast a glance of compassion over their suffering and if You see fit, to terminate them.

Good Spirits, you who are ministers of the Almighty, I beseech you to second my request to alleviate their sufferings. Direct my thought so that a balsam may be poured over their body and consolation poured into their soul.

Inspire them with patience and submission to God's will. Give X... *(name)* enough strength to support the pain with Christian resignation, so that the fruits of this test may not be lost. (See the prayer in item No. 57.)

80. PRAYER *(To be said by the Healing Medium)* - Dear God, if it pleases You to use me as an instrument, although I am unworthy, may I cure this infirmity if You so desire, because I have faith in You. But I know I can do nothing alone. Permit the Good Spirits to concentrate their beneficial fluids in me, so that I may transmit them to this sick person, and free me from all thought of pride and selfishness that might alter its pureness.

FOR THOSE WHO ARE BEING OBSESSED

81. PREFACE - Spiritual obsession is the persistent action that an inferior or evil spirit exercises over an individual. It may present many varied characteristics, from a simple moral influence with no perceptible exterior sign, to a complete organic and mental perturbation. It may obstruct all mediumship faculties. In 'automatic-writing', this may be displayed through the insistence of only one Spirit communicating, to the exclusion of all other spirits.

Evil spirits constantly encircle the Earth, due to the moral inferiority of its inhabitants. Their malevolent action forms part of the afflictions that face humanity. Spiritual obsessions, just as much as infirmities and all life's tribulations, should be considered as tests or atonements and accepted as such.

In the same manner that sicknesses are the result of our physical imperfections that make the body accessible to pernicious exterior influences, obsession is always the result of moral imperfections that allow access to influences from evil spirits. Physical causes pit themselves against physical forces; a moral cause must always be opposed by a moral force. In order to prevent sicknesses we fortify our bodies; to protect ourselves from obsession it is necessary to fortify the soul. This means that the disturbed person must work for their own moral betterment, which is frequently sufficient to free them from the obsessor without resorting to help from others. However, if an obsession degenerates into subjugation and apparent possession, then the help of other people becomes indispensable, because not infrequently the patient loses both their will power and their free will.

Obsession usually manifests a desire for vengeance by a spirit. This is frequently rooted in the relationship they had with this person in a previous life. (See chap. 10, item 6 and chap. 12, items 5 & 6.)

In the case of a very serious obsession, the person being obsessed is enveloped and impregnated by pernicious fluids that repels and neutralises the action of healthy fluids. Therefore, it is very important to free the person from these vaporous negative fluids. However, similar negative fluids cannot eliminate evil fluids. Therefore, it is necessary to expel the evil substances with the help of healthier fluids by applying a similar action to that exercised by a Healer in the case of sickness. This produces an effect of mechanical action and reaction. However, this is not sufficient in itself, because *it is also necessary and very important to act directly upon the actual intelligent spiritual being.* This can only be done by someone with greater authority than the perturbing spiritual entity. The greater the moral superiority of this person, the greater will be their authority.

Nevertheless, this is not all that is required in order to guarantee liberation from the obsessing spirit. It is also necessary to induce the perverse spirit to renounce their evil intentions, to awaken repentance in them and a desire to do Good. This can be done through skilfully directed counselling, given during private meetings organised specially for this purpose, with the objective of offering moral education to this spirit. Then it may be possible to have the double satisfaction of liberating an incarnate person and converting an imperfect spirit.

This task is made easier when the obsessed person, understanding their situation, joins in with the prayers and adds their cooperation in the form of a desire for recuperation. The same does not happen when, being seduced by the obsessing spirit, the person remains deluded as to the qualities of the entity that dominates them, even taking pleasure in the errors this spirit induces them to commit. In this case, instead of helping, the person repels all assistance offered. This is what happens in cases of fascination, which are infinitely more rebellious to treat than even the most violent case of subjugation. (See The Mediums' Book – Second Part, Chap. 23.)

In all cases of obsession, prayer is the most powerful means of help for anyone assisting in this process and acting upon the obsessing spirit.

82. PRAYER *(To be said by the person being obsessed)* - Dear God, permit the Good Spirits to liberate me from the malefic spirit that has linked itself to me. If this spirit is seeking vengeance because of wrongs I might have practised against them in another existence, then you have permitted this, Lord, and I suffer for my own faults. May my repentance make me deserving of Your pardon and my liberation! But whatever the motive, I beseech Your mercy for my persecutor. Lord, help it to find the pathway to progress that will turn it away from the practise of evil. May I, on my part, repay evil with goodness, so inducing it to better sentiments.

Dear God, I also know that it is my own imperfections that make me accessible to the influences of imperfect spirits. Give me the necessary enlightenment so I may recognise these imperfections, and above all remove the pride in me that makes me blind to my own defects.

How great must be my unworthiness, to have allowed an evil spirit to dominate me!

Dear God, may this blow to my vanity be a lesson for the future. May it fortify the resolution I have made to cleanse myself by means of the practise of goodness, charity and humility, so that from now on I may put up a barrier against all evil influences.

Lord, give me strength to support this test with patience and resignation. I understand that, just as with all other tests, it will aid my progress if I do not spoil the fruits by complaining. Since it offers me an opportunity to demonstrate my submission and practise charity towards an unhappy brother/sister by forgiving any evil they may have done to me. (See chap. 12, items 5 & 6; chap. 28, item 15 and subsequent, also items 46 & 47.)

83. PRAYER *(For the obsessed person)*[19] - Almighty God, may it please You to give me the power to liberate X... (*name*) from the influence of the spirit that is obsessing them. If it is Your wish to put an end to this test, concede me the grace of speaking to this spirit with the necessary authority.

Good Spirits, may you help me, and you, their Guardian Angel, may you give me your assistance; help me to free this sufferer from the impure fluids that envelop them.

In the name of Almighty God, I urge the evil spirit that torments this person to withdraw!

84. PRAYER *(For the obsessing spirit)* - Lord of infinite goodness, I implore Your mercy for the spirit who is obsessing X... (*name*) Help it to see the Divine Light so that it may recognise the falsity of the path it follows. Good Spirits, help me make it understand that it has everything to lose by the practise of evil, and everything to gain by the practise of goodness.

To the spirit who is tormenting X... (*name*), listen to me since I speak to you in the name of God!

If you would but reflect, you would understand that evil could never outdo goodness and that it is not possible to be stronger than God and the Good Spirits.

They could have protected X... (*name*) from your attacks. If this was not done, it is because they had to go through this test.

---

[19] The Counsellor undertaking the task of liberating the obsessed person can offer this prayer. (Translators note.)

However, when this test reaches its end, then all action against your victim will be blocked. The evil that you have done, instead of causing harm, will have contributed towards their progress and happiness. In this manner, you will have employed your wickedness to no avail and it will rebound upon yourself.

God, Who is all-powerful, and the Superior Spirits who are His delegates, being more powerful than you, are capable of putting an end to this obsession, and your tenacity will fail before this supreme authority. Nevertheless, because He is in fact the Good, He wants to leave you the merit for having ceased of your own free will. This is a respite that is being offered to you; if you do not take advantage of it, you will suffer deplorable consequences. Great punishment and cruel suffering will await you! You will be forced to plead for mercy and for prayers from your victim, who has already forgiven you and prays for you, which constitutes a great merit in the eyes of God and will hasten their liberation.

So, reflect while there is still time, seeing that God's justice will fall upon you as it does on all rebellious spirits. Consider that the evil you do now necessarily has a limit, whereas, if you persist in being obstinate, you will only increase the extension of your own sufferings.

When you were upon Earth, did you ever consider it stupid to sacrifice a great goodness for a small momentary satisfaction? It is the same now you are a spirit. What will you gain from what you are doing? The misguided pleasure of tormenting someone does not stop you being wretched, even if you refuse to admit it, leaving you even more unhappy.

On the other hand, see what you are missing! Look at the Good Spirits around you and tell me if their lot is not preferable to yours. The happiness they enjoy can also be yours, whenever you like. What do you have to do for this? Pray to God and instead of doing evil, practice the Good. I know that you cannot transform yourself immediately, but God does not demand the impossible; He only asks for your Good will. Try to follow this advice and we will help you. Make an effort so that very soon we may offer up in your name the prayer for those who are repentant (No. 73), and no longer rank you amongst the evil spirits as you await the time when you can be counted among the Good Spirits. (See also No. 75 - Prayers for Hardened Spirits).

COMMENTS: The cure for grave obsessions requires much patience, perseverance and devotion. It also demands tact and ability in order to direct those who are frequently perverse, hardened and astute towards Goodness, since there are those who are extremely rebellious. In the vast majority of cases, we must be guided by the circumstances. Nevertheless, whatever the characteristics of the disturbed spirit, it is an incontestable fact that nothing is obtained by either constraint or threats: All influence resides in moral superiority. Another truth, equally well proven by experience, as well as by logic, is *the complete ineffectiveness of exorcism, formulas, sacramental words, amulets, talismans, exterior practises or any kind of material symbols.*

Prolonged spiritual obsession may cause pathological disorders, which frequently demand simultaneous or consecutive treatments, be these magnetic and/or medical, in order to be able to restore organic health. When the causes have been destroyed, it remains for the effects to be remedied. (See *The Mediums' Book*, 2nd part, Chap. 23 – "Obsession" - also '*Revue Spirite*', February and March, 1864 & April, 1865 - examples of cures for obsession.)

APPENDIX

BIOGRAPHICAL SKETCHES OF SOME OF THE SPIRIT COMMUNICANTS WHOSE MESSAGES ARE PUBLISHED IN THIS BOOK

ERASTUS (A disciple of Paul) - Treasurer of Corinth, he was a disciple of Paul of Tarsus, having accompanied him on his mission to Ephesus. He is cited in the book of Acts, 19:22. – "So he sent into Macedonia two of them that ministered unto him, Timotheus and Erastus; but he himself stayed in Asia for a season." In the book of Romans, 16:23. – "Gaius mine host, and of the whole church, salutes you. Erastus the chamberlain of the city salutes you and Quartus a brother." In 2 Timothy, 4:20. – "Erastus abode at Corinth: but Trophimus have I left at Miletum sick."

FÉNELON, François de Salignac de la Mothe - A French prelate born in 1651 who discarnated in 1715. He belonged to a family famous in the field of arms and diplomacy. An ordained Priest, he dedicated himself to his ministry. His works are entitled "The Fables," "Dialogue with the dead" and "Telemaco". This last book fell out of favour due to the question of Quietism that was a doctrine preached by Madame Guyon. Fénelon defended Quietism, whereas Bossuet condemned it. Later on he was condemned by the Pope, so becoming just a simple priest again. He left many literary works, mostly on matters of politics, religion and education.

GIRARDIN, Delfina de - To be exact her maiden name was Delphine Gay. She published many poetical works under the name of Delphine Gay. In 1827, when she was twenty-three, she found herself acclaimed in the Capitolian when journeying through Italy. On marrying Emile de Girardin, a politician and a man of letters, she became Mrs Emile de Girardin. After her marriage, she published various poems and romances. She was most certainty a great inspirational medium. On 6th September 1853, she disembarked on the Isle of Jersey for the purpose of spending a short time with the family of Victor Hugo, where she held numerous mediumship sessions by means of the 'talking-tables'.

HAHNEMANN, Samuel-Chrétien-Fréderic - Of German origin he was born in Meissen on 10th April 1755. Graduating in Medicine from Erland University in 1779, he exercised his profession until 1789, when he abandoned his medical practice due to a great dissatisfaction with the total lack of guidance at that time in the administration of remedies. He finally discovered Homeopathy about 1790, and continued to research and experiment in this area, managing to survive by translating books. In 1796, he presented his discovery to the world in the form of a monograph, going on to practise his newly found discovery. As Homeopathy was very rational it soon became a success, which caused him to suffer persecution from his ex-colleagues, and so was given protection by the reigning duke of Anhalt-Cohen, where he went to live in 1821. Nevertheless, the hate followed him, the local doctors incited the people against him and on one occasion, his house was stoned. Despite this, he continued to live there and became rich and greatly sought after for his treatments. In 1835, he moved to Paris and in 1843, returned to the spiritual world at the age of eight-eight. He was laid to rest in the Montmartre Cemetery. In 1900, his mortal remains were transferred, by members of the International Homeopathic Congress, to a monument erected by his disciples in the Père Lachaise Cemetery. On the same day and time President Mackinley, of the United States of America, inaugurated a statue to Hahnemann in

Washington that had cost American Homeopathic doctors seventy thousand dollars.

HEINE, Henri - He was a German poet born in Düsseldorf in 1797, discarnating in Paris in 1856. He was the author of poems of a painfully melancholic nature (Intermezzo, Sketches of a Journey and Song, Essays on Modern German Literature, The Romantic School and Germany) all written with sparkling brilliance but tainted with profound scepticism.

JOHN THE EVANGELIST - The Apostle of Jesus Christ, son of Zebedee and brother to the Apostle James. He was the author of the fourth Gospel and three epistles. While exiled on the Greek island of Patmos he received the 'Apocalypse' through the means of mediumship. He lived almost one hundred years. Together with the Apostles Peter and James the Elder, he was invariably called upon by Jesus to witness the most important events that occurred during His mission.

LACORDAIRE, Jean-Baptiste-Henri - This is the Priest Lacordaire referred to in the Revue Spirite, the Spiritist magazine initiated by Allan Kardec in 1858. He also had a brother of some note, Jean-Thédore Lacordaire who was a naturalist, teacher and journalist, born in 1801. It is certain that we are dealing with the first brother, born in 1802 who discarnated in 1861. He was a Dominican, a brilliant preacher and disciple of Lamennais, with whom he broke off relations in 1834. He was vicar of Notre-Dame and after five years of retreat entered the Dominican Order in 1839. He was a member of the French Academy, his principle works being two very different lectures: 'The Life of Saint Domingos' and 'Considerations on the Philosophical System of M. de Lamennais'.

LAMENNAIS, Félicité Robert de - Born in Saint-Malo in 1782, he discarnated in Paris in 1854. He was ordained a priest in 1816. The following year he published 'Essays on religious indifference and its bearing on political and civil order', which was a translation of 'Imitation of Jesus Christ' and 'Modern Slavery'. He founded the newspaper 'L'Avenir' (The Future) in which he extolled the alliance of the Church with Liberty. Pope Gregory XVI denied his authority to hold such opinions in a circular letter entitled 'Mirari Vos' (Looking at Ourselves). Following this he published 'Words of a Believer', which was condemned in the circular 'Singulari nos'. Nevertheless, he continued writing without interruption: 'The Book of the People', 'An Outline of a Philosophy', etc. In 1840, he was condemned to prison. In 1848, he was elected to the National Assembly. He asked that he be buried amongst the poor.

MORLOT, François Nicolas Madeleine - A French prelate and Archbishop of Paris and a Cardinal. Born in 1795, he discarnated in 1862.

PAUL, THE APOSTLE - Born in the flourishing town of Tarsus in Cilicia, possibly in the year 10 or 12 of this epoch. He was martyred in Rome in the year 67 AD. Nicknamed 'The Apostle of the Gentiles', he was one of the most outstanding disseminators of Christian ideas, taking the words of Jesus Christ to the great centres of population of that time, these being Antioch, Athens, Ephesus, Corinth, Macedonia, Jerusalem and Rome. He wrote a great number of Epistles that are contained in the book of 'The Acts of the Apostles' where many elucidative descriptions of his Apostleship and his incomparable activities in favour of the birth of Christianity are also to be found. His original name was Saul that was later changed to Paul after at the event on the road to Damascus. Although he was not one of the Apostles of Jesus, he deserves the title of Apostle due to the magnificent tasks that he accomplished.

PASCAL, Blaise - A French geometrician, physicist, philosopher and writer, born in Clermont-Ferrand, France in June

1623, he discarnated in Paris in 1662. When he was eleven years old he composed a treatise on sound; at twelve he discovered the thirty-second theorem of the first book of Euclid. At sixteen, he wrote his "Essay on Conics." At nineteen, in order to help the mathematical work of his father, he conceived his machine for mathematics that took him ten years. He also wrote works on space and calculations of possibility. After a period spent living a worldly life, he then returned to religion and dedicated himself to the production of works of a metaphysical and spiritual nature. He was in fact one of the great exponents of religious and philosophical thought of his time.

SAINT AUGUSTINE, (Aurelius Augustinus, 354-430 AD) - Bishop of Hipona, he was a theologist, philosopher, moralist and dialectician. After a disturbed boyhood, the Spirit of the enlightened Ambrose attracted him to a religious life. On the insistence of his mother, Monica, he left Africa to go to Italy hoping to seek a more promising career in the Roman Empire. He wrote many sermons, helped the poor and, during the second part of his life, maintained the firm objective of serving the Church and Christ. He became the most celebrated of all the doctors of the Catholic Church. He sought to harmonise the doctrine of Plato with the Catholic dogmas and intelligence with faith. His chief works were "The City of God", "Confessions" and a treatise on grace.

SAINT LOUIS (Louis IX) - A King of France, he lived from 1215 until 1270. He began his reign under the tutorage of his mother, Blanche de Castille. He took part in the seventh and eighth Crusades and discarnated as a victim of a plague on disembarking in Cartages. He was a good and pious man. He was canonised by the Catholic Church in 1297. He is constantly cited in the 'Revue Spirite' thanks to the numerous communications received from his Spirit.

SAINT VINCENT DE PAUL (1576-1660) - He was a French priest celebrated for his acts of charity. He was the instigator of crèches and hospitals of charity. When war and famine devastated the provinces of Lorraine, Picardie and Champagne, this apostle of charity gave all he had in order to minimise the hardships of the population of those regions.

VIANNEY, Jean Marie Baptiste - Lived from 1786 until 1859. While on Earth, he was the Vicar of Ars. During his life, he gained great popularity due to the numerous cures he managed to realise, as well as the brotherly attention he dispensed to the sick of whatever nature, who sought him out in his obscure village. He protected his parish through the sheer force of mediumship phenomena, for which he was the intermediary and which the people saw as authentic miracles. His fame caused the other priests to feel inferior, even though his parish was considered one where 'there was not even place to rest one's head'. They said, "He is an illiterate who was ordained out of commiseration and charity. He does not know even three words of Latin and nothing of theology, who dares to offer confession to the multitudes and frequently treats complex and dangerous cases" and with these accusations they prohibited his followers from visiting him. The Abbot of Borjon wrote to him, "Dear Vicar, when you have as little theology as you have, you should be reluctant to enter into a confessionary". - On receiving this letter, the Vicar of Ars broke into sobs and exclaimed, "It is true!" On replying to this critic, he pondered, "My very venerable brother, I have so much reason to love you! You are the only one who knows me well. Please help me to obtain the grace that I have been requesting for so long. Then on being substituted in my position in whose exercise I do not consider myself worthy due to my great ignorance, I might retire to some small village where I can weep over my poor life."

(Permission to include the translation of these brief biographical sketches in this book was kindly given by the SPIRITIST FEDERATION OF THE STATE OF SÃO PAULO, BRAZIL, as taken from their publication (1982) of 'O EVANGELHO SEGUNDO O ESPIRITISMO'.)